935
LIES

935
LIES

The Future of Truth
and the Decline of
America's Moral Integrity

CHARLES LEWIS

PublicAffairs
New York

PublicAffairs books are available at special discounts for bulk
purchases in the U.S. by corporations, institutions, and other organizations.
For more information, please contact the Special Markets Department at
the Perseus Books Group, 2300 Chestnut Street, Suite 200,
Philadelphia, PA 19103, call (800) 810-4145, ext. 5000,
or e-mail special.markets@perseusbooks.com.

Book design by Linda Mark

Lewis, Charles, 1953–
    935 lies : the future of truth and the decline of America's moral
integrity / Charles Lewis.—First Edition.
    pages cm
    ISBN 978-1-61039-117-7 (hardback)—
    ISBN 978-1-61039-118-4 (ebook) 1. Political ethics—United
States. 2. Business ethics—United States. 3. Truth—Political
aspects—United States. 4. Truth—Social aspects—United States.
5. Political culture—United States. 6. United States—Moral
conditions. 7. United States—Politics and government—Moral and
ethical aspects. I. Title. II. Title: Nine hundred and thirty-five lies.
    JK468.E7L494 2014
    323.44'50973—dc23
                                                    2014005739

First Edition
10 9 8 7 6 5 4 3 2

For my wife, Pamela Gilbert

Time's glory is to calm contending kings,
To unmask falsehood and bring truth to light.
—WILLIAM SHAKESPEARE, 1594[1]

If a nation expects to be ignorant and free, in a state of
civilization, it expects what never was and never will be.
—THOMAS JEFFERSON, 1816[2]

Contents

Prologue: 935 Lies   *xi*

1. Our First Casualty   1

2. The Public's Right to Know: The Pentagon
   Papers, Watergate, and a Triumph for Truth   27

3. Race: The American Delusion   55

4. America's Secret Foreign Policy and
   the Arrogance of Power   83

5. Doubt Is Their Product: The Corporate War
   on Truth   115

6. Where Have You Gone, Edward R. Murrow?   153

7. A Watchdog in the Corridors of Power   179

8. The Future of Truth   199

   A Note from the Author   239
   Appendix A: Real-Time Truth Charts   249
   Appendix B: The Iraq War Card   253
   Notes   261
   Bibliography   337
   Index   349

Prologue: 935 Lies

> When regard for truth has been broken down or even
> slightly weakened, all things will remain doubtful.
> —ST. AUGUSTINE, C. 395[1]

> The result of a consistent and total substitution of lies for
> factual truth is not that the lies will now be accepted as
> truth, and the truth be defamed as lies, but that the sense
> by which we take our bearings in the real world—and the
> category of truth vs. falsehood is among the mental
> means to this end—is being destroyed.
> —HANNAH ARENDT, 1967[2]

AT THE END OF **2004,** a series of public opinion polls offered disturbing news. More than half of all Americans, we learned, believed that there had been weapons of mass destruction (WMDs) in Iraq—the principal raison d'être for George W. Bush's war of choice there—despite the fact that numerous widely publicized bipartisan and international reports had definitively shown that no such weapons existed. This stubborn refusal to face the facts about Iraq continues today for millions of Americans.[3]

Facts are and must be the coin of the realm in a democracy, for government "of the people, by the people, and for the people," in

Abraham Lincoln's words, requires an informed citizenry.[4] But in regard to the Iraq War, it seems, facts are now irrelevant or at least debatable, a mere matter of opinion, for a majority of Americans. And if facts no longer matter to millions of our fellow citizens, then what becomes of the traditional role of the journalist as the independent watchdog digging through obfuscation, secrecy, and deception by the powerful in search of what Carl Bernstein once called "the best obtainable version of the truth"?

This is a question that touches me personally—not just as a concerned citizen, but as someone who has dedicated his life and work to the pursuit of truth. In more than three decades as an investigative reporter in Washington, DC, my approach toward those in power, regardless of party or ideology, has followed the principle "Watch what they do, not what they say." Politicians, captains of industry, and their zealous aides too often resemble circus barkers, shilling for attention and advantage, with little regard for accuracy or veracity, using the press and the news media not to enlighten but to bamboozle the public in pursuit of votes, profits, and power. When necessary, they even employ the wiles of deception to conceal, disguise, or justify unseemly and sometimes outright criminal behavior. As George Orwell wrote, in words that still ring true more than half a century after they were written, "Political speech and writing are largely the defence [*sic*] of the indefensible . . . Political language . . . is designed to make lies sound truthful and murder respectable, and to give an appearance of solidity to pure wind."[5]

So as a professional truth-seeker, I have always been skeptical of statements by those in power, preferring to ignore the official versions of events in my quest for the (sometimes ugly) underlying realities. That quest continues. But when I learned the extent to which the public had swallowed and accepted the official lies about WMDs in Iraq, I realized that I actually could no longer ignore what those in power had said. Their shameless manipulations and misrepresentations, I now saw, were a crucial element in the tragedy of that dubious war of choice, and therefore deserving of investigation and analysis in their own right. Precisely what had US government officials said to cause most Americans and their elected representatives to completely ignore facts, logic, and reason in the rush to war? Exactly who was involved and to what extent?

I began systematically to investigate the answers to those and other related questions, enlisting the help of a team of reporters, researchers, and other contributors that ultimately included twenty-five people. Nearly three years later, the Center for Public Integrity published *Iraq: The War Card*, a 380,000-word report with an online searchable database whose overall findings are summarized graphically in Appendix B of this book.[6] It was released on the eve of the five-year anniversary of the invasion of Iraq and was covered extensively by the national and international news media.

Our report found that in the two years after the terrorist attacks of September 11, 2001, President George W. Bush and seven of his administration's top officials made at least 935 false statements about the national security threat posed by Iraq. The carefully orchestrated campaign of untruths about Iraq's alleged threat to US national security from its WMDs or links to al Qaeda (also specious) galvanized public opinion and led the nation to war under decidedly false pretenses. Perhaps most revealing: the number of false statements made by top Bush administration officials dramatically increased from August 2002 to the time of the critical October 2002 congressional approval of the war resolution and spiked even higher between January and March 2003, between Secretary of State Colin Powell's address before the United Nations General Assembly and the fateful March 19, 2003, invasion.[7]

Within hours of the release of our report, White House press secretary Dana Perino responded with scorn: "I hardly think that the study is worth spending any time on. It is so flawed in terms of taking anything into context or including—they only looked at members of the administration rather than looking at members of Congress or people around the world. Because as you'll remember, we were part of a broad coalition of countries that deposed a dictator based on a collective understanding of the intelligence."[8] This sophistry was at least consistent with the administration's track record of distorting reality. In fact, neither Congress nor America's international allies was demanding an invasion of Iraq before the administration started beating the war drums. The so-called Coalition of the Willing was a face-saving artifice cobbled together after the UN Security Council failed to approve the US-instigated invasion, rendering it a violation of the UN Charter and thus "illegal." Furthermore, "the intelligence" referred to by Perino proved to be anything but intelligent; indeed, it had been mostly manufactured by the administration in accordance with its political agenda.[9]

Three months after the Center for Public Integrity Iraq report, David Barstow of the *New York Times* reported more details about how the Iraq deception had been orchestrated. Barstow revealed that the Pentagon had quietly recruited and coached seventy-five retired military officers to be "independent" paid consultants and radio and television analysts whose true role was to make the case for war in Iraq. Many had significant, undisclosed financial ties to defense companies and were thus benefiting hugely from the very policies they were "analyzing."[10]

Earlier, Barstow had reported (with colleague Robin Stein) that "at least 20 federal agencies, including the Defense Department and the Census Bureau, have made and distributed hundreds of television news segments between 2001 and 2005 . . . Many were subsequently broadcast on local stations across the country without any acknowledgement of the government's role in their production." David Walker, the then comptroller general of the Government Accountability Office, who happened to be a Republican, declared that such taxpayer-paid propaganda by the government is unethical and violates federal law. However, the Bush administration publicly disagreed, and Congress meekly declined to pursue the matter any further.[11]

The broadcast and cable news media, which had overwhelmingly failed to investigate or challenge the administration's flawed case for war, shamelessly ignored Barstow's revelations, neither reporting on their own dubious use of such compromised news sources nor apologizing to the public for the resulting gross misrepresentations of fact.

And a month after the stunning *Times* stories, one of the White House officials who had actually made several false statements in the lead-up to the Iraq invasion, former press secretary Scott McClellan, wrote a "surprisingly scathing" memoir admitting that his own public comments at White House briefings about Iraq had been "badly misguided," that President Bush had not been "open and forthright on Iraq," and that instead he had relied on "propaganda."[12]

There were a few honorable exceptions in Washington to the general failure of the news media to challenge the pro-war deceptions. They included the fine independent coverage by then Knight Ridder (now McClatchy) Washington bureau reporters Warren Strobel and Jonathan Landay; the prescient articles by Walter Pincus, buried in the back pages by his nervous *Washington Post* editors; and, in early 2004, the Abu Ghraib prison-abuse scandal stories by CBS News *60 Minutes II* and Seymour Hersh in the *New Yorker*. Later, in 2005, beyond the Iraq deceptions, there were Dana Priest's exposés in the *Washington Post* about the Central Intelligence Agency's secret "black site" prisons and James Risen and Eric Lichtblau's stories in the *New York Times* revealing how the Bush administration had quietly authorized the National Security Agency (NSA) to secretly eavesdrop on Americans and others inside the United States, without warrants usually required for domestic surveillance.[13]

But in the context of the overall performance of the media, these valiant efforts to get beyond the official version to uncover the truth about our involvement in Iraq were too little, too late. The full extent of deference to power and self-censorship by our obsequious major news media during the run-up to war is still not fully known; it will gradually seep out—or not—over the coming years. Some major news organizations later grudgingly acknowledged that their coverage was insufficiently critical of government pronouncements. But that did nothing to ameliorate the tragic consequences of an unnecessary war, including a financial toll of more than $2 trillion, a sum that is likely to increase substantially with benefits to war veterans over time and other expenses, as well as—far more important—the deaths of thousands upon thousands of soldiers and innocent civilians, including women and children.[14]

Could the Iraq War have been prevented if the public had been better informed before the invasion about the specious official statements, faulty logic, and breathtaking manipulations of public opinion and governmental decision-making processes? I believe the answer to that grim question is very possibly yes, and it will haunt me and others in my profession for years to come.[15]

Did President Bush and other officials from his administration lie about Iraq intentionally and deliberately? It's hard to tell without unfettered access to the principals and their internal communications. Certainly, we should never underestimate the human capacity for self-delusion—too often, we find it easy to believe what we want to believe. But the fact is that they have avoided the glare of formal scrutiny about their personal responsibility for the litany of repeated, false statements in the run-up to war. Under the Republicans in 2005 and 2006, and the Democrats in 2007 and 2008, there was no congressional investigation into this specific question. Congressional oversight focused almost entirely on the *quality* of the US government's pre-war intelligence—not the veracity of the highest-ranking US officials' public statements or the objectivity and logic of their decision making in instigating the war. Nor in 2009 did the new Democratic president Barack Obama, his administration, or the Democratic Congress evince any interest in investigating this politically sensitive subject. There may be no more telling example of what has happened to congressional oversight in Washington in recent decades.

Investigating this tale of dishonesty by those in power and ac-quiescence on the part of those charged with reporting the truth has been a disheartening experience for me. Even more sobering, however, is the fact that the Iraq War deception, with its 935 public, shameless lies, is simply the latest and most egregious story of truth betrayed that I've witnessed or reported on over the past five de-cades. My career in journalism has coincided with a tragic period in American history—one in which falsehood has increasingly come to dominate our public discourse, and in which the bedrock values of honesty, transparency, accountability, and integrity we once took for granted have been steadily eroded.

During this period, we have been lied to innumerable times, by our government, by various corporations, and by other organiza-tions. Not only does it happen often, it happens with impunity, with little or no public accountability for these gross misdeeds. The mis-begotten Iraq War reflects the astonishing extent to which there are clearly discernible patterns of deception by those in power. The sad truth is that as citizens of this republic, we almost never have access to "real-time truth" about the most egregious abuses of power—that is, truth revealed as events are unfolding, so that we and our elected representatives can act to prevent or remedy the crimes.

As a result, we are increasingly benumbed by our politicians' prevarications, which include not just what they say, but what they *don't* say. For example, during the 2008 presidential campaign, how many Americans imagined that decisions by President Barack

Obama would lead to the deaths of hundreds of unarmed civilians in Pakistan by *quintupling* the use of drones as compared to the last four years of President George W. Bush's administration? The deployment of drones against alleged terrorists was barely mentioned during the 2008 presidential campaign, and it has taken journalists years to piece together the truth about these controversial killings.[16]

On the domestic front, Obama said repeatedly during the 2008 campaign that he would introduce national health-care-reform legislation, and the bill he championed—the Affordable Care Act—was indeed passed by Congress and has since been implemented. But along the way, Obama also reassured Americans that their existing health insurance would not be threatened, saying repeatedly, "If you like your health care plan, you can keep it." Since then, 4 million Americans have discovered that the president's statements were simply untrue. He was given the "Lie of the Year" award in 2013 by the Pulitzer Prize–winning, fact-checking website, PolitiFact.[17]

Deceptions like these—some by omission, others by commission—make a mockery of our political discourse.

Of course, lying by those in power is not new. History tells us that millions have died because of bold, confident falsehoods by those in positions of public or private authority. This kind of public nightmare keeps recurring across time and cultures, across economic and education levels, regardless of systems of governance or the extent of political independence and civil liberties. Examples include the crimes committed—and lied about—by humankind's most psychopathic mass murderers, from Adolf Hitler to Josef Stalin, from Mao Tse-tung (whose "Cultural Revolution" has been more accurately characterized as "China's Holocaust") to Pol Pot (whose Khmer Rouge were responsible for the "killing fields" in Cambodia). During the 1990s, in Rwanda, the minority Tutsi population was demonized for weeks on the airwaves as *inyenzi* (or "cockroaches") that needed to "disappear once and for all"; very soon thereafter, up to 1 million Tutsis were murdered within just a few short months.[18]

Around the same time, in Bosnia, the Serbs described Islam as a "malignant disease" that would "infect" Europe, and their "ethnic cleansing" between 1991 and 1995 resulted in roughly 200,000 Muslim casualties.[19] Even more recently, in the first mass brutality of the twenty-first century, Arab Islamic Janjaweed militias in the Darfur region of Sudan, working in tandem with the Sudanese government, murdered hundreds of thousands of African tribal members and displaced millions more, with the brutality also spreading into Chad and the Central African Republic.[20]

Although the details of the carnage certainly have varied, the means by which it was achieved have not. In each case, those in power strictly controlled the flow of information, corroding and corrupting its content, using newspapers, radio, television, and other means of mass communication to consolidate their authority and cover their crimes in a veneer of fervent racialism or nationalism. And always with the specter of an imminent public threat—what the twentieth-century political theorist Hannah Arendt called "objective enemies"—as an excuse for their tyrannical actions.[21]

At one time, we Americans assumed we were immune from such ruthless, systematic criminality—that a combination of our commitment to democracy, the integrity of our public leaders, and the vigilance of our news media would ensure that our citizenry would always have access to the truth and thereby be equipped to make wise, informed decisions about matters of national interest. Unfortunately, this assumption—always somewhat dubious—has become much shakier over time. And over the past half century, the American track record in regard to public truth has grown steadily worse.

That's the story I seek to explore in this book—how and why our national commitment to integrity has been eroded; how a relative handful of reporters, activists, and other truth-seekers have tried to fight back in an increasingly unsupportive, vacuous media environment; and what we can do as a nation to reverse this tragic trend.

935 Lies is made up of three main strands. The first is a retrospective review of the struggle for truth in the recent past, including some of my own experiences as an investigative reporter. If you've lived through the decades since 1960, you may think that some of the stories I'll tell are familiar—but many of the details included here, including some of the most shocking, are still relatively little known. And my emphasis on the ways in which the truth was hidden or distorted by those in power—until it was ultimately exposed, often years or decades later—provides a unique perspective on the importance of real-time truth that is crucially important for the future of our democracy.

In a case that foreshadowed the Iraq debacle, the American people were misled by the Johnson administration and the Pentagon into a war in Vietnam that cost 58,000 US lives and hundreds of thousands of Vietnamese lives and ultimately led to a humiliating defeat. Some in the media fought back against the assault on truth. The publication of the Pentagon Papers and the exposure of the Nixon Watergate scandal still represent US history's high-water mark in the long-standing struggle between raw political power and democratic values. But much important information about the abuses by those in power took years to become known to the public. As Benjamin C. Bradlee, executive editor of the *Washington Post* at the time, reflected more than two decades later, "What might have happened had the truth emerged in 1963 instead of 1971? . . ."[22] Perhaps the tragedy of America's war in Vietnam might have been avoided altogether. We will delve more deeply into this intriguing subject in Chapter 1.

Unfortunately, the Vietnam and Iraq War deceptions are only two of the most egregious examples of abuses of power by the US government in the past century. I describe some of the others in later chapters—for example, America's secret wars in Latin America during the 1980s. Appendix A lists and details the most grievous of these transgressions and delineates when the public epiphany or official recognition about them precisely occurred, and when and who the first journalists were to discover and write about them.

At the same time, private corporations have certainly also been guilty of covering up and lying about their misdeeds, from financial manipulations by investment banks to the manufacture and sale of harmful products like tobacco, asbestos, and lead paint. For example, in September 2008, Lehman Brothers filed for the largest bankruptcy in history, imperiling the nation's entire financial system. The company had systematically concealed more than $100 billion of risky assets from investors and regulators, using a technique it called "Repo 105," then lied outright when later asked about its duplicitous bookkeeping.[23] E-mails that subsequently surfaced showed that senior Lehman executives clearly understood the practice was wrong. Most business journalists failed to uncover the deception in a timely fashion, part of a "general system failure," according to the *Columbia Journalism Review*.[24]

Many of these corporate offenses against the truth are discussed in detail in later chapters of this book; they are catalogued and described in Appendix A. Like the governmental deceptions recounted in these pages, these private duplicities illustrate the disturbing frequency with which those in power have managed to conceal their misdeeds from the public. One important purpose of this book is simply to document this pattern in the hope that other concerned citizens will find it as troubling—indeed, as enraging—as I do.

The second major strand of this book is an examination of what has happened to commercial journalism in recent years and how this change has affected the quality and quantity of news coverage—in particular, the historically significant, difficult, expensive, and sometimes dangerous work of journalists investigating the unpalatable truths that those in power seek to conceal.

I think you'll find that some of my experiences in the world of commercial media—especially my years at *60 Minutes*, perhaps our country's most significant mainstream effort to consistently supply serious news coverage to the general public—vividly illuminate both the power of these traditional outlets as purveyors of crucial truths and the pitfalls they increasingly encounter as they strive to do their work.

Finally, I'll consider the future of truth—the path we can take as a society to reverse the decline in public integrity and restore the Jeffersonian ideal of a truly informed citizenry with control of its national destiny. I'll assess the significance of new technologies, global information platforms, and the emerging new journalism ecosystem in the United States and globally, and I'll detail my view of "the possible" when it comes to the future of investigative reporting and how citizens around the world may be able to obtain credible, independent information about those in power in the twenty-first century.

If I am right in believing that truth today is under siege—that those in power have become more skilled than ever at obscuring the truth and twisting our perceptions of reality itself, and that the truth-telling capacity of journalists in our society has become correspondingly debilitated—then where does that leave us as citizens, as voters, as consumers? Under such distorted circumstances, how can we make important decisions about our collective destiny? How can we begin to seek and obtain redress when we are wronged, if we cannot even ascertain what exactly happened and why? We are like a boat that has lost its moorings, adrift.

But there's no need for us to yield to despair. This is also a book about hope, about the indomitable human spirit and how, across the world, kindred souls have gotten mad as hell, decided not to take it anymore, and in many cases have left conventional, commercial journalism to launch their own nonprofit news organizations. I'll explain how my own frustration led me to quit my job as a producer for senior correspondent Mike Wallace at *60 Minutes* in 1988 and found a new, nonpartisan, watchdog journalism organization in Washington called the Center for Public Integrity. The Center eventually grew to become the largest nonprofit investigative reporting publisher in the world, winning scores of national journalism awards. [25] And the movement that the Center helped to spawn has grown rapidly. Today there are roughly one hundred nonprofit news publishers in the United States, most of which have begun operation just since 2006. The most important accountability reporting in the United States will increasingly emanate from this new journalism ecosystem.

Those in power can be held accountable for their actions. I have been inspired by hundreds of people, from professional journalists to citizen activists working in traditional and nontraditional media outlets, who have made it their mission to investigate "the bastards" and expose their monstrous lies, greed, and abuses of power. In many countries, these watchdogs put their lives on the line, risking everything from incarceration and financial ruin to physical injury including death.

Their indomitable will is animated by the timeless hope that French novelist Émile Zola immortalized: "Truth is on the march and nothing can stop it."[26] Their courageous commitment to the unadorned, raw truth humbles and inspires me, and their example should inform and encourage us all.

Our First Casualty

God offers to every mind its choice between truth and
repose. Take which you please. You can never have both.
—RALPH WALDO EMERSON, 1841[1]

A S A CHILD GROWING UP in the 1950s and 1960s, and as a
young adult into the 1970s, I thought I had a clear, unmistakable view of what constituted truth. And like millions of
baby boomers living through that tumultuous, painful epoch, I was
shocked and dismayed when many of the presumed certainties I'd
grown up with melted away.

I had a Norman Rockwell childhood in Newark, Delaware, as
a fifth-generation native of that small city. I grew up literally on
Main Street—the less affluent end of Main Street, as it happened—
and my mother was a member of the Daughters of the American
Revolution. I was an Eagle Scout and president of my high school
student body, born into a middle-class, Republican-voting (though
not politically active), Christian (though not regular churchgoing)
household where the Ten Commandments, the Golden Rule, and
other core teachings were indelibly imbued. These values were not
repressively imposed on my younger sister and me by our parents,

Charles and Dorothy Cherry Lewis, but they were quietly understood amid the irreverence and humor that pervaded our home, from my father's dry wit to my mother's earthy and hilarious farm stories.

My parents lived through the Great Depression and World War II, and those events informed their—and our—perceptions of the world. When their farmhouse in Ridgely, Maryland, burned to the ground during the Depression, my mother's entire family was forced into a drafty wooden barn for a year, with no indoor plumbing and only a Home Comfort cookstove for heat. Friends and neighbors provided clothes and food, and within a year, they'd built a new house with beams and boards they'd bartered for raw timber harvested from their land.

Later, my parents met while working at a war materiel plant in Newark and were married in that same Ridgely farmhouse in July 1945, as the war was winding down. Three of their five brothers had gone off to fight, one nearly killed by shrapnel that remained forever lodged in his back. Years later, we learned over one Thanksgiving dinner that my mother had volunteered to be a wartime "plane spotter" for the Civil Air Patrol. Among my parents' wedding presents were war-rationed gas stamps that they used to take a honeymoon drive to Baltimore and Luray, Virginia.

Growing up in the shadow of these times, my sister and I were inevitably imbued with values like hard work and patriotism. The United States, we were taught, is a powerful but inherently peace-loving nation, fighting wars reluctantly and conscientiously adhering to international human-rights standards that we helped to establish. And of course we knew that American presidents—that noble line of heroes stretching from FDR and Teddy Roosevelt back through Lincoln and Washington—would never lie to the people or otherwise abuse their power.

And then things started to change.

Our First Casualty

The shocks began when I was ten. In the middle of an ordinary school afternoon, we got word that President Kennedy—our nation's youngest elected president—had been gunned down. Along with tens of millions of other Americans, I was mesmerized by the three days of searing TV news coverage: the initial sense of disbelief, confusion, and horror; the killing of the presumed assassin—on live national TV, no less; and the spectacle of the funeral, with the flag-draped coffin, the riderless horse, the grief-shattered widow, and the fatherless children even younger than me.

For me, as for countless others, those three days in 1963 were my first visceral encounter with the tragic side of life. We didn't yet realize how familiar that sense of shared horror would become. But then, as the 1960s wore on, it became clear even to a young teenager that something very terrible—and perhaps very wrong—was happening to our country in a distant, once-unknown land known as Vietnam.

I vividly recall when the reality of that steadily worsening war hit home for us in Newark. It was in March 1967, when Marine Corporal Lawrence Lee LaSalle—my friend Randy LaSalle's older brother, Larry—was killed in Vietnam. Suddenly the war was more than a flickering image on our TV set—it was a living threat, real enough to claim the life of a Newark boy.

Months later I accompanied Randy and his father, our kind-hearted assistant scoutmaster, on a visit to Larry's grave at Arlington National Cemetery. I recall the mind-numbing enormity of it all—the cemetery with its thousands of white crosses, each representing a young man or woman fallen in one of the nation's conflicts as well as (I now understood) the inescapable lifelong sorrow of a family and a community.

But at least Larry and his fellow soldiers had died for a worthy cause, fighting to preserve our nation's freedom in an unavoidable war against tyranny much like the world wars that an earlier generation had won. So we believed.

We'd learned from the news and in our discussions of current events at school that the escalation of US military involvement in the war between the Communist government of North Vietnam and our allies in South Vietnam had been authorized by congressional passage of the Gulf of Tonkin Resolution in August 1964. That resolution, in turn, had been prompted by a series of events in the coastal waters off North Vietnam earlier in the month. On August 2, North Vietnamese patrol boats had approached the US naval destroyer *Maddox*, whose crew opened fire. The crew of the USS *Ticonderoga* also fired on the patrol boats, sinking one and damaging two others.[2]

Then, on the morning of August 4, the *Maddox* reported another attack by unspecified vessels. When President Lyndon Johnson authorized a military response, sixty-four US naval planes bombed four North Vietnamese PT boat bases and a petroleum storage area. According to the Pentagon, twenty-five of the thirty boats there were either destroyed or damaged, and the smoke from an oil depot "was observed rising to 14,000 feet."[3]

On August 5, 1964, in a televised address to the nation, Johnson described what had happened. "Renewed hostile actions against the United States ships on the high seas in the Gulf of Tonkin . . . have today required me to order the military forces of the United States to take action in reply." Johnson claimed the US warships had been on "routine patrol in international waters," and that the North Vietnamese "attacks were deliberate. The attacks were unprovoked. The attacks have been answered . . . The government of North Vietnam is today flouting the will of the world for peace."[4]

The very next day, the Senate Foreign Relations Committee and the House Foreign Affairs Committees held closed-door hearings to vote on this requested joint resolution, which decreed that the United States would be "prepared, as the President determines, to take all necessary steps, including the use of force" to help any Southeast Asia Treaty Organization (SEATO) member "requiring assistance in defense of its freedom." During these secret sessions, legislators were told vaguely about US covert activities in the Tonkin Gulf vicinity beforehand. It had been the South Vietnamese forces, they were informed, that had conducted covert raids, using boats and other military support from the United States.

There was only one dissenting vote in the two committees, by Senator Wayne Morse, Democrat of Oregon, who bluntly told Defense Secretary Robert McNamara to his face: "I think we are kidding the world if you try to give the impression that when the South Vietnamese naval boats bombarded two islands a short distance off the coast of North Vietnam, we were not implicated."[5]

On August 7, just three days after the second, suspicious attack on the *Maddox*, Congress gave the president his Gulf of Tonkin Resolution. The measure passed the House of Representatives by a vote of 416 to 0, and the Senate by 88 to 2. Joining Wayne Morse in opposition was Senator Ernest Gruening, Democrat of Alaska. Together they argued that the resolution was a "predated declaration of war power," which of course it was.[6] That day on the Senate floor, Morse declared, "I believe that history will record that we have made a great mistake in subverting and circumventing the Constitution of the United States . . . by means of this resolution . . . we are in effect giving the President . . . war-making powers in the absence of a declaration of war. I believe that to be a historic mistake."[7]

At the time—and for years afterward—Morse's dissent was scoffed at by most American political leaders. But his words would prove prophetic. Over time, many of those who had unhesitatingly supported our involvement in Vietnam gradually came to recognize the depth of their mistake. And so did much of the general public, though very slowly and incompletely.

In 1982, eighteen years after the Gulf of Tonkin Resolution, George Ball, the highest-ranking skeptic about the escalating Vietnam policies inside the Johnson administration, would describe that measure as a "terrifyingly open-ended grant of power." "I had counted on Congress to insert qualifying language," he complained, "but Congress had abdicated."[8]

So had the national news media, which trumpeted the Johnson administration policies. "The nation's united confidence in the Chief Executive is vital," the *New York Times* wrote. The *Washington Post* editorialized that "President Johnson has earned the gratitude of the free world."[9] No wonder the vast majority of Americans rallied behind the president's call to arms. Not only had the leader of the free world testified to a grave danger threatening our nation's interests, but the independent newspapers that serve as public watchdogs had backed him to the hilt. Ordinary citizens could do no less.

And so the war came. The boys from Newark, and countless other cities and towns and villages, were shipped off to Southeast Asia. And as the weeks turned into months and years, their numbers continued to grow, even as thousands began coming home in body bags.

∽∂∾

It was only years later that I, and millions of other Americans, began to learn, little by little, what had really happened between the United States and Vietnam during those shadowy months of 1964. And the slow, haphazard emergence of those revelations was to prove as devastating to our sense of normality and national identity as the death of John F. Kennedy and the Vietnam War itself.

The Gulf of Tonkin Resolution, we would learn, which had authorized direct US involvement in the Vietnam War and nearly all the resulting carnage, was a monumental misrepresentation.[10] Prior to enemy hostilities there, the US government had been engaged in Top Secret intelligence-gathering activities in violation of another country's sovereign land, air space, and territorial waters, including consciously planned, aggressive military provocations against North Vietnam.

No one in the Congress was aware of this, nor did lawmakers know about the clandestine high-level war diplomacy that had been going on for months—talks in which the United States threatened the North Vietnamese with a dramatic escalation of American military involvement there. All of these activities had been authorized and secretly set in motion by President Lyndon Johnson. But telling the truth about them would have been simply too politically embarrassing and legally problematic, so instead Johnson and his top administration officials repeatedly fed the American people, the Congress, and US allies falsehoods they considered more palatable.

There had been no unprovoked attack on the US destroyer *Maddox* and other naval vessels, as the nation was told; in fact, our small patrol boats had attacked the North Vietnamese *first*, and separately, our destroyers had already entered their territorial waters. The *Maddox* and other destroyers were on a secret intelligence mission known as the "DESOTO patrols." Their mission: to enter the territorial waters of the North Vietnamese and provoke them to turn on their coastal radar systems, thereby revealing their defense systems in hopes of providing intelligence for future air or sea attacks. The collected data were then passed on to the National Security Agency (NSA) for decryption and translation.[11]

Another covert action program, OPLAN 34A, which President Johnson approved in early 1964 and was carried out the night of July 30, authorized the shelling of two North Vietnamese islands in the Gulf of Tonkin by high-speed patrol boats known as Nastys.[12] These operations were controlled by the Central Intelligence Agency (CIA) and the Pentagon's Military Assistance Command, Vietnam (MACV), working closely with the US Navy.[13] They led directly to the confrontations involving the *Maddox* and the *Ticonderoga*, as well

7

as the bombing of the North Vietnamese boat bases and the oil depot smoke that "was observed rising to 14,000 feet." After that attack, in an anecdote that only emerged years later, Johnson proudly bragged to a few selected reporters, "I didn't just screw Ho Chi Minh, I cut his pecker off."[14]

Only in time did it emerge that there had not, in fact, been a second attack against the *Maddox* on August 4. In 1982, for example, we learned that moments after Congress passed the Gulf of Tonkin Resolution, Johnson told Undersecretary of State George Ball, "Hell, those dumb, stupid sailors were just shooting at flying fish."[15]

In 1990, one of the navy pilots flying over Tonkin that night, squadron commander James Stockdale, told the *Chicago Tribune*, "I had the best seat in the house to watch that event and our destroyers were just shooting at phantom targets—there were no [North Vietnamese] PT boats there . . . I reported that, and Washington received it promptly, but we went to war anyway."[16]

Even one of the war's chief architects, former secretary of defense Robert McNamara, eventually had to acknowledge Stockdale's observation. In his 1995 memoir, *In Retrospect*, McNamara admitted that "the facts remain in dispute even now, thirty years later."[17] And in November 1995, as a participant in a US-Vietnam historic conference in Hanoi, McNamara became convinced that the supposed second attack on US ships had, in fact, *never* occurred. Had he known this in 1964, he said, "We would not have carried out that military attack."[18]

One of his Defense Department special assistants in August 1964, Daniel Ellsberg, best known for leaking the classified Pentagon Papers, was privy to all secret cable and communications traffic between Vietnam, McNamara's office, and the highest levels of the White House. In his 2002 memoir, Ellsberg wrote that he had become certain "beyond reasonable doubt" by 1971 that there had been no second attack.[19]

But the real evidentiary coup de grâce was delivered in 2005, when the National Security Agency officially confirmed—four decades after the fact—that no second attack on US ships had occurred in Tonkin on August 4, 1964. Declassifying more than one hundred incident-related documents, including an article by National Security Agency historian Robert Hanyok explaining what really happened, the NSA essentially admitted its officials had "mishandled" signals intelligence (known as SIGINT) and provided the president, the secretary of defense, and others with "skewed" intelligence supporting "the notion that there had been an attack."[20] In *Legacy of Ashes*, his 2007 Pulitzer Prize–winning history of the CIA, Tim Weiner characterized the NSA disclosure and its larger significance this way: "It was not an honest mistake. The war in Vietnam began with political lies based on fake intelligence."[21]

The whole Tonkin affair, with its geographical obscurity, lack of local, on-the-scene reporting, or other independent sources of information, and very tight time pressures, could not have been more convenient for Johnson. The attack on US military forces, dramatically announced by the president and the Pentagon, would make the Congress willing to approve a blank-check authorization of force.[22]

Curiously enough, the former Senate majority leader, vice president, and now president, Lyndon B. Johnson, had quietly ordered his aides to prepare just such an open-ended Vietnam resolution months earlier, *prior* to the Tonkin Gulf incident. There would never be a formal declaration of war by the Congress about Vietnam; none was needed. The Gulf of Tonkin Resolution would do just fine.

∽∾

All of this multilayered subterfuge and manipulation, though, paled in magnitude to what Johnson was secretly doing at the military and diplomatic levels, unbeknownst to Congress, the nation, and the world. The president had assured Americans in his August 5, 1964, address that "we seek no wider war." But for months, in fact, he and his administration had been making precise, elaborate plans to do just that and had also delivered an explicit threat to Ho Chi Minh, president of the Democratic Republic of Vietnam (DRV), and his Hanoi regime. The message: call off the current fighting or risk a much deeper, wider US war involvement.[23]

Furthermore, since the spring of 1964, the Joint Chiefs of Staff had secretly been drawing up precise plans for direct air attacks on North Vietnam. By the end of May, they had recommended ninety-four specific bombing targets.[24]

The need for secrecy was heightened by domestic political considerations. Johnson was running for a full term as president in 1964 on a "peace platform," branding the Republican presidential nominee, Arizona Republican senator Barry Goldwater, as a warmonger willing to use nuclear weapons. Yet at the same time, the US government at its highest levels was secretly girding for a major escalation of the Vietnam War.

On August 18, 1964, the US ambassador to South Vietnam, Maxwell Taylor, proposed a direct "carefully orchestrated bombing attack" on North Vietnam with "January 1, 1965, as a target D-Day." And the Joint Chiefs of Staff in the Pentagon were continuing to advocate air strikes.[25]

Just two months before the presidential election, John McNaughton, assistant secretary for international security affairs and perhaps Robert McNamara's closest adviser, wrote a chilling memo discussing potential options in light of the deteriorating situation in South Vietnam. McNaughton mentioned that the United States could "enlarge significantly the US military role in the pacification program inside South Vietnam—e.g., large number of US special forces, divisions of regular combat troops, US air, etc., to 'interlard' with or to take over functions or geographical areas from the South

Vietnamese armed forces." This could begin to occur around October 1, but "it postpones probably until November or December any decision as to serious escalation."[26]

McNaughton also proposed various "extra-territorial" covert actions in North Vietnam and Laos, which would not only cause "apprehension . . . they should be likely at some point to provoke a military DRV [North Vietnamese] response . . . the provoked response should be likely to provide good grounds for us to escalate if we wished." The "timing and crescendo should be under our control, with the scenario capable of being turned off at any time. . . ."[27]

Under the heading "*Special considerations during next two months*" (italics in the original), McNaughton wrote: "During the next two months, because of the lack of 'rebuttal time' before election to justify particular actions which may be distorted to the U.S. public, we must act with special care—signaling to . . . [the South Vietnamese] that we are behaving energetically despite the restraints of our political season, and to the U.S. public that we are behaving with good purpose and restraint."[28]

It is noteworthy that within weeks of this memorandum and all of the other growing internal energies toward massively escalating the war, Lyndon Johnson was assuring voters in campaign stops that "we are not about to send American boys nine or ten thousand miles away from home to do what Asian boys ought to be doing for themselves."[29]

Johnson's duplicity worked in the short term: he was elected in a landslide. But he never really sought and certainly never received the American people's informed consent to the policies he'd planned to follow. As Sissela Bok later wrote in *Lying: Moral Choice in Public and Private Life*, "Believing they had voted for the candidate of peace, American citizens were, within months, deeply embroiled in one of the cruelest wars in their history. Deception of this kind strikes at the very essence of democratic government."[30]

Beginning in 1965, fragments of the truth began to trickle out. Yet the lies about Vietnam continued. And as they did so—not only through Johnson's administration but into that of Richard Nixon—the moral authority of the presidency ebbed away.

∽∂∾

Within months of the 1964 Tonkin incidents, support for the Vietnam War and the Johnson administration had begun to erode in Congress and among the general public. And with the deployment of 100,000 fresh US troops by August of that year and double that by the end of 1965, those tensions only escalated.

Along with the buildup of troops in Vietnam came an increase in the number of journalists dispatched there, including network television crews. Some reporters were embarrassed by their own obsequiousness to power and angry at the way they'd been so easily manipulated during the Tonkin affair. Among those who apparently felt no such uneasiness was Chet Huntley, the highly regarded co-anchor of the NBC evening news show *The Huntley-Brinkley Report*, who actually narrated the US Navy's official film about the Tonkin incidents.[31] But by all accounts, though, a culture shift was beginning to occur inside the profession about how war and government officials ought to be covered, and that change appears, in part, to have been generational.

The first reporters to develop a new skepticism were the young war correspondents based in Saigon in the earliest years of the US involvement. Their ranks included David Halberstam, Neil Sheehan, Malcolm Browne, Peter Arnett, and Charles Mohr; among the television correspondents doing fearless war reporting were two from CBS, Morley Safer, thirty-three, and Jack Laurence, twenty-six.[32]

In January 1968, with the United States deep into the quagmire, the North Vietnamese stunned the world by launching the huge Tet

Offensive, attacking thirty-six of forty-four provincial capitals and five of the six major cities in South Vietnam.[33] This was clearly at odds with what most Americans had been led to believe over the previous few years—that victory in Vietnam was practically imminent. As a result, the Johnson administration's false image of reality there finally came crashing down.

And this time the news media were there in full force. For example, with the war a growing political issue—especially on the eve of the 1968 presidential campaign—Walter Cronkite reported from Saigon in late February and early March of 1968. The famous CBS *Evening News* anchor augmented four successive daily broadcasts with personal commentary critical of the situation in Vietnam, and he also weighed in with a critical prime-time special report on Vietnam.

Cronkite, a former United Press correspondent who had reported from the front in World War Two and covered the Nuremberg trials before joining CBS, had also briefly reported on the Korean War and had been to Vietnam. He had always supported the anti-communist containment strategy of the United States, and his reporting had always been generally favorable to the military. But by 1968 he recognized that American casualties and opposition to the war were steadily mounting. Not only had this conflict now dragged on longer than those earlier wars, it appeared to be hopeless, with no end in sight. His trip to Vietnam in February and March cemented this impression and convinced Cronkite that the White House and the military had been misleading the public about the war.[34]

In Vietnam, Cronkite was acutely aware of the difference between what he was being told by the full-press military officials and what he actually witnessed. Amid the piles of body bags and other jarring sights and sounds of war, General William Westmoreland and other top brass kept telling Cronkite that things were exactly as they'd hoped. In fact, the military and the Johnson administration declared

13

the Tet Offensive to be a decisive US victory, noting, for example, that the enemy had suffered more casualties than the Americans had. Yet Cronkite and his producer had difficulty even *landing* in the country—all of the airports were closed, and when they finally arrived in Saigon, there was fighting all around them. As Halberstam later described it, "It was an Orwellian trip—Orwell had written of a Ministry of Truth in charge of Lying and a Ministry of Peace in charge of War—and here was Cronkite flying to Saigon, where the American military command was surrounded by defeat and calling it victory."[35]

For the first time since he had become the public face of the network news division, the respected anchorman decided to speak out personally and provide his own commentary about what he had seen and concluded. Cronkite understood the potential risk to his credibility, given his standing as a national oracle of objectivity. But in conversations with his producers, and angered by the years of deception by federal officials, he believed "that this was one instance in which traditional objectivity was probably the more misleading, the more dishonest position."[36]

On February 27, 1968, in the prime-time TV viewing hours, Cronkite concluded his special report about Vietnam:

> We have been too often disappointed by the optimism of the American leaders, both in Vietnam and Washington, to have faith any longer in the silver linings they find in the darkest clouds . . . For it seems now more certain than ever that the bloody experience of Vietnam is to end in a stalemate . . . To say that we are closer to victory today is to believe, in the face of the evidence, the optimists who have been wrong in the past. . . . It is increasingly clear to this reporter that the only rational way out then will be to negotiate, not as victors, but as an honorable people

who lived up to their pledge to defend democracy, and did the best they could.[37]

Within five weeks, the domestic politics of the war had shifted dramatically. Two Democratic senators, Eugene McCarthy and Robert F. Kennedy, mounted successful presidential bids challenging Johnson's Vietnam policy. And in a nationally televised speech on the night of March 31, Johnson announced that he'd rejected a request from his top generals to further escalate the war by adding *another* 206,000 new troops. Furthermore, he revealed a halt to US bombing above the twentieth parallel in Vietnam. Finally, Johnson dramatically told the nation: "I shall not seek, and will not accept, the nomination of my party for another term as your President."[38]

∽◦∾

In the ensuing four decades, more of the truth about the Vietnam War—including the intricate political, diplomatic, and military decisions that guided US policies—has gradually emerged in articles, books, documentaries, conferences, and declassified documents. So too have scholarly analyses of the news coverage of that war, assessing its fairness, accuracy, and impact on public opinion.

It is clear that the vast bulk of American news media failed in their watchdog role during the early, critical months of the war, when a skeptical evaluation of the administration claims surrounding the Tonkin incident might have helped prevent the tragic escalation of our involvement. But the blame doesn't lie solely with a compliant media. The president and his administration, in fact, had severely limited the circumstances for any independent, high-quality reporting, making it virtually impossible for the unvarnished truth to emerge in real time.

Consider the plight of Murrey Marder, the distinguished *Washington Post* veteran whose coverage of Senator Joseph McCarthy in the early 1950s had been among the most unflinching and discerning, and who, in 1957, had become the first overseas correspondent for that paper's foreign service.

On the night of August 2, 1964, Marder happened to be in the State Department press room when the Associated Press (AP) reported that North Vietnamese patrol boats had attacked two US destroyers. Marder told me years later about his skeptical reaction to the report. "I looked at this and I thought, well, that's strange. I have been on torpedo boats. And torpedo boats are not equipped to attack destroyers."

Marder got a trusted State Department intelligence source on the phone and asked him bluntly, "What were we doing to them to provoke them to do this?" Marder wheedled out of his source an admission that "yes, we had been conducting some operations there."[39]

But Marder's source refused to be quoted by name, and time to get out this alternative version of the story was quickly ebbing. And there was another problem by the time Johnson uttered his first public statements about the attack. Marder learned, to his great dismay, that his own newspaper—notoriously close to Johnson for years, to the extent that former publisher Philip Graham had helped broker Kennedy's selection of Johnson as his running mate in 1960—had just editorially endorsed the Gulf of Tonkin Resolution. In fact, practically every major American newspaper did likewise, and 85 percent of Americans polled backed the US bombing raids. Just three months before the election, the president's overall approval rating jumped to 72 percent from 42 percent.[40]

Under the circumstances, there was little chance that a dissenting view of the official Tonkin Gulf story, backed only by an anonymous quotation from a State Department source, would be featured prominently—or at all—in a leading US newspaper.

Until his death in 2013, Marder was haunted by his failure to do everything he could to push his story about the truth behind Tonkin Gulf more aggressively. Remarkably, Marder donated fully two-thirds of his life savings to create the Nieman Watchdog Project, a nonprofit project within Harvard University's Nieman Foundation, dedicated to help the press ask penetrating questions, critical questions, questions that matter, questions not yet asked about today's news.[41] (I'll have more to say about this project and similar ones in Chapter 8.)

At the time, the toughest critic of the US military actions was liberal muckraker I. F. Stone, known for eschewing exclusive interviews with Washington newsmakers and instead actually *reading* government documents, no matter how obscure. In his *Weekly* newsletter distributed to 70,000 subscribers, Stone wrote that the United States had violated the League of Nations Covenant, the Kellogg Pact, and the United Nations Charter, as well as internal government-policy edicts from such obscure publications as the "old War Department manual, *Rules of Land Warfare.*"[42]

Standing quite alone, Stone published one of the first investigative reports of the Tonkin Gulf incidents on August 24, 1964, intricately delineating how "the American Government and the American press have kept the full truth about the Tonkin Bay incidents from the American public." He raised serious factual contradictions in the official version of events surrounding what he called the "alleged" second Tonkin attack, noting that no photographs had been provided, nor "flotsam and jetsam as proof of the wreckage" from the incident at sea. Whatever the true story, Stone wrote, "the second incident seems to have triggered off a long planned attack of our own."[43]

Stone also explained one of the reasons for the uncritical coverage by the press, and its susceptibility to being misled: "The process of brain-washing the public starts with off-the-record briefings for newspapermen in which all sorts of far-fetched theories are suggested to explain why the tiny North Vietnamese navy would be mad enough to venture an attack on the Seventh Fleet, one of the world's most powerful. *Everything is discussed except the possibility that the attack might have been provoked* [italics in original]."[44]

The president had placed the news media, the Congress, and the entire country in an extremely tight bind, as journalist David Halberstam put it in words hauntingly familiar today, "at the level of patriotism and emotion. He would give them, when he was ready, the flag, and they would salute it."[45]

What about the performance of the media later in the Vietnam War? Is it true, as claimed in a persistent mythology embraced by some military officers and others, that the news media, especially television, turned American opinion against the war?

Television was actually still a relatively new medium in the late 1960s, though TV sets were ubiquitous: there were 10,000 television sets in the United States in 1941, 10 million by the time of the Korean War, and 100 million at the peak of the Vietnam War.[46] So Vietnam was essentially America's first "living room war," as many media analysts have noted. But the public implications of that fact are not clear, particularly in the context of mounting casualties, crushing budgetary costs, and years of stalemate. In fact, one study found that of roughly 2,300 stories from South Vietnam that were televised on evening news programs, only seventy-six "showed anything approaching true violence—heavy fighting, incoming small arms and artillery fire, [soldiers who had been] killed and wounded within view."[47]

According to John Mueller, author of *War, Presidents and Public Opinion*, there are no polling data to support the notion that "largely uncensored day-by-day television coverage of the war and its brutalities made a profound impression on public attitudes."[48] There is, however, a direct polling-data relationship between casualties and public opinion. Support for the Vietnam war fell fifteen points every time casualties increased by a factor of ten.[49]

What's more, detailed content analysis of newspaper and television coverage of US involvement in Vietnam by scholar Clarence R. Wyatt and others reveals that "more often than not, the press reported official information, statements, and views with relatively little dissent." Notwithstanding the courageous reporting of many individual journalists, some of whom lost their lives or were severely wounded, the sad, simple truth is that the Vietnam War showed that "the ability and inclination of the Executive Branch to restrict and manipulate information is largely beyond the press' ability to resist."[50]

Even the biggest exception to that overall pattern is revealing. One of the most significant investigative news stories about the Vietnam War revealed the March 16, 1968, massacre of hundreds of innocent civilians in the village of My Lai, including children and the elderly. My Lai became a byword for atrocity, and one of its alleged perpetrators, Lieutenant William Calley, became a potent symbol for both opponents and supporters of the war.

But the My Lai story was not broken by any Vietnam- or Washington-based correspondent for a major news organization. There had been no reporter on the scene that horrific day, there were no TV cameras, and the troops involved were ordered not to discuss the incident. Finally, *twenty months* after the atrocity, it was exposed by a young, former Associated Press reporter and author named Seymour Hersh.

The story behind the story is equally significant. Hearing about the US Army's court martial prosecution of Calley, Hersh—aided by a grant from the new Washington-based Fund for Investigative Journalism—traveled to Fort Benning, Georgia. He managed to find Calley there, living under house arrest, and interviewed him for five hours.[51] In Claremont, California, Hersh then interviewed

Ron Ridenhour, the former GI who had learned about My Lai from others and, in March 1969, blew the whistle about it in a five-page letter to President Richard Nixon, members of Congress, and other US officials, which prompted the army's internal investigation. Yet Hersh couldn't find anyone in the major news media to publish his story. An editor at *Life* said "it was out of the question." [52]

Sy Hersh has told me, "Nobody wanted it. Nobody . . . I couldn't get anybody to touch this story, and it was pretty scary, so we decided . . . to syndicate. I had a wonderful friend named David Obst, who said, let's just put it out ourselves, our own news service." Hersh filed his first story about My Lai with a new, little-known syndication outfit called Dispatch News Service, and it ran on November 13, 1969, in the *St. Louis Post-Dispatch* and other newspapers.

By the next day, the army was under such public pressure it took correspondents from the *New York Times, Newsweek,* and ABC News to see what was left of My Lai. There were no signs of life in the village, but reporters saw several mounds of earth that appeared to be mass graves. Eventually, shocking, undeniable photographs of the human carnage taken by US Army photographer Ronald Haeberle and others became public.

One major problem affecting the overall quality of Vietnam War news coverage was that virtually all of the US reporters sent by major news organizations to cover the conflict took a US-centric view of the affair. Phillip Knightley, author of the seminal book about the history of war reporting, *The First Casualty,* has noted that early on, American correspondents did not question the US policy of intervention in Vietnam but instead wrote about its effectiveness. Even the great correspondent Neil Sheehan, who reported alongside David Halberstam for United Press International (UPI) and later for the *New York Times,* wrote in his Pulitzer Prize–winning book, *A Bright Shining Lie,* about how American reporters shared the US military's "sense of commitment" to the war. "We regarded the conflict as our war too. We believed in what our government said it was going to accomplish in Vietnam, and we wanted our country to win this war just as passionately as [they] did."[53]

Another vexing problem for news organizations was the relative ease with which officialdom could play reporters in the field against their editors in Washington. One of *Time* magazine's correspondents in Vietnam, John Shaw, told Knightley, "For years the press corps in Vietnam was undermined by the White House and the Pentagon. Many American editors ignored what their correspondents in Vietnam were telling them in favor of the Washington version. Yet the Pentagon Papers proved to the hilt that what the correspondents in Saigon had been sending was true." The "Washington version" was the politically spun version, the Big Schmooze, over drinks, meals, phone calls, and other intimate access "granted" by major officials to editors, publishers, executive producers, and other network bigwigs.[54]

The dichotomy within the news media between Washington and Saigon reflected to some extent the conflicting perceptions of a reality problem afflicting the Department of Defense. When Halberstam returned to Vietnam for three months in the fall of 1967, he was disillusioned by "the optimism I found among the top Americans in Saigon, which struck me as essentially self-deception . . . It reflected once again the immense difference between what people in the field thought was happening and what people in the Saigon command, responding to intense political pressure from Washington, wanted to think was happening." Johnson press secretary George Christian remembered, "It was pretty obvious to me that the impact on the public of [the 1968] Tet [Offensive] was very detrimental to the President's war effort. But the impact on our military in Vietnam was actually considerably the other way. You know, it was quite a victory in their eyes . . . (laughs) It is all in the eye of the beholder."[55]

∿⁀

Humans, of course, have a remarkable capacity for self-delusion. To those in power, the control of information is regarded as utterly essential to achieving success, regardless of subject or policy, of administration or even country. The lessons of the Vietnam War for cold-blooded, pragmatic wielders of national power were not that excessive government secrecy was wrong. Or that waging something as gravely consequential as war without the informed consent of the governed is wrong, indeed immoral. Or that the political control of information in times of war, including misstating or overstating the facts, corrupts the government's internal decision-making ability and circumvents the central tenet of self-government of the people, by the people, and for the people.

In fact, serious power practitioners believe such sensibilities are quaint and naïve do-gooder sentiment, to be disregarded. Realpolitik, they contend, requires the rigorous, sometimes ruthless control of information, and the longer it takes for the public to learn the truth, the better. Strict discipline and careful execution are absolutely essential, the goal being to severely limit internal and external access to information, whether it's documents and calendars or memoranda, phone logs, and e-mails. This is rarely discussed publicly, but when salient information about significant government decisions disappears inexplicably or is simply never made available, perhaps for decades, such actions connote a contemptuous disregard for the public and the consent of the governed.

In 1917, Senator Hiram Johnson famously said, "The first casualty when war comes is truth." In an era when the lines between war and peace have long been blurred—first by a half-century-long

Cold War between East and West, then by a seemingly endless "war on terror" launched in the aftermath of September 11, 2001—it's no wonder that truth has become an increasingly rare commodity in our national discourse.

But the Founding Fathers understood this power dynamic 150 years before detonation of the first atomic bomb. In 1798, James Madison wrote to Thomas Jefferson, "Perhaps it is a universal truth that the loss of liberty at home is to be charged to provisions against danger, real or pretended, from abroad."[56]

Democratic senator J. William Fulbright of Arkansas, the longest-serving chairman of the Senate Foreign Relations Committee (1959–1974), became incensed by the Gulf of Tonkin deception by the president of the United States, and he soon turned against the Vietnam War. In his 1966 book, *The Arrogance of Power*, Fulbright wrote:

> Power tends to confuse itself with virtue and a great nation is particularly susceptible to the idea that its power is a sign of God's favor, conferring upon it a special responsibility for other nations—to make them richer and happier and wiser, to remake them, that is, in its own shining image. Power confuses itself with virtue and tends also to take itself for omnipotence. Once imbued with the idea of a mission, a great nation easily assumes that it has the means as well as the duty to do God's work.[57]

One of the means to do God's work apparently involves invoking omnipotent control over all information. For example, during Fulbright's 1968 hearings into the Gulf of Tonkin deception, Secretary of Defense McNamara insisted that he could not answer one of the chairman's probing questions "because the [committee] staff has not been cleared for certain intelligence. . . ." Members and staff of the most important congressional committee dealing with matters of foreign policy were astonished; as one senator exclaimed, "I never heard of this . . . I thought Top Secret was Top Secret." McNamara subsequently revealed: "There are a host of different [security] clearances. I would guess I have perhaps twenty-five."[58]

The problem is that when access to government information is so tightly controlled, with multiple clearances representing many levels of classification, by definition you've created carefully delineated layers of truth. In essence, you have formally "institutionalized lying," as David Wise characterized this phenomenon in his 1972 book, *The Politics of Lying*. "Policy makers who consider it desirable to mask their decisions or their objectives, or who wish to mislead the public or withhold information, can do so as easily as reaching for the nearest rubber stamp. In short, lying and secrecy are two sides of the same coin."[59]

Early in this chapter, I talked about how Larry LaSalle's death in Vietnam was one of the first incidents that shocked me into an awareness of the tragic reality of the war. Regrettably, this heartbreaking incident had a troubling footnote: more than three decades after Larry's death on March 17, 1967, the family, according to Randy, learned that the chaplain who'd informed them of his demise had "lied to us about how and where he was killed."

Lying becomes a habit, one that's indulged even when it's unnecessary and purely hurtful.[60]

Little did I know, when I visited the grave of Larry LaSalle at Arlington National Cemetery, that the shocks and traumas of the 1960s and 1970s were just beginning. In 1968, Martin Luther King Jr. and Robert F. Kennedy would be assassinated within two months of one another, cutting short the lives of two of the most inspiring progressive leaders of our time. In July 1969, Senator Edward M. Kennedy would crash his black Oldsmobile off a bridge in Massachusetts, causing the drowning death of campaign worker Mary Jo Kopechne and sabotaging his hopes for the White House. In

1972, another presidential candidate, race-baiting, segregationist Alabama governor George Wallace, was shot and paralyzed while campaigning in Maryland. In October 1973, Vice President Spiro Agnew resigned in disgrace over improprieties committed while he was the governor of Maryland. And ten months later, for the first and (so far) only time in US history, a US president would resign from office because of his role in a political scandal, in Nixon's case the massive Watergate cover-up.

All of us living through those years understood that something had changed in America. It wasn't just the astonishing realization that a bullet could take out a national leader at any time. It was something even more insidious: the growing sense that long-standing betrayals of our trust, in the most consciously calculating ways, by multiple presidents and their appointees, might be not merely thinkable, but actually routine.

In the decades that have ensued, that sense, I'm afraid, has become our national reality. For millions of us, it began with Vietnam. The lies that got us into a pointless and unwinnable war back in 1964 didn't just lead to the deaths of Larry LaSalle and more than 58,000 other Americans but also to the death of something real and precious inside all of us. For us, as a nation built on the notions of democracy, freedom, and truth, that death was our first casualty.

The Public's Right to Know:
The Pentagon Papers, Watergate, and a Triumph for Truth

In the First Amendment, the Founding Fathers
gave the free press the protection it must have to fulfill
its essential role in our democracy. The press was to serve
the governed, not the governors. The Government's power
to censor the press was abolished so that the press would
remain forever free to censure the Government. The press
was protected so that it could bare the secrets of government
and inform the people. Only a free and unrestrained press
can effectively expose deception in government.

—SUPREME COURT JUSTICE HUGO BLACK, PENTAGON PAPERS DECISION
(CONCURRING OPINION), JUNE 30, 1971[1]

W E'VE ALREADY SEEN how the Johnson administration's desire to expand the Vietnam War with minimal
interference from the news media—or, for that matter,
from skeptical citizens—led to one of the most significant concerted
projects of secrecy and deception in modern American history: the
lies surrounding the Gulf of Tonkin incidents, which helped win
congressional and public acquiescence to war.

Sadly, the malign impact of that war on our political culture was
just beginning. But governmental dishonesty in regard to the Vietnam

War would also help lead, indirectly, to the proudest victories of an aroused and vigilant press corps—victories that today seem like forgotten relics of an almost impossible past.

On March 12, 1971, *New York Times* reporter Neil Sheehan was given access to a leaked Defense Department history of the Vietnam War that unequivocally revealed government deception and incompetence. The source was former Defense official Daniel Ellsberg, and the history was the trove of documents that came to be known as the Pentagon Papers.[2]

Sheehan was told that he needed to quickly and discreetly copy and return the documents that same weekend. He called Bill Kovach, the *Times* New England Bureau chief, who helped Sheehan get everything reproduced in nearby Medford, Massachusetts, personally writing a check for $1,500 to cover the costs.[3] On April 20, after an important meeting in the *Times* Washington Bureau attended by Sheehan and top New York and Washington editors, the massive "Project X," as it had been dubbed, was editorially approved for development with great excitement. Sheehan and other *Times* editorial staffers began working under very tight security, as they would do for months, at the New York Hilton Hotel, reading, analyzing, and preparing stories from some 7,000 pages.[4]

At the same time, often heated discussions were being held about whether or not to publish the Pentagon Papers. Among the participants were publisher Arthur "Punch" Sulzberger; executive vice president (and former State Department legal adviser) Harding Bancroft; in-house counsel James Goodale; Abe Rosenthal, James "Scotty" Reston, and other top *Times* editors; and representatives of Lord, Day and Lord, the newspaper's outside law firm.[5]

More than two decades later, Sulzberger recalled to authors Susan Tifft and Alex Jones, "The more I listened, the more certain I became that the entire operation smelled of twenty years to life." Although he did not say much in the meetings about publication, he confided to a trusted company adviser, "I'm not sure we should publish this stuff."[6]

At one meeting late in the deliberation process, company executives and retained counsel argued strongly that publication of the Pentagon Papers would be legally, politically, and financially disastrous. One of the newspaper's outside attorneys, Herbert Brownell, the former US attorney general under Eisenhower, told Sulzberger that if his newspaper published the Pentagon Papers, he and others would likely go to jail, and the *Times* would be damaged irreparably. Although Sulzberger later recalled that Brownell had "scared the bejesus out of me," deep down, he also believed Brownell had overstated the danger: "I didn't think they were going to come and lock me up, but I thought they could fine us one hell of a lot, and we didn't have all that much money."[7] But Goodale and the newspaper's editors contended otherwise. Sulzberger told executive editor Rosenthal to continue preparing the materials, but he also confided that he'd not yet made up his mind about whether to publish them.

"Well, if the *Times* doesn't publish them," Reston said, "I'll publish them in the *Vineyard Gazette*!" This was a small local newspaper Reston had recently purchased on the fashionable island of Martha's Vineyard, off the coast of Massachusetts.[8]

Ultimately, Sulzberger made the momentous decision by remembering the poignant question former executive editor Turner Catledge had once asked him: Who is the *New York Times* written for? As the publisher recalled to authors Tifft and Jones years later, "We weren't writing for the benefit of the government; we were writing for the benefit of the reader, who is entitled to know."[9]

By the eve of publication, in June, *Times* executives were so worried about a possible federal injunction that the paper's building security at 7 West 43rd Street had become "shut down tight . . . checking everybody who wants to come in or out."[10] But no injunction was forthcoming. On Sunday, June 13, 1971, the front page of the *New York Times* boasted a large headline that spanned four columns: "Vietnam Archive: Pentagon Study Traces 3 Decades of Growing U.S. Involvement." Bearing the byline of Neil Sheehan, the story was the first installment of a ten-part series that had finally been approved by *Times* officials.

Unable to obtain copies of the Top-Secret material, the *Washington Post* and a few other major newspapers began the humiliating task of rewriting the *Times* exclusive for their Monday editions. But few US newspapers initially paid much attention to the Pentagon Papers story. In fact, the *Chicago Tribune*'s only mention was a front-page editorial criticizing the *Times* for publishing classified government information.

Very soon after the *Times* story was published, two Federal Bureau of Investigation agents appeared at the doorstep of Bill Kovach early one morning. The *Times* New England Bureau chief and his wife, Lynne, were frying eggs and sausage for breakfast, and Kovach answered the doorbell in his underwear. The visitors said they'd come to discuss the Pentagon Papers; the FBI had apparently identified which photocopy shop had been used to duplicate the secret papers and had traced Kovach's personal check to the transaction.

"Look, either come in the house or put me under arrest or get the hell out of here," Kovach told the agents. "I am not going to stand here in the door in my underwear."[11]

The agents soon departed. The government didn't want Kovach or even Sheehan but rather Daniel Ellsberg, the whistleblower who had leaked the classified papers. But while the administration pursued Ellsberg, it was desperate to prevent the release of any more of the embarrassing papers. On Monday, June 14, Attorney General John Mitchell sent a late-day telegram to the publisher of the *New York Times*, urging that it "publish no further information of this character," which he claimed was "directly prohibited" by the Espionage Act of 1917. Further publication, Mitchell added, would "cause irreparable injury to the defense interests of the United States." Mitchell separately called Herbert Brownell, whom he had seen socially just days earlier. Mitchell bluntly informed him that if the *New York Times* did not stop publication of the Pentagon Papers, the Justice Department would proceed immediately against it.[12]

Intense deliberations ensued, with executive editor Rosenthal insisting that Sulzberger, on travel in London, be awakened for a 2:00 a.m. phone consultation from his hotel. After listening to the latest developments and the opposing views—acting publisher Harding Bancroft had advised against continuing publication—Sulzberger declared that the newspaper would continue to publish the Pentagon Papers. Rosenthal announced Sulzberger's courageous decision, in direct defiance of a federal government legal and financial threat, to 150 cheering staffers in the *Times* newsroom. The newspaper then sent the attorney general a reply telegram: "*The Times* must respectfully decline the request of the Attorney General, believing that it is in the interest of the people of this country to be informed of the material contained in this series of articles."[13]

With legal repercussions looming, Brownell, in his role as senior partner of Lord, Day and Lord, called in-house counsel James Goodale at 11:00 p.m. to say that he and his firm would no longer represent the *New York Times*. The newspaper needed someone to prepare arguments and write a brief to present in US district court the very next morning. Somehow Goodale found distinguished Yale Law professor Alexander M. Bickel and his former student, Floyd Abrams, of the firm Cahill, Gordon, Sonnett, Reindel and Ohl, who agreed to work through the night.[14]

On June 15, the *Times* published the third page-one installment by Neil Sheehan, but the newspaper's lead story, by Max Frankel, was headlined, "Mitchell Seeks to Halt Series on Vietnam But *Times*

Refuses." Months later, executive editor Rosenthal wondered aloud what it would have meant if the headline had been "Justice Department Asks End to Vietnam Series and *Times* Concedes." "I think it would have changed the history of the newspaper business," Rosenthal remarked.[15]

Later that day in federal court, the Pentagon Papers case was presented before Murray Gurfein, a new judge appointed by Nixon who had served in army intelligence during World War II. Literally on his first case, Gurfein granted the US government a temporary restraining order, ruling that "any temporary harm that may result from not publishing during the pendency of the application for a preliminary injunction is far outweighed by the irreparable harm that could be done to the interests of the United States government if it should ultimately prevail" in the case.[16]

Never before had the US government legally barred a newspaper from publishing information. As Daniel Ellsberg described it decades later, the Nixon administration was "asking federal courts to violate or ignore the Constitution or in effect to abrogate the First Amendment. It was the boldest assertion during the cold war that 'national security' overrode the constitutional guarantees of the Bill of Rights."[17]

Ellsberg was by now a fugitive, meeting discreetly with friends and journalists amid growing indications that FBI agents were seeking him all over the Boston-Cambridge area. With no new installment of the Pentagon Papers in the *New York Times* on June 16, Ellsberg feared his year of leaking classified documents about the deceptions of the Vietnam War might ultimately be for naught. He needed another nationally respected newspaper to publish them, and he remembered an acquaintance from the Rand Corporation, Ben Bagdikian, who had returned to the *Washington Post* as assistant managing editor for national affairs. He decided to try contacting him through an intermediary.[18]

The Pentagon Papers situation had thus far been a frustrating experience for the ambitious *Washington Post*. Under publisher Katharine Graham and Ben Bradlee, the charismatic, fiercely competitive executive editor she had hired, the *Post* had been steadily improving in quality and stature. Now the Pentagon Papers threatened to deal the *Post* a major competitive blow. As Bradlee told me in 2007, "We heard for months [that] the *New York Times* had this great story. And they were going to lay it on. And we would never recover. It would bring the *Post* to their knees, and all that crap. And . . . the day they led their paper with the Pentagon Papers, we led the newspaper with Tricia Nixon's wedding. And the contrast was just killing."[19]

Bagdikian remembered the internal newsroom angst more than thirty-five years later: "Bradlee couldn't stop pacing around. He had to get the Pentagon Papers. The *Times* had been stopped." He also vividly recalls emerging from a staff meeting to find an intriguing phone message: call a "Mr. Boston" at a 617 area code, from a secure (that is, bug-free) phone. So Bagdikian crossed the street and called an intermediary "cutout" from a pay phone inside the Statler Hilton Hotel. In a few moments, he found himself talking to former Rand colleague Daniel Ellsberg.[20]

Ellsberg offered the *Post* the Pentagon Papers, but only on condition the newspaper commit to printing them. So Bagdikian returned to the *Post* and asked Bradlee whether he'd agree to printing the papers. Bagdikian recalls Bradlee's response: "'I'd give my left one for that.' And I said, 'Well, if we get them, will we print them?' He said, 'If we don't print them, there is going to be a new executive editor at the *Washington Post*.'"[21]

Bagdikian secured the papers at a meeting with Ellsberg at a "rundown motel" in the Boston area and brought them to Bradlee's Georgetown home, where a who's who of the newspaper's editorial staff was assembled, including Murrey Marder, others knowledgeable about Vietnam, and editorial page editor Phil Geyelin and his deputy,

Meg Greenfield. They were later joined by two attorneys from the *Post*'s outside law firm, Roger Clark and Anthony Essaye, as well as Frederick R. "Fritz" Beebe, chairman of the board of the Washington Post Company.[22]

The *Post* reporters and copy editors set about the task of combing through thousands of pages of government documents, trying to craft comprehensible stories about them in a day or two, as opposed to the three months the *New York Times* writers had been allowed. More complicated was the dicey legal and financial landscape the newspaper faced. The *Times* had been censored by a federal judge for publishing the same subject matter. A former senior partner in the law firm retained by the *Post*, William S. Rogers, happened to be President Nixon's secretary of state and was known to be upset about the disclosure of the Pentagon Papers. In addition, the Washington Post Company owned several radio and TV stations, half of whose broadcast licenses would be up for review by the Federal Communications Commission (FCC) the next year. An accused or convicted felon may not hold a broadcast license.[23] As Beebe put it, "If we're indicted and convicted of a crime, we lose valuable parts of our company."[24]

Even worse was a quirk of bad timing: the *Post* had gone public two days earlier, with investment banker Lazard Frères and Co. floating more than a million shares of Post Company stock on the American Stock Exchange. But the *Post*'s agreement with its underwriter would not fully take effect for another week, and it contained a worrisome clause that provided for the possible—and financially calamitous—cancellation of the stock issue if an imprecisely defined "disaster" or "catastrophic event" were to befall the company. "I cannot put the company under that risk," Beebe declared.[25]

But the editorial staff pushed back, urging publication. At one point, Bradlee, Beebe, and the lawyers left the gathering to call *Post* publisher Katharine Graham. They returned to the living room to announce "a compromise": the *Post* would not publish a story the next day, but would state in a page-one box that it had the Pentagon Papers and intended to run stories about them the following day.[26]

Bradlee obviously wasn't sold: "That's inviting the attorney general to stop us," he said. "It's begging him to stop us." The reporters and researchers, who'd already spent some six hours preparing the stories, were aghast. "And [Don Oberdorfer] said, 'That's the shittiest idea I ever heard of.'"[27] Chalmers Roberts, one of the paper's most senior and respected reporters, scolded the lawyers and editors for "crawling on your belly to the Attorney General . . . If you don't want to risk running it, then to hell with it, don't run it."[28] "Tomorrow," he added, "I will put my name to a public statement that I disassociate myself with this decision." Bagdikian warned that a full-scale staff revolt might be in the offing.[29]

Bradlee knew full well that the stakes couldn't be any higher: "Not publishing the information when we had it would be like not saving a drowning man, or not telling the truth. Failure to publish without a fight would constitute an abdication that would brand the *Post* forever, as an establishment tool of whatever administration was in power. And end the Bradlee era before it got off the ground, just incidentally."[30]

But he also realized the apparent intractability of the financial and legal issues, and he decided that he "had to massage the lawyers, especially [board chairman] Beebe, into at least a neutral position." His strategy: get another legal opinion, ideally from someone of great credibility and stature. So he placed an urgent call to Edward Bennett Williams, an old friend who was regarded as one of the nation's preeminent lawyers. For ten uninterrupted minutes, Bradlee explained the situation "and then I shut up. Nothing from Williams for at least sixty seconds. I was dying. And then, finally: 'Well, Benjy, you got to go with it. You got no choice. That's your business.' I hugged him, long distance."[31]

Bradlee returned to the group discussion, and "when I had the right opening, I told them what Williams had said, and I could see the starch go out of Clark and Essaye, and I could see the very beginning of a smile on Beebe's face."[32]

After another hour of arguing, Bradlee called Katharine Graham; joining him from the other phones in his house were Beebe, Phil Geyelin, and *Post* assistant managing editor Howard Simons. Graham later recalled, "I well remember Phil Geyelin's response when I said that deciding to publish could destroy the paper. 'Yes,' he agreed, 'but there's more than one way to destroy a newspaper.'"[33]

Ultimately, Graham recalled years later in her memoir, "Frightened and tense, I took a big gulp and said, 'Go ahead, go ahead, go ahead. Let's go. Let's publish.' And I hung up."[34] According to Bradlee, "I dropped the phone like a hot potato and shouted the verdict, and the room erupted in cheers."[35]

The next day, after the *Post* published its first article about the Pentagon Papers, Assistant Attorney General William Rehnquist called Bradlee to request that the *Post* halt any further publication. Bradlee's reply: "I'm sure you will understand that I must respectfully decline." That afternoon, the United States sought an injunction against the *Post*, alleging that the newspaper had violated the Espionage Act of 1917 by publishing sensitive information that "could be used to the injury of the United States." Judge Gerhard Gesell, who previously worked as both a reporter and a national security official, quickly ruled against the government, asserting that the Espionage Act had never been intended to justify federal "censorship of the press."[36]

A day later, in New York, Judge Gurfein heard further arguments about the Pentagon Papers matter, and on June 19, he lifted his temporary restraining order against the *New York Times*. In a seventeen-page opinion, Gurfein said, "The security of the nation is not at the ramparts alone. Security also lies in the value of our free institutions. A cantankerous press, an obstinate press, an ubiquitous press must be suffered by those in authority in order to preserve the even greater values of freedom of expression and the right of the people to know."[37]

Although the *Times* and *Post* won important victories in US district court cases in New York and Washington, US court of appeals judges in both cities nevertheless sided with the government, setting up a showdown at the Supreme Court. On Friday, June 25, the High Court agreed to review both cases together, scheduling a highly unusual Saturday session to hear oral arguments.[38]

On June 28, 1971, the Supreme Court rejected the government's argument that prior restraint was justified and, by a vote of 6–3, upheld the First Amendment. Justice Potter Stewart wrote in his opinion for the majority:

> In the absence of governmental checks and balances present in areas of our national life, the only effective restraint upon executive policy and power in the areas of national defense and international affairs may lie in an enlightened citizenry—in an informed and critical public opinion which alone can here protect the values of democratic government. For this reason, it is perhaps here that a press that is alert, aware, and free most vitally serves the basic purpose of the First Amendment. For without an informed and free press there cannot be an enlightened people.[39]

The *New York Times* and the *Washington Post* immediately resumed publication, and the following spring the *Times* won the Pulitzer Prize for meritorious public service. But beyond the euphoria and affirmation of the role of independent reporting in our society, it was sobering how close to the precipice the press had come. As Ben Bradlee later reflected, "For the first time in the history of the American republic, newspapers had been restrained by the government from publishing a story—a black mark in the history of democracy . . . What the hell was going on in this country that this could happen?"[40]

⟡

Bradlee's question is indeed the crucial one. And what was going on was nothing less than raw presidential power and paranoia out of control. What is not well remembered or understood to this day is how President Richard Nixon's obsession with the war in Southeast Asia, the Pentagon Papers (along with the man who brought them to the world's attention), and "national security" in general helped to subsequently spawn so many of the crimes we came to glibly lump together under the rubric of Watergate.

Daniel Ellsberg, who had continued to leak Pentagon Papers material to roughly twenty other newspapers, granted an exclusive interview to CBS News anchor Walter Cronkite on the afternoon of June 23, 1971, which aired on the *CBS Evening News* and later that night in a prime-time special.[41] Within two days, a federal warrant was issued for Ellsberg's arrest, and on June 28, he surrendered to the FBI in Boston; on that same Monday, he was indicted in Los Angeles on federal felony charges that included unauthorized possession of "documents and writings related to the national defense."[42]

A week earlier, in a conversation with aides, Nixon had urged "the criminal prosecution" of Ellsberg, and following his indictment, the president told aide Charles Colson, "If you can get him tied in with some communist groups, that would be good . . . that's my guess that he's in with some subversives."[43] On the very day the Supreme Court rendered its Pentagon Papers decision, Nixon told Attorney General John Mitchell and National Security Adviser Henry Kissinger, "Try him in the press. Everything, John, that there is on the investigation, get it out, leak it out. We want to destroy him in the press."[44]

And a day later, bitter about the Supreme Court decision and obsessed with Ellsberg, Nixon told H. R. Haldeman, Charles Colson, and John Ehrlichman in the Oval Office, "I don't want that fellow Ellsberg to be brought up until after the [1972] election. I mean, just let—convict the son of a bitch in the press. That's the way it's done."[45]

So the president and his administration got down to business, launching a campaign of secret and illegal activities that two years later would be his undoing. As *Washington Post* special Watergate editor Barry Sussman observed in his book, *The Great Cover-Up*, "It seems certain that if not for Nixon's appetite for political gain out of Ellsberg, there never would have been a Watergate affair."[46]

In fact, Nixon's appetite was so insatiable that on July 2, 1971, two days after the Supreme Court's Pentagon Papers decision, he met with Haldeman and Ehrlichman about using the Ellsberg situation to revive the old House Un-American Activities Committee (HUAC, at that time called the House Internal Security Committee) to investigate a "spy ring." The president told them, "Don't you see what a marvelous opportunity for the committee. They can really take this and go. And make speeches about the spy ring . . . [Y]ou know what's going to charge up an audience. Jesus Christ, they'll be hanging from the rafters . . . Going after all these Jews."[47]

In another Oval Office conversation around this time with Haldeman, Ehrlichman, and Colson, Nixon said, "We have to develop now a program, a program for leaking out information. We're destroying these people in the papers . . . This is a game. It's got to be played in the press." Because he believed agencies such as the FBI could not be trusted, Nixon recommended that this operation be "run from the White House without being caught."[48]

Within days of the completed newspaper publication of the Pentagon Papers, and frustrated that the FBI had not found more damaging information to discredit Ellsberg, the president authorized the creation of the White House Special Investigations Unit, the infamous "plumbers" tasked with stopping leaks. Its operations included burglaries, illegal physical and electronic surveillance, forgery of secret documents, misuse of the Internal Revenue Service (IRS), misuse of CIA technical and psychological profiling assistance for illegal political activities, and an array of other government abuses of power. The plumbers were headed by John Ehrlichman's assistant, Egil Krogh, and David Young, formerly from Henry Kissinger's National Security Council staff; personnel included former CIA covert operative E. Howard Hunt, transferred from Charles Colson's office, and former FBI agent G. Gordon Liddy. They had a basement office in the Old Executive Office Building, but a phone number billed to a residence in Alexandria, Virginia.[49]

Four weeks later, Hunt sent Colson a memo entitled "Neutralization of Ellsberg," which described a "skeletal operations plan" to "destroy his public image and credibility." It proposed to interview Ellsberg's first wife, to pull "the full holdings on Ellsberg" from all of the intelligence agencies, and to "obtain Ellsberg's files from his psychiatric analyst." On August 11, after deciding that the full CIA psychiatric profile of Ellsberg was "disappointing and very superficial," Krogh and Young apprised Ehrlichman—whose official title was chief domestic policy adviser to the president—of the progress of two secret grand jury investigations and planned wiretaps. They recommended, "that a covert operation be undertaken to examine all the medical files still held by Ellsberg's psychoanalyst covering the two-year period in which he was undergoing analysis." Ehrlichman approved the burglary, with the notation "if done under your assurance that it is not traceable."[50]

On September 3, 1971, Liddy, Hunt, and three anti-Castro Cubans, all veterans of the CIA Bay of Pigs fiasco a decade earlier, broke into the Los Angeles office of Ellsberg's psychiatrist, Dr. Lewis Fielding, and broke open locked file cabinets—a futile effort, because Ellsberg's files weren't there. The expenses for this illegal farce had been paid for with thousands of dollars in cash delivered to Krogh's office by a friend of Colson's, who had an advertising contract with the White House, and reimbursed via a political front group called People United for a Good Government Committee.[51]

Although there was chagrin and frustration over the break-in debacle, the Special Investigations Unit and its small staff of plumbers were not reprimanded inside the White House. Indeed, a more damaging CIA psychological profile of Ellsberg was ordered up—this time suggesting that Ellsberg was motivated by aggression against his father, the president, and even his analyst—which Colson leaked to reporters.[52]

Why the obsession with Ellsberg by Nixon and his squad wielding the full force of the federal government? As the man who had co-directed the plumbers unit, Egil Krogh, told federal judge Gerhart Gesell in his January 1974 sentencing statement after pleading guilty to approving the break-in at Fielding's office:

> To discredit Dr. Ellsberg would serve to discourage others who might be tempted to emulate him in disclosing information. It would also make him less able to mobilize opposition to President Nixon's chosen Vietnam policy. The freedom of the President to pursue his chosen foreign policy was seen as the essence of national security.[53]

And independent reporting and leaked government documents, even when they revealed true information vital to the public's understanding, were seen as fundamentally antithetical and potentially detrimental to the president's "freedom" to pursue his foreign policy. In his unrepentant memoir published four years after his resignation, Nixon wrote that, in retrospect, the "break-in at Ellsberg's psychiatrist's office seems wrong and excessive . . . But I do not accept that it was as wrong or excessive as what Daniel Ellsberg did."[54]

US district judge William Matthew Byrne Jr. obviously disagreed: on May 11, 1973, he dismissed all of the charges against Ellsberg and his co-defendant, Anthony Russo, a friend who had helped him photocopy the Pentagon Papers. (Russo, however, ended up being the only person to serve any prison time regarding the Pentagon Papers case, for contempt of court for refusing to testify in secret before a federal grand jury.) Byrne dismissed the charges against Ellsberg because he had learned of the "unprecedented" government misconduct against the defendants that "offend[s] 'a sense of justice' . . . bizarre events [that] have infected the prosecution of this case." Specifically, Byrne—and the American people—learned of how operatives working directly for the Nixon White House had violated local and federal laws in their elaborate efforts to investigate and discredit the defendants, the kind of illicit behavior never publicly associated with a president of the United States.[55]

The administration had also tried to interfere in the Ellsberg case directly. The *Washington Star-News* reported that during the trial, Nixon and Ehrlichman had invited Judge Byrne, a former federal prosecutor, to a meeting at the president's "Western White House" in San Clemente, California, where the position of FBI director was "dangled" in front of him as a possible presidential appointment. It should also be noted that in April 1973, Nixon ordered the head of the Justice Department's Watergate investigation, Henry Petersen, *not* to provide information about the burglary of Dr. Fielding's office and other White House Ellsberg activities to Judge Byrne, saying, "I know about that. That is a national security matter. You stay out of that." Petersen was troubled by Nixon's response and felt he had an ethical obligation to inform Judge Byrne of the illicit activity, which he did.[56]

Within minutes of the dismissal of the charges against Ellsberg, a frustrated Nixon told his former chief of staff, H. R. Haldeman, "that sonofabitching thief is made a national hero and is going to get off on a mistrial. And the *New York Times* gets a Pulitzer Prize for stealing documents. . . . *What in the name of God have we come to?*" (italics in the original).[57] What we'd come to, of course, were the full throes of the Watergate scandal.

But a stubborn Nixon said that in his "frame of mind," he was "driven to preserve the government's ability to conduct foreign policy and to conduct it in the way that I felt would best bring peace. I believed that national security was involved. I still believe it today, and in the same circumstances I would act now as I did then."[58] In other words, the president of the United States wanted to preserve the national security of the United States as defined exclusively by himself, waging war in Laos and Cambodia with no cumbersome congressional oversight or public discussion, with the United States taking numerous actions in defiance of state and federal laws if necessary. As he told television interviewer David Frost in 1977, "When the President does it, that means it is not illegal."[59]

∽∾

With that kind of mindset, all else is incidental, including the parameters of secrecy about the government's policies and activities. Thus, the *truth itself* as understood by the public is substantially defined by the commander in chief and the state, through his chosen representatives. And unbeknownst to the American people and most national reporters, from 1969 through early 1972, the Nixon White House was veering out of control from its power, paranoia, and political ambition. Besides Ellsberg, for example, Howard Hunt and others were investigating muckraking journalist Jack Anderson, whose India-Pakistan reporting had also upset the president. The

White House put the nationally syndicated columnist under surveillance, tapped his telephone, investigated his staff, and audited his taxes; at one point, Hunt apparently even hatched plans to assassinate him but fortunately did not proceed.[60]

Other members of the media were targeted by the administration. According to author Sanford Ungar, at one point CBS was so beset by legal attacks, complaints from the Federal Communications Commission, and other problems that the network literally employed more lawyers than reporters. Between January 1969 and July 1971, CBS and NBC alone received 122 subpoenas for film or reporters' testimony in court proceedings.[61]

In 1970, White House special assistant to the president Charles Colson began coordinating the creation of an "Enemies List," which ultimately targeted some two hundred individuals and eighteen organizations to receive "'special' government attention." The roster included actors, Democratic politicians, foundations, university presidents, and more than fifty journalists, including James Reston, Marvin Kalb, and Daniel Schorr, a CBS News correspondent hired in 1953 by Edward R. Murrow.[62]

Schorr was seen as a "real media enemy" by the Nixon White House. During live network television coverage of the Senate Watergate hearings in 1973, after former White House counsel John Dean first testified and revealed that there had been a White House "Enemies List," Schorr and his producers quickly obtained the list, and the veteran correspondent began to read the names live, on the air. "I had not seen it. I had not prepared for it . . . I didn't faint. I didn't say 'Wow.' I didn't do anything. I read my name with the other names just as though it was another name."[63]

In fact, he had been extensively investigated by the FBI after reporting a story skeptical of the president's promise to give federal aid to parochial schools. Schorr recalled that Bob Haldeman, Nixon's chief of staff, called FBI director J. Edgar Hoover and said that

Nixon wanted some background on him. Hoover and his agents apparently misunderstood and thought Schorr was being considered for a federal appointment. They haplessly interviewed Schorr himself about the position, to Haldeman and Colson's later chagrin and consternation. So to preempt any adverse news story, the White House put out the word that Schorr was being considered for an administration job. (Schorr told me that twenty years later, not long before former president Richard Nixon's death, he found himself ironically at a dinner with Nixon. Afterward, Schorr said to him privately, "'Mr. Nixon, I am not sure you remember me, but, uh. . . .' And he turned, 'Sure, Dan Schorr. I damn near hired you once.'") [64]

Hoover eventually got clear about Nixon's real interest in Schorr, who recalled, "Hoover opened up a wide-open investigation, sending people to talk to my boss and my brother and others." [65] In 1974, that federal investigation of citizen Schorr became part of Article 2 of the House Judiciary Committee's Articles of Impeachment, under "Abuse of Presidential Powers."

More than three and a half decades later, Schorr, the senior news analyst for National Public Radio (NPR), who passed away in 2010 at the age of ninety-three, told me that being a "part of history" in this way "is one of the greatest honors of my life." [66]

But the Schorr fiasco was merely a single episode among an entire array of surveillance programs and activities orchestrated by the Nixon White House. The president and his aides ordered the FBI to record all "inflammatory" speeches by antiwar protestors. The Justice Department, through the FBI, began tracking the "income sources of revolutionary groups," in turn handing over this information to the White House, the CIA, the State Department, the Secret Service, and other intelligence agencies. At the urging of the White House, the CIA—in violation of its charter—conducted domestic-surveillance activities, sending more than a thousand monthly reports to the FBI. And the administration ordered the Internal Revenue Service to establish the Special Service Staff to "collect relevant information on organizations predominantly dissident or extremist in nature and on people prominently identified with these organizations." Four years later, the SSS had files on 8,585 individuals; the dossiers were distributed to the White House and key agencies, the aim being to "deal a blow to dissident elements" through tax investigations and audits.[67]

The abuses of power extended far beyond the supposed misdeeds of the media or claimed damage to national security. The White House, joined later by the Committee to Re-elect the President (also known as the Committee for the Re-election of the President), also began conducting illegal political intelligence and surveillance operations and "dirty tricks" to disrupt, embarrass, and smear the likely 1972 Democratic presidential candidates. For example, on September 8, 1971, Nixon said to Ehrlichman in the Oval Office, "We have the power but are we using it to investigate contributors to [Nixon's vanquished 1968 Democratic presidential opponent] Hubert Humphrey, contributors to [Democratic senator Edmund] Muskie, the Jews, you know, that are stealing every— . . . are we going after their tax returns? Do you know what I mean? . . . Are we looking into Muskie's return? . . . Teddy [Kennedy]? Who knows about the Kennedys? Shouldn't they be investigated?"[68]

And the hapless White House plumbers, who apparently had learned nothing from the botched burglary to steal Ellsberg's psychiatric files nine months earlier, forged recklessly ahead with another nocturnal black-bag job.

What happened in the earliest morning hours of June 17, 1972, at offices of the Democratic National Committee in the Watergate office complex in Washington, DC, profoundly altered politics and journalism in America and remains indelibly etched in our cultural consciousness and history. The story of the Watergate burglary and the journalistic quest to uncover the truth about the Nixon White House's involvement in the crime has been told many times, most notably in *All the President's Men*, the 1974 best-selling book written by *Washington Post* reporters Bob Woodward and Carl Bernstein, and the gripping 1976 movie of the same name.[69] But it's easy to forget how much serendipity was involved in the journalistic triumph that Watergate ultimately became.

The *Washington Post* "got off to a running head start," as Ben Bradlee later recalled in his memoir, on what many other national news organizations wrongly took to be merely a weekend local crime story.[70] The newspaper knew about the break-in just before 8:00 a.m., tipped off by Joseph Califano, the *Washington Post's* outside lawyer who was also general counsel to the Democratic National Committee. He had called *Post* managing editor Howard Simons at home, who then called metropolitan editor Harry Rosenfeld, who in turn called Barry Sussman, the (district) city editor, who immediately sent Al Lewis, the *Post's* police reporter, to the Watergate and dispatched an ambitious young metro reporter named Bob Woodward to cover the arraignment of the five arrested burglars. That same day, Simons apprised *Post* publisher Katharine Graham, who liked to be in touch with her editors on weekends. So the very first public day of the biggest political scandal in US history, everyone from the newspaper owner to its top editors down to its youngest street-level reporters was in sync about the importance of the Watergate story.

It was at the district courthouse that Saturday that Woodward heard "that one of the people being arraigned, [James W.] Mc-Cord, said that he worked at the CIA. [He] didn't say it very loudly, but that's kind of big news. So we had an awful lot of people on this right off the bat for that reason . . . In all, that day I had ten reporters and editors working on the story," Sussman told me.[71] As Bradlee put it more bluntly, "No three letters in the English language, arranged in that particular order, and spoken in similar circumstances, can tighten a good reporter's sphincter faster than C-I-A."[72] Another first-day staffer was Carl Bernstein, a colorful young metro reporter assigned to cover suburban Virginia. Within days, Sussman recommended that the two very hardworking, hungry metropolitan reporters, Woodward and Bernstein, be assigned full-time to cover the unfolding scandal, and Sussman himself was assigned to be the newspaper's "special Watergate editor."[73]

During the crucial first six months of the scandal, the *Post* published 201 staff-written stories, and by October, Sussman and his colleagues realized how high the stakes had gotten: "We were out on a limb. There was no turning back. We just had to keep going with our stories. We were under massive attack by the White House, the Nixon Reelection Committee and the Republicans in the Senate. It was a unified massive attack."[74]

"The real story that changed our perception of Watergate," Woodward recalls, "was on October 10, 1972. The [Donald] Segretti story that said Watergate was only part of a whole of espionage and sabotage activities directed at the Democrats . . . Mark Felt [the confidential source known for thirty years as "Deep Throat"] had said there were fifty such saboteurs and spies, like Donald Segretti, whom Carl had chased down. And people thought, 'Oh come on, fifty?' Well, go look at the Watergate [Congressional and Special Prosecutor] investigations. I once went back and counted sixty-six . . . This is the operation that [Howard] Hunt and [G. Gordon] Liddy were running, aimed at Democrats. [Watergate] was a series of illegal sabotage and espionage activities run and financed by the White House and Nixon campaign."[75]

Over time, the journalistic exposés spawned criminal prosecutions and congressional investigations, presided over by heroic figures such as Judge John Sirica, a Republican appointee, in his federal courtroom, and Democratic committee chairmen Senator Sam Ervin and

Representative Peter Rodino, who in nationally televised hearings insisted on the truth and on government accountability. As a result, Americans learned that President Richard Nixon had violated his oath of office, systematically and illegally abusing power in the most wide-ranging ways ever documented, much of it obvious from the White House audiotapes of meetings and phone calls to and from the Oval Office. To compound matters, Nixon clumsily orchestrated the cover-up within days of the Watergate break-in, and in October 1973, shamelessly ordered his appointees to fire Watergate special prosecutor Archibald Cox, in the "Saturday Night Massacre." And for more than two years he lied to the American people, straight-faced before the cameras, about his involvement, knowledge, and criminal misconduct.

In the end, Nixon was caught in his own web of deceit and abandoned by even his most stalwart Republican supporters; his impeachment and removal from office unavoidable. He resigned on August 9, 1974. Altogether, more than seventy people, including White House aides and Cabinet officials, were convicted of crimes related to the Watergate scandal.[76]

Respected author Theodore H. White summed up the whole sorry saga back then: "The true crime of Richard Nixon was simple: he destroyed the myth that binds America together . . . that all men are equal before the law and protected by it; and no matter how the faith may be betrayed elsewhere, at one particular point—the Presidency—justice will be done beyond prejudice, beyond rancor, beyond the possibility of a fix. It was that faith that Richard Nixon broke."[77]

The historic impact of journalists during this period cannot be overstated. And some of that impact was at the most basic, human level, as Woodward has often mused about. As a reporter, he says, you sometimes ask yourself: Who are you writing for? And sometimes the answers can be surprising:

You are writing for the newspaper readers, all of them. But in this case, there were two people who had subscriptions to the *Washington Post* who, it turned out, were really important. One was Judge Sirica, who was the judge in the first Watergate trial. And Sirica later told me about this. . . .

It's very important to understand how the investigative ball goes from the media, to the courts, to the Senate. And in our stories, we were essentially saying, "This is an illegal White House run, criminal conspiracy." In the first Watergate trial, the only people charged were the five burglars and the bosses, Howard Hunt and Gordon Liddy. And the [Nixon Justice Department] prosecutors presented the case such that Gordon Liddy was the mastermind of all of this, out on his own. Judge Sirica was reading the *Washington Post* that had a whole other line. Sirica was the one who hammered, and asked questions, gave really large sentences, and finally got James McCord, the lead burglar, to crack and write this famous letter saying, essentially, the *Washington Post* version is the right one. And that was critical.

The second reader was [Senator] Sam Ervin . . . And he called me in January 1973, and said, "I have read these stories. And we are going to investigate." . . . It was kind of "Okay, We are going to figure out what this was." But if those two people didn't have subscriptions to the *Washington Post* . . . [78]

The *Post* was awarded the 1973 Pulitzer Prize for Public Service for its outstanding Watergate coverage, and Woodward and Bernstein became international celebrities. Suddenly, every kind of abuse of power was fair game for reporters; investigative journalism in the United States reached its unmistakable apogee. In fact, four of the six Pulitzer Prizes for newspaper writing in 1974 were awarded for investigative reporting, with *Time* magazine branding it the "Year of the Muckraker."[79]

All of that said, the full truth about Watergate has taken decades to unfold, with the publication of memoirs and the release of government documents and White House tape recordings. And beneath the triumph and the glitter, it should also be recognized that the *Washington Post* had been substantially alone and courageously withstood the considerable political and financial pressure brought against it. Who can forget Nixon's first attorney general, John Mitchell, warning Carl Bernstein that *Post* publisher Katharine Graham is "gonna get her tit caught in a big fat wringer."[80] The same day the Watergate burglars were indicted, September 15, 1972, Nixon told his aides, "The *Post* is going to have damnable—*damnable*—problems out of this one. They have television stations . . . and they're going to have to get them renewed. . . . [T]he game has to be played awfully rough."[81]

And it was. By early 1973, the company's stock had dropped to $21 a share from $38, after two *Post* Florida TV station licenses had four challenges filed against them. (In the preceding four years, only eleven such challenges had been brought against the nation's 701 commercial TV stations combined.) Each challenge cost roughly $1 million in legal fees and audience surveys for the *Post* to stave off. "And yet," author Alicia Shepard observed, "the *Post* and its editors still backed their young reporters."[82]

And that included protecting its reporters from legal harassment. Bernstein remembered one day inside in the *Post* newsroom: "I got the call that there was a subpoena server in the building. And I told [Ben] Bradlee. And he said, 'Get out of here.' And, 'where are your notes?' And I said, 'They are in those file cabinets there' . . . And I went to see *Deep Throat*, the movie. . . ." And when he returned to the office, Bernstein learned that the newspaper's lawyers had told lawyers representing the Republican National Committee, "Look, you want to subpoena somebody, subpoena Katharine Graham. And she is ready to go to jail if you want to mess with that. . . .We were blessed with this publisher."[83]

Compare that kind of institutional support with two other national news organizations that more recently chose *not* to back their reporters. In 1994, ABC settled a multibillion-dollar lawsuit (and even issued a public apology) brought by corporate giant Philip Morris over the objection of its award-winning reporters Walt Bogdanich and John Martin, and in 2005, *Time* magazine relinquished reporter Matt Cooper's notes against his wishes in the so-called Valerie Plame scandal, part of the drama that eventually culminated in the perjury conviction of Lewis Libby, Vice President Dick Cheney's chief of staff.[84]

About the late Katharine Graham, who had hired him as the *Washington Post* executive editor, Bradlee said, "I think it was fabulous for the press to see what we used to call the embattled widow stand up to the president of the United States and say, 'Yes, we can.' And I think that gave publishers all over the world a sense that, by God, they could stand up to authority. And just because somebody told you that you couldn't do something, it didn't necessarily mean that you couldn't."[85]

The Pentagon Papers case and the Watergate scandal still represent the high-water mark in the long-standing struggle between raw political power and democratic values, poignantly affirming the public's right to know about its government. Even then, in both celebrated sagas, critical information about those in power still took *years* to become public. These episodes also provide invaluable perspective today, as we ponder what has happened to truth and truth-telling in the disquieting and intervening decades.

Facing similar circumstances today, would contemporary publishers and the current Supreme Court demonstrate the same courageous commitment to the First Amendment and the essential role of an informed citizenry in this democracy? Hypothetical questions are always difficult to answer, but I fear the answer is no.

Jane Kirtley, executive director of the Reporters Committee for Freedom of the Press in Washington, DC, from 1985 to 1999 and the Silha Professor of Media Ethics and Law at the University of Minnesota School of Journalism and Mass Communication, isn't so sure. When asked whether papers like the *New York Times* and the *Washington Post* would stand up to the US government in court today, Kirtley responded in the affirmative. "After all," she said in a 2008 interview, "both newspapers have published controversial classified information in the last couple of years, for which they've been honored by their peers and vilified by supporters of the administration."[86] (The "administration" she referred to was that of George W. Bush, though it would be possible to make much the same observation about relations between the press and the subsequent administration of Barack Obama.)

But here's what troubles Kirtley: "I fear that 'big media' are becoming increasingly irrelevant in this equation. . . . You know as well as I do that the big First Amendment cases of the 1960s through '80s were mostly fought and won by the 'legacy press.' I am not at all sure that will continue to be the case. And this is significant because if the legacy media don't do it, I'm not sure who will step in." The reality, she added, is that if today's news media owners "don't see that the First Amendment is the prerequisite to making money, then they won't" take risks, publish, and defend their legal right to do so later in court. "The legions of bloggers are good at making noise, but I'm not sure they'll join forces to litigate—assuming that, as a group, they'd have enough money to do it."[87]

What has perhaps been most surprising is the unexpected national security obsessiveness of President Barack Obama, whose administration has waged protracted prosecutions of leakers like army private Chelsea (formerly Bradley) Manning, who had illegally passed classified documents to WikiLeaks, as well the journalists who work with leakers, for example, James Risen of the *New York Times*. What's more, more than 4 million government employees and contractors now have national security clearances. And in 2010, a jaw-dropping 77 million documents were classified, up 44 percent from the year before![88] According to James Goodale, the *New York Times'* lead counsel during the historic Pentagon Papers case, "In many respects, President Obama is no better than Nixon. Obama has used the Espionage Act to indict more leakers than any president in the history of this country." And Goodale wrote that in his memoir *before* the Obama Justice Department secretly obtained two months of telephone records for reporters and editors at the Associated Press (AP), an act unprecedented in US history.[89]

And all of this makes what happened over four decades ago invaluable to understanding the delicate and endangered state of journalism, democracy, and truth itself in America today.

3

Race: The American Delusion

The chances of factual truth surviving the
onslaught of power are very slim indeed; it is
always in danger of being maneuvered out of the
world not only for a time but, potentially, forever.
—HANNAH ARENDT, 1967[1]

AVING GROWN UP IN a conservative Republican family
in Delaware, I found myself mesmerized by the unfolding Watergate scandal. The sense of living, historic drama
happening in real time was galvanizing, and the reporting in the
Washington Post, particularly by Bob Woodward and Carl Bernstein, made a profound impression on me. I found it inspiring that
two young reporters and their newspaper could play such a significant watchdog role in our society. As the evidence uncovered by
Woodward, Bernstein, and other investigators mounted, along with
millions of other Americans I had personally come to believe that
Richard Nixon was guilty of "high crimes and misdemeanors," and
therefore should be impeached.

In early 1974, as this drama was nearing its climax, I went to Washington to intern for Senator William V. Roth, a Delaware Republican

who had served on the staff of General Douglas MacArthur in World War II and later received a law degree and an MBA from Harvard University.[2] I found the congressional offices, hallways, and cafeterias teeming with embryonic politicians, or at least young wannabes, and I suppose I was no different. It was exhilarating to be in our nation's capital, and on evenings, before heading home to the dilapidated attic room I'd rented in a Constitution Avenue row house, I'd gaze endlessly at the beautifully lit Capitol dome just blocks away. On weekends I would sit atop the Lincoln Memorial steps, peering out across the National Mall. Or I'd perch myself by the Lee Mansion atop Arlington Cemetery, directly above the graves of John and Robert Kennedy, with its astonishing view of Memorial Bridge and the city of Washington. Months before he was slain, President Kennedy had visited the Lee Mansion and admired the extraordinary view, commenting, "I could stay here forever."[3]

My Washington internship had been arranged through the political science department at the University of Delaware, where I was studying. Of course, in addition to politics, I'd already become interested in journalism. I'd been working in the sports department of the *Wilmington News-Journal*, to which I returned that summer of 1974, and I'd earlier been a columnist and the editorial editor of my high school paper, the *Yellowjacket Buzz*. This journalistic background raised some suspicions about me in the senator's office, so I dutifully kept my opinions about Nixon and Watergate to myself. Republican politicians were suffering through the excruciating ordeal, fearful of being perceived by voters as either too loyal to Nixon or too critical of him, which might risk alienating their own party and base. As a result, most Republican incumbents tried to duck questions about Nixon and the Watergate scandal by urging Americans to "allow the various investigations to run their course."

But that lame strategy of avoidance didn't prevent a massive anti-Republican backlash in the 1974 midterm elections, weeks after

Nixon had resigned. In fact, the public's wrath was so severe that former Senator Bill Brock, the respected Republican national chairman in the 1970s, told me years later that Republican elders, fearful that the party name had become indelibly besmirched by Watergate, had seriously considered changing it.[4]

I had never imagined that politicians could be so fearful of public sentiment. I remember wondering why anyone would bother going through the ordeal of getting elected, only to hide from the public so as not to offend any powerful constituency. Everything seemed to be about image. For example, I often watched one famous politician who happened to be noticeably short standing on a wooden box during press conferences in a Dirksen Senate Office Building hallway, hoping to look taller to constituents watching on TV. It struck me as an apt metaphor for the disjunction between appearance and reality in politics.

Not everything in Washington was so disillusioning. I couldn't miss the fact that an epic constitutional drama was playing itself out in the buildings I walked through every day. And there were politicians who rose to the occasion: the independent, thoughtful Republicans on the Watergate committees, such as Senator Lowell Weicker and Representatives William Cohen, Hamilton Fish, and Tom Railsback, who had publicly criticized the Republican president or would soon summon the fortitude to do so, as well as Attorney General Elliot Richardson and Deputy Attorney General William Ruckelshaus, who had famously resigned on principle rather than carry out the White House order to fire Watergate special prosecutor Archibald Cox.[5]

But much of what I witnessed on Capitol Hill played havoc with my youthful idealism and my romantic conviction that politics is a noble profession. And the more I read and studied history, the more inconsistencies emerged between the myths I'd learned as a child and the realities of American democracy.

Nowhere was the gap between image and truth greater than in the field of race relations. Those stirring words from the Declaration of Independence—"All men are created equal"—had pertained, when written, only to wealthy white men who owned property (the only Americans then qualified to vote). The motto "Equal Justice Under Law" engraved atop the US Supreme Court Building belied the disproportionately high rate of incarceration suffered by African Americans. And despite such historic triumphs as the Emancipation Proclamation of 1863 and the 1954 landmark case of *Brown v. Board of Education*, black-white racial inequities and discrimination, stereotypes and bias, continued to surround us.

My high school years, starting in the fall of 1968, came during a tumultuous time of racial turmoil nationwide. Following the murder of Dr. Martin Luther King Jr. in April of that year and the shocking riots throughout the nation that spring and summer—including violence in Wilmington, just a few miles away—there were ugly fights in my own Delaware high school, where racial hatred, anger, threats, and taunts were a daily phenomenon. Like millions of other young people, I found myself wondering whether the national problem of racism, supposedly resolved a century earlier, had ever truly been addressed.

These stark realities of race in America became even more apparent to me in 1977, when I was hired by veteran journalist Sander Vanocur at the ABC News bureau in Washington and assigned to investigate the infamous 1963 bombing of the Sixteenth Street Baptist Church, in Birmingham, Alabama—a Sunday-morning explosion that killed four young black girls and maimed a fifth. For ten months I investigated these murders and others from the early years of the civil rights movement, most notably the 1965 slaying of Viola Liuzzo, a white mother of five who had traveled to Alabama from Michigan for the historic Selma-to-Montgomery march.

What I learned in the process shocked me. If I'd previously accepted the notion that the march to equality for black Americans had ended in a clear-cut victory for the forces of freedom, my naïveté was swiftly shattered. I quickly discovered that equal justice regardless of color was still an unattained American ideal. And perhaps even more disturbing, I learned that most Americans are blissfully unaware of this shameful reality—and that government, much of the news media, and many Americans themselves have quietly succumbed to this state of willful, comfortable blindness.

‿ॐ‿

Two months before his death, President John F. Kennedy asked FBI director J. Edgar Hoover to aggressively investigate the Sixteenth Street bombing case. More than two hundred FBI agents were assigned to the case, but the federal government didn't prosecute anyone in the years that immediately followed. Worse, in 1980 it finally emerged that Hoover had unilaterally *blocked* any prosecution for the heinous civil rights crime, even though his agents had identified the perpetrators within weeks.[6]

A quarter century later, another piece of that puzzle emerged in a powerful 2005 book, *The Informant*, by historian Gary May. According to May, the FBI in Birmingham knew ten days *before* the girls were murdered that the most dangerous local Klansmen—believed responsible for other bombings months earlier—had just obtained a crate of dynamite. Yet the FBI did not question or apprehend the men, or even alert the Birmingham police.[7]

It should be noted that nearly forty years after the Birmingham church bombing, the Justice Department did finally successfully prosecute sixty-two-year-old Thomas Blanton for the crime. (I interviewed Blanton in Birmingham in 1977 while at ABC News; he steadfastly and unconvincingly denied his involvement in the bombing, then and always.) In 2001, Blanton was convicted in US district court in Birmingham for murder.

In his closing argument to the jury, then US attorney Doug Jones said, "It's never too late for the truth to be told. It's never too late for wounds to heal. It's never too late for a man to be held accountable for his crimes."[8] That's true, of course; and justice delayed by forty years is better than no justice at all. But there's no credible excuse for the FBI's willful failure to prosecute in the 1960s, as soon as it had knowledge of the perpetrators of the crime. Swift action would have sent a strong message that violence against the civil rights movement would not be tolerated, perhaps deterring some of the other attacks that followed.

Sadly, the failure of the authorities to respond in a timely fashion to the Sixteenth Street bombing was no anomaly. The outrageous truth is that there are still more than *one hundred* unsolved civil rights–related murders of African Americans from the era between the 1954 Supreme Court *Brown* decision and the 1968 murder of Dr. Martin Luther King Jr.[9]

Not everyone has simply acquiesced in this tragic state of affairs. Some of the killings from the civil rights era have been solved through the tireless work of a handful of courageous reporters. Chief among them is investigative reporter Jerry Mitchell, of the *Clarion-Ledger* (Jackson, Mississippi). Over more than two decades, Mitchell has methodically tracked down new witnesses and uncovered key evidence in unresolved or unprosecuted killings, including the 1963 murder of Medgar Evers and the 1964 killing of three civil rights workers later dramatized in the movie *Mississippi Burning*.[10]

Having braved numerous death threats over the years, Mitchell readily acknowledges that "it has not been an easy journey. There were many people who wanted me to stop, including friends, family and fellow journalists."[11] The *Clarion-Ledger* had a dreadful reputation in the 1950s and 1960s; indeed, its coverage of the civil rights struggle "reeked of racism." But over the past two decades, that same newspaper has enabled Mitchell's courageous accountability journalism, which in 2005 earned him a career recognition award from the organization Investigative Reporters and Editors (IRE). Mitchell told me, "The *Clarion-Ledger* has been extremely supportive of me and my work."[12] Sad to say, there are few investigative journalists today who can say the same about the newspapers for which they work.

To this day, Mitchell continues his brave truth-telling efforts—and as a result, he continues to be the target of hatred and abuse. When I asked him in 2008 about receiving threats because of his work, Mitchell shared the latest one with me: "Why don't you come to Philadelphia (Mississippi) . . . I wish you would. But these people down here, they wouldn't bury your sorry ass. You don't deserve a fucking burial. They'd let you lay out and rot . . . You gonna get it before it's over with and I hope to hell I see it—you and that fucking no-good nigger-loving damn newspaper up there."[13]

Where race is concerned, the willingness of most Americans *not* to know the truth has deep historical roots. The end of the nineteenth century and the first decades of the twentieth century featured unspeakable and systematic racial abominations—widespread racial cleansings, for example, in which whites drove thousands of blacks from their homes. The truth about this period in our nation's past is only now being revealed through the painstaking work of reporters and historians. For example, in his book *Buried in the Bitter Waters*, Pulitzer Prize–winning investigative reporter Elliot Jaspin methodically documented how from 1890 to 1930, in two hundred Deep South counties spread across Kentucky, North Carolina, Texas, and other states, blacks disappeared completely from "sundown towns."[14] And a year after Jaspin's book was published, Douglas A. Blackmon, Atlanta Bureau chief for the *Wall Street Journal*, exposed the system of "neoslavery" by which 100,000 or more African Americans were coerced into involuntary servitude in his book *Slavery by Another Name*.[15]

What particularly frustrated truth-tellers like Elliot Jaspin were the denial and the revisionism many decades later by white communities—including their white-owned and white-operated newspapers—about what blacks have painfully understood all along: the larger "silence" about the burning, racial purges, and land thefts and the way in which local whites feel "a need to either deny or shade its history."[16]

The problem, of course, is that most of white America doesn't know—or perhaps doesn't want to know—about our sordid past. After Reconstruction, for example, and after the first decades of the twentieth century, racial discrimination and white supremacy throughout the South became so endemic and institutionalized that in 1937 the Carnegie Corporation commissioned a comprehensive study of race in America. Carnegie expressly sought out a respected scholar from a country associated with neither colonialism nor racial segregation. Gunnar Myrdal of Sweden, with the help of over one hundred researchers, conducted a three-year field investigation that produced 15,000 pages of raw written material. His seminal 1944 book, *An American Dilemma: The Negro Problem and Modern Democracy*, influenced the Supreme Court's *Brown v. Board of Education* decision a decade later.

Myrdal was taken aback at what he had found. "The economic situation of the Negroes in America," he wrote, "is pathological. Except for a small minority enjoying upper or middle class status, the masses of American Negroes, in the rural south and in the segregated slum quarters in southern cities, are destitute. They own little property; even their household goods are mostly inadequate and dilapidated. Their incomes are not only low but irregular. They thus live day to day and have scant security for the future."[17]

Myrdal also found "a legal system of discrimination against Negroes in evasion of the Constitution" throughout the South, from the courts, to sentencing, to prison conditions, to capital punishment.[18] Overall, it was quite apparent that "Negro criminals serve longer terms for crimes against whites and are pardoned and paroled much less frequently than white criminals in comparable circumstances."[19] Such systemic discrimination could hardly have been more pervasive, extending to voting, education, employment, housing, politics. But Myrdal also saw signs of hope: "A great many Northerners, perhaps the majority, get shocked and shaken in their conscience when they learn the facts . . . *To get publicity is of the highest strategic importance to the Negro people* . . . There is no doubt, in the writer's opinion, that a great majority of white people in America would be prepared to give the Negro a substantially better deal if they knew the facts" (italics in the original).[20]

At the time Myrdal's book was published, the truth about race, class, and the gaping economic and social disparities in the South had been almost entirely ignored for decades by the national news media. Indeed, according to the Pulitzer Prize–winning book *The Race Beat*, by Gene Roberts and Hank Klibanoff, no major publication, including the *New York Times*, even had a bureau in the South. Between 1935 and 1940, the *Times* published only one story on its front page mentioning America's Negro anti-segregation leaders, as part of a piece about Negro labor leader A. Philip Randolph.[21] In the South, there were only a few white editors with liberal-minded views about race, including Harry Ashmore in Charlotte, North Carolina, Hodding Carter Jr. in Mississippi, and Ralph McGill in Atlanta, but they were the courageous exceptions to their journalistic brethren.[22]

There was, however, a meaningful counterpoint to the white-owned and white-managed newspapers. From 1827 on, some 2,700 Negro newspapers largely came and went, each lasting on average nine years; by 1951, fewer than 175 were still publishing.[23] Most whites, including journalists, were completely unaware of what Myrdal termed the "fighting press," the Negro newspapers that provided weekly "bitter and relentless criticism" of whites to "practically all Negroes who can read." The growth of these papers reflected "two interrelated trends: the rising Negro protest and the increase of Negro literacy."[24] If for decades the white press was largely aloof and uninterested or unwilling to cover race, black newspapers not only covered it but also unabashedly advocated for human rights and racial equality. Their historic importance cannot be overstated; one observer in 1926 called the Negro press "the greatest single power in the Negro race."[25]

Black and white truths across America finally began to converge—though only partially and painfully—in the mid-1950s, when the burgeoning civil rights movement captured the attention of the national news media. One reporter with a unique perspective on the process was Moses Newson of the *Tri-State Defender*, a black-owned newspaper in Memphis.

Newson and his colleagues in the black press had covered the race story for years, often traveling alone at night on unlit country roads, staying in rooming houses, using easily hidden "sawed-off steno pads" so they wouldn't appear to be reporters. As explained by Gene Roberts, co-author of *The Race Beat* and legendary former executive editor of *The Philadelphia Inquirer*, they were the most physically vulnerable journalists in America. It "was a tough assignment for a black reporter to go into a racially charged town. And arguably there wouldn't have been a civil rights movement without the black press, which basically sensitized a couple of generations of Americans to want and then ultimately demand [the] full rights of citizenship in the United States."[26]

But for years, most Americans knew nothing about the reporting being done by people like Moses Newson. Mainstream awareness that something was happening on America's racial front lines stirred fitfully to life in 1954 with the unanimous *Brown* decision. It crystallized with the torture and murder of fourteen-year-old Emmett Till in Mississippi in the summer of 1955. The Till murder proved to be the kind of teaching moment for American whites that Myrdal had presciently foreshadowed. Two weeks later, more than fifty black and white reporters and photographers sat side by side in the courthouse in tiny Sumner, Mississippi, covering the trial of Till's accused murderers.[27]

Roy Bryant and J. W. Milam were found not guilty by the all-white jury. Weeks later, however, they recounted in gruesome detail to *Look* magazine exactly how they had made "an example" of Emmett Till.[28]

Moses Newson, then twenty-eight, covered the Till trial. He suddenly found white reporters on the race beat, and "they were from everywhere. Not only the United States, but they came from abroad . . . we never had that sort of dramatic appearance and dramatic coverage that came with that Till case situation."[29]

It was, he recalled half a century later, "a case that shook up a lot of people. Black people decided that if this is the kind of thing they are going to do to our kids, then it's time for us to start being a little more bold in what we do and to try to get this monkey off our backs. And, I don't know this. I am not a historian. [But] I think this played a lot into the situation in Montgomery, Alabama, later that same year."[30]

As Newson's words recall, the process of shared truths, "publicity," and consciousness-raising about the race issue continued in 1955 with the 381-day Montgomery bus boycott, following the arrest of Rosa Parks for refusing to relinquish her seat to a white passenger. That arrest and the unprecedented civil rights boycott that followed also marked the national emergence of an eloquent, charismatic, twenty-six-year-old Baptist minister named Martin Luther King Jr. The public enlightenment process continued in 1958, with the forced federal desegregation of public schools in Little Rock, Arkansas, by President Dwight D. Eisenhower, who announced it on television to 100 million Americans. Within hours, 11,000 troops from the 101st Airborne Division and federalized members of the Arkansas National Guard moved to quell the angry white mob for its street violence and physical beatings of journalists, especially black reporters.[31]

Little Rock marked the full-throated arrival on the civil rights scene of the national TV networks, which supplemented their evening newscasts by repeatedly breaking into daytime programming with special reports. Over the next several years, Americans began finally to see the ugly, unavoidable truth about "democracy and fairness and justice" in their country, as Moses Newson put it. And, indeed, how could they not, "when [they] started seeing people sic dogs on people and knocking people down with fire hoses, buses being burned up with people on the buses and that sort of thing. I think people just didn't feel that that was something the country should tolerate. And I think that included people who were not necessarily for desegregation."[32]

The civil rights movement efforts led by Dr. King and others moved throughout the South, nowhere impressed upon the nation's consciousness more graphically or indelibly than in Alabama. Busloads of Freedom Riders on the highways couldn't be more obvious, and they found themselves in great personal peril. In May 1961, Newson was among those on a bus in Anniston, Alabama, that was firebombed, its occupants badly beaten.

"People were crawling around," he recalls, "and were coughing and trying to get the smoke out of their chest . . . It was one of the more horrible scenes you would see. You know, just to think that some Americans were doing that to other Americans."[33]

At this point in his career, Newson was a reporter for the *Baltimore Afro-American*. He was "the last person off the Greyhound bus as it was burning outside of Anniston, Alabama," Gene Roberts told me. "And Simeon Booker [a black reporter for *Jet* and *Ebony* magazines] was on the other bus in which the Freedom Riders came into Birmingham and were beaten in the bus station . . . They both opted to sit in the very back row [of their respective buses] so that they could be observers."[34]

Journalists at the time understood that they were caught in a kind of deadly minuet playing itself out. Martin Luther King Jr. was strategically forcing the race issue while also informally forging kindred sensibilities with reporters on the race beat and with successive presidents, Kennedy and then Johnson.

"He sought out the most promising settings for creating dramatic confrontations that would serve as moral passion plays," Pulitzer Prize–winning journalist and author Nick Kotz has written. "A successful performance would reveal to the nation the stark contrast between peaceful African American demonstrators and brutal southern racists. King, too, was a gambler and provocateur . . . he knew he risked his own life and the lives of others. When his campaigns stumbled, he could act with cool ruthlessness to attract national media attention."[35]

One of the most obvious examples of this occurred in the spring of 1963, seven years after the successful Montgomery bus boycott. Mere oratory without palpable systemic change throughout the South was getting old for civil rights leaders, who were frustrated by the Kennedy administration's cautious support. Although the president had sent a message to Congress decrying discrimination and inequality in America, no major civil rights legislation had been proposed. Something had to give. Movement leaders decided to focus their energies on Birmingham, Alabama, one of the most notorious, racially repressive cities in the South.[36]

But the campaign to end discrimination in downtown stores, from their lunch counters to their employment practices, stalled. The white establishments responded shrewdly to the demonstrations, and the cartoonish thuggery of Birmingham's racist police commissioner, Eugene "Bull" Connor, had not yet been exposed by the national news media. The local black newspaper was unconvinced by the protests, the white newspapers were predictably hostile, and conservative black ministers and their congregations generally were not engaged. King decided that the situation required more aggressive measures, and he opted for personally demonstrating while under a court order not to do so. Upon his incarceration, King penned his landmark "Letter from Birmingham Jail" to fellow clergymen. "I cannot sit idly by in Atlanta," he wrote, "and not be concerned about what happens in Birmingham. Injustice anywhere is a threat to justice everywhere." Suddenly, Birmingham was back in the news.[37]

King also turned to one of his edgiest, most brilliant Southern Christian Leadership Conference strategists, Reverend James Bevel, who recommended the almost unthinkable: make the Birmingham campaign a "children's crusade."[38] King agreed, and on May 2, 1963, more than one thousand young black people congregated at Birmingham's Sixteenth Street Baptist Church, then marched downtown.[39] There were six hundred arrests. Four days later, the procession of young blacks swelled to 3,000, and another eight hundred arrests overflowed the Birmingham jail to outdoor pens on the state fairgrounds. By the time it was all over, 10,000 children had been arrested, transported to their outdoor prison in school buses.

The use of children had "caught the Birmingham authorities completely by surprise," David Halberstam wrote years later in *The Children*. "Soon Bull Connor had his people turn high-velocity fire hoses on the children and use police dogs to assault them. All of these scenes were captured in their full cruelty by the national media. Birmingham became, to the rest of the nation, not so much a city but an image, and a devastating one at that, where white cops could use maximum force on children trying to exercise constitutional rights."[40]

Within six weeks, 15,000 people had been arrested in 758 demonstrations in 178 cities across the nation.[41] As the civil rights crisis escalated, President Kennedy sent federal troops to Alabama and prepared to federalize that state's national guard. Kennedy told a group of White House visitors that he was "sickened" by the picture of a white policeman unleashing a dog on a black teenage demonstrator.[42]

On May 18, in a speech at Vanderbilt University in Tennessee, the president publicly embraced the concept of civil rights for all, in the "highest traditions of American freedom." And other such statements followed, most notably after a federal judge ruled that the all-white University of Alabama must admit black students. Governor George Wallace had stood in the schoolhouse doorway to block the admission of two matriculating summer-session black students, who had successfully sued the state. But Wallace physically withdrew upon the arrival of national guardsmen the president had ordered to Tuscaloosa to enforce the court ruling. It was all dramatically captured on national television. And that evening, June 11, 1963, Kennedy spoke to the American people at length about civil rights, framing it for the first time as "a moral issue."[43]

"It is as old as the Scriptures and is as clear as the American Constitution," Kennedy said. "The heart of the question is whether all Americans are to be afforded equal rights and equal opportunities, whether we are going to treat our fellow Americans as we want to be treated."[44] Just hours after Kennedy's speech, Medgar Evers, director of the Mississippi National Association for the Advancement of Colored People, was assassinated outside his home in Jackson. A week later, after having met with Evers's grieving family at the White House, the president submitted to Congress what would become the 1964 Civil Rights Act. The legislation passed the US Senate by a vote of 73–27 exactly one year later, adeptly shepherded into law by Lyndon Johnson after Kennedy had also been assassinated.[45]

It would be pleasant to look back on this victory for equality and consider the issue of equal voting rights settled once and for all. However, nearly forty years later, the conservative US Supreme Court "effectively struck down" the heart of the Voting Rights Act of

1965, allowing nine mostly Southern states to change their election laws without "advance federal approval."[46] The battle, it appears, will continue.

⟨ঙ⟩

The peculiar, mutually dependent dynamic between newsmakers and newsmen (men did nearly all of the national news reporting on the civil rights struggle) was particularly evident during the arduous and deadly Selma campaign in 1965. Although the 1964 Civil Rights Act outlawed discrimination in housing, education, public access to transportation, and employment, while empowering the federal government to prosecute violations of the law, voting rights were substantially unaddressed.

In January 1965, just months after King had been awarded the Nobel Peace Prize, he and other movement leaders felt certain that the unabashedly racist authorities in Selma and the rest of Dallas County would respond to their planned civil rights demonstrations with violence. Instead of Bull Connor, the incumbent sheriff was Jim Clark, known for punching civil rights protesters in the mouth or whacking them with his billy club; his deputized "volunteers" also used cattle prods. By February, more than 3,000 nonviolent demonstrators had been jailed. At one protest in Marion, twenty-three miles from Selma, Alabama, state troopers clubbed both marchers and onlooking journalists; two UPI cameramen and NBC correspondent Richard Valeriani were badly beaten. Worse, a twenty-six-year-old black man named Jimmie Lee Jackson was shot and killed by a trooper, according to witnesses.[47]

Not surprisingly, such blatant inhumanity also strained the conformities of journalistic neutrality and objectivity, not to mention the precise parameters of journalistic conduct amid the street violence and police brutality in this historic good-versus-evil morality play.

For example, *Life* magazine photographer Flip Schulke "saw a small child being roughed up by a sheriff's posse in Selma, Alabama," Gene Roberts recalled. "And [Schulke] dropped his camera, let it dangle around his neck while he went to the rescue of a child. And Martin Luther King heard about it, and said, you know, we need to talk about what our different roles are. I have got plenty of civil rights demonstrators. When you stopped shooting today, the world missed what you would have captured in your camera. And that's more important than wading into the fray."[48]

To honor the sacrifice of Jimmie Lee Jackson, and also to give the horde of national news media something significant to cover, King decided on a march from Selma to the state capitol building in Montgomery, fifty-four miles away via the Jefferson Davis Highway. Governor Wallace declared that "such a march cannot and will not be tolerated."[49] But on the afternoon of March 7, starting from Selma's Brown Chapel Church, civil rights leaders John Lewis and Reverend Hosea Williams led over five hundred marchers, walking two abreast, through the city's streets to the Edmund Pettus Bridge, named after a local Confederate brigadier general. Atop the bridge, Lewis later recalled, "I stopped dead still . . . there, facing us at the bottom of the other side, stood a sea of blue-helmeted, blue-uniformed Alabama state troopers, line after line of them, dozens of battle-ready lawmen . . . behind them were several dozen more armed men—Sheriff Clark's posse, some on horseback. . . ."[50]

At the bottom of the bridge, the marchers were told that "this is an unlawful assembly," and to "turn around and go back to your church." Lewis, Williams, and the demonstrators behind them, all of whom had stopped, quietly knelt to pray. Within seconds, the command was given: "Troopers, advance!" Lewis was promptly beaten, his skull fractured. Roy Reed, of the *New York Times*, wrote the next day: "The first 10 or 20 Negroes were swept to the ground screaming, arms and legs flying, and packs and bags went skittering . . . The troopers continued pushing, using both the force of their bodies and the prodding of their nightsticks. A cheer went up from the white spectators lining the south side of the highway." Sheriff Clark's deputies continued chasing and beating the retreating marchers all the way back to Brown Chapel Church.[51]

Later that night, ABC interrupted its prime-time airing of *Judgment at Nuremberg*, which chronicled how the German people had enabled Nazi-era atrocities, with a fifteen-minute special report featuring remarkable footage of "Bloody Sunday" in Selma. Within moments, millions of Americans went from seeing a movie about brutal Nazis to seeing vicious Alabama law enforcement officials, at one point hearing Sheriff Clark order his men to "get those goddamned niggers. And get those goddamned white niggers."[52]

The next day, people began streaming into Selma from across America, while demonstrators in eighty cities protested the Bloody Sunday violence. Within just forty-eight hours of that nationally televised brutishness, King and others led some 2,000 people without incident across the Pettus Bridge; they then reversed course, honoring a temporary federal injunction against a march to Montgomery because of public-safety concerns. The atmosphere was extremely tense. About 450 clergymen from around the country had amassed in Selma; also congregating were throngs of local white segregationists, raw with racist anger over the arrival of "outside agitators." Later that night, James J. Reeb, a white Unitarian minister from Boston, was beaten with a baseball bat while walking back to Brown Chapel Church after dinner with two others. Reeb died two days later amid wall-to-wall coverage of his fate by the national news media.[53]

Just eight days after Bloody Sunday, with the country fully engaged over the crisis in Alabama, President Johnson proposed voting-rights legislation before a joint session of Congress and 70 million TV viewers. In a powerful speech interrupted by applause forty times, Johnson said:

I recognize that outside this chamber is the outraged conscience of a nation, the grave concern of many nations, and the harsh judgment of history on our acts . . . Even if we pass this bill, the battle will not be over. What happened in Selma is part of a far larger movement which reaches into every section and state of America. It is the effort of American Negroes to secure for themselves the full blessings of American life. Their cause must be our cause too. Because it is not just Negroes, but really it is all of us, who must overcome the crippling legacy of bigotry and injustice.

Then Johnson paused for effect and, with his Texas drawl, said emphatically, "And we *shall* overcome!"

According to John Lewis, who watched the speech in Selma with other movement leaders, Martin Luther King "wiped away a tear at the point where Johnson said the words, 'We shall overcome.'" Later that evening, King called Johnson to thank and congratulate him. He added: "It is ironic, Mr. President, that after a century, a southern white President would help lead the way toward the salvation of the Negro." In a subsequent telegram, King told Johnson his speech was "the most moving, eloquent, unequivocal and passionate plea for human rights ever made by any President of the nation."[54]

∽ා∾

Johnson's speech was a turning point in the civil rights movement. But the struggle—and the violence—were far from over.

On March 25, ten days after Johnson's address, Viola Liuzzo, a white mother of five who had come to Selma from Detroit to demonstrate peacefully, was shot and killed while ferrying marchers in her Oldsmobile in "bloody Lowndes" County.

The news of her ambush shocked the country, and in a stunning development literally the next day, President Johnson announced in a televised event that the FBI had already arrested the accused killers: Ku Klux Klansmen William Eaton, Gary Thomas Rowe, Eugene Thomas, and Collie Leroy Wilkins. Days later, however, Jack Nelson of the *Los Angeles Times* and, soon after, Fred Graham of the *New York Times* reported that in fact, Rowe was a paid FBI informant and had been riding inside the murderers' car. Hours later, it was reported, he provided the names of his fellow travelers to the FBI.[55]

But as a career in investigative journalism has repeatedly taught me, the whole truth often takes years or decades to emerge—if it ever does.

The story of the Liuzzo killing took a strange twist thirteen years later, in July 1978, when the *New York Times* and ABC News reported about what ABC called "the strange career of Gary Thomas Rowe . . . who may have instigated the racial violence he was hired to prevent." He had been a "rogue" informant in the Birmingham area, participating directly in Klan racial violence for years—which the FBI had overlooked—and then receiving cash for confidentially providing the Bureau with information about the crimes he had helped commit.[56]

The two surviving perpetrators of Liuzzo's murder, who had been convicted in federal court a decade earlier in large part based on Rowe's eyewitness testimony, told ABC News that it was Rowe who had fired the fatal shots from the car. Rowe's accusers each passed polygraphs administered by a nationally respected examiner; Rowe vehemently denied the crime on camera, but his polygraph, administered by another nationally respected examiner, indicated deception.

In 1978 and 1979, I devoted ten months at ABC News to investigating this subject under the mentorship of Sander Vanocur and veteran reporter and former NBC *Nightly News* executive producer Wallace Westfeldt, both of whom had covered the civil rights struggle in the late 1950s. My colleagues and I tracked down and interviewed scores of people inside the civil rights community, the Klan, and the Liuzzo family. We interviewed Liuzzo's surviving passenger that night, Leroy Moton, as well as the three surviving men in the ambush car (who have all since died). We talked to their polygraph examiners. We talked to the federal, state, and local criminal investigators and prosecutors. And we talked to law enforcement personnel directly involved in the matter. In addition, we combed through thousands of pages of files from the FBI and Alabama authorities, and we further studied state and federal trial transcripts.[57]

Based on this information, Carol Blakeslee produced two *20/20* segments on the case that aired in July 1978, prompting, along with Howell Raines's *New York Times* page-one stories, a Justice Department investigation, a civil lawsuit against the FBI and Justice Department, and a state murder indictment.

The following year, a special Justice Department task force report, compiled in response to the news stories, criticized the FBI's informant system and identified Rowe's role as "one of a handful most intensely involved" in some of the most notorious racial violence in Birmingham. But the task force attorneys, devoting half of their three-hundred-page report to the Liuzzo shooting, were unable or unwilling to identify her killer, finding none of the four Klansmen in the assailant car that night, including Rowe, to be believable.[58]

And so today, four-plus decades after Liuzzo's murder, and despite the massive effort dedicated to the case by reporters and law enforcement officials alike, it remains clear to me that we will *never* know the full truth about this crime or Rowe's precise, complicated role in it.[59]

Personally, I find this conclusion excruciatingly painful. It goes against everything in my investigative reporter's DNA. But sometimes inexorable circumstances (such as lack of physical evidence or lack of witness credibility) simply preclude ever knowing the full truth. For journalists, as well as judges, juries, prosecutors, and others operating in a postmortem, criminal-justice context, real-life circumstances can sometimes erode certainty "beyond a reasonable doubt." And there are the investigator's own individual or organizational limitations, usually related to finite time and resources, including money. Within the journalism milieu, the financial, legal, and corporate sensibilities, usually subtle and unstated, can directly affect what a reporter, editor, or corporate executive is willing and able to even attempt at the outset.

The saga of this particular civil rights crime underscores the immense difficulties journalists and others face in attempting to ascertain the truth regarding almost any public situation. Patience, perseverance, measured editorial judgment, honesty in assessing the available facts, and, in the end, humility are essential traits for those afflicted with a gnawing curiosity about the truth of the matter, whatever it may be.

∽∾

In March 2007, as part of our continuing fascination with the American struggle over race, my wife and I, along with our six-year-old son, accompanied a dozen bipartisan members of Congress and others on a three-day pilgrimage to Birmingham, Montgomery, and Selma to revisit the sites of the historic bombings, murders, churches, and marches of 1961 to 1965. This was one of the biannual trips organized by Representative John Lewis, beaten or imprisoned forty times in the 1960s, and one of the "Big Six" black leaders in the civil rights movement with King. Lewis spoke at the great 1963 March on Washington, at the age of twenty-three, and after King's murder, in 1968 was a presidential campaign aide to Senator Robert Kennedy, with him in Los Angeles just minutes before his assassination.[60] As you can imagine, revisiting these hallowed sites for the first time in thirty years in the presence of John Lewis was a remarkable experience for me.

Sometime during that extraordinary weekend, we all learned from Representative Lewis of an unusual political situation: Illinois senator and recently announced presidential candidate Barack Obama had been invited weeks earlier to speak Sunday morning at the Brown Chapel Church, prior to the culminating reenactment of the great march across the Edmund Pettus Bridge. It was the iconic Selma church where Malcolm X had once spoken while Martin Luther King was in a city jail, and where weeks later, in March 1965, King addressed the congregation at the start of the Selma march. And apparently in response to Obama's Brown Church invitation, the front-runner in the 2008 presidential campaign, Senator Hillary Clinton, had decided to speak that same Sunday morning at the nearby First Baptist Church.[61] Former president Bill Clinton—so close to the black community he'd been dubbed "the first black president"—was also coming to town, for his induction into the National Voting Rights Museum's Hall of Fame. What was supposed to be a special remembrance weekend was becoming a full-blown political and media circus.

Congressman Lewis asked members of the traveling delegation to decide two or three days in advance, because of scarce seating and security, which church service they'd prefer to attend. Because we were Lewis's guests and knew he would be speaking at Brown Chapel Church, and because of its historic significance, we attended that service. We heard Senator Obama frame in majestic, biblical terms what Martin Luther King and others had done in Selma and elsewhere. "So don't tell me I don't have a claim on Selma, Alabama," he concluded. "Don't tell me I'm not coming home when I come to Selma, Alabama. I'm here because somebody marched. I'm here because y'all sacrificed for me. I stand on the shoulders of giants."[62]

It was an eloquent and impressive speech. But few people fully imagined that day what would occur over the ensuing twenty-two months: the election of the first African American president of the United States, and then, from the west portico of the US Capitol, his inauguration before a shivering crowd of roughly 2 million jubilant people. That evening of January 20, 2009, the Obama family slept in the White House, which slaves had built two centuries earlier.

But in spite of the understandable yearning now to think and talk in "post-racial" terms, the idea that racism is now dead remains an American delusion. Unfortunately, in the decades since the height of the civil rights movement, the majority of Americans, their elected representatives, and the national news media have moved on, as if they've decided that the problems of ethnic poverty and discrimination either have been solved or perhaps are unsolvable. And against this backdrop of inaction, it is fair to say that most editors working for overwhelmingly white-owned and white-managed media corporations, dependent on mostly white business advertising, are not exactly pining for their reporters to undertake enterprising stories on this sensitive topic—despite the fact that white-nonwhite disparities in our society remain stark, as a mere glance at statistics regarding unemployment, family income, incarceration rates, educational achievement, and countless other factors makes obvious.[63]

Since the 1960s, there has been both a lack of policy consensus and a lack of strategic political leadership and vision within the civil rights movement, the Congress, and various presidential administrations. At the same time, one of our leading political parties has adopted an unspoken but long-standing electoral strategy of preying upon white fear and anger toward blacks.

That "Southern Strategy" began with the successful 1968 "law and order" candidacy of Richard Nixon, who frequently talked about crime in thinly veiled racial terms while some two hundred riots traumatized urban America. It continued in 1988 with what Republican

Party general chairman Lee Atwater called on his deathbed "our successful manipulation" of various campaign themes in the 1988 presidential contest from which George Herbert Walker Bush emerged victorious—including the fraudulent linking in a scurrilous political ad of opponent Michael Dukakis and a black convicted murderer, William Horton, incorrectly nicknamed "Willie" by the voiceover as his police mug shot was displayed.[64] The Bush campaign and the Republican Party benefited hugely from the emotive, inflammatory ad. And there's no doubt that the strategy was completely conscious and deliberate. In the heat of that political battle, Atwater had proclaimed about Democrat Dukakis that, as Bush's 1988 campaign manager, he had intended to "strip the bark off the little bastard" and "make Willie Horton his running mate." But two years later, dying of terminal brain cancer, Atwater said in *Life* magazine that he was sorry "for both statements: the first for its naked cruelty, the second because it makes me sound racist, which I am not."[65]

Despite Atwater's disclaimer, there's no doubt that a brutal, heavy-handed manipulation had indeed occurred. Republican media consultant Roger Ailes, later founding president of Fox News Channel, said at the time of the infamous commercial, "The only question is whether we depict Willie Horton with a knife in his hand or without it."[66] In the words of eminent communications scholar Kathleen Hall Jamieson at the University of Pennsylvania Annenberg School, "William Horton and Michael Dukakis are now twinned in our memory. The fact that the memories are factually inaccurate does not diminish their power. Dukakis did not pardon Horton nor did the furloughed convict kill . . . in politics as in life, what is known is not necessarily what is believed, what is shown is not necessarily what is seen, and what is said is not necessarily what is heard . . . Abetted by news reports, amplified by Republican ads, assimilated through the cognitive quirks of audiences, William Horton came to incarnate liberalism's failures and voters' fears."[67]

Similar subtle and not-so-subtle race-baiting tactics have been used by other Republican candidates for state and local offices for decades. These appeals have often been successful, at least in part, because so many white Americans prefer to believe that racial injustice is a thing of the past—or perhaps never even really existed.

In their effort to maintain that comfortable delusion, some political leaders have resorted to obfuscation of the truth and to downright dishonesty.

In 2005, in the immediate aftermath of Hurricane Katrina, for a brief, appalling moment, the American people saw poor black people penned for days inside a downtown football stadium without food and water. The federal and state government incompetence and de facto abandonment of the poor in New Orleans and elsewhere in the Gulf region resulted in numerous entirely preventable deaths, severely damaging President George W. Bush's standing in public opinion polls.

Rather than accepting blame, the administration sought to deflect it. Four days after the hurricane, Bush tried to suggest that no one had seen this coming: "I don't think anybody anticipated the breach of the levees." Actually, the New Orleans *Times-Picayune*, in a multipart series three years earlier, had exposed the unreliability of the levees.[68] And months after Katrina, the Associated Press released confidential government video footage showing that Bush had been clearly told in a briefing days before the hurricane hit that "the storm could breach levees, put lives at risk in New Orleans' Superdome and overwhelm rescuers."[69] Worse still, the administration even tried to prevent any media photographs of the injured or dead, a hide-the-truth policy that had proven to be much more feasible in a tightly controlled Iraq war zone than in five Gulf Coast states.[70]

For a time, national television news presenters seemed genuinely shocked and angry over the suffering and public neglect of the hurricane victims. But the media's interest proved fickle and fleeting.

Pulitzer Prize–winning author David Shipler ably described the media's attention deficit disorder weeks after Katrina:

> There is no more telling indictment of reporters and editors than the surprise felt by most Americans in seeing the raw poverty among New Orleans residents after Hurricane Katrina . . . The fissures of race and class should be "revealed" every day by America's free press. Why aren't they? . . . When government ignores a problem, the problem festers and usually fades into the shadows of coverage until a Hurricane Katrina ravages New Orleans or a riot tears through South Central Los Angeles. If the White House pursues an issue, either at home or abroad, the bright searchlight of attention focuses for a while, and once the beam swings away, the subject disappears.[71]

I've come to see that when it comes to race and class, candor and truth are excruciatingly rare. How can any white politician, desperate to win an election in a majority white district, speak honestly about race? A white candidate who talks too much about issues like inequality is often dismissed by both voters and the media as hopelessly idealistic or naïve. And his or her opponent will almost certainly use code words to inflame racial fears and incite white voters. Reporters are generally expected to inform the public about what is said, verbatim, but not what is unsaid but intuitively understood—which means that latent race-baiting messages are quietly ignored or even passively transmitted by the media rather than being challenged or exposed.

Of course, American society has experienced racial progress since the 1960s, as the election of Barack Obama reflects. And in the broader context of history and democracy, as author Nick Kotz has noted, "The civil rights movement directly inspired and led to successful protest movements against the Vietnam War, and on behalf of women's rights, the rights of older workers, rights for the hand-icapped, and struggles overseas for human rights."[72] But continued progress on all these fronts depends on the truth-telling role of the news media in a democracy.

We must never forget that once the Northern news media finally began to take notice of the plight of blacks in America, beginning with the *Brown* decision and the murder of young Emmett Till, most Americans "got shocked and shaken in their conscience when they learned the facts," just as Gunnar Myrdal had predicted they would in *An American Dilemma*.

As Representative John Lewis recalled in 2005, on the fortieth anniversary of Bloody Sunday and the fiftieth anniversary of the Montgomery bus boycott:

> I have often said that without the media, the civil rights movement would have been a bird without wings. I am not certain where we would be today as a nation, if the American public had not been made to acknowledge the struggles we faced in the American South . . . without the media's willingness to stand in harm's way and starkly portray events of the movement as they saw them un-fold, Americans may never have understood or even believed the horrors that African Americans faced in the deep South.

Print and broadcast journalists, Lewis added, "overcame their fear and decided to tell the American story."[73] Yet there is so much more of that story still untold. Who will have the courage to uncover the unpalatable facts and share them with the world? It's a question with enormous implications for all who value freedom—and the truth.

America's Secret Foreign Policy and the Arrogance of Power

Political language . . . is designed to make lies
sound truthful and murder respectable, and to
give an appearance of solidity to pure wind.
—GEORGE ORWELL, 1946[1]

S INCE THE **1890s,** the United States has deposed or helped to
depose more than a dozen foreign governments, often for the
benefit of US commercial interests operating in those countries.[2] This track record flatly contradicts our cherished self-image as
a reluctant warrior—a powerful but inherently peace-loving nation,
one that enters other people's frays only when attacked or in imminent danger, and only at the direction of the president with the informed consent of the Congress. No wonder our government rarely
acknowledges the crassly commercial motives underlying many
of these foreign adventures. Instead, we defend our actions using
euphemistic phrases like "the national interest." And most Americans—including many members of the news media—are content to
quietly accept such evasions. As with race, the disconnect between

our vision of ourselves and the reality of our behavior is too painful to acknowledge, and so we ignore it, sacrificing truth in the process.

One of my closest encounters with the harsh realities underlying America's supposedly idealistic foreign policy came in early 1975, when I was researching and writing an undergraduate thesis about the role of the United States in Chilean politics in the early years of the decade. As part of this project, I was able to meet with Dr. Orlando Letelier, who had been the Chilean ambassador to the United States under its former president, Salvador Allende, as well as the country's defense minister at the time of the September 11, 1973, military coup d'état that ended Allende's regime—and his life.

Letelier himself had been arrested that day and imprisoned along with other top government officials in a "desolate concentration camp" on Dawson Island, "a cold and barren rock" in the Straits of Magellan, not far from Antarctica.[3] Following a yearlong international campaign to have him released, Letelier was expelled by the Chilean government under its then head, General Augusto Pinochet. But before he left Dawson Island, according to authors John Dinges and Saul Landau, the camp commander ominously warned him, "General Pinochet will not and does not tolerate activities against his government" and punishment could be rendered "no matter where the violator lives."[4]

Letelier relocated to Washington, DC, and was hired as director of the Transnational Institute, the international operations of the liberal Institute for Policy Studies (IPS). Over the ensuing months, in his traveling, writing, and speaking, he lobbied members of Congress, as well as UN and European officials, for human-rights sanctions against the murderous military regime ruling Chile. His long, distinguished background in government, including a stint as a senior economist for the Inter-American Development Bank, and his forceful, fearless public statements about the military junta in Chile, made him that country's most prominent political figure in exile.[5]

We met at his suburban Washington home, on a cul-de-sac in Bethesda, Maryland. The slim, mustachioed Letelier could not have been more gracious during my hourlong visit. But the information he wanted to share with me was very disturbing for anyone who harbored illusions about the American overseas role.

Letelier showed me secret Chilean intelligence cables indicating that US naval forces had been off the coast of Santiago on that fateful morning of September 11. He spoke of his strong sense of anger and personal betrayal toward Secretary of State Henry Kissinger, who had repeatedly assured him that the United States was not trying to foment dissent in Chile. These reassurances, which Letelier had passed on directly to Allende, were all bald-faced lies, delivered by a master diplomat with no compunctions about deceiving and manipulating a high official of another government.

As Seymour Hersh years later wrote in his seminal book *The Price of Power: Kissinger in the Nixon White House*, "Letelier, with his old-world manners and civility, was no match for Kissinger."[6] Those who might wonder how Kissinger himself would defend his actions will turn to his three volumes of memoirs in vain. Kissinger did not mention Letelier once—not even in a footnote.[7]

Letelier was also convinced that a May 1972 break-in at the Chilean Embassy in Washington, which he described to me in intricate detail, had been the handiwork of the White House Watergate "plumbers" as part of the US "infernal machine" of covert intervention against Allende. We now know he was correct.[8] In 1999, newly available Oval Office recordings from May 1973, revealed President Nixon telling his aide General Alexander Haig, "There are times, you know, when, good God, I'd authorize any means to achieve a goal abroad," including "the breaking-in of embassies and so forth."[9]

Days later, in another conversation, Nixon told White House lawyer J. Fred Buzhardt, "When we get down, for example, to the break-in, the Chilean Embassy—that thing was a part of the burglars' plan, as a cover . . . a CIA cover."[10] Indeed, electronic surveillance planted during the break-in enabled the CIA to learn the Chilean government's intentions about its nationalization efforts, which the White House then secretly passed on to the US companies with operations there, all major Nixon and Republican Party donors.[11]

I left my conversation with Letelier feeling troubled, as almost any American would, over the notion that our nation's highest authorities would unhesitatingly undermine a duly elected foreign government and then brazenly lie about it, all in the service of US financial interests. But the denouement of my encounter with Letelier would be even more horrific.

Roughly eighteen months after our conversation, in the darkness before dawn just outside his Bethesda home, an assassin sent to Washington by the Chilean secret police—with the personal knowledge of General Pinochet—taped a remote-control bomb to the driver's-side chassis of Letelier's Chevrolet Chevelle. On the morning of September 21, 1976, driving with his young, recently wed IPS colleagues Michael and Ronni Moffit to work downtown, one of the assassins trailing them "pressed the button on an electronic paging device," triggering a massive explosion that was heard at the State Department half a mile away. A piece of shrapnel cut twenty-five-year-old Ronni Moffitt's jugular vein, and she literally drowned in her own blood. Letelier's legs were blown off, and he died before the ambulance reached George Washington University Hospital. The backseat passenger, Michael Moffitt, only slightly injured by comparison, tried in vain to help the pair amid the bloody mayhem.[12]

It was the first time in US history that a foreign government had conducted a political execution on the streets of Washington, DC—at least, so far as we know. Of course, it took years for the truth to seep out, and it's still not all out yet. But, in time, the world learned that Augusto Pinochet had authorized a series of political assassinations outside Chile, with Letelier just one of the victims. Pinochet's deadly secret police, the Directorate of National Intelligence (DINA), headed by Colonel Manuel Contreras, who reported directly to him, was responsible for the years of terror after the coup. Contreras had overseen the Letelier hit, along with other "Operation Condor" state-sponsored terrorism. Michael Townley, a US citizen who had emigrated to Chile, had placed the bomb under the car and earlier had recruited as accomplices a trio of anti-Castro Cubans, all of whom were eventually apprehended, tried, and convicted, although their convictions were later reversed on appeal.[13]

Throughout his brutal seventeen-year dictatorship, Pinochet and his regime denied any involvement in the murders. But truth eventually caught up with him. In 1987, a member of the Letelier assassination team agreed to plead guilty and provide testimony in exchange for protection in the United States. He directly implicated Pinochet in the cover-up of the crime. In 1988, Pinochet lost a constitutionally required, national plebiscite, and on January 6, 1990, Christian Democrat Patricio Aylwin was inaugurated as Chile's new president. In October 1998, Pinochet was arrested in London in connection with a Spanish government prosecution against him; he was held under house arrest for sixteen months before being allowed to return to Chile. But upon his arrival, facing over seventy judicial cases, he was stripped of his immunity. He was placed under house arrest in January 2001 and interrogated by the authorities, but the Chilean Supreme Court ruled in July 2002 that Pinochet, eighty-seven, was "mentally unfit due to dementia" to stand trial.[14]

In 2004, the National Commission on Political Imprisonment and Torture in Chile concluded in a 1,200-page report that during the Pinochet years, "torture was a state policy, meant to repress and terrorize the population." The report specifically identified 27,255 people who were tortured at 1,200 sites, and it named the military, political, and intelligence units that inflicted this torture. Shortly afterward, a judge placed the aged Pinochet under house arrest for kidnapping and murder. He died in 2006.[15]

It's a terrible story. But also terrible, for me as an American citizen, is the fact that the US government helped to bring about Chile's decades-long international nightmare. To this day, no American president has ever apologized to Chileans for the violence our government helped to cause.

⌒∽∿⌒

The history of American interference in Chile goes back at least to the early 1960s. Shortly after Fidel Castro's Communist revolution, the Kennedy and Johnson administrations—knee deep in the Cold War—sought to prevent another Cuba in the hemisphere. That concern helped spawn such social-welfare and development-aid programs as the Alliance for Progress. Chile, for decades one of the most stable democracies in Latin America, had also had a recent "history of popular support for Socialist, Communist and other leftist parties," which to Washington was seen as a "flirtation with communism."[16] Chile thus was chosen as "the showcase" country for Alliance for Progress assistance, and between 1962 and 1969, it received more than $1 billion in direct US aid—more per capita than any other country in Latin America.[17]

Against that backdrop, the Kennedy and Johnson administrations, with help from the CIA, had also decided to secretly intervene "on a massive scale" in the 1964 presidential election in Chile, approving the expenditure of nearly $4 million (the equivalent of $29 million in 2011 dollars) for fifteen covert-action projects.[18] Secretary of State Dean Rusk, in a Top Secret memorandum to President Lyndon Johnson weeks before the election, wrote, "We are making *a major covert effort to reduce chances* of Chile being the first American country to elect *an avowed* Marxist president [emphasis in original]. . . ."[19] The goal was to "prevent or minimize the influence of Chilean Communists or Marxists" in the government and specifically to thwart the presidential candidacy of Socialist Party candidate Salvador Allende Gossens. Ultimately, the CIA "underwrote slightly more than half of the total cost" of the entire Christian Democratic campaign, whose candidate, Eduardo Frei, received a 57 percent majority in a three-way race.[20]

The CIA's anti-Communist propaganda, support of right-wing media outlets, and other activities inside Chile—"twenty covert action projects" costing nearly $2 million—continued between 1965 and 1969. Despite such efforts to stoke public opinion over the dangers of communism, Chile, as the Church Committee later put it, actually was "a country where nationalism, 'economic independence' and 'anti-imperialism' claimed almost universal support."[21] Frei, for example, had supported "Chileanization," or partial nationalization of the copper industry, a mainstay of the country's economy. But in 1970, with Frei unable to run for reelection because of the constitutional term limit for presidents, the stage was set for another dramatic election.

Allende was again the leftist, multiparty candidate, this time atop a Popular Unity coalition; his campaign platform urged wage increases, agrarian reform, and complete nationalization of the copper industry, which was substantially owned and operated by US multinational corporations Anaconda and Kennecott. He also urged closer relationships with Socialist and Communist countries. The conservative National Party candidate was seventy-four-year-old ex-president Jorge Alessandri, and left-leaning Radomiro Tomic was the Christian Democratic nominee. Like Allende, Tomic favored nationalization of the copper industry.[22]

US multinationals in Chile, not surprisingly, were extremely concerned about the prospects of an Allende presidency. Allende had made it clear, for example, that he also intended to nationalize the country's telephone company, Chiltelco, which at that time was 70 percent owned by International Telephone and Telegraph, Inc. ITT officials contacted the CIA in both Santiago and Washington. In coordination with the company's chairman, board member John McCone, who had served as director of central intelligence during the height of the Cold War, called CIA director Richard Helms with a proposal: ITT wanted the agency to secretly launder its $1 million contribution to the Alessandri campaign. The CIA declined, but ITT later found another way to move $350,000 to Alessandri's campaign (and $100,000 to the conservative newspaper *El Mercurio*). Other US multinationals did likewise.[23]

But those efforts, as well as a $425,000 CIA-funded "spoiling operation" of anti-Allende propaganda activities, were unsuccessful: on September 4, 1970, Allende narrowly won the presidential election, with 36.3 percent of the vote—roughly the same plurality Abraham Lincoln received in his multiparty election in 1860.[24] Because no candidate had gotten 50 percent, the Chilean Congress would have to choose between him and Alessandri, the runner-up. Based on historic precedent, the Nixon administration understood, correctly, that the Chilean Congress, scheduled to meet in joint session seven weeks later, would very likely ratify Allende's constitutional ascent to power.

On September 15, 1970, in a White House meeting with Kissinger, Mitchell, and CIA director Helms, Nixon ordered Helms to stop Allende from being inaugurated on November 4. The following day, Helms told subordinates that Nixon had authorized the CIA to "prevent Allende from coming to power or to unseat him. The President had authorized ten million dollars for this purpose, if needed. Further, The Agency is to carry out this mission without coordination with the Department of State." One item in Helms's handwritten notes from that Oval Office meeting was "make economy scream." And over the ensuing weeks, the administration would do everything conceivable to create a "coup climate" economically in Chile; at one point, Helms cabled Kissinger: "a suddenly disastrous economic situation would be the most logical pretext for a military move." The name of the overall secret operation to block Allende from becoming president: Project FUBELT.[25]

On September 16, in an off-the-record White House briefing for reporters, Kissinger outlined his "domino theory" regarding Chile: "I have yet to meet somebody who firmly believes that if Allende wins, there is likely to be another free election in Chile . . . There is a good chance that he will establish over a period of years some sort of Communist Government . . . in a major Latin American country . . . [ad]joining . . . Argentina . . . Peru . . . and Bolivia . . . So I don't think we should delude ourselves that an Allende takeover in Chile would not present massive problems for us, and for democratic forces in Latin America, and indeed to the whole Western Hemisphere."[26] Of course, although US officials were not pleased with the election outcome, there wasn't a whisper that the president had just authorized the CIA to do something about it, including attempting to instigate an internal coup d'état.

After the brief consideration of myriad, convoluted ways to prevent the Chilean Congress from ratifying Allende's electoral victory—which even included an aborted plan to bribe legislators—a takeover of the government by the Chilean military was decided to be the best option. Back on September 9, six days *before* Nixon's decision to unseat Allende, the CIA head of the Western Hemisphere had told the Agency's station chief in Santiago, Henry Hecksher, "The only prospect with any chance of success whatsoever is a military *golpe* [coup d'état] either before or immediately after Allende's assumption of power." Hecksher was told to establish "those direct contacts with the Chilean military which are required to evaluate possibilities and, at least equally important, could be used to stimulate a *golpe* if and when a decision were made to do so."[27] The United States had gradually increased training and aid to the Chilean military in recent years, deepening personal contacts with its top officers. Between October 5 and 20, the CIA had twenty-one conversations with key military and police officials in Chile, and "those Chileans . . . inclined to stage a coup were given assurances to strong support at the highest levels of the U.S. Government both before and after a coup."[28]

However, it soon became clear that a stumbling block to any coup solution was the Chilean commander in chief of the army, General René Schneider, a constitutionalist strongly opposed to military interference in the electoral process. In Santiago, US military attaché Paul Wimert was in contact with "several groups of military plotters," and by mid-October a single "full-fledged conspiracy" had emerged involving two Chilean generals (one active, one retired), an admiral, and a team of "kidnappers," who supposedly would abduct Schneider and take him to neighboring Argentina. The plan: the military would announce that Schneider had "disappeared" and blame it on "leftists," then President Frei would resign and a new military junta would assume power.

Wimert gave $50,000 to the unidentified kidnappers, along with six submachine guns and ammunition that had been sent in the overnight diplomatic pouch from Washington "specially wrapped and falsely labeled to disguise what they were from State Department officials." Two unsuccessful attempts to intercept Schneider occurred on October 19 and 20, and on October 22 his car was rammed by a Jeep. Five people surrounded the vehicle and started firing; Schneider was shot three times and died days later.[29]

CIA director Helms and his top deputies sent a cold-blooded, congratulatory cable to Santiago: "The Station has done excellent job of guiding Chileans to point today where a military solution is at least an option for them. COS [Chief of Station] [and others involved] are commended for accomplishing this under extremely difficult and delicate circumstances."[30] Nixon disingenuously wired the former president of Chile, Eduardo Frei: "The shocking attempt on the life of General Schneider is a stain on the pages of contemporary history. I would like you to know of my sorrow that this repugnant event has occurred in your country."[31] Of course, there was widespread public revulsion to the violence, and on October 24, 1970, the Chilean Congress, by a margin of 153–37, ratified Salvador Allende as president. The Schneider assassination had caused exactly the *opposite* effect of what had been intended.

That left the CIA scrambling to cover up the incriminating evidence. Wimert was instructed to retrieve the $50,000 bounty, and in so doing he was forced to pistol-whip Brigadier General Camilo Valenzuela, who had not yet paid the kidnappers. And on orders to dispose of the guns, he dumped them in the Pacific Ocean, seventy miles from Santiago. Over the ensuing decades, the CIA attempted to airbrush the history of its involvement in the Schneider debacle. Agency Santiago personnel were ordered to "stonewall all the way," even to other US officials, about what had transpired. But in late 2000, around the time the CIA was forced to declassify a particularly sensitive 1970 cable alluding to requests for money from some of the Schneider assassination plotters, the Agency finally acknowledged that it had paid money directly to the assassins.[32]

From the time of Schneider's death, Henry Kissinger, in sworn deposition, congressional testimony, and his subsequent memoirs, steadfastly maintained that he had halted Project FUBELT a week *before* Schneider's killing, on October 15, 1970, and that he "never received another report on the subject."[33] In fact, there are White House telephone-call transcripts confirming that on the day Kissinger informed Nixon he had ordered the CIA to stop the military coup-plotting in Chile, he said: "That looks hopeless. I turned it off. Nothing could be worse than an abortive coup." But as respected historian Robert Dallek has noted, according to a once-secret CIA

"Memorandum of Conversation" on that very same day, CIA deputy director Thomas Karamessines told Kissinger in a White House meeting that he did not think "wide-ranging discussions with numerous people urging a coup could be put back into the bottle."[34] Indeed, the fact remains that the Schneider murder almost certainly would not have occurred without their covert maneuverings, which set certain tragic, inexorable events in motion. Nonetheless, after leaving government, both Kissinger and Nixon steadfastly maintained a "who, me?" posture, which is belied by reams of bellicose internal cables, telephone transcripts, and secret memoranda at that time. But, of course, that was always the plan—the diplomatic, public posture and the much tougher, private reality.[35]

In the months following Allende's inauguration, Nixon was coolly, cagily deceitful. Regarding the Chilean election, he told a panel of TV journalists, "For the United States to have intervened—intervened in a free election and to have turned it around—I think would have had repercussions all over Latin America that would have been far worse than what has happened in Chile . . . we recognize the right of any country to have internal policies and an internal government different from what we might approve of. . . ."[36] Around the same time, in his 1971 "State of the World" message, Nixon publicly declared, "We are prepared to have the kind of relationship with the Chilean government that it is prepared to have with us."[37] And later that year, to the annual convention of the American Society of Newspaper Editors, he said, "The Chilean people voted for it. So as far as our attitude toward Chile is concerned, it will be affected by what Chile's attitude is toward us . . . We are waiting to see what they will do. As long as they treat us properly, we'll treat them properly."[38]

Meanwhile, over the next three years, the United States privately made the Chilean economy scream, dropping US bilateral aid from $35 million in 1969 to $1.5 million in 1971 and, by 1973, just $800,000. The United States used its international financial clout to "dry up the flow of new multilateral credit or other financial assistance," from $76.4 million in 1970 to $8.2 million in 1972.[39] And separately, approximately $7 million was spent on covert activities inside Chile during Allende's presidency, some of it going to opposition political parties and nearly $2 million funneled to the anti-Allende newspaper *El Mercurio*. And during this same time, the CIA's relationships with the military quietly deepened.[40]

Finally, on September 11, 1973, amid rising signs of hardly coincidental "destabilization," including nationwide strikes against truck, bus, taxi, and shop owners, President Salvador Allende died in a brutal military coup led by General Augusto Pinochet, who became president and dissolved the Congress two days later.[41] In the subsequent months and years of the Pinochet regime, 3,197 Chilean citizens and at least four US citizens were tortured, mutilated, and murdered by the new US-supported regime.[42]

With the world aghast at the carnage, the Nixon administration delayed recognizing the new military junta government for two weeks, with discreet back-channel apologies directly to Pinochet in Santiago *the day after* the coup.[43] Within seventy-two hours of the coup, the United States secretly began the process of lifting its "invisible blockade" against Chile, with an interagency task force called the "Washington Special Action Group" meeting to assess "anticipated short, medium and long term Chilean assistance requirements."[44] Soon Chile began receiving more bilateral and multilateral aid than ever.[45]

But in the immediate aftermath of the death of Allende and his democratically elected government, the military coup and the apparent US role in instigating it were universally condemned. A few days after Allende's removal, in the White House Oval Office, Kissinger complained to Nixon, "Of course, the newspapers [are] bleeding because a pro-Communist government has been overthrown." Nixon replied, "Isn't that something." Kissinger continued, "I mean, instead

of celebrating—in the Eisenhower period we would be heroes."
Nixon said, "Well, we didn't—as you know—our hand doesn't show
on this one." Kissinger agreed: "We didn't do it. I mean we helped
them—created the conditions as great as possible." "That is right,"
Nixon replied. "And that is the way it is going to be played."[46]

∽∂∾

What intrigued me then and now was this tacit understanding in
the diplomatic community that governments speak and act on different levels, with differing levels of truth. In the case of Chile and
Allende, "covert" meant, I was appalled to learn, that the president
and other top US officials could secretly subvert the elected government of another country without ever acknowledging it publicly.
International law and congressional oversight seemed to be less than
an afterthought. It seemed there were two realities: one, a sooth-
ing bromide for the unknowing public and journalists; and another,
the unmitigated, unaccountable truth of dubious legality or outright
crime, knowable only to a select few.

And so it might have remained, if not for House and Senate
committees controlled by a different political party, in this case the
Democrats. The committees were able to disgorge and publish secret government and corporate documents concerning the coup in
Chile, setting forth precisely what abuses of power had occurred.

In 1975, the Senate Select Committee to Study Government Activities with Respect to Intelligence, chaired by Idaho Democratic
senator Frank Church—the so-called Church Committee—issued
its first of fourteen reports about a wide range of covert government
intelligence activities "and the extent, if any, to which such activities were 'illegal, improper or unethical.'" The work of the Church
Committee represents one of the most remarkable investigations
Congress has ever undertaken, as indicated in particular by its two

stunning, starkly detailed reports, "Covert Action in Chile, 1963–73" and "Alleged Assassination Plots Involving Foreign Leaders." These reports formally concluded that covert US activities in Chile between 1963 and 1973 had been "extensive and continuous."[47]

Investigative reports by journalists with access to leaked government documents helped bring the facts to the American public. For example, on September 8, 1974, Seymour Hersh authored a front-page story in the *New York Times* titled, "CIA Chief Tells House of $8 Million Campaign Against Allende in '70–'73," using information drawn from a leaked letter by Democratic representative Michael Harrington of Massachusetts. Hersh's reporting hugely influenced the rest of the news media, including the CBS News Washington Bureau, which assigned Daniel Schorr to "develop what, in effect, would be a television version of Hersh's stories."[48]

In late February 1975, CBS News correspondent Daniel Schorr broke the story about the CIA's past efforts contributing to the attempted assassinations of various foreign leaders, including Fidel Castro; Patrice Lumumba, prime minister of the Republic of the Congo; and General René Schneider. (Several of ITT's CIA-Chile internal memoranda had been reported on by syndicated columnist Jack Anderson as early as 1972, providing the first public whiff of the CIA's extensive covert efforts against Allende.)[49] A few months later, in the summer and fall of 1975, Schorr and others reported the details of these CIA activities, as "an unbelievable array of witnesses began parading before closed hearings of the Church Committee."[50] Schorr also reported closely on the House of Representatives Pike Committee's findings and he managed to obtain a leaked copy of its unpublished final report.

Remembering how the *New York Times* published the Pentagon Papers in their entirety in book form, Schorr asked CBS News to publish the report via one of its two book companies. But CBS declined, and Schorr later recalled, "I learned what I should have long since known—that a television network, operating in a regulated environment, concerned about its local affiliates and advertisers, does not display the same First Amendment courage as a major newspaper." Schorr gave the leaked report to the *Village Voice*, where it was published, and he was subsequently investigated for months by the House Ethics Committee, which eventually voted 6–5 *not* to recommend a contempt citation over his refusal to reveal his source. Schorr left CBS, twenty-three years after being hired by Edward R. Murrow.[51]

As exceptional as these stories were and remain, however, they all exposed controversial covert CIA activities many years after they had occurred. Truth delayed is truth denied. When the facts are bottled up by secrecy and deception, it means that the public and its elected representations can do nothing to prevent or reverse abuses. And it often means that officials responsible for misconduct are never held accountable for their actions, including their misleading comments to the US Congress and to the public.

The record shows that the only public official prosecuted for lying to Congress following Hersh's revelatory Chile stories was former CIA director Helms. The famously "urbane and dashing spymaster" was represented by the celebrated defense lawyer Edward Bennett Williams—ironically, the same attorney whose telephoned advice to Ben Bradlee had stiffened the spine of the *Washington Post* and helped ensure the publication of the Pentagon Papers. Having worked out a deal with the Carter administration, Helms pleaded nolo contendere to a two-count misdemeanor, for which he was sentenced to two years in prison (suspended) and fined $2,000. Judge Barrington Parker castigated Helms in a tirade culminating in the words, "You now stand before this court in disgrace and shame." Helms silently accepted the judge's rebuke, appearing contrite. But outside the courthouse, a smiling Helms proclaimed to reporters, "I wear this conviction like a badge of honor . . . I don't feel disgraced at all."[52] Later that day, his former CIA colleagues gave Helms "a standing, cheering ovation" and passed a hat around, raising the full amount of his fine.

Helms died in 2002. In his posthumously published memoir, he matter-of-factly acknowledged that in his dramatic meeting with Kissinger and Nixon in the Oval Office on September 15, 1970, which led to the Schneider assassination, "President Nixon had ordered me to instigate a military coup in Chile, a heretofore democratic country. Moreover, the knowledge of this presidential directive was to be kept from the U.S. officials most directly concerned. Within CIA this directive was to be restricted to those with an absolute need to know. And I was to report to the President through Henry Kissinger."[53]

In 1974, there was some thoughtful soul-searching about the quality of the reporting while Allende was in power, some of it published in the *Columbia Journalism Review*. Veteran CBS News correspondent Robert Schakne, who had done several stories from Chile for the *CBS Evening News with Walter Cronkite*, acknowledged, "It is a failing of our brand of journalism that we headline what governments choose to announce and ignore too often possibly more important policies which may not be secret but which governments don't talk publicly about . . . With regard to the CIA role, a number of reporters had their suspicions, but none were able to document them. Certainly the public evidence of the U.S. policy . . . could have and should have been examined more extensively." Months later, he wrote about the Chile reporting again, observing, "More than anything else, the experience of American journalists in Chile suggests that foreign reporting may begin at home, that the sources, the leaks, and the documentation are more likely to surface in Washington than abroad. U.S. policy originates in the White House and the State Department and that is where the story is frequently to be found."[54]

Today, many Americans probably know something about the US involvement in the coup that toppled Allende. But much of the truth remains obscure. For example, most Americans don't realize that the ostensible reasons for interfering in the affairs of Chile were seriously flawed. Nixon and Kissinger simply misread—or ignored—US intelligence assessments about the supposed "threat" posed by the election of Salvador Allende. According to the Church Intelligence Committee investigation two years after Allende's death:

> Throughout the Allende years, but especially after the first year of his government, the American Government's best intelligence—National Intelligence Estimates, prepared by the entire intelligence community—made clear that the more extreme fears about the effects of Allende's election were ill-founded; there never was a significant threat of a Soviet military presence; the "export" of Allende's revolution was limited, and its value as a model more restricted still; and Allende was little more hospitable to activist exiles from other Latin American countries than had been his predecessor, Eduardo Frei . . . Chile was charting an independent, nationalist course.[55]

Furthermore, few Americans fully understand the repellent nature of the Pinochet regime we helped to install. In 2004 and 2005, reports issued by the Senate Permanent Subcommittee on Investigations made it clear that Pinochet was not only a thuggish murderer and dictator, but also a drug trafficker for whom Riggs National Bank—the Washington bank for seventeen presidents—had laundered millions of dollars of dirty money through its Bahamian trust company and two offshore shell corporations.[56]

Even the Letelier murder can be laid, at least indirectly, at the feet of US influence. Over the years, it has become evident that US officials understood the deadly nature of Operation Condor and the state-sponsored terrorism it was supporting around the world, including the possibility it might also occur in Washington. Hewson

Ryan, deputy assistant secretary of state in the Ford administration, acknowledged not long before his death, "We knew fairly early on that the governments of the Southern Cone countries were planning, or at least talking about, some assassinations abroad in the summer of 1976 . . . Whether if we had gone in, we might have prevented this, I don't know. But we didn't. We were extremely reticent about taking a forward public posture, and even a private posture in certain cases, as was this case in the Chilean [Letelier] assassination."[57]

The plot thickened in April 2010, when historian Peter Kornbluh posted on the National Security Archive website newly declassified documents indicating that five days before the Letelier bombing, Secretary of State Kissinger *withdrew* an order he planned to deliver to the Pinochet government, warning against orchestrating assassinations abroad. Why did Kissinger do that? He's never said.[58]

Other questions linger more than thirty-five years after the murder of Letelier. For example, why was Colonel Contreras, the head of Pinochet's deadly Directorate of National Intelligence, on the CIA's payroll in 1975? Why did the CIA provide training to DINA, as John Dinges reported in *The Condor Years*? Why didn't the CIA cooperate fully with the Justice Department lawyers prosecuting Letelier's killers? And in the weeks following the assassination, why did the CIA plant stories in major media outlets alleging that the intelligence community believed Letelier may have been assassinated by Chilean left-wing extremists rather than by agents of the Chilean military junta?[59] Curiously, this falsehood was parroted by the likes of North Carolina senator Jesse Helms, 1976 Republican presidential candidate Ronald Reagan, and *National Review* founder William F. Buckley Jr.

The Buckley connection to this story is a particularly complicated and interesting one. Buckley worked briefly in the CIA for nine months in 1951 in Mexico City, reporting to E. Howard Hunt, who two decades later became a convicted felon after organizing the botched Watergate burglary. By the 1970s, founder and editor in chief Buckley and three other former CIA employees worked on the staff of the *National Review*; between 1976 and 1978, he wrote articles suggesting that the Pinochet Chilean regime had nothing to do with the Letelier assassination, writing as late as September 1978 that "there are highly reasonable, indeed compelling, grounds for doubting that Pinochet had anything to do with the assassination." The public didn't know that Buckley had helped Marvin Liebman to create the American-Chilean Council (ACC), which was deeply involved with and even funded by the Pinochet government, a public relations effort that, among other things, robustly attempted to discredit Letelier after his death as a "Cuban agent," even though the ACC's own hired researcher, a former FBI agent named Robert Shortley, told Liebman and Buckley and his *National Review* editors that this was actually not true. In 1978, the Justice Department found that the ACC had failed to register as a foreign agent of the Pinochet Chilean government, and it was shut down; the government filings also explicitly revealed Buckley's role in helping to create ACC.[60]

The Clinton administration, to its great credit, initiated the Chile Declassification Project, which resulted in the release of roughly 24,000 secret documents pertaining to the two-decade US foreign policy disaster. The most stubbornly intransigent agencies, not surprisingly, were the CIA and the National Security Agency, which to this day refuse to declassify hundreds of documents. Kissinger had, for decades, prevented anyone from accessing records related to his tenure as National Security adviser and secretary of state to two presidents; when he left government, he literally took with him his recorded telephone conversations between 1970 and 1976. Public officials frequently pull such shenanigans—absconding with public documents and getting others declassified for their high-priced memoirs, while withholding the negative, unflattering, or even potentially criminal material. Kornbluh calls it "holding history hostage."[61] Call it whatever you want, it obscures and distorts the truth as we know it. And that's wrong.

~∞~

US involvement in the Chilean coup of 1973 is scarcely the only episode in recent history in which illegal, immoral, or simply politically untenable acts by American governments abroad have been mired in webs of secrecy, obfuscation, and lying. We opened the first chapter of this book with another such episode, the Gulf of Tonkin incident, which seemingly set the pattern for similar escapades, including the one that lends the book its title—the brazen use of 935 lies by the administration of George W. Bush to mislead America into war in Iraq. There certainly have been other examples of foreign policy adventures that were of questionable legality or in which the Congress, the public, and the news media were misled, including the US invasion of the Dominican Republic (1965) and the invasion of Panama (1989), in which hundreds of people were killed and US reporters were kept from the field of action.[62]

Sadly, in the field of US foreign policy, seriously assessing the morality of government decision making is rare, generally regarded as quaint and foolish by realpolitik policymakers, regardless of party or administration. When it does occur, it often seems to degenerate into self-serving pomposity and self-justifying, in-the-eyes-of-the-beholder rhetoric.[63]

One of the most striking—and revealing—examples of executive deception in the conduct of US foreign policy is the Reagan-era scandal that came to be known as Iran-Contra. It had its origins in decades of history in which the United States and the poor Latin American nation of Nicaragua had been tragically embroiled.

The "Somoza dynasty" of Nicaraguan presidents had been, in the words of foreign policy historian Walter LaFeber, "a subsidiary of the

United States since 1936." In fact, there had been eleven US military interventions in Nicaragua between 1853 and 1933, *before* the Somozas. But by 1979, the Somoza dynasty was ready to collapse under pressure from the left-wing Sandinista National Liberation Front. The Carter administration had stopped supporting Somoza and his National Guard in the waning months before he fled Nicaragua, and ultimately Carter also refused to grant Somoza political asylum in July 1979 when he fled the country he and his family had ruled since 1937. Somoza had been responsible for the deaths of thousands of Nicaraguans and a looted national treasury left with only $3 million. He was assassinated in exile in Paraguay just over a year later.

Meanwhile, the Sandinistas had taken over the country and installed a ruling junta, led by future president Daniel Ortega. While the Carter administration had serious misgivings about the leftist Sandinistas' close ties to Fidel Castro's Cuba, it had also sent emergency earthquake relief to Nicaragua and sought $75 million from Congress in US economic aid. For nearly a year, however, House conservatives stalled the legislation, and it was finally approved in September 1980.[64]

By then, Nicaragua had become a political football, with the Sandinista-led country cast as "a second Cuba." A few months before the demise of Somoza's regime, Ronald Reagan, in a syndicated radio talk, proclaimed that Castro "is a powerful, charismatic leader [who] has a vision that extends beyond the 'walls of his Palm prison in Cuba.' His idea of peace is to spread Russian-style communism throughout the world and certainly throughout Latin America and the Caribbean." He continued by saying that "the troubles in Nicaragua bear a Cuban label also. While there are people in that troubled land who probably have justified grievances against the Somoza regime, there is no question but that the rebels are Cuban trained, Cuban armed and dedicated to creating another communist country in this hemisphere."[65]

After Reagan became president in 1981, his ambassador to the United Nations, former Georgetown University professor Jeane Kirkpatrick, signaled the new administration's change in foreign-policy thinking by declaring that "Central America is the most important place in the world for the United States today."[66] And in fact, over the next several years, Reagan and his appointees helped to turn the poor and substantially illiterate region into a major Cold War combat zone, orchestrating and bankrolling secret wars "fought in the main by proxy warriors." In February 1983, the president told a national meeting of the American Legion, "The specter of Marxist-Leninist-controlled governments in Central America with ideological and political loyalties to Cuba and the Soviet Union poses a direct challenge to which we must respond." Unfortunately, the decades-in-the-making social and political inequality and inevitable turmoil in Nicaragua, El Salvador, and Guatemala had finally overheated into full-fledged armed conflict, and as historian LaFeber put it, "the Reagan administration sought to fight fire by pouring on gasoline."[67] The result was widespread human suffering in those three countries, plus Honduras, the base of operations for the anti-Sandinista Contras in Nicaragua.[68]

The wars created economic devastation, as well; by one estimate, the already poor region suffered $30 billion in financial losses. Moreover, the gap between rich and poor widened, and those billions of dollars in military assistance *doubled* the size of each country's army, making these already fragile democracies more so.[69]

No country in Central America suffered more atrocities than Guatemala during its civil war, which raged from 1960 to 1996. According to the Commission for Historical Clarification report, released in early 1999, Guatemalan government security forces were responsible for 93 percent of the more than 200,000 civilian deaths or disappearances. According to Christian Tomuschat, coordinator of the commission, "until the mid-1980s, the United

States Government and U.S. private companies exercised pressure to maintain the country's archaic and unjust socio-economic structure. In addition, the United States Government, through its constituent structures, including the Central Intelligence Agency, lent direct and indirect support to some illegal operations." The voluminous report also detailed "acts of genocide" by government security forces between 1981 and 1983, "extermination en masse of defenseless Mayan communities," which "came about with the knowledge, or by order, of the highest military authorities."[70]

Over the years that followed, more sordid truths began to seep out, including the symbiotic, enabling relationship between US military and intelligence personnel and the various repressive regimes and their militaries. Thanks to the United Nations, in the 1990s Guatemala and El Salvador created truth commissions, enabling them to formally ascertain the extent of the human rights abuses and begin the process of accountability and reconciliation. Although the US government assisted the Guatemalan truth commission—declassifying documents, for example, that revealed Guatemalan military cover-up efforts to destroy secret torture and burial sites—we certainly still do not know the full extent of the CIA's complicity in the Guatemalan civilian murders.

But we've certainly learned a lot: after the commission released its report, the nonprofit watchdog National Security Archive managed to obtain and publicly release internal intelligence documents detailing the close relationship between the CIA and the Guatemalan army, revealing, among other things, that US officials were aware of the Mayan massacres *at the time they were occurring*. And in 2005, an archive of at least 80 million pages of detailed files of the notoriously brutal, now defunct National Police was discovered, prompting an extraordinary international restoration and digitalization project that has so far resulted in the arrest of two former, very senior Guatemalan officials on charges of genocide and other crimes against humanity. The prosecutions of many others may eventually follow.[71]

However, when the atrocities were occurring, the chief response of American officials was to deny, obfuscate, and mislead—and then to attack the journalists who sought the truth. Consider, for example, what happened to Raymond Bonner of the *New York Times* when he dared to reveal facts that undermined the administration's preferred narrative about the conflicts in Latin America.

In January 1982, Bonner (traveling with photojournalist Susan Meiselas) and Alma Guillermoprieto of the *Washington Post* separately journeyed to the El Salvadoran village of El Mozote. Later that month, each wrote powerful page-one stories about a massacre committed there weeks earlier by the Salvadoran Army's elite, American-trained Atlacatl Battalion. Their stories featured interviews with survivors and reported that several hundred civilians, including women and children, had been murdered there, their decomposing bodies and charred skulls and bones still visible.[72]

The US and Salvadoran governments swiftly denied that any massacre had occurred. President Reagan audaciously sent to Congress his written certification, required by law should legislators decide to authorize any more funding and weapons, declaring that El Salvador was "making a concerted and significant effort to comply with internationally recognized human rights." And with a straight face, Assistant Secretary of State Thomas Enders told Congress, "There is no evidence to confirm that government forces systematically massacred civilians in the operations zone, or that the number of civilians remotely approached the 733 or 926 victims cited in the press." Representative Gerry Studds, Democrat from Massachusetts, angrily told Enders he didn't believe Reagan's assurances: "The President has just certified that up is down and in is out and black is white, and I anticipate his telling us that war is peace. We have said to the military by this certification in El

Salvador, 'No matter what you do—we're going to certify that you are in compliance. . . .'"[73]

A few days later, Elliott Abrams, the assistant secretary of state for human rights and humanitarian affairs, told the Senate Foreign Relations Committee that not only were the sheer number of El Mozote casualties "not credible . . . it appears to be an incident which is at least being significantly misused, at the very best, by the guerrillas." Some media outlets also began criticizing the El Mozote stories—from the very conservative *Wall Street Journal* editorial page, which called Bonner and Guillermoprieto "overly credulous reporters," to *Time* magazine and news accounts of US ambassador to El Salvador Deane Hinton's characterization of Bonner as an "advocacy journalist."

Some of the pressure was brought directly upon *Times* publisher Arthur "Punch" Sulzberger, who in turn reportedly complained to executive editor Abe Rosenthal.[74] Months later, following a meeting Rosenthal had with Ambassador Hinton in San Salvador, Bonner—a marine captain in Vietnam and a graduate of Stanford University Law School—was recalled to New York City to work on the metro desk and the business desk. The *Times* Washington Bureau chief at the time, Bill Kovach, told me, "I know the Reagan administration called the *Times* to complain" about the Mozote story. He continued, "I didn't know Ray, I just knew his work . . . I asked Abe [Rosenthal] to send him to the [Washington] bureau, I would like to have him in the Bureau to work as an investigative reporter. And he tells me, no, he couldn't do that, said he had to be broken. He said 'broken' and then he added 'in,' to get him trained in reporting."[75]

Rosenthal, who died in 2006, had claimed in 1982 that "at no time, in no way, did any official of the U.S. embassy or government suggest to me, directly or indirectly, that we ought to reassign Bonner." But not long afterward, Bonner quit the *Times*. And the journalism profession immediately understood what had happened: the Reagan administration and the US embassy in San Salvador had just gotten the *New York Times* correspondent "kick(ed) out." To the *Columbia Journalism Review*, Bonner's recall "seemed to send a signal. The once-tough press went soft."[76]

Few journalists, including Bonner, found Rosenthal's comments credible. "You tell me that [Ambassador] Deane Hinton, who's been beating the hell out of me, didn't raise me at lunch with the executive editor of the *New York Times*?" It was clear to Bonner then and now, three decades later, "It wasn't the massacre [coverage], it was the totality of my [Central America] reporting that both the embassy didn't like and that Abe didn't like."[77]

Eleven years after this episode, in early 1993, the UN-sponsored Un Commission on the Truth for El Salvador brought Argentine forensic anthropologists to El Mozote, where they spent thirty-five days removing the underbrush and then carefully digging and sifting. They discovered the skulls and other remains of 143 bodies, nearly all of them under age twelve. All but one of the 245 rifle cartridge cases found had come from American M-16 rifles, "manufactured for the United States Government at Lake City, Missouri." From this evidence and substantial eyewitness testimony, the commission concluded that "more than 500 identified victims" had perished at El Mozote and in other nearby villages "during the same temporal event," not "later than 1981."[78]

In March 1993, CBS News *60 Minutes* correspondent Ed Bradley covered the exhumations and also interviewed the vindicated reporters. Alma Guillermoprieto told him, "This administration, the Reagan administration, simply didn't want to know. They didn't want the truth to get in the way of a policy, and that was terribly wrong." Bonner told me thirty years after the El Mozote massacre, "They covered up, there's no question."[79]

In mid-1993, a special review panel on El Salvador, appointed by Secretary of State Warren Christopher, concluded that the State Department had mishandled the El Mozote investigation in 1982 and had undermined "the Department's credibility with its critics—and probably with the Salvadorans—in a serious way that has not healed." Not only had no one from the State Department ever actually gone to El Mozote to eyeball the carnage, department officials then misled the American people about what had happened there. Now, in the spirit of the courageous El Salvador Truth Commission, the record was being set straight: "a massacre had indeed occurred and the U.S. statements on the case were wrong."[80] The report concluded that there was "no effort in Washington to obtain and analyze the numerous photographs that had been taken at the site by the American journalists. The Embassy does not seem to have been inclined to press, and Washington preferred to avoid the issue and protect its policy then under siege."[81]

In retrospect, what is most striking about the 1980s Central America secret wars, to a massive extent spurred financially and militarily by the United States through local, "proxy" governments, was the unswerving, righteous arrogance of the Reagan administration—publicly mum and morally obtuse to their repressive comrades-in-arms' wanton violence against civilians, even children; willing to lie to Congress and the American people, if necessary, about politically inconvenient truths and activities; and undeterred in the slightest by pesky and nettlesome US and international laws that might impede full implementation of the administration's foreign policy agenda—i.e., aggressively supporting numerous covert, paramilitary wars around the world, a policy that came to be known as the Reagan Doctrine.

It was this arrogance that led the administration to scoff at multiple votes condemning US support for the anti-Sandinista Contras by the International Court of Justice at the Hague, the UN Security Council, and the UN General Assembly—together testifying to the near-unanimity of international opinion. It was this same arrogance that led the administration to defy the US Congress, which had voted in late 1984 to end all US assistance to the Nicaraguan rebels, by quietly creating a "private contra aid network," which raised millions of dollars from individual donors and such foreign countries as Saudi Arabia, Taiwan, and Brunei.[82] The inevitable result was the Iran-Contra scandal, an illegal, Rube Goldberg–like scheme to sell arms to Iran (a pariah nation under an international arms embargo), and in exchange, attempt to both secure the release of US hostages in Lebanon and provide funding to the Contras in Nicaragua. Known as the "Enterprise," and led by Lieutenant Colonel Oliver North, it had "its own airplanes, pilots, airfield, operatives, ship, secure communications devices, and secret Swiss bank accounts. For 16 months, it served as the secret arm" of the White House National Security Council, carrying out an illegal covert Contra aid program that Congress had prohibited.[83]

Ultimately, when the embarrassing details emerged, Reagan had to fire several top aides over the scandal. And Iran-Contra independent counsel Lawrence E. Walsh prosecuted fourteen administration officials, nine of whom pleaded guilty—five for withholding information, making false statements, or committing perjury before Congress.[84]

◦◦◦

In retrospect, beyond the particulars of the Latin American wars and the Iran-Contra scandal, something in Washington had seriously changed, undoubtedly for the worse. The will and the ability to hold those in power accountable had perceptibly weakened, in three specific ways.

First, although we had divided government in 1987 just as in the 1973–1974 Watergate period, with a Republican president and a Democratic-controlled Congress, the leaders of the Iran-Contra House and Senate Committees evinced no real interest in seriously investigating Ronald Reagan, the aging, affable, immensely popular president who had survived an assassin's bullet in 1981. Iran-Contra Committee staffers have complained to me for years about the various ways the scope of their investigative efforts was limited from the outset by senior members of the two committees.

Seymour Hersh's *New York Times* magazine article in 1990, based on over one hundred interviews, detailed the fundamental "failure of the legislators to accept the Iran-Contra investigation as a constitutional confrontation between Congress and the White House." Peter Rodino, the respected chairman of the House Judiciary Committee during the Watergate hearings, who retired in 1989, told Hersh, "It was a sham, if anything . . . we didn't get all the documents that could be retrieved," including Oval Office tapes.[85]

Second, the Washington press corps essentially missed the Iran-Contra story. As veteran journalist Eleanor Randolph put it in the *Washington Post*, "How did such a big story tiptoe almost silently past the most powerful media establishment in the world?" She concluded that the cause was an all-too-familiar pattern of factors that most journalists will recognize—a combination of "coziness with sources," "time pressure," "national security jitters," and so on.

There were a few examples of excellent Iran-Contra reporting, including work by Robert Parry of the Associated Press and then *Newsweek*, who won the 1984 George Polk Award, and Alfonso Chardy, who, with his colleagues at the *Miami Herald*, won the 1987 Pulitzer Prize.[86] But perhaps *New York Times* columnist Anthony Lewis best summed up the news media's anemic coverage: "Fundamentally, the press lost interest in Iran-Contra because Congress did not develop sustained outrage. In this as in other matters the American press, for all its independence, relies on the official institutions of Washington to legitimize its choice of what is news."[87]

And finally, in attempting to hold accountable those responsible for the Iran-Contra abuses of power, the rule of law in the United States was seriously subverted.

On December 2, 1986, President Reagan called for an independent counsel, and just over two weeks later, a three-judge panel named to the post Lawrence Walsh, a former US district court judge and deputy attorney general appointed by President Eisenhower. Within a mere two months, and for years afterward, Reagan and Bush attorneys general and their assistants, along with individual Republican lawmakers, began a drumbeat of public criticism of Walsh and the expense of the independent counsel investigation. Despite being under siege, Walsh and his staff dutifully attempted to fulfill his very difficult task. Then, on Christmas Eve, 1992, President George H. W. Bush effectively shut down the investigation by granting "full, complete and unconditional" pardons to former secretary of defense Caspar Weinberger, former national security adviser Robert McFarland, assistant secretary of state Elliott Abrams, and three others. Bush—who had been present in Iran-Contra meetings with Reagan and others while serving as vice president, and who had withheld his own notes from Walsh for six years—cited Weinberger's health and his own concern about "the criminalization of policy differences" as the reason for the pardons.

Walsh's reflections, literally the last words of his 1997 memoir about the Iran-Contra conspiracy and cover-up, were:

> Ronald Reagan's advisors succeeded in creating a firewall around him. He escaped meaningful interrogation until it was no longer of use, and he escaped prosecution altogether, while subordinates suffered. The delay in producing government records and the concealment of personal notes were crucial to the strategy. George Bush's misuse of the pardon power made the cover-up

complete. What set Iran-Contra apart from previous political scandals was the fact that a cover-up engineered in the White House of one president and completed by his successor prevented the rule of law from being applied to the perpetrators of criminal activity of constitutional dimension.[88]

Indeed, the cover-up continues to this day. In 2001, a few months after becoming president, George W. Bush signed the unprecedented Executive Order 13233, which sharply restricted public access to the papers of former presidents, including Ronald Reagan and Bush's father. The Bush order overrode the post-Watergate, 1978 Presidential Records Act, requiring that a president's papers must be made available to the public twelve years after leaving office. Steven L. Henson, the president of the Society of American Archivists, told the *Washington Post*, "The order effectively blocks access to information that enables Americans to hold our presidents accountable for their actions."

On his first full day in office, January 21, 2009, President Barack Obama signed Executive Order 13489, revoking the earlier Bush order and also explicitly stipulating that vice presidential records are considered a part of "Presidential records." Nonetheless, two decades after the pardons, George H. W. Bush's Iran-Contra papers have still not been declassified at the Bush presidential library.[89]

From the manipulations, misrepresentations, and misconduct in Chile, to Guatemala, El Salvador, and Nicaragua, culminating in the Iran-Contra scandal, the United States displayed a callous contempt for transparency, laws, and human lives. It's not hard to see a direct line leading from this outrageous and unaccountable conduct to an unnecessary war of choice in Iraq in 2003.

When respect for the truth is eroded, the barriers that protect us from official arrogance and, ultimately, tyranny inevitably begin to crumble.

Doubt Is Their Product:
The Corporate War on Truth

Just as the most poisonous form of disorder is the
mob incited from high places, the most immoral act
the immorality of a government, so the most destructive
form of untruth is sophistry and propaganda by those
whose profession it is to report the news.
—WALTER LIPPMANN, 1920[1]

I WAS DELIGHTED IN JUNE 2001, when the *Washington Post*'s
Bob Woodward accepted my invitation to deliver the keynote
luncheon address to the Center for Public Integrity's International Consortium of Investigative Journalists (ICIJ). We'd convened
sixty to seventy preeminent investigative reporters from around the
world to explore the growing global opportunities and challenges
facing those dedicated to ferreting out the truth and providing it
to the public. And for many in the news business, and even more
among the general public, Bob Woodward epitomized fearless journalistic tenacity and integrity. His collaboration with Carl Bernstein
in doggedly unraveling the Watergate scandal had demonstrated the
power of truth-telling to inform and galvanize the citizens of a democracy, had helped to topple a US president, and had inspired a

generation of young people to consider journalism as a career. He'd even been portrayed in an Oscar-nominated movie by actor Robert Redford.

But when Woodward concluded his speech, the first question from the audience took the air out of the room and seemed to stun Woodward. The gist of it was: Why is it that, over your long and distinguished career, you have always investigated government abuses of power, but never those of corporations?

After a discernible pause, Woodward startled the audience by saying, essentially, "Maybe I didn't have the courage to do that kind of reporting." And then he continued:

When I was, on a daily basis, running the investigative unit at the *Post*, Morton Mintz, one of the reporters, kept pounding me to write—he wanted to write more and investigate the tobacco companies. Morton was what you would call a very aggressive advocacy reporter. He was convinced they were lying, that [smoking] was a health hazard, that it was immoral. I had, I must confess, a very conventional view of, well, this is a product, it's out there; yes, if you can bring us evidence, we'll publish it. And he brought evidence that sort of got his toe in the water of the issue, but I didn't have the foresight or intelligence to see what he was on. If I were to go back to those moments, instead of resisting I would have said, "Morton, go to it, go look, we will be patient."

A newspaper, a news organization or an editor—the biggest gift they can give a reporter is honest patience, and say, "Follow your instinct, I know it's going to take time, I know it's going to be hard." There were a number of times when, unfortunately, I did not see the possibilities in his story, and he did and was quite right about it.

I've asked myself—you do what in the CIA they call "back bearings"—if we knew what we know now, when would we have first seen it? On the tobacco issue, the first sign was Morton Mintz, week after week, exploding in my office. He did not have the evidence, he did not know, he was operating on an assumption and an instinct that happened to be correct, and we should have done it.[2]

Woodward's critical self-appraisal may have surprised many in the audience. But it was a candid reflection of the intense and growing pressures faced by reporters and editors when considering investigative projects. Woodward himself, despite his status as journalistic superstar, had felt those pressures. During an ill-fated stint as the *Post*'s deputy managing editor for metropolitan news, he had assigned Patrick Tyler, a talented young reporter, to an intricate investigative story about Mobil Oil, alleging major improprieties by its president, William P. Tavoulareas. Woodward edited the piece, whose publication generated a highly publicized $50-million libel lawsuit against the newspaper that dragged on for eight years; by the time the full US Court of Appeals for the District of Columbia Circuit finally affirmed the truth and validity of the published story, the litigation had cost the *Washington Post* nearly $1 million.[3] After it was all over, Ben Bradlee said, "If you come to me and ask me to run that story and say it's going to cost a million dollars in legal fees and all the back and forth, I wouldn't run it." Woodward publicly disagreed with that sentiment.[4]

Later, Woodward oversaw and edited Janet Cooke's Pulitzer Prize–winning article, "Jimmy's World," the heartrending story of an eight-year-old heroin addict. When it was discovered to be entirely bogus, the *Post* had little choice but to return the Pulitzer, the first time in history that any newspaper had been so humiliated. Woodward accepted responsibility for the debacle and even offered to resign, writing in the paper days later, "My skepticism left me. I was personally negligent."[5] According to his biographer, Alicia C. Shepard, the Janet Cooke fiasco spelled the end of any chance that Woodward would become the *Post*'s executive editor.

So by the time Woodward was put in charge of an eight-person investigative reporting team that included Morton Mintz, would he and the *Post* have had a strong appetite to take on a wealthy, powerful, and legally aggressive industry like tobacco? Possible—but not likely.

When I asked Mintz about Woodward's comments, he said, "I recall no discussions with Bob Woodward about covering the tobacco industry, the explanation being that I had occasion to cover tobacco while on the National and Financial staffs, but not while in Woodward's investigative unit."[6] In fact, "in 1983, Woodward unceremoniously exiled me without consultation. . . ."[7]

Although Morton Mintz has never enjoyed one-tenth the public acclaim experienced by Bob Woodward, he has had a distinguished career as an investigative journalist. His story epitomizes many of the trials facing anyone who dedicates his life to the pursuit of truth in a world where powerful interests prefer secrecy and deception.

In 1962, Mintz wrote a remarkable front-page story for the *Post* about Dr. Frances Oldham Kelsey, a Food and Drug Administration (FDA) official who had resisted intense pressure from the pharmaceutical industry to approve the sedative thalidomide (trade name Kevadon) for sale to pregnant women suffering from morning sickness. Of course, thalidomide was later found to cause severe deformities in the children of pregnant mothers who used it, including missing arms or legs. His incisive journalism inflamed and emboldened Congress to enact legislation giving the FDA greater authority to require that drug companies scientifically test and prove that their products are safe.[8]

Within weeks of Mintz's story, President John F. Kennedy specifically commended Kelsey during a nationally televised press conference, and days after that awarded her the President's Award for

Distinguished Federal Civilian Service.[9] Congress unanimously passed
and Kennedy signed into law tougher federal controls regulating the
safety and effectiveness of pharmaceutical drugs.[10] Mintz, a World
War II navy veteran who'd begun his journalism career in St. Louis,
won the George Polk Award for his reporting and, in 1965, published
his first book, *The Therapeutic Nightmare: A Report on Prescription
Drugs, the Men Who Make Them, and the Agency That Controls Them.*[11]

Even though thalidomide had been approved in Canada and in
over twenty European and African countries, Kelsey was not at all
convinced it was safe, and she had continued to ask questions and request more information. Mintz himself vividly recalls the impact his
interview with Kelsey made on him: "I was just absolutely shocked
to hear that this drug company had applied pressure on her. I mean
it was outrageous, pressuring a medical officer of the FDA . . . It was
the first personal awakening that really mattered as to what corporate conduct can be. How bad it can be. How criminal it can be in
some cases."[12]

Mintz went on to author or coauthor ten books. He exposed
numerous unsafe or ineffective medicines and medical devices, including Oraflex, a lethal anti-arthritis drug withdrawn by the man-
ufacturer, and the Dalkon Shield (IUD), which "exposed millions of
women to serious infection, sterility, and even death."[13] And off and
on for a quarter century, Mintz investigated the tobacco industry.
"As far back as I can remember," he told me, "I saw tobacco as a
hugely important story."[14]

But despite his reporting prowess, Mintz was not particularly
well-liked at the highest echelons of the newspaper. Indeed, publisher
Katharine Graham once called Mintz "the thorn in all of our sides." It
seems "at *Post* luncheons he would interrogate heads of multinational
corporations and other guests instead of maintaining the superficial
conversations" she wanted.[15] As former *Post* reporter and former
executive director of the Fund for Investigative Journalism John

Hanrahan recalled, "It seemed that Mort often had front-page-type stories that appeared somewhere inside the paper, rather than on the front page where they belonged."[16] According to Barry Sussman, the special Watergate editor who oversaw Woodward and Bernstein and others during that momentous time, "There were very few editors at the *Post* who shared Mort's fervor. Editors like self-starter reporters, but not necessarily self-starters who take on injustice, corporate wrongdoing, and powerful institutions the way Mort incessantly did."[17]

Given all these factors, it's no wonder that Morton Mintz was never given carte blanche by the *Washington Post* to take on the tobacco industry. Instead, he became one of a long series of dedicated truth-seekers to do battle in an arena where powerful economic forces, public health, journalistic honor, and scientific integrity collide. And history tells us that this is a battle in which truth rarely prevails.

⌒∽⌒

Tobacco is no ordinary consumer product. It is both highly lucrative for a handful of giant corporations and lethally harmful for millions of consumers. And for almost a century, it has been the subject of a vast, deliberate effort to manipulate the minds of the public—a war on truth waged in the interest of corporate profit.

The story begins with Edward Bernays, a nephew of Sigmund Freud, the founder of psychoanalysis, who was indelibly influenced by his famous uncle's theories about how the human subconscious profoundly affects what people do, and who used those theories to help mold the mentality of the masses by helping to found the modern practice of publicity.[18]

Bernays made no bones about his philosophy. In his 1928 book *Propaganda,* he wrote, "The conscious and intelligent manipulation of the organized habits and opinions of the masses is an important element in democratic society . . . We are governed, our minds molded, our tastes formed, our ideas suggested, largely by men we have never heard of . . . who understand the mental processes and social patterns of the masses. It is they who pull the wires which control the public mind, who harness old social forces and contrive new ways to bind and guide the world."[19]

The following year, Bernays had a chance to field-test his theories, in concert with another early PR wizard named Ivy Lee. (In later years, Ivy Lee would serve as an informal adviser on propaganda strategy to Germany's Nazi regime through a lucrative 1933 contract with industrial giant I.G. Farben—an admittedly extreme example of the readiness of many corporate public relations experts to apply their talents on behalf of virtually any paying customer. Public outrage over Lee's services to the Nazis eventually led to passage of the 1938 Foreign Agents Registration Act, requiring that anyone in the United States who "acts at the order, request, or under the direction or control of a foreign principal" must report to the Department of Justice.)[20]

Bernays and Lee were enlisted by the American Tobacco Company to rectify a very costly, commercial problem with the "public mind": American women were reluctant to smoke cigarettes on the streets of their communities. As Bernays explained it, "A woman seen smoking in public was labeled a hussy or worse." Change that, he was told, and the company could "double the female market."[21]

Bernays retained a psychiatrist, A. A. Brill, who advised him that cigarettes for women represented "a sublimation of oral eroticism; holding a cigarette in the mouth excites the oral zone." And therefore, he concluded, "Cigarettes, which are equated with men, become torches of freedom."[22] Based on this "motivational research," Bernays orchestrated, in the name of "equality of the sexes," a "freedom march" of debutantes who smoked their way up six blocks of

New York City's Fifth Avenue during the Easter Sunday parade. The highly unusual public event became national news. Bernays later wrote, "Age-old customs, I learned, could be broken down by a dramatic appeal, disseminated by the network of media."[23]

Despite heavy newspaper coverage, no one apparently realized or reported that the event had been orchestrated by Bernays and American Tobacco.[24] Almost two decades later, in an essay entitled, "The Engineering of Consent," Bernays proudly declared that "the engineer of consent *must create news* [emphasis added] . . . Newsworthy events, involving people, usually do not happen by accident. They are planned deliberately to accomplish a purpose, to influence our ideas and actions."[25]

But by 1950, the tobacco industry had to do more than create news. That year, five scientific studies linking smoking to lung cancer were published, none more stunning than one by Dr. Richard Doll, a biostatistician on Britain's Medical Research Council. He and colleague A. Bradford Hill, in their paper "Smoking and Carcinoma of the Lung," found that heavy smokers were fifty times as likely as nonsmokers to contract lung cancer.[26] That was followed by publication of fourteen similarly dire, smoking-cancer studies, including the largest, most substantive study to date about cigarettes and longevity, released by the American Cancer Society to the American Medical Association in 1954.[27] For the first time, there was compelling scientific evidence of what had been suspected, but not officially proven, for centuries: smoking kills.

"And that should have been the end of the debate about whether smoking is dangerous," according to Dr. David Michaels, a nationally respected epidemiologist who in late 2009 became the administrator of the US Occupational Safety and Health Administration.[28]

But with billions of dollars in future profits at stake, the tobacco industry responded by hiring the president of the public relations company Hill and Knowlton, John W. Hill, who ironically had himself quit smoking in the early 1940s for health reasons. Hill developed an aggressive counterstrategy that to this day dominates corporate anti-regulation efforts for a slew of dangerous products: engineer "controversy" instead of consent.[29]

Hill told his clients they should be perceived as "embracing" scientific research instead of ignoring it, that as an industry they should support the principle that "public health is paramount to all else." On January 4, 1954, the companies collectively issued "A Frank Statement to Cigarette Smokers," written by Hill and Knowlton, which appeared as an advertisement in newspapers nationwide. It announced the creation of the Tobacco Industry Research Committee to explore "all phases of tobacco use and health" and declared, among other things, "We always have and always will cooperate closely with those whose task it is to safeguard the public health."[30]

It sounded sincere and for years managed to bamboozle scientists, journalists, and millions of smokers. But with the benefit of decades of hindsight and roughly 40 million internal tobacco company documents made public via discovery during litigation, we now know that TIRC was nothing more than a mere front group for big tobacco. Brown and Williamson chief counsel Addison Yeaman actually admitted so in a confidential memo to other industry executives: "It [the TIRC] was conceived as a public relations gesture and . . . it has functioned as a public relations operation."[31]

Perhaps the most obvious tip-off was that TIRC's administrative offices were located at Hill and Knowlton. Another was that the organization's executive director, Tom Hoyt, had no scientific qualifications and was literally "loaned" by Hill and Knowlton to the tobacco industry. And when respected scientists inquired about funding for their own smoking-cancer research, they soon discovered the industry's incuriosity about the health effects of its products. Indeed, the TIRC never sponsored direct epidemiological research about cigarettes and disease; the many cancer-related studies trumpeted by the tobacco industry during the early 1960s, for example, were all, according to David Michaels, "motivated by the same principle: Find other causes for disease, find smokers who do not have disease, find new associations of whatever sort, find this, find that, find anything—but the truth."[32]

Perhaps the closest thing to a "smoking gun" from inside the millions of pages of industry documents amassed through decades of discovery litigation was a memo written in 1969 by a Brown and Williamson executive, who proclaimed, "Doubt is our product since it is the best means of competing with the 'body of fact' that exists in the mind of the general public. It is also the means of establishing a controversy . . . Doubt is also the limit of our 'product.' Unfortunately, we cannot take a position directly opposing the anti-cigarette forces and say that cigarettes are a contributor to good health. No information that we have supports such a claim."[33]

A similarly frank reference to the industry's modus operandi was made in a 1972 internal Tobacco Institute document, about its "brilliantly conceived and executed" approach "to defend itself on three major fronts—litigation, politics and public opinion . . . It has always been a holding strategy, consisting of creating doubt about the health charge without actually denying it; advocating the public's right to smoke, without actually urging them to take up the practice; encouraging objective scientific research as the only way to resolve the question of health hazard."[34]

No matter what the scientific evidence linking cigarettes to ill health, no matter how aggressive government efforts to impose new regulations or legislation, industry executives and their legions of lawyers, lobbyists, and public relations flacks defiantly stayed on message. In April 1994, for example, amid mounting public anti-tobacco frustration, the heads of the seven leading US tobacco companies were called before a House subcommittee on health and the environment, chaired by Representative Henry Waxman (D–California).

To a man, they testified that they did not believe cigarettes were addictive.[35] (The CEO of RJR Nabisco, James W. Johnston, even insisted that "cigarette smoking is no more 'addictive' than coffee, tea or Twinkies.") And despite that 1964 surgeon general's report, which concluded that lung cancer and chronic bronchitis are "causally related" to cigarette smoking and that studies of male cigarette smokers put the death rate from lung cancer at "almost 1,000 percent higher than in nonsmokers," the tobacco executives maintained that the health evidence related to smoking "is not conclusive."[36]

For the first time, the American people saw cigarette sophistry in the full light of day, directly from the top company executives themselves, personally and on videotape. What they saw was appalling. Perhaps the *Baltimore Sun* put it best: "Good thing no one asked those tobacco executives whether they think the world is round or flat." The media circus had been a public relations debacle for the companies; the Justice Department began a perjury investigation of all seven tobacco CEOs, and within roughly two years, they were all gone from the industry.[37]

Such defiance of federal attempts to curb the tobacco menace was nothing new for this industry. Two former surgeons general, Dr. C. Everett Koop (who served in the Ronald Reagan administration) and Dr. Richard Carmona (the George W. Bush administration) described being constantly pressured over their anti-tobacco reports and statements. Carmona said he "fought for years" to release his significant surgeon general's report, *The Health Consequences of Involuntary Exposure to Tobacco Smoke*.[38] And Koop described the human impact of more than *half a century* of sustained, systematic misrepresentations: "In the course of my years as surgeon general and since, I have often wondered how many people died as a result of the fact that the medical and public health professions were misled by the tobacco industry."[39] All we can precisely say is that 100 million people around the world died from smoking-related illnesses in the twentieth century, according to the World Health Organization. And that number is expected to soar to an estimated *one billion* smoking-related deaths in this century, thanks to an aggressive export strategy aided and abetted by trade officials from the Jimmy Carter administration to that of Barack Obama.[40]

⌒⌒⌒

During the decades when the tobacco industry and its PR partners were diligently working to confuse the public and obscure the truth, their efforts did not go unnoticed or unchallenged. Consider the story of veteran reporter George Seldes, who covered "wars, assassinations, peace conferences, coronations and the rise to power of dictators," who met and interviewed the likes of Sigmund Freud, Benito Mussolini, Vladimir Lenin, and many others.[41] Frustrated over interference with his reporting by conservative newspaper magnates in the 1920s, Seldes became a freelance journalist, and in 1929 wrote the first of his twenty-one books, *You Can't Print That! The Truth Behind the News, 1918–1928*; two years later he penned *Can These Things Be!*, in both works venting his spleen and telling "the stories that he could not tell in the *Tribune*."[42]

In 1940, Seldes launched *In Fact*, a four-page weekly newsletter "For the Millions Who Want a Free Press" (he later added the subtitle: "An Antidote to Falsehoods in the Daily Press"). It was America's "first successful periodical of press criticism"; at its peak, in 1947, it counted 176,000 subscribers—more than the combined circulations of the *New Republic* and the *Nation*. Among the newsletter's pioneering areas of interest: how the press, receiving millions of dollars in tobacco company advertising, was, not coincidentally, "censoring" important, new scientific information showing that smoking cigarettes kills.[43]

In 1938, for instance, Dr. Raymond Pearl, a respected biologist at Johns Hopkins University, published the first major study identifying a correlation between an increase in tobacco use and a shorter life expectancy. The study was largely ignored by the press. Incensed, Seldes wrote in the January 13, 1941, edition of *In Fact*, "The facts [from the Hopkins study] . . . constitute one of the most important and incidentally one of the most sensational stories in recent American history, but there is not a newspaper or magazine in America (outside scientific journals) which has published all the facts."[44]

In the next decade, Seldes published roughly one hundred tobacco-related articles in the five hundred issues of *In Fact*, including the latest scientific findings, tobacco-company newspaper-advertising contracts stipulating that "no news or and [*sic*] no adverse comments on the tobacco habit must ever be published," and public policy issues: the urging of citizens, for example, to send cigarettes to members of the armed forces to "Keep 'Em Smoking," and the post–World War II export of nearly $1 billion worth of cigarettes to Europe as part of the Marshall Plan. Ultimately, very few of Seldes's revelations about the industry were picked up by the major news media, so the American people were substantially in the dark about the dangers of smoking and the extensive manipulations by the tobacco industry to maintain the public-ignorance status quo.[45]

Over the next sixty years, many other reporters would come to share Seldes's exasperation at the unconscionable complicity and spinelessness of their own publishers and profession when it came to reporting on tobacco.

One unlikely "mainstream" publication that stood up to the tobacco industry was *Reader's Digest*, hardly known, then or now, for courageous public-service journalism. However, because its business model at the time was based on paid subscriptions, not advertising, the magazine was able to withstand the "considerable pressures of tobacco company advertising." In 1941, an article under retired world heavyweight boxing champion Gene Tunney's name warned "that serious smokers would smell bad, cough in their sleep and die young." In 1942, an article titled "Cigarette Advertising Fact and Fiction" revealed that tests of two dozen cigarette brands produced only miniscule differences in "irritation properties," which prompted the Federal Trade Commission to file false advertising complaints against four tobacco companies.[46]

And in 1952, after several smoking-related studies had been published in various medical journals, *Reader's Digest*, then the nation's largest-circulation magazine, published its toughest smoking-related article to date, "Cancer by the Carton." According to Richard Kluger, author of *Ashes to Ashes*, the Pulitzer Prize–winning history of the tobacco industry, by "charging the cigarette industry with covering up the real peril of smoking"—lung cancer—*Reader's Digest* "had taken the unmentionable subject out of the medical journals and laid it bare for the masses."[47]

Other major news organizations, such as the *New York Times*, *Time*, and *Newsweek*, reported on the increasing number of scientific studies showing a clear causal link between cigarette smoking and such diseases as lung cancer.[48] And so did CBS News, where Edward R. Murrow, a heavy smoker rarely seen on TV or in photos sans cigarette, devoted two scrupulously balanced *See It Now* programs to the confirmed link between smoking and lung cancer, commercial television's first extensive news coverage of the subject.[49]

Murrow himself died of lung cancer in April 1965.[50] Adding to the irony, William Paley, the man who built and oversaw CBS for half a century, was able to do what he did only because of the personal wealth he'd amassed from his family's cigar business, whose seven factories produced more than 1 million cigars daily. Soon after he merged two broadcasting companies to create the Columbia Broadcasting System, Paley hired none other than Edward Bernays, the preeminent public relations expert and longtime tobacco-industry flack. Paley exulted, "I thought, my God, to be important enough to have a public relations man. Somebody who could tell you what to do and what not to do."[51]

But the *See It Now* reports about the connection between smoking and lung cancer were the exception for network television news shows, which otherwise "virtually ignored" that inconvenient subject. As Thomas Whiteside of the *New Yorker* later reported, those programs were "nearly all sponsored by cigarette companies."[52] By the late 1960s, according to the Federal Trade Commission, every US household with a TV set was annually exposed to roughly 800 cigarette commercials, and "four out of every five promotional dollars spent by cigarette makers" in the United States were spent annually on television.[53] In 1969 alone, that amounted to $230 million on television advertising spent by the tobacco companies.[54]

That same year, a half decade after the surgeon general's report on smoking, Congress and federal regulators contemplated a complete ban on broadcast cigarette advertising—a proposal that brought lobbyists from the National Association of Broadcasters and the tobacco industry out in force. NAB president Vincent T. Wasilewski harrumphed that the federal government, in particular the Federal Communications Commission, "has arrogated to itself the formulation of a national policy . . . outside its area of expertise." He extolled, instead, the virtues of self-regulation, claiming—falsely, it was revealed in congressional testimony—that the NAB's Advertising Code Authority was "rigorously vetting cigarette commercials."[55]

At one point, in response to an inquiry by a Senate subcommittee chairman, the three television network presidents declared they would not voluntarily release the tobacco companies from their multiyear advertising contracts. Leonard Goldenson, the president of ABC, complained that a cigarette advertising ban would be unfair and financially calamitous, and in fact, "it could well mean a substantial cutback in our news and public affairs operations almost immediately . . . We do not believe that the Congress would look with favor on any such forced curtailment of network service to the American public." In other words, as journalist Whiteside adroitly put it at the time, "ABC owed it to the public to keep the cigarette commercials on the tube."[56] Ultimately, despite the substantial industry pressure and sophistry, not to mention campaign contribution largesse, Congress passed and President Richard Nixon signed into law the Public Health Cigarette Smoking Act of 1970, banning all television and radio cigarette commercials starting January 1, 1971.[57]

Of course, the new law didn't end cigarette advertising but merely relocated it. In the first year of the ban, the tobacco industry spent $157.6 million on newspaper and magazine advertising in the United States—up dramatically from $64.2 million in 1970.[58] Whiteside, the most prominent tobacco industry muckraker during this time, was livid over the sudden advertising bonanza the print media had no compunction accepting. "How," he asked, "can any publisher— anyone—*make money* out of selling advertisements for a product that is known to cause death on a disastrous scale year after year?"[59] But the coffin cash kept flowing. Newspapers and magazines cumulatively took in $10.9 billion worth of cigarette advertising between 1976 and 2008, with $649 million in 1981 alone.[60] During those same three-plus decades, approximately 12 million people in the United States died prematurely from smoking-related illnesses.[61]

What few Americans realized in the early 1970s was that in the wake of the stunning cigarette advertising ban, the tobacco industry had also quietly maneuvered itself out of any meaningful federal government oversight. With the help of Congress, the industry had made sure that cigarettes were "all but exempt" from regulation by the Consumer Product Safety Commission, the Food and Drug Administration, the Occupational Health and Safety Administration, and other agencies.[62]

With the exception of Whiteside and a few others, there was little noteworthy print or broadcast investigative reporting—no Pulitzer, Peabody, or National Magazine Award winners—about the tobacco industry in the 1960s and 1970s. The news media's anemic coverage of the nation's deadliest industry, while simultaneously reaping billions of dollars in revenues from it, is particularly ironic considering that this coincided with the historic apogee of high-quality, public-service journalism in America, namely, publication of the Pentagon Papers in 1971 and the Watergate scandal coverage between 1972 through 1974.

Indeed, everyone in journalism spent the late 1970s and early 1980s looking for the next "-gate," myself included. But perhaps inevitably, at least until the mid-1980s Iran-Contra scandal, government abuses of power were neither major nor historic in dimension. And as memories of the glory days of reporter-sleuths like Woodward and Bernstein began to fade, so too did some of the independent spirit of American journalism.

Political forces played a role. The election of conservative Republican Ronald Reagan in 1980 ushered in a period when the GOP would control the White House for twenty out of twenty-eight years, moving the nation's political agenda and outlook to the right as well. The nation's leading newspapers followed suit. From the 1960s to the late 1990s, many of the nation's most prominent newspaper companies went public, among them the *Wall Street Journal*, owned by Dow Jones and Company (1963), the Times-Mirror Company (1964), Gannett Company (1967), the *New York Times* (1967), Knight Ridder (1969), *Washington Post* (1971), the Tribune Company (1983), the Pulitzer Company (1986), and E.W. Scripps Company (1998).[63] The shift from private to public ownership made Wall Street a player in the newspaper business, making corporate concerns even more influential in media circles.

The television networks, too, experienced a painful transition. The news divisions of ABC, CBS, and NBC reached their pinnacles in terms of staffing and audience during the 1980s, which also saw the advent of CNN and, eventually, other cable news networks. But between 1980 and 2010, the average number of viewers per night fell from 52.1 million cumulatively for the three network evening news programs to 23.2 million, a 55 percent drop. Funding and staffing levels began to fall as a result. [64]

In the mid-1980s, when I was a producer for the CBS News program *60 Minutes*, I got an unforgettable glimpse of the first round of layoff carnage. I watched and winced as the most respected producers were unceremoniously fired. Because I was relatively young (and low paid), I was spared. Within months of becoming the chief executive officer of CBS Inc., Laurence "Larry" Tisch in 1987 "launched the biggest single staff and budget reduction in network TV history. When the dust had settled, hundreds had lost their long-secure jobs, news bureaus had been shuttered, and CBS was but a shell of its former self."[65] Unfortunately, there have been numerous staff reductions from the news division since.

That same year, Richard Bonin and I began co-producing a *60 Minutes* segment entitled "Tobacco on Trial" for senior correspondent Mike Wallace about the increasingly aggressive civil litigation against the cigarette companies, and their muscular and very expensive efforts to fight back. No smoker had ever successfully sued a cigarette company in the United States, despite more than three hundred civil lawsuits filed against the industry since 1954, after their product's lethal qualities had become scientifically well established. In an attempt to ward off more lawsuits, and to help ensure victory in the courtroom, the tobacco industry hired eighty-seven of the premier law firms in the United States, made aggressive use of private investigators, and conducted brutal interrogations of plaintiffs and related witnesses that lasted for days—all entirely legal, of course.

But by 1987, big tobacco was facing its most formidable plaintiff lawsuit. A smoker since 1943, Rose Cipollone had begun having serious, smoking-related health problems in the late 1960s. She died of lung cancer in October 1984, a year after filing a lawsuit against Liggett, Philip Morris, and Lorillard, the manufacturers of the five different brands of cigarettes she had smoked. The lawsuit was continued by her husband, and the lead plaintiff lawyer was Marc Edell, whom Mike Wallace interviewed in late 1987.[66] This was the background against which Bonin and I began producing "Tobacco on Trial" for *60 Minutes*.

It was certainly not a risk-free project for us, nor for correspondent Mike Wallace—especially because Larry Tisch, the principal shareholder and CEO of CBS, was also a part owner of Loews Corporation. In 1969, Loews had purchased Lorillard—one of the three tobacco companies being sued by Rose Cipollone. Of course, we formally requested an on-camera interview with Tisch, which he declined, obligating us to include in our script: "For this broadcast no one from any of the major tobacco companies would talk to us on camera, not Philip Morris or R.J. Reynolds, Brown and Williamson, Lorillard, American Brands, or Liggett. Laurence Tisch, president of CBS and also chairman of Lorillard, declined to comment or appear."[67]

Only later did Wallace tell Bonin and me that Larry Tisch had asked him, over dinner, not to run our tobacco story—to which Wallace said he replied, "Go to hell." I don't know whether those were his exact words. In any case, what we were doing was probably about as cheeky and insubordinate as a correspondent or producer can be within the confines of a commercial television network.

The Loews-Lorillard connection wasn't the only potentially embarrassing element in the story. One of the issues in the Cipollone trial was the question of whether the cigarette companies had misled the public, with deceptive cigarette advertising slogans such as "Just what the doctor ordered" and "Play Safe—Smoke Chesterfields," falsely suggesting that smoking was good for your health. In preparing our *60 Minutes* segment, we pulled some TV commercials from the 1950s and found some in which a much younger Mike Wallace was smoking cigarettes and urging viewers to try a particular brand. In an internal rough-cut screening, I suggested that we "preempt" any potential viewer criticism of Wallace or *60 Minutes* for hypocrisy by including one of these particular commercials in the segment. It was an awkward subject to broach, and Wallace predictably thought that it was a terrible idea. But thankfully, executive producer Don Hewitt, senior producer Phil Scheffler, and co-producer Rich Bonin agreed with me, and we included one of his cigarette ads, with Wallace's newly written and tracked voiceover now in the piece.

"Tobacco on Trial" was broadcast on Sunday night, January 3, 1988. Weeks later, I attended a lavish, evening celebration of the twentieth anniversary of *60 Minutes* at the Tavern on the Green restaurant in New York City, the only such corporate event I was invited to during my relatively short time at CBS. In the midst of the festivities, Mike Wallace came up to me with, I noticed nervously, a familiar, mischievous twinkle in his eye. Standing just a few feet away was Laurence Tisch. Mike yelled out, "Hey, Larry, there's someone I'd like you to meet." Tisch turned politely toward us. And Mike said, energetically, "Larry, I want you to meet Charles Lewis. He produced that tobacco story we shoved right up your ass!"

The three of us laughed and shook hands, Tisch and I both blushing. I don't know which Mike enjoyed more—saying that to Tisch or watching us awkwardly squirm afterward.

In June 1988, six months after "Tobacco on Trial" aired, New Jersey US district court judge H. Lee Sarokin presided over a jury trial that found that one of the companies, Liggett, should have warned consumers before 1966 and "therefore had contributed to Cipollone's smoking, lung cancer and death."[68] Mr. Cipollone was awarded $400,000, although it proved to be a Pyrrhic victory: Liggett appealed all the way to the Supreme Court of the United States, where that verdict and award was overturned. In addition, the tobacco industry lawyers got the Third Circuit Court of Appeals to remove Judge Sarokin from hearing any future tobacco liability cases, successfully arguing that some of his court ruling language had given "the appearance of bias against the defendant companies."

Meanwhile, the surviving Cipollone children, after nine years of litigation, decided to end the case (even though the charges of conspiracy and fraud against the tobacco companies had been remanded back to the district court for possible re-trial). And Marc Edell's New Jersey law firm, looking at nearly $3 million in uncollected fees on the Cipollone matter, had no interest in continuing to subsidize the case. So it ended there, and indeed, after the appellate court rulings, "the filing of new (plaintiff) litigation slowed to a trickle."[69]

❧

The airing of "Tobacco on Trial" on *60 Minutes* was a small victory for truth in the face of corporate financial interests. But just a small one. And in the next several years, a series of disturbing episodes revealed just how shaky the commitment of the three major broadcast networks to fearless reporting of the facts about tobacco had become.

During the 1990s, the central battleground over regulation of tobacco products was the US Food and Drug Administration, then being run by David Kessler, a gutsy doctor and lawyer first appointed by President George H. W. Bush and reappointed by Bill Clinton. In 1993, Kessler decided to aggressively explore the prospects of the FDA earning the legal authority to regulate nicotine and tobacco as drugs. He called on three men to spearhead that effort: former investigative reporter and author Jack Mitchell, who helped run the FDA's Office of Special Investigations, and Gary Light and Tom Doyle of the agency's Office of Criminal Investigations.

On January 20, 1994, in a hotel suite in Virginia Beach, Virginia, Light and Doyle interviewed a former R.J. Reynolds employee with a doctorate in engineering, thereafter known by the code name "Deep Cough." She revealed the innermost secrets of the cigarette manufacturing processes. The investigators briefed the FDA commissioner by phone immediately after their meeting, and according to Kessler, "I heard certain key words: 'body fluids,' 'nicotine levels,' 'spray-dried tobacco extract,' 'buy nicotine extract from flavor houses,' 'adjusting the pH of the extract to affect nicotine delivery.' If Deep Cough's statements were true, they were evidence of nicotine manipulation. And if the company was manipulating nicotine, that was evidence, under the drug definition, of the company's intent."[70]

But the R.J. Reynolds whistleblower hadn't been talking exclusively to FDA officials. For months, ABC News investigative producer Walt Bogdanich, winner of a Pulitzer Prize while at the *Wall Street Journal* for his stories about faulty testing by medical labs, had been digging into the nicotine story with associate producer Keith Summa. As luck would have it, Bogdanich sought out Cliff Douglas, an immensely respected anti-tobacco lawyer and advocate who had been quietly encouraging Deep Cough to come forward for nearly three years before she'd agreed to speak with the FDA. And thus Bogdanich had gotten to interview her as well, and he'd also repeatedly attempted, without success, to interview Commissioner Kessler on camera.

Kessler learned that Bogdanich and correspondent John Martin would be breaking the nicotine story on the ABC News primetime program *Day One* on February 28, 1994. Not wanting it to appear that the FDA was simply reacting to the show, Kessler and his staff crafted a preemptive strategy. On the Friday before the scheduled Monday *Day One* broadcast, Kessler's staff leaked a letter to the *New York Times* and the *Washington Post*, in which he stated that "evidence brought to our attention is accumulating that suggests that cigarette manufacturers may intend that their products contain nicotine to satisfy an addiction on the part of some of their customers. In fact, it is our understanding that manufacturers commonly add nicotine to cigarettes to deliver specific amounts of nicotine." That was a major, newsworthy shift in the agency's policy. It raised eyebrows on Capitol Hill and caught the tobacco industry temporarily flat-footed.

When the *Day One* episode, entitled "Smoke Screen," aired, it contained this opening statement: "Late last week when word of our investigation got out, the Food and Drug Administration announced that it is now considering whether to regulate cigarettes as drugs." Kessler's preemptive strategy hadn't quite worked. As he wryly observed years later, "So much for the two years we had spent in preparation."[71]

However, the eighteen-minute segment, touted as revealing "the last best secret" of the tobacco industry, proved to be a powerful blow against big tobacco. It included an on-screen interview with Deep Cough as well as comments from former surgeon general C. Everett Koop and anti-tobacco lawyer Cliff Douglas, who said, "The industry manipulates nicotine, takes it out, puts it back in, uses it as if it were sugar being put in candy." Of course, a tobacco industry spokesman forcefully denied "artificially spiking" cigarettes "in any way."[72] But as Bogdanich recounted, "It was a serious threat to this industry. I think a kind of threat they hadn't come against in a very long time."[73] "Smoke Screen," which would later win the prestigious George Polk Award, was followed by two other *Day One* stories offering other critiques of the tobacco business.

Nor was that all. Another ABC News prime-time program, *Turning Point*, had in the works an hourlong investigative documentary about tobacco, to be aired in early 1994. Co-produced by four-time Emmy winner Marty Koughan and his nephew, Frank Koughan, "Tobacco Under Fire" focused on Philip Morris's specific actions and policies in quietly nudging US Department of Commerce and

US trade representatives to spend millions of taxpayer dollars to pry open foreign markets to American cigarettes, thereby quintupling exports to the "untapped market of Asian women and children."[74] By early March 1994, the final rough cut of "Tobacco Under Fire" had been approved by the show's top producers, screened by network news president Roone Arledge and others, and approved by ABC lawyers.[75] Music and other post-production stylistic touches were being added to "tart it up a bit," as Marty Koughan put it, in anticipation of an air date, possibly as early as April.[76]

Big tobacco had to fight back—and to do so in a timely, dramatic fashion. As Bogdanich put it, "What they wanted was to cast doubt to undermine our story. And what better way to do that than on national television, to announce that they are going to file the biggest slander suit in history against journalists."[77]

So on March 24, 1994, the tobacco giant announced that it was filing a $10 billion libel lawsuit against ABC, Walt Bogdanich, and John Martin for the "false and defamatory" February 28 and March 7 *Day One* stories, which it said had been produced "knowingly, recklessly and with malice."[78] The libel lawsuit was filed in the city of its corporate headquarters, Richmond, Virginia. ABC predictably stood by its stories, both companies hired very expensive law firms, and the battle lines were drawn.

Hours after Philip Morris announced its lawsuit, Marty Koughan received a telephone call from *Turning Point* senior producer Betsy West, "the very same person," he told me in an interview, "who was in the room when everything was passed and approved, maybe two months before, and she said 'We now have problems, we have to make changes, we've got to make revisions in your hour.'"

Koughan recalls, "I was accommodating because I knew of the style issues anyway, so I said 'Sure, we can rework this.' A series of meetings were scheduled between March and the end of May, none of which happened . . . at no time did we ever have a sit-down with these people." At some point in May, when an ABC lawyer called Koughan and asked him "for all of my notes, outtakes, tapes, it was abundantly clear to me by then that they weren't doing that so they could rework the material for air. They were doing that to kill everything."[79]

Koughan, who had never before had a documentary killed, refused to turn over those materials, even though they legally belonged to ABC. In short order, inconvenient news coverage about the internal spiking of his documentary appeared in the *Washington Post*, *American Journalism Review*, *Village Voice*, *New York Daily News*, Project Censored, and elsewhere, and things got uglier. Koughan told the *Washington Post* in August 1995, "A half-million dollars was flushed down the toilet, and a tough look at the tobacco industry was snuffed out." With its lawsuit, he said, Philip Morris had shown that "for a paltry $10 million or $20 million in legal fees . . . you can effectively silence the criticism."[80]

Paul Friedman, ABC's executive vice president, denied that the network was caving to pressure. He told the *Post* that "the lawsuit 'didn't even enter my mind' when he killed Koughan's program. Most of it was 'boring,' he said, or rehashed what ABC already had reported."[81] But the denial strains credulity. At the time, ABC News was already facing a $2.47 billion lawsuit for a 1992 *Primetime Live* story alleging unsanitary food practices at the supermarket operator Food Lion. Now, with a $10 billion lawsuit being brought by Philip Morris, how could ABC News *not* become more risk averse?[82]

For this book, I contacted former Capital Cities-ABC chairman Thomas Murphy, but the day before our scheduled interview in New York City, he canceled.[83] Roone Arledge, the visionary ABC News president who passed away in 2002, made no mention of Koughan's documentary in his posthumously published memoirs, nor were his donated personal papers at Columbia University very revealing about this.[84] However, what is clear from his appointments calendar is that he met with ABC lawyers and his top executives just two hours after the Philip Morris lawsuit was publicly announced. How long would it have taken for one of the two ABC News vice presidents with direct authority over *Turning Point* producers to flatly inform participants in that tense meeting that an equally tough, or even tougher, tobacco documentary simply could not be broadcast?

I contacted them to find out, starting with Paul Friedman, now a professor of journalism at the Quinnipiac University School of Communications in Connecticut. Nearly two decades later, his perspective had not changed. He stood by his previous comments and insisted to me, "I was never given any kind of directive from either [Capital Cities-ABC chairman Thomas] Murphy or the lawyers" to kill the *Turning Point* documentary . . . I've never felt at any point that I couldn't do a story."[85]

Alan Wurtzel, the ABC News senior vice president directly overseeing *Turning Point* and other long-form programs at the time, who is now at NBC, declined to talk with me about why the Koughan documentary was killed. But he may have answered my primary question—at least in part—in this short, possibly revealing message: "This was handled by lawyers and I had no personal involvement so I'm afraid I don't have anything I can offer you on the subject." Despite follow-up e-mails and phone calls, he did not elaborate.[86]

Richard Wald, who was a longtime senior vice president at ABC News and, by 1994, specifically responsible for "editorial quality," told me, "At a point before the [*Turning Point* tobacco] program was to go on the air, the Corporate guys [*sic*] called Roone Arledge, the President of the division, to say that they wanted to kill it, and he acquiesced. I think his words at the time were that they owned the football and ultimately, it was their call. He may have had reasons of his own to kill it, but I do not know them."[87]

I saw the *Turning Point* rough cut in February 1994, weeks before it was killed, and it was an excellent investigative documentary, shot on four continents and revealing significant new information. But perhaps such a serious documentary was not up to the high journalistic standards of *Turning Point*, which instead that year ran segments such as "The Manson Women: Inside the Murders," "Baby, Oh, Baby: The Six Pack Turns Two" (about a family of sextuplets), and "Inside the O.J. Simpson Story."[88]

∽∂∾

Meanwhile, by the spring of 1994, Walt Bogdanich and others at ABC News found themselves in legal hell. Bogdanich was the first US journalist to obtain the thousands of pages of internal Brown and Williamson documents known as the "Cigarette Papers." But to his immense consternation, ABC lawyers would not allow the network to report the story. His voice mails had been checked and all of his documents had been seized—and this was *before* the Philip Morris subpoenas.[89] Bogdanich says he was told by a corporate lawyer, "'You are to turn over all the documents you have on this case. You are not to do this story' . . . The experience was like I was in some Central American banana republic where the junta comes in and smashes the typewriters and takes the evidence. That's how I felt."[90]

It only got worse. His deposition, before a large team of lawyers, lasted ten days. What's more, Philip Morris subpoenaed American Express, AT&T, MCI, Sprint, Bell Atlantic, and other companies, in an attempt to glean from billing records the identities of Bogdanich's sources, including Deep Cough. "I made all of my calls from pay phones," he told me. "And I imagined people were following me. I mean, with all the money in the world, why wouldn't they do this? So it was a difficult period of time in my life."[91]

Bogdanich was instructed not to speak to the news media, despite all kinds of criticism and accusations that were appearing in the press. But "by the end of our subpoenas and depositions and everything, our lawyers had put together a summary judgment that was just devastating, asking for the lawsuit to be dismissed, backing up what we had written or reported and broadcast. And this was the moment, all my lawyers had been saying, 'You know, Walt, be patient, it will happen. Your day will come.'"

But it didn't come: Bogdanich discovered that ABC had quietly asked its lawyers to file the defense's summary judgment motion to dismiss under seal. As he put it, "You don't have to be an investigative reporter at that point to know that the game has been rigged. Something bad is going to happen. And something bad did happen."[92]

On August 21, 1995, with ABC's own lawyers saying the network had a two-in-three chance of winning its case, the network settled its lawsuit with Philip Morris. The settlement came weeks after Disney and Capital Cities-ABC had agreed to merge, at the time the second-biggest corporate takeover in US history, worth an estimated $19 billion (and worth millions individually for Murphy's top executives). "Of course, we knew the corporation was nervous," Friedman recalls. "He was trying to sell the company."

Arledge happened to be out of the building that day, and Capital Cities-ABC chairman Thomas Murphy urgently summoned executive vice president Paul Friedman to his posh corporate office. Murphy began reading the settlement statement that had been hammered out with Philip Morris, telling Friedman it was nonnegotiable, that not a single word could be changed. According to Friedman, "I realized he was giving me deniability" for after the meeting, when he returned to the ABC News offices and publicly announced the agreement.[93]

ABC issued a formal apology to Philip Morris and, as part of the settlement, Diane Sawyer read it during halftime of *Monday Night Football*.[94] Bogdanich and correspondent John Martin refused to sign the apology. One of the terms of the settlement was that both sides would not talk publicly. But days later, Philip Morris bought full-page ads in roughly seven hundred newspapers, with the banner headline "Apology Accepted."[95] ABC was widely attacked as having sold out journalism. Under the headline "The Cave on Tobacco Road," Jonathan Alter wrote in *Newsweek*, "ABC caved—not entirely, but enough to send a true chill through the entire news business." And Murphy was heavily criticized as a "corporate sellout."[96]

ABC News employees were stunned by what appeared to be a crass corporate capitulation at the expense of their own credibility as journalists. Bogdanich told me, "There was no doubt in my mind, none, that this was an attempt to clean the record, hand off a company that didn't have a $10 billion potential liability on its books, even though . . . our lawyers kept assuring us that we are going to win this case."[97]

After the settlement, Bogdanich resigned from ABC News, but he was quickly talked into returning by Roone Arledge and Peter Jennings; he signed a one-year contract and helped produce a prime-time investigative documentary showing how "through clever marketing, aggressive lawyering and big-money lobbying the tobacco industry not only survives, but even thrives." In 1996, "Never Say Die: How the Cigarette Companies Keep On Winning" was anchored by Jennings, who discussed his own smoking habit on the air. In 2005, Jennings died of complications from lung cancer.[98]

ᗌᗍ

Just three weeks after the controversial ABC settlement, CBS ordered the most popular and honored prime-time news program in US history to withhold a news story because of the mere possibility of a lawsuit—an act without historic precedent. CBS lawyers told *60 Minutes* executives and producer Lowell Bergman to stop reporting a story about tobacco whistleblower Dr. Jeffrey Wigand. The former vice president for research and development at Brown and Williamson had signed a nondisclosure agreement with his tobacco-industry employer, and therefore if CBS aired senior correspondent Mike Wallace's interview with him, the network could supposedly face a billion-dollar lawsuit for "tortious interference"—persuading someone to break a legal contract. *Vanity Fair* speculated that perhaps the real concern at Black Rock (CBS corporate headquarters) was that the interview might open CBS chief executive Laurence Tisch's son, Andrew, the CEO of Lorillard, to perjury charges because of his controversial testimony denying any industry wrongdoing before Representative Henry Waxman's House committee a year earlier. Whistleblower Wigand, in fact, knew *exactly* what the state of internal scientific research and knowledge was—also known as the truth—within the industry.[99]

On November 12, 1995, *60 Minutes* aired only a heavily edited version of the Wigand interview. Afterward, executive producer Don Hewitt acknowledged publicly that ABC's recent experiences with Philip Morris had played a role in the decision not to air the full interview.[100] The *New York Times* editorially slammed the corporate decision to withhold reporting "out of fear of a lawsuit that the industry had not even threatened to file. This act of self-censorship by the country's most powerful and aggressive television news program sends a chilling message to journalists investigating industry practices everywhere."[101]

Even Walter Cronkite, the venerable anchor of the CBS *Evening News* during the turbulent 1960s and 1970s, was disgusted, telling the Public Broadcasting System (PBS) program *Frontline*:

[T]he management of *60 Minutes* has the power there, quite clearly, to say, "I'm sorry. We're doing this because we must do it. This is a journalistic imperative. We have this story and we're going with it. We've got to take whatever the legal chances are on it." Well, they didn't. They felt it was necessary to buckle under the legal pressures and that must send a message to every station across the country where they might have any ambitions to do investigative reporting. "Hey, look, if *60 Minutes* can't stand the pressure, then none of us ought to get in the kitchen at all."[102]

The CBS capitulation completed the trifecta of the 1990s Network Television "Corporate Mergers and Abdications from Journalism" sweepstakes. It demonstrated unmistakably that something had changed throughout network television. Under questioning by *Frontline* correspondent Daniel Schorr, Mike Wallace acknowledged that it had never occurred to him to quit in protest, and though never publicly stated, that obviously was also the case with Hewitt.

I've known Lowell Bergman since we met in 1979 in the ABC News office of Washington Bureau chief Carl Bernstein, trying to play catch-up to NBC when the FBI's ABSCAM investigation of Congress scandal broke. To my knowledge, there is no other journalist in the United States today who has won a wider variety of national awards for his work in both print and television, from the Pulitzer Prize to the Peabody, Polk, DuPont Columbia, and Emmys. We have quietly commiserated over the years when our respective stories were killed at two networks, and during the *60 Minutes*–Wigand saga, I got an earful, separately, from Bergman and Mike Wallace.[103]

"In the Wigand case," Bergman recalls, "the *day* I met Jeffrey Wigand, I was in touch with the [CBS] legal department. So that's the irony here. From the very beginning, I smelled trouble from the first phone call to him, first attempt to contact him . . . I told the lawyers at the beginning, a year and a half before, if Wigand ever gave us an interview, that if he ever talks, this is trouble."[104]

ABC's settlement of the Philip Morris lawsuit, along with a Justice Department criminal inquiry into possible perjury committed by the seven tobacco CEOs testifying before Congress (including Laurence Tisch's son, Andrew), had, according to Bergman, "put a chill into the general counsel and the corporation." What's more, as Bergman points out, "CBS was also up for sale." In fact, one day after the ballyhooed Disney-Capital Cities-ABC merger, in August 1995, CBS announced that it too was looking for suitors; in the end, the company accepted a $5.4 billion offer from Westinghouse Electric Corporation, which reportedly earned more than $500 million for Larry (and brother Preston) Tisch's Loews Corporation, the largest shareholder of CBS. The sale, which was approved a few days after the embarrassing, truncated *60 Minutes* interview with Wigand, also made millions for CBS general counsel Ellen Kaden and CBS News president Eric Ober, the very executives who told Bergman, Wallace, Hewitt, and their cohorts to halt their work on the tobacco project.[105]

But despite all the attention given to this matter, Bergman says that what is not well understood by the public is that "there was [still] a lot of reporting to do . . . This story was killed before it was ever done . . . The normal process would be to finish your rough cut of the story and show it to the bosses. [But] they didn't let it get that far . . . Their own process, the formal process we had, changed." For the first time in Don Hewitt's tenure at CBS News, dating back to 1948, the corporate general counsel put the kibosh on a news story *before it was even finished.* And Bergman was incensed. "I went to the president of CBS News at the time, Eric Ober. I called him on the phone on October 3, 1995. And I said to him, 'You're the president of the News Division. The general counsel says we shouldn't run this story, this interview. But she is just a lawyer. What do you say?' And he said, 'The Corporation will not risk its assets on this story.'"[106]

In June 2000, soon after the release of the movie *The Insider*, in which Bergman was portrayed heroically by Al Pacino, the anger of Mike Wallace and Don Hewitt toward Bergman spilled into public view at the national conference of Investigative Reporters and Editors, in New York City.

With Wallace seated nearby, Hewitt used his keynote address to angrily excoriate Bergman, who was in California that day. When Hewitt said that no one should let Lowell Bergman within one hundred miles of a newsroom, the ballroom of the Waldorf Astoria Hotel erupted in raucous outrage. And bedlam followed his address, with hundreds of journalists—armed with cameras, recorders, and questions—swarming around Hewitt and Wallace.[107] The uproar was tragic because of what it revealed about two iconic figures in American journalism and the once collegial, mutually supportive world of television network journalism.

Hewitt continued his diatribe against Bergman in his 2001 memoir: "After *The Insider* came out, Bergman seemed to be making a new career for himself touting the virtues of truth here, there, and everywhere. But when a journalist who professes to be dedicated to *the truth, the whole truth, and nothing but the truth* conspires with a screenwriter to concoct a movie about himself that portrays him by name doing things he never did and saying things he never said, and is so comfortable with the fraudulent portrayal that he lends himself to 'hyping' the movie, that is not someone I would want within a hundred miles of my newsroom or a thousand miles of a journalism school."[108]

Marty Koughan, reflecting on the demise of his documentary "Tobacco Under Fire," told me he had misgivings similar to those Bergman felt:

Despite the fact that I never felt particularly appreciated by my bosses for the kind of work I did, I always felt that it was, on its merits, unassailable, and therefore I would be supported. I naively believed that in this case with ABC. Yeah, I knew they had this [legal] thing going on, but nonetheless, what we had was solid—we had the characters, we had the people, all the situations were factual. I didn't believe for a second that in some form or other, this story wouldn't air . . .

147

In this specific case, what was truth? From the moment that lawsuit went on, truth then had to be, "Wait a minute, we need to reshape this now." They didn't say change the facts, we had to just "reframe" how we were doing this because of new events or evolving situations. So truth now gets a little murkier. Within a couple of months after that, when it becomes clear, on the corporate level, that this merger was going to happen and therefore in order to make it happen the Philip Morris lawsuit had to go away, the only way it could go away was to cut a deal with Philip Morris. So the humiliating apology on Walt Bogdanich's piece, and the disappearance of my hour—and the truth then became "Oh, there's no news here." From out of the mouths of the very people who a year before said, "This is terrific stuff."

. . . The new truth was defined by the economic realities of the corporation. Truth became, "Well, this is something that is not worthy of airing. . . ."

I think there was a whole evolution that started during this period. It was the new corporate news environment that happened as a result of all these mergers that really changed what the definition of news was. And I think a lot of the old school rules were, if not thrown out the window, quietly buried over a period of time. They moved to more innocuous kinds of news reporting. There was very little support, not that there ever was, for serious investigative stuff. I think it became harder and harder to do.[109]

And what did this unheralded shift in the media's definition of "truth" mean to concerned citizens?

According to public-interest lawyer Cliff Douglas, who now teaches at the University of Michigan School of Public Health and is a consulting adviser to the US Department of Health and Human Services on tobacco-control policy issues, "It was devastating when the networks' bosses threw their own brilliant and courageous reporters, along with the First Amendment, under the bus. Right before our eyes, the corporate brass were shredding the principle that news coverage be conducted 'without fear or favor,' thus seriously jeopardizing the institution of American investigative journalism."[110]

❦

Tragically, the cigarette companies' cold-blooded, calculated cover-up over many decades—blowing smoke about their lethal, addictive products while knowing full well they were causing death and suffering—also has been the modus operandi of numerous other industries. Manufacturing uncertainty for years and often decades and attempting to thwart regulation while raking in the cash from their mortally dangerous products is what the asbestos, coal, lead paint, dyes (beta-Naphthylamine [BNA], benzedrine), metal (beryllium), pesticides (DDT), plastics (vinyl chloride), pharmaceutical drug (ephedra, Vioxx, Rezulin), and other industries have done throughout the past century.[111]

As with tobacco, the deadly "doubt is our product" deception is implemented by soulless public relations and law firms and earnest-sounding front groups, and sometimes their coordinated strategy is no more complicated than to attack the professional credibility of an inconvenient, inquiring journalist before, during, and after publication. On occasion, these efforts have even been continued for *decades* after exposure of the damaging truth.

Prior to the 1962 release of *Silent Spring*, Rachel Carson's classic bestseller exposing the dangers of DDT and other pesticides and herbicides, one agricultural chemical company, Velsicol, tried unsuccessfully to intimidate publisher Houghton Mifflin, while another, Monsanto, published and distributed nationwide a satirical article called "The Desolate Year," imagining a pesticide-free America, overrun by insects. Chemical industry associations increased their PR budgets to fund a smear campaign against Carson. The National Agricultural Chemicals Association (today it is CropLife America) distributed thousands of book reviews, smearing both Carson and *Silent Spring*. [112]

At the time, E. Bruce Harrison worked as manager of environmental information for Manufacturing Chemists Association, his precise task to help orchestrate the industry's campaign against the book, working closely with public relations professionals at DuPont, Dow, Monsanto, Shell Chemical, Goodrich-Gulf, and W.R. Grace. According to public relations industry watchdogs John Stauber and Sheldon Rampton, Harrison's "crisis management" techniques included "emotional appeals, scientific misinformation, front groups, extensive mailings to the media and opinion leaders and the recruitment of doctors and scientists as 'objective' third party defenders of agrichemicals."[113]

Harrison, not surprisingly, disagrees with this description. Half a century later, he labels Carson's book a direct affront to the chemical companies, saying that her thesis "was not only that pesticides would wreak unintentional harm—the hypothetical spring when birds would not sing—but also that because it *knew* of the potential damage of chemicals to wildlife and humans, the industry was *evil*." Harrison told me that whatever tactics he and his PR colleagues used in 1962 were "responsive to less informed and less accurate communication and they were, at least to my mind, rational." And he asked me, "Do you sense or see anything that seemed irrational or incoherent?"[114]

The Carson crisis helped catapult Harrison's career. The E. Bruce Harrison Company, which he co-founded with his wife, Patricia Harrison, began operation in Washington in 1973 and subsequently opened offices throughout the United States and in Europe, with scores of corporate clients such as R.J. Reynolds, Monsanto, Dow

Chemical, and, more recently, the Climate Change Coalition, which opposes environmental regulation regarding global warming. To some environmentalists, Harrison is the father of "green-washing," the practice of fashioning an "environmentally responsible public image, while covering up their abuses of the biosphere and public health."[115] Interestingly, Patricia Harrison later became co-chair of the Republican National Committee and, since 2005, has been president of the Corporation for Public Broadcasting.

The anti-Carson smear campaign failed to achieve its short-term goals. *Silent Spring* became a bestseller, was publicly praised by President Kennedy, and helped to spawn the environmental movement and the banning of most uses of DDT in the United States in 1972.

And yet, in 2007, a Senate resolution to honor Carson on the one-hundredth anniversary of her birth was successfully blocked by ultraconservative senator Tom Coburn, Republican of Oklahoma, who accused her of using "junk science" to turn the public against chemicals, including DDT.[116] His cited evidence? The website RachelWasWrong.org, created and funded by the Competitive Enterprise Institute in Washington, which is "dedicated to advancing the principles of limited government, free enterprise, and individual liberty." CEI doesn't disclose its donors, perhaps because they include such controversial companies as Koch (pronounced "coke") Industries, a privately owned Kansas-based conglomerate of oil, chemical, and many other interests.[117] Its owners, billionaire brothers Charles and David Koch, have quietly spent hundreds of millions of dollars in recent years trying to reduce federal regulation of their corporation by "educating" the public and Washington policymakers via seemingly unrelated, third-party cutout organizations that espouse limited government, deregulation, free enterprise, and so on.

In fact, a two-year analysis by the Investigative Reporting Workshop at American University in Washington, DC, found that Koch

Industries has "developed what may be the best funded, multifaceted, public policy, political and education presence in the nation today." From 2007 through 2011 alone, while Koch Industries spent $53.9 million lobbying for its federal and state policy agenda, Koch private foundations were giving $41.2 million to eighty-nine nonprofit public-policy-related organizations and $30.5 million to 221 US colleges and universities. Koch Industries and the Koch brothers contributed $8.7 million to congressional or presidential candidates and the Republican Party. In 2011, these mutually reinforcing, private and public "deregulation" efforts helped the oil and gas industry kill climate change legislation in the House of Representatives.[118] The Kochs and their foundations have also founded or substantially underwritten the organizing entities behind the conservative, antigovernment Tea Party movement, the Americans for Prosperity Foundation, and Freedom Works.[119]

Corporations, labor unions, left-leaning and right-leaning donors have been lavishly funding Trojan horse policy-oriented nonprofits with highfalutin names for decades, but in my forty years in Washington, I have never seen a single corporation like Koch Industries so aggressively and shamelessly bent on secretly furthering its crass financial, deregulation agenda through other, more noble-sounding shills.

The Koch brothers and the organizations they run have joined the tobacco companies, the chemical industry, and many other industry front groups in mastering the use of don't-let-the-facts-get-in-the-way tactics designed to sway lawmakers, intimidate reporters, and confuse the public.

Doubt is their product. And their enemy? The unpalatable truth.

6

Where Have You Gone, Edward R. Murrow?

Our history will be what we make it. And if there are any
historians about fifty or a hundred years from now, and
there should be preserved the kinescopes for one week
of all three networks, they will there find recorded in black
and white, or color, evidence of decadence, escapism and
insulation from the realities of the world in which we live . . .
If we go on as we are, then history will take its revenge.

—EDWARD R. MURROW, 1958[1]

TWENTY-NINE-YEAR-OLD Edward R. Murrow, with no
prior on-the-ground reporting experience, began his il-
lustrious broadcasting career with coverage of the Nazi
Germany Anschluss annexation of Austria in March 1938. "This
is Edward Murrow speaking from Vienna," he told his CBS radio
audience. "It's now 2:30 in the morning and Herr Hitler has not yet
arrived." It was the first of Murrow's more than 5,000 broadcasts,
none more memorable, perhaps, than those he delivered during the
Battle of Britain from a London rooftop while the German Luft-
waffe bombers wreaked their devastation from above. Between September 1940 and May 1941, millions of Americans were riveted to

their radios during Murrow's dramatic "This . . . is London" nightly reports, in which he vividly portrayed the stubborn resolve of the British people in the face of the terrifying nightly air raids known as the Blitz.[2]

Later in the war, Murrow reported about Allied aerial combat missions from England to Berlin, traveling on twenty-five of these dangerous bombing and reconnaissance sorties, at one point ignoring the suggestions of anxious CBS owner William Paley that maybe he'd courted death often enough.[3] In April 1945, Murrow covered the liberation of the Nazi Buchenwald concentration camp in Germany, accompanying General George Patton's Third Army. Three days later, he filed what, according to his biographer, A. M. Sperber, was his "most harrowing report" of the war: "There surged around me an evil-smelling horde," Murrow said after entering the camp's main gate. "Men and boys reached out to touch me; they were in rags and the remnants of uniforms. Death had already marked many of them, but they were smiling with their eyes." At the crematorium, he saw "two rows of bodies stacked up like cordwood. They were thin and very white. Some of the bodies were terribly bruised, though there seemed to be little flesh to bruise . . . I was told that there were more than 20,000 in the camp. There had been as many as 60,000. Where are they now?"[4]

Years of such dramatic, evocative stories had made Murrow America's most famous journalist. As early as the autumn of 1941, during a months-long stateside respite, he was given a hero's welcome, his ship met at the New York City dock by reporters and well-wishers. CBS feted him with a posh dinner at the Waldorf Astoria Hotel, with a tribute from Congressional Librarian Archibald MacLeish and congratulatory telegrams from President Franklin Roosevelt, the director general of the BBC, and other luminaries read aloud to the 1,100 VIP guests and a nationwide radio audience. On the evening of December 7, 1941, just hours after the Japanese had attacked

Pearl Harbor, Murrow dined at the White House with Roosevelt and First Lady Eleanor. Then he left on a national speaking tour.[5]

Ironically, despite their violence and immense suffering, the World War II years were the least complicated in Murrow's journalism career, with little ambiguity or controversy surrounding his reporting. As Nicholas Lemann, former dean of the Columbia School of Journalism, has noted, Murrow "was an important player in the Allied war effort, and, under the circumstances, that did not conflict with his journalistic role. Murrow's special significance was making Americans see, through his broadcasts about the Blitz, that the European war was not something faraway and irrelevant."[6]

As with most of his media brethren, Murrow's coverage during the war generally echoed the official public positions of both the American and British governments—so much so that, in early 1942, Murrow was offered a high-level radio position in the newly created, propagandistic US Office of War Information, which he declined. (His boss William Paley, however, accepted a consultant position in the OWI Psychological Warfare Branch, and was assigned to General Eisenhower's headquarters in Algiers, prior to the invasion of Italy.) Shortly thereafter, one of President Roosevelt's closest aides, Harry Hopkins, courted Murrow via telegram: "IT SEEMS TO ME YOU SHOULD BE RELATED TO THE GOVERNMENT."[7] And in mid-1943, Winston Churchill, through his minister of information, recruited Murrow to become the de facto "editor in chief" of all BBC programming, which he also declined.[8] Major media figures comingling so closely with top government officials might be deemed unseemly by today's journalistic sensibilities, but it was uncontroversial and little-remarked-upon during those life-or-death times.

Following the war, Paley gave Murrow the top news-management position at CBS, reporting directly to the chairman himself. But both men soon realized that being an executive didn't suit Murrow, and by September 1947, he had returned to the radio airwaves.[9] Of course, there was now an important new medium on the horizon: in 1948, CBS and NBC began short, televised nightly newscasts, and as politicians began playing to the cameras (Harry Truman's inauguration was a televised first), there was a growing sense of inevitability inside CBS that Murrow and his cohorts would soon migrate to this new broadcast platform.[10]

But Murrow had misgivings about television, which were widely shared by "Murrow's Boys," the team of remarkable young reporters (Eric Sevareid, Charles Collingwood, Howard K. Smith, among others) widely considered the "giants of broadcast journalism." As CBS News historian Gary Paul Gates noted, they wanted no part of television: "Sevareid more or less spoke for the entire Murrow team when, to a friend, he lamented, 'That damn picture box may ruin us all.'"[11]

Perhaps for this reason, although Murrow had done some on-camera reporting at the 1948 political conventions, his weekly television news program, *See It Now*, didn't debut until November 18, 1951. Sig Mickelson, the first director of CBS television news, describes *See It Now* as the first successful long-form, news-related program that was pure television rather than "a feeble copy of techniques used in either radio or newsreels, though it borrowed from both."[12] The program was an immediate hit with the public and the print press. The *New York Times* gushed, "Edward R. Murrow's program 'See It Now' . . . [is] a striking and compelling demonstration of the power of television as a journalistic tool, lifting the medium to a new high in maturity and usefulness."[13] As author Bob Edwards has observed, "Finally, educated people would admit without shame that they owned a TV set. For the second time, Edward R. Murrow had introduced a broadcasting medium to in-depth news."[14]

See It Now would become the model for all of the popular and important prime-time TV news programs that followed. In its seven-year run, *See It Now* examined such subjects as the Suez Canal crisis, book banning in California, the 1954 *Brown vs. Board of Education*

Supreme Court case, apartheid in South Africa, US immigration policy, and the future of Communist China (including an exclusive interview with Premier Chou En-lai).[15]

With the benefit of hindsight, however, it is starkly apparent that Murrow and his *See It Now* staff were working under extremely precarious conditions. This time, the fabled broadcast journalist was not in danger of being bombed out of his office as he had been during the London Blitz. Instead, he faced the possibility of being forced out, incrementally and insidiously, by his own employer. And it is Murrow's ultimate martyrdom and its implications for the future of television journalism that make him a figure of enduring fascination and importance today.

~∾

In retrospect, there were ominous signs from the beginning. With the advent of the Cold War, the embryonic CBS and NBC networks found themselves under public pressure to adhere to acceptable political standards. In 1946 alone, they fired two dozen "left-leaning correspondents" amid demands "to 'tone down' news which is sympathetic to organized labor and to Russia."[16] In 1947, a popular newsletter founded by three former FBI agents called *Counterattack* and another publication called *Red Channels*, which listed 151 broadcast journalists and entertainers "who allegedly had Communist leanings," began turning up the heat, criticism to which Paley and others at CBS were very sensitive. After the House Un-American Activities Committee began hearings later that year into "subversives" in the US film industry, the Red Scare also deepened within broadcasting. According to *Variety*, "any actor, writer or producer who has been even remotely identified with leftist tendencies is shunned."[17]

Things got even more precarious in February 1950, when Senator Joseph McCarthy declared that the State Department had been substantially infiltrated by Communists. Murrow soon questioned McCarthy's claim on his radio newscast, drawing many letters of protest to Murrow's corporate sponsor, Campbell Soup, which withdrew its sponsorship in June. Indeed, *Edward R. Murrow with the News* never again had a national sponsor, only regional sponsors.[18]

Within six months, CBS required all of its 2,500 employees—including Murrow—to sign a loyalty oath that they were not, nor had ever been, a member of the Communist Party or any other group advocating the overthrow of the US government.[19] And according to author Edward Alwood, between 1952 and 1957, HUAC, the Senate Internal Security Subcommittee, and Senator McCarthy's Subcommittee on Government Operations subpoenaed over one hundred newspaper journalists to testify, some of them publicly. Fourteen who refused to do so, including four *New York Times* reporters, were fired.[20]

The specter of political intimidation from Washington hung over the entire industry as Congress held a series of highly publicized investigative hearings about the motion picture industry and broadcast television. Broadcasters feared increasing scrutiny and government regulation of the TV industry, worrying, for example, that the Federal Communications Commission might refuse to renew broadcast licenses of those TV station owners supposedly linked to the Communist Party. In the words of broadcasting historians Robert L. Hilliard and Michael C. Keith, "The FCC and the rest of the government in the 1950s—like the attitudes and behavior of most of the United States, business and public alike—were being held hostage by McCarthyism."[21]

The response of the networks to this intimidation was less than heroic. Both CBS and NBC unabashedly blacklisted employees, and network executives also quietly shared personnel-related security information. Equally disturbing, during this grim time, CBS founder Paley was allowing "CIA operatives to screen CBS News film, to eavesdrop on conversations between CBS news officials in New York and the field and to debrief CBS correspondents on their return from overseas assignments." And he was also aware that "CIA agents from time to time operated as part-time CBS correspondents."[22] It was obviously one of the darkest periods in US history for the "due process" clauses of the US Constitution, freedom of the press, and the ideal of an independent media serving as a watchdog over government power.

It was in this portentous environment that Murrow experienced his first palpable pushback at CBS. In August 1950, an eight-minute radio dispatch raising serious questions about General Douglas MacArthur's conduct of the Korean War, which Murrow filed from Tokyo, was censored by CBS—with Paley personally killing the story—on the grounds that it violated the army's wartime prohibition against "unwarranted criticism." It was the first time Murrow had "been blacked out on his own show," and he briefly considered resigning from CBS because of it. *Newsweek* reported the ugly episode as part of a story about foreign correspondents formally protesting General MacArthur's censorship policies related to Korean War coverage. The piece, accompanied by a photo of a grim-faced Murrow, reported that "Murrow's stormy objections brought the censorship problem to a head in the network's newsroom and for other Americans trying to report the war in Korea."[23]

It was the first of a number of once-unthinkable affronts to Murrow by Paley and other top CBS executives. The storied journalist was gradually being cut down to size within the fast-growing network.

In the fall of 1953, Murrow and *See It Now* reporter-producer Joe Wershba planned to tell the riveting story of Milo Radulovich, a University of Michigan student who weeks earlier had been removed from the US Air Force Reserve as a security risk. Radulovich was not accused of being a Communist, or even of being disloyal;

rather, his father and sister were accused of being "Communist sympathizers," because he read a pro-Communist Slavic newspaper and she had once picketed a Detroit hotel to protest its discrimination against the black singer Paul Robeson, who had been openly supportive of the Soviet Union and was a target of the House Committee on Un-American Activities.[24]

The story made the brass at CBS nervous. Fearing that the program's sponsor, defense contractor Alcoa, might object to the subject matter, the network refused to promote the episode. So Murrow and *See It Now* executive producer Fred Friendly, a TV news visionary who drove the show's staff hard to produce great programming, personally purchased a $1,500 advertisement in the *New York Times* touting the broadcast.

When the story aired on October 20, Radulovich was eloquent in his own defense: "Are [my children] going to be judged on what their father was labeled? Are they going to have to explain to their friends . . . why their father's a security risk? . . . I see a chain reaction that has no end. . . ." The show struck a strong public chord: CBS and Alcoa received 8,000 letters and telegrams, overwhelmingly in support of Radulovich. Five weeks later, he was reinstated by the US Air Force Reserve.[25]

But Senator Joe McCarthy—who had not even been mentioned in the segment—took the Radulovich story as a personal affront. At a Senate hearing in Washington, McCarthy's lead investigator, Donald Surine, told Wershba privately that they had a 1935 story from a Pittsburgh newspaper about Murrow's work for the Institute of International Education (IIE); the story, Surine said, implied that American educators sent by the institute to the Soviet Union were being indoctrinated there, then returning home to similarly indoctrinate US schoolchildren. In fact, the IIE had been created in 1919 by Nobel Peace Prize winners Nicholas Murray Butler, president of Columbia University, and former secretary of state Elihu Root to foster international educational exchange programs.

After learning from Wershba about this not-too-subtle threat against him, Murrow didn't back off but rather asked his staff to begin collecting films of McCarthy's speeches and the congressional hearings he chaired. These were stitched together for a March 9 *See It Now* segment entitled "Report on Senator McCarthy."[26] CBS refused to promote this show as well, but moments before the broadcast, Paley called Murrow and said, "Ed, I'm with you today, and I'll be with you tomorrow." As author Gary Paul Gates wryly observed many years later, however, "The real question was whether Paley would be with Murrow the day *after* tomorrow, and in the years ahead. The answer was no."[27]

Murrow's report was one of the first national broadcasts to challenge McCarthy, using film clips to highlight some of the many self-contradictions in the senator's public statements. At the end of the dramatic program, Murrow closed his commentary this way:

> We proclaim ourselves—as indeed we are—the defenders of freedom, what's left of it. But we cannot defend freedom abroad by deserting it at home. The actions of the junior Senator from Wisconsin have caused alarm and dismay among our allies and given considerable comfort to our enemies. And whose fault is that? Not really his. He didn't create this situation of fear. He merely exploited it, rather successfully. Cassius was right: "The fault, dear Brutus, is not in our stars, but in ourselves."
>
> Good night and good luck.[28]

Paley hadn't asked to screen the program before it aired, and after the broadcast, he had a personal "proxy," his wife, Babe Paley, call Murrow to congratulate him. As David Halberstam noted in his magisterial, contemporary history of the major news media, *The*

Powers That Be, "The deniability had to be kept open in case the storm was too great and Murrow or the program eventually had to be sacrificed."

A few days later, CBS president Frank Stanton called Fred Friendly to his office and told him, "A lot of people think that you may have cost us the network." Friendly disagreed, noting that CBS had received 100,000 telegrams voicing support. But Stanton showed him the results of a special Roper poll he had commissioned, which revealed that more people trusted McCarthy than Murrow, and that one-third of the respondents considered Murrow to be a "Communist or a Communist sympathizer."[29]

CBS and Murrow offered McCarthy a full half-hour in which to respond, which he did on April 6, angrily calling Murrow "the leader and the cleverest of the jackal pack which is always found at the throat of anyone who dares to expose individual Communists and traitors."[30] The nation soon saw much more of the erratic, bombastic senator in the Army-McCarthy hearings, gavel-to-gavel televised coverage of which began on April 22. The hearings filled 187 hours over thirty-six days and culminated in the dramatic confrontation when army counsel Joseph Welch pointedly asked McCarthy, "Have you no sense of decency, sir?"

Months later, on December 2, 1954, the US Senate voted 67–22 to "condemn"—although not to expel—McCarthy. Rejected and bitter, he literally drank himself to death and died two and a half years later. In the end, not a single proven act of espionage or subversion was ever uncovered by his subcommittee.[31]

In the months and years that followed, Paley and Stanton hid behind the corporate veil, incrementally cutting Murrow down to size as the network grew larger and as they grew richer and more powerful. The slights and the indignities just kept coming.

At the end of the 1955 spring schedule, Alcoa stopped sponsoring *See It Now*; the public pressure over McCarthy and other controversial subjects had finally gotten to the company, and other would-be corporate sponsors were reluctant to lend their name to the program. Meanwhile, prime-time programming had become a bonanza for CBS, with the advent of TV quiz shows such as *The $64,000 Question* confirming Murrow's darkest concerns about television and its potential for crass, unabashed commercialism. Suddenly, the news seemed dry, pedestrian, and out of place amid the glitz and the screams from live audiences that lent excitement and drama to the game shows. Murrow knew that the politically unpalatable *See It Now* could never compete financially. He said to Fred Friendly, "Any bets on how much longer we'll keep this time period?"[32]

The answer: not long at all. As Halberstam put it: "Now, quite systematically, CBS moved to emasculate Ed Murrow . . . it was all done very deftly . . . corporations are often good at this, the increments of limitation were small, just enough to cut him down but never really enough to drive him away in anger." Paley and Stanton first reduced *See It Now* to occasional special reports rather than keeping it as a weekly staple of the network lineup. Ratings naturally suffered. Then it was taken off the air completely. As the final insult, Friendly, the show's co-creator, was named executive producer of the new documentary program *CBS Reports*, which tapped the very disillusioned, indeed depressed, Murrow as merely an occasional correspondent.

Murrow's last important journalism, which stands for the ages as one of network television's finest single news programs, was "Harvest of Shame," a powerful documentary on the plight of migrant farm workers. Soon after that November 1960 broadcast, Murrow left television. He briefly served as director of the US Information Agency under President John F. Kennedy. In 1965, he died of lung cancer.[33]

Separately, Fred Friendly rose to become CBS News president, but he resigned in protest in 1966, when CBS executives beneath

Stanton and Paley refused his request to broadcast live coverage of the historic Senate Foreign Relations Committee hearings, chaired by Senator J. William Fulbright, in which crucial public questions were raised about America's involvement in the Vietnam War. To honor Friendly's request, the network would have had to break into its regular daytime programming, which would have cost millions in advertising revenue. So CBS aired its lucrative reruns of *I Love Lucy* rather than cover the hearings. That, as Halberstam concluded, was simply too much money to spend—"a higher price for democracy than most network executives would be willing to pay."[34]

Half a century later, the entire Murrow and Friendly saga at CBS still epitomizes the core conundrum of commercial television news. TV is an immensely powerful medium, but its potential to make astonishing sums of money is typically realized only by appealing to the lowest-common-denominator instincts of viewers. As a result, serious journalism—particularly investigative or other expensive-to-produce, in-depth reporting—will necessarily be undertaken by commercial TV news executives with great caution, inevitably taking a back seat to more crowd-pleasing, less costly, and thus more lucrative programming.

Yet in the early years of television, the potential for a different path existed. Few people realize that, as author Chad Raphael has pointed out, the "high point of the (network television) documentary boom" in America was in 1962, when ABC, NBC, and CBS collectively produced 447 news reports (not all investigative in nature, of course).[35] Raphael has argued that "television's contribution to the mainstream media's first sustained period of muckraking since the Progressive era compares more favorably to print than is usually thought." But he has also documented how the most aggressive and best-known television documentaries of that period—such as Murrow's "Harvest of Shame" in 1960, Charles Kuralt's "Hunger in America" in 1968, Roger Mudd's "The Selling of the Pentagon" in 1971—all engendered substantial controversy and even government investigations.[36]

Now the hourlong network TV documentary is virtually extinct. Some of the most respected, pioneering network TV documentarians I know quietly blame *60 Minutes*—with its three-stories-in-one-hour modus operandi, and original investigative segments now a rarity—for its demise. Even *60 Minutes* creator Don Hewitt, who firmly believed in the "small doses" approach of his extremely profitable program, ironically became somewhat frustrated late in his life that most television shows had become "little more than cesspools overflowing into our nation's living rooms." And he lamented how the internal production ethos within network television news had changed over time from the Murrow-Friendly era sensibility of "make us proud" to "make us money!"[37]

But what, exactly, created the move to shorter snippets of serious information? Was it television's apparently natural impulse to simplify everything for its millions of viewers? Or did a complex combination of factors in our increasingly frenetic, mass-media world make the change inevitable? Whatever the answer, in the decades since Murrow and Friendly plied their trade, I've seen more than a dozen investigative-reporting units at the TV networks come and then go, usually for all the wrong reasons. Ultimately, well-meaning, immensely talented on-air and off-air journalists were figuratively ground up and spit out, departing their posts in bitterness and frustration, and leaving truths our citizenry desperately needs to know unexplored.

Other trends in television news are equally disheartening. With the advent of cable television in the United States, not to mention over-the-air TV channels, the Internet, mobile phones, and social networks, roughly 30 percent of the population "stopped watching any news at all."[38] For me, the most troubling statistic of all is that as additional sources of online news, entertainment, and other information have proliferated, consumer "use of newspapers, news magazines, and television is at a 50-year low" in the United States, according to Robert Picard, the director of research at Oxford University's Reuters Institute.[39]

In the words of Paul Starr, a two-time Pulitzer Prize–winning author and a longtime Princeton University professor: "The digital revolution has been good for freedom of expression because it has increased the diversity of voices in the public sphere. The digital revolution has been good for freedom of information because it has made government documents and data directly accessible to more people and has fostered a culture that demands transparency from powerful institutions. But the digital revolution has both revitalized and weakened freedom of the press." Starr has also noted what I have certainly discerned in the past decades: studies throughout the world indicate "that corruption flourishes where journalism does not . . . The less news coverage, the more entrenched political leaders become and the more likely they are to abuse power."[40]

Meanwhile, "most Americans still get their news from their favorite local TV news team," according to an authoritative government study, "The Information Needs of Communities."[41] Unfortunately, network television news and newsmagazine staffs are roughly half what they were in the 1980s, whereas most local TV stations have increased the amount of news programming while also reducing their editorial positions.[42] As Matthew Zelkind, the news director of WKRN-TV in Nashville, Tennessee, told the Federal Communications Commission, "Long-form stories are dying because they're not financially feasible . . . It's all economically driven."[43] Throughout the United States today, only 20 to 30 percent of the population has access to a local all-news cable channel, and one-third of commercial TV stations offer "little or no" news.[44] Sadly, far too many local stations today still rely on slick, "happy talk" anchor banter, as well as the familiar 1970s-era formula of "Action News" in notorious "if it bleeds, it leads" form, followed by weather, sports, and such "human interest" video fare as a water-skiing squirrel or a snowboarding opossum.[45]

Obviously, none of the deteriorating national- and local-news media trends bode well for original reporting and truth-telling in the foreseeable future. We would do well to remember what Edward R. Murrow told the radio and television news directors one October evening in Chicago in 1958. His disquieting words were eerily prophetic, especially considering the abysmal state of commercial TV, cable, and radio news today, and the mutually assured delusion of the commercial media and the public, year after year after year, to hold our most serious truths in abeyance:

> We are currently wealthy, fat, comfortable and complacent. We have currently a built-in allergy to unpleasant or disturbing information. Our mass media reflect this. But unless we get off our fat surpluses and recognize that television in the main is being used to distract, delude, amuse and insulate us, then television and those who finance it, those who look at it and those who work at it, may see a totally different picture too late.[46]

❧

At the same time that television news has been losing its way, unfettered financial considerations are also crippling American newspapers. Throughout the twentieth century, the most original reporting and the most substantive public-service journalism in America has always been initiated, supported, and published by newspapers. As previously discussed, the courageous publication of the Pentagon Papers by the *New York Times* and the *Washington Post* in 1971, and their and other news organizations' coverage of the Watergate scandal, culminating in the only resignation of a sitting US president, remains the apogee of independent journalism in America. Along with muscular reporting about the Vietnam War by David Halberstam, Neil Sheehan, Seymour Hersh, and others, as well as the national news media's coverage of race and the civil rights struggle between 1955 and 1968, these cumulatively represent the high-water mark in the long-standing struggle between raw political power and democratic values, including freedom of the press, in America.

But by the 1980s, financial tensions within the newspaper business began to erode the commitment to serious reporting. Many major US newspapers had gone public beginning in the late 1960s, and to journalism professionals, it seemed as though out-of-town shareholders were increasingly insisting on higher quarterly earnings at the expense of quality news coverage.

The toll on America's newspapers has been profound. Between 1992 and 2009, the number of commercial newspaper editorial employees in the United States dropped by 33 percent, to 40,000 from more than 60,000, according to a Columbia University study written by Leonard Downie Jr. and Michael Schudson.[47] Most of those cuts have occurred recently (13,400 jobs lost between 2007 and 2010),[48] thanks in large part to a 47 percent decline in newspaper advertising revenue between 2005 and 2009. The fact is, according to the Federal Communications Commission, even though the country's population grew to 308 million in 2010 from 203 million in 1970 (a gain of roughly 50 percent), today we have approximately the same number of journalists watching those in power as we did then. What's more, we have half as many television network news staffers as we had in the 1980s.[49]

This means that newspapers in twenty-seven states now have no reporters in Washington covering their members of Congress and myriad other state-relevant subjects. Moreover, the number of reporters covering state governments in the United States fell by one-third between 2003 and 2008 alone, their thinning ranks clearly not up to the task of following some 22,000 laws passed each year in state capitals. And coverage of global events has been similarly affected: between 2003 and 2011, the number of American foreign correspondents dropped by 24 percent, to 234 from 307, according to the *American Journalism Review*.[50]

Against this backdrop of drastically reduced coverage, the number of entries for the Pulitzer Prize for in-depth, nondaily reporting, the most prestigious award for print journalism, has also dramatically dropped. From 1985 to 2010, applications for the public service "Gold Medal" category fell to 70 from 122, for the investigative reporting category to 81 from 103, and for explanatory journalism to 104 from 181.[51] The organization Investigative Reporters and Editors, of which I have been a proud member since 1982, saw its dues-paying membership drop to 4,000 in 2010 from 5,391 in 2003.[52]

The sharp decline in the number of professional journalists and Pulitzer entries is not occurring in a vacuum. In a society increasingly beset by public relations, advertising, and other artificial sweeteners manufactured by message consultants and communications flacks, how does an ordinary citizen decipher truth amid the "pseudo-events" and vast "thicket of unreality which stands between us and the facts" so aptly described by Daniel Boorstin in his classic 1962 book, *The Image: A Guide to Pseudo-Events in America*. Our late Librarian of Congress Emeritus and one of our most distinguished historians, who died in 2004, called for Americans to "disillusion ourselves. What ails us most is not what we have done with America, but what we have substituted for America. We suffer primarily not from our vices or our weaknesses, but from our illusions. We are haunted, not by reality, but by those images we have put in place of reality."[53]

Tragically, Boorstin's prophetic vision about America's substantial illusions was not heeded; indeed, that thicket of unreality today, nearly half a century later, has become practically impenetrable. In 1960, the ratio of public relations specialists to professional journalists in the United States was roughly 1:1. By 2012, the ratio had increased to 4:1, likely leading to an even worse thicket of unreality if the current, disturbing trends continue, according to authors Robert McChesney and John Nichols.[54]

As a result, the sad, simple truth is that a disturbing percentage of daily newspaper stories today are based upon press releases. British journalist Nick Davies labeled this lamentable practice "churnalism" in his 2008 book *Flat Earth News*, and by 2011, the nonprofit organization Media Standards Trust (United Kingdom) had launched churnalism.com, which "lets people compare press releases with published news articles."[55] Does that sound exaggerated? A study by Cardiff University, in Wales, of the four "most prestigious and serious media outlets" in Britain (the *Times*, the *Guardian*, the *Independent*, and the *Daily Telegraph*) found that 60 percent of the news stories "consisted wholly or mainly of wire copy and/or PR material," another 20 percent contained "clear elements" of such material, and the source was unclear in 8 percent of the stories. In only 12 percent of the stories did researchers find that all of "the written material was generated by the reporters themselves."[56] They concluded:

> Taken together, these data portray a picture of journalism in which any meaningful independent journalistic activity by the press is the exception rather than the rule. We are not talking about investigative journalism here, but the everyday practices of news judgment, fact-checking, balance, criticizing and interrogat-

ing sources, etc., that are, in theory, central to routine, day-to-day journalism.[57]

Other research, both in the United States and elsewhere, confirms this basic trend. A study of ten newspapers in 2009 by the Australian Centre for Independent Journalism, at the University of Technology in Sydney, found that "55 percent of the stories analyzed were driven by some form of public relations."[58] The *Columbia Journalism Review* analyzed one edition of the *Wall Street Journal* and found that more than half of the news stories "were based solely on press releases" reprinted "almost verbatim or in paraphrase."[59]

Similarly, local TV stations in the United States are increasingly running stealth commercials masquerading as "news," in which expert reviewers of various consumer products are quietly paid to plug those products, with "minimal to nonexistent disclosure" to viewers and hardly any federal prosecution for such illegal "plugola."[60] One-fourth of local TV news executives acknowledged "a blurring of lines between advertising and news" in a 2010 Pew survey, and these sleazy "pay-to-play" arrangements prompted the Association of Health Care Journalists and the Society of Professional Journalists to issue a joint statement urging local broadcast stations to curtail such practices.[61] Unfortunately, in this audacious mercenary environment, well-intentioned moral suasion probably only goes so far.

❧

For iconic former newspaper editors like Gene Roberts, these various developments in the corporate journalism world are enormously depressing. For eighteen years, Roberts was executive editor of the *Philadelphia Inquirer*, the flagship of Knight Newspapers, a chain of fifteen papers at the time it went public in 1969. During Roberts's tenure, the paper won seventeen Pulitzer Prizes. But as the corporate obsession with profits increased throughout the 1980s, he became more and more frustrated and, in 1990, he finally quit.

Roberts spoke with me about the pressure on newspapers to maintain profit margins to 20 to 30 percent, which he described as almost a "prescription for suicide":

> That's a profit margin far, far above what the typical American business had. So to keep the profit margins up and please Wall Street, newspapers began eating their seed corn. And they started cutting the space for news, and then the staff that gathered the news. And at the very moment in time when computers were becoming competition and you had twenty-four-hour cable television coming along during the same period, and newspapers were being challenged as never before.
>
> But many of the managers of newspapers looked at it [as though] there was no competition anymore, not direct competition with other newspapers. There are few competitive markets left. So they, in effect, began to speak of newspapers as a franchise which basically could give the reader less and charge more. And, of course, readers reacted to that . . .
>
> At a very moment in time when newspapers should have been responding to a changing world, digitalization, all of this, instead of giving the reader more, we ended up giving the reader significantly less. And newspapers are becoming less relevant. And this is a tragedy for democracy.[62]

A little over a decade later, in March 2001, the publisher of the *San Jose Mercury News*, Jay T. Harris, resigned his post. (At the time, "The Merc" was part of Knight Ridder Newspapers, formed in 1974 by the merger of Knight Newspapers and Ridder Publications. The company, for a time the nation's largest newspaper publisher, was sold in 2006.) Harris warned his bosses that their profit goals for the financially troubled newspaper risked "significant and lasting harm to the *Mercury News* as a journalistic enterprise." Regarding Harris's resignation letter, former *Des Moines Register* editor Geneva Overholser told the *New York Times* that "all of us in newspapers are indebted to this honorable man."[63] Three months later, Overholser moderated a panel Harris and I were part of at the national conference of Investigative Reporters and Editors, and Harris got very warm applause from the eight-hundred-plus journalists, who clearly appreciated his courage and sacrifice in publicly refusing to gut the newsroom. His comments were thoughtful and reflective, at one point expressing his concern that if journalists "do a news report that is a little less good than the year before . . . it feeds on itself."[64]

By 2006, when Knight Ridder sold its thirty-two newspapers and ceased to exist, the *Philadelphia Inquirer* had half as many reporters covering the Philadelphia metropolitan area as it had in 1980.[65] As Gene Roberts had foreseen a decade and a half earlier, Knight Ridder was a casualty of many things, including greed and mismanagement. But by having gone public, the company had also fallen victim to what the *American Journalism Review* termed "the first big-time hostile takeover of a U.S. newspaper." The instigator of this coup was Florida money manager Bruce S. Sherman, a major shareholder (representing other rich out-of-town individuals and institutions) who was deeply concerned about the falling stock price. What happened to the *Inquirer* after that became even grimmer, as it was sold and resold to investors with no past interest in or association with journalism, downsizing the staff repeatedly and selling its iconic building in Center City Philadelphia. By 2013, the entire debacle had become the subject of the scathing PBS documentary *Black and White and Dead All Over*, which mocks the appalling greed and mismanagement in the *Inquirer* corporate suites and, more broadly, laments the decimation of the commercial newspaper industry in recent years and what it means for democracy.[66]

By the mid-1990s, Roberts had become so concerned about what he called the "corporatization of newspapers" that he launched the Project on the State of the American Newspaper, funded by the Pew Charitable Trusts, which produced two books and twenty articles in the *American Journalism Review*. That important work illuminated, among other things, the extraordinary extent of newspaper consolidation that had occurred. Between 1994 and mid-2000 alone, roughly 40 percent of America's daily newspapers were sold at least once, with small papers (circulation under 13,000) accounting for 70 percent of that total.[67] According to journalist Mary Walton, "the frenzy of buying and selling has produced a new breed of 'financial owner' for whom small newspapers are just another business . . . Because the bulk sales from old to new chains typically have involved a large number of leanly run 'mature papers' in no- to slow-growth communities, the only way the new owners can increase revenue is to find fresh properties and cut costs." Buyers were especially interested in finding groups of newspapers that could be "clustered" around one printing plant, with newsroom staffs in some instances also being shared and presumably made more "efficient."[68]

The project identified, throughout the United States, "125 major regional concentrations, involving more than four hundred papers—or well over a fourth of the nation's dailies." Journalist Jack Bass properly wondered "why hasn't the growth of newspaper clusters—especially in huge monopoly-like concentrations—drawn the attention of the Justice Department? Why wasn't it an antitrust issue, for example, when Gannett ended up owning every daily paper in a dozen adjacent counties of Wisconsin?" One of the very few times the Justice Department did address the antitrust implications of a newspaper merger, a federal judge voided the sale of the *Northwest Arkansas Times*, and Washington and Benton Counties there eventually ended up with "one of the most competitive daily newspaper markets in the country." That would seem to suggest what should have been obvious elsewhere: "that preserving editorial competition can improve newspaper quality and provide for a better-informed citizenry."[69]

But in the absence of antitrust activity and other countervailing forces, the corporatization of newspapers continued. The new owners began harvesting their "mature" investments by boosting profit margins through cuts in overhead, shrinking the daily news hole, and reducing the newsroom staff—strategies that made many newspapers thinner and less readable, year after year. These pressures began to be noticeable in newsrooms nationwide in the 1980s, which culminated in the calamitous events of the past decade: thousands of reporters and editors lost their jobs, news bureaus closed, several newspapers shut down, and others opted for Chapter 11 bankruptcy protection.

The problem has been clearly articulated by Iowa State University professors Gilbert Cranberg, Randall Bezanson, and John Soloski:

Today, in the publicly traded newspaper company, the business of news is being transformed into the business of business. News is not its product, upon which the enterprise depends for its long-term survival. News is instead increasingly an instrument by which advertisers are lured, customers are efficiently reached, advertising rates are increased, news staff is cut, and margins are increased, and increased, and increased. At its worst, the publicly traded newspaper company, its energy entirely drawn to the financial market's unrealistic and greedy expectations, can become indifferent to news and, thus, ultimately to the fundamental purposes served by news and the press. Some of the publicly traded

175

companies are today acting as if . . . they see themselves as simply a channel for consumption, a broker and distributor of commerce.[70]

Indeed, as Jack Fuller, the former editor and publisher of the *Chicago Tribune*, painfully acknowledged in his 2010 book, *What Is Happening to News*, "every newspaper company, even those led by people totally committed to striking a proper balance between the financial and social missions of journalism, has been beaten down."[71] So beaten down, in fact, that in 2011, print advertising revenues dropped for the sixth consecutive year, and Gannett—the nation's largest newspaper publisher as measured by daily circulation—purged the word "newspapers" from its home page. And according to the Newspaper Association of America, although online advertising in 2011 increased by $207 million compared to 2010, print advertising over that same period dropped by $2.1 billion. "So the print losses were greater than the digital gains by 10 to 1."[72]

❧

To sum up, then: The intense financial pressures that drove Edward R. Murrow and other conscientious reporters out of the television news business have only become more powerful and universal in recent decades. And the shortsighted greed and increasing corporatization of the newspaper industry have led to a dire downward spiral in the quantity and quality of independent journalism.

The quest for truth, it seems, has become more marginalized than ever before in our recent history.

What does this bode for the future of truth in America? Are we doomed to live in a quasi-democracy in which the forms of freedom—such as elections—are preserved but the factual underpinnings essential to informed debate have substantially eroded? Will truth-seeking and truth-telling become mere artifacts of a simpler, more naïve time, when people actually *cared* about such quaint concepts as honesty, integrity, and accountability?

I don't think so, for two reasons. First, my life in journalism has convinced me that the urge to discover and report the truth is a deep human instinct that even powerful political, economic, and social pressures can never extinguish. If commercial TV networks and traditional newspapers will no longer provide sufficient independently gathered information to citizens about the powers that be, then alternative media outlets must and will be found.

Second, I've seen and experienced the extraordinary potential of some of the earliest alternative outlets, and what is possible in the foreseeable future thrills the imagination. I believe we are witnessing the dawn of a new nonprofit journalism ecosystem in which the most ambitious reporting projects will increasingly emanate from the public realm, not from the private, commercial outlets.

In the remaining chapters of this book, I'll recount some of the adventures, good and bad, that have led me to conclude that the search for truth remains an essential element of the human condition. And I'll describe some of the hopeful signs of the remarkable new forms that I believe the great journalism of tomorrow is likely to take.

A Watchdog in the Corridors of Power

The right to search for truth implies also a duty; one must
not conceal any part of what one has recognized to be true.
—ALBERT EINSTEIN, 1954[1]

ERNEST HEMINGWAY FAMOUSLY SAID that "the most essential gift for a good writer is a built-in, shock-proof shit
detector. This is the writer's radar and all great writers have
had it."[2] He was talking about the novelist, I suppose. But his dictum applies to the investigative journalist, in spades. It is the born
reporter who insistently, even masochistically, clings to the notion
that things are *not* what they outwardly seem and pursues the hidden
truth in any situation even when other people prefer to ignore it.
For most people—except, perhaps, detectives, forensic accountants,
research scientists, and certain historians—this simply is not normal
human activity.[3]

What possesses someone to intensely scrutinize a single subject
for months or years in search of information that is secret, impenetrable, covered up, or otherwise obscured? Why is the investigative

179

reporter willing to accept rejection by scores of possible sources, physical threats, financial and legal repercussions, and almost universal calumny in pursuit of what Carl Bernstein calls "the best obtainable version of the truth"?

It certainly isn't the money, the institutional prestige, or the perks of the profession. As we've seen, fewer commercial news organizations support investigative journalism today than at any time in recent history, and reporters today—especially those who aggressively seek the truths that government, business, and other powerful institutions seek to conceal—are arguably more alone, more exposed, and more vulnerable to professional and even physical harm than are the practitioners of other professions.

I have firsthand knowledge in this regard. Over the years, those unhappy with my investigations have tried just about everything to discourage me. They have issued subpoenas, stalked my hotel rooms, escorted me off military bases, threatened me with arrest or with being thrown from a second-story window, hired shills to pose as reporters asking disruptive questions at nationally televised news conferences, and even arranged to have death threats delivered by concerned state troopers who urged me to leave town immediately (I didn't). And of course they've launched frivolous libel lawsuits that took years and cost hundreds of thousands, even millions, of dollars to fight before they were dismissed.

It takes a strange sort of zeal to accept such treatment as part of the cost of doing business. And despite having spent a lifetime with this peculiar form of affliction, I'm sure I can't fully explain it.

To understand a little better what propels some souls toward careers in enterprise journalism—a term that embraces investigative journalism as well as other forms of in-depth, original reporting on topics whose importance transcends that of the usual flow of daily events—let's consider the formative years of three of the best.

Journalist Florence Graves decided that investigative journalism was for her at a very early age. "I would read biographies of women," she told me. "And I remember reading biographies of Nellie Bly and Ida Tarbell when I was a kid in elementary school and thinking, 'Wow. That's what I want to do.'" Their compelling personal stories of exposing outrageous abuses of power in settings ranging from a mental asylum to the most powerful corporation in America provided Graves with a "picture that this was possible. Because in the '50s and '60s Texas that I grew up in, that was not possible."[4]

"I saw that [Bly and Tarbell] were able to use their brains," Graves says. "They were able to use their curiosity, their determination to actually go out and do stories that were important, that would make a difference that in many cases could lead to changes in society. Because even as a kid, I could see that there were things that needed to be changed in the world. And journalism was a way to bring truth to people, or a form of the truth."[5]

Graves forged a career that enabled her to follow in the footsteps of her early heroes. As founding editor of the now-defunct *Common Cause Magazine*, Graves helped earn the muckraking journal a coveted National Magazine Award for General Excellence in 1987. In 1992, as a freelance writer, Graves teamed up with a *Washington Post* staff reporter to produce an exposé revealing sexual misconduct by Senate Finance Committee chairman Bob Packwood of Oregon. That revelation led to his censure and resignation, and prompted the passage of legislation making Congress more accountable in matters related to employment and sexual harassment.[6]

Bill Kovach grew up poor in the Appalachian region of Johnson City, Tennessee, where his Albanian parents ran a little coffee shop in the Trailways bus station. "My dad was an illegal immigrant. He worked his way over on a steamer as a fourteen-year-old boy. And my mother was brought over by her older brother . . . she and her sisters and her brother were orphaned in the first war when the Italians bombed their home, killed their parents."[7]

Kovach's father died when he was twelve, and young Bill developed into an observant and angry adolescent:

> I grew up in the streets, because my mother was working all the time . . . And in the streets of that town . . . there was a veteran's hospital that was one of the biggest industries. And that veteran's hospital had a lot of World War I gas victims, both Canadian and U.S., whose lungs were destroyed by the gas attacks. They were incapacitated for life and living at the hospital. And they were emaciated, sad people who just needed a drink to forget about things. So I was always, as a kid, watching cops kicking these guys around, you know, people taking advantage of them. And it infuriated me, in part, because, you know, we were outsiders. In East Tennessee there weren't a lot of Albanians.[8]

Kovach's keenly felt personal frustrations manifested themselves in "my first journalism. I wrote letters to the editor, something about the way they treated some of these people." Following four years in the navy during the Korean War, after which he earned a bachelor's degree, Kovach was hired by the *Johnson City Press Chronicle*, where his exposés about abuses of power convinced him that "I can make a difference here."[9] He eventually became the Washington Bureau chief for the *New York Times*, editor of the *Atlanta Journal-Constitution*, curator of the Nieman Foundation for Journalism at Harvard University, and an internationally respected author.

Daniel Schorr realized his calling earlier than most. He grew up in a ground-floor tenement apartment in the Bronx in the 1920s, fatherless when he was five and with a younger brother afflicted with polio. "On one hot summer's day with the windows open, I heard a big plop outside. And I went to the window to see what it was. And it was a man lying on the stone, dead. He had jumped or fallen." The twelve-year-old Schorr went outside with paper and pencil, asked the police who the man was and why they thought he had fallen, and then called in the story to the local newspaper. His natural instinct, even then, was that "my job is to report it and explain what it's about. It's very strange." Schorr was paid $5.00 for that first scoop.[10]

From breaking major Watergate scandal stories to exposing secret assassinations of foreign leaders by the United States and so many other significant scoops, Daniel Schorr had an extraordinary career over six momentous decades, winning every major US broadcast journalism award. Hired by Edward R. Murrow at CBS News in 1953 and getting the first televised interview with Soviet premier Nikita Khrushchev in 1957, Schorr developed a reputation as a tenacious reporter who, according to the *Washington Post*, "broke major national stories while also provoking presidents, foreign leaders, the KGB, the CIA and his bosses at CBS and CNN." He spent the last twenty-five years of his life as a senior news analyst for National Public Radio.[11]

I wouldn't presume to put myself in the same constellation as the great investigative reporters I admire. But when I look back on my life, I can see the early development of some of the same traits that mark people like Graves, Kovach, and Schorr. As a child, I found myself taking quiet, unstated umbrage over perceived inequities, injustices, or improprieties in the world around me. What's more, I frequently found assumptions, assurances, and apparent truths uttered by people in positions of authority to be false, even in my formative years. Combined with my innate desire to see justice done and my natural tendency toward skepticism, I'd soon begun to see myself as an outsider, a scrapper, someone born to live by my instincts, wits, and Hemingway's shit detector. I didn't know it yet, but I was assembling some the weapons found in the arsenal of most successful investigative journalists.

But at bottom, what most outstanding enterprise journalists all seem to have in common is the trait that surfaced on the summer's day in the Bronx when some unfortunate soul met his end on the sidewalk in front of Daniel Schorr's apartment—an indomitable, almost primal, need to report what they have just learned, what they absolutely *know* to be the truth. Without that drive, it's doubtful that anyone would choose the difficult, often frustrating life of an investigative reporter—particularly today, when political, economic, and social trends all seem to be conspiring to make that life less secure and more dangerous than ever.

⌒∽⌒

In October 1977, a few weeks before I turned twenty-four, I was hired as a "reportorial producer" for a fledgling Special Reporting Unit at ABC News. The project was headed up by veteran journalist Sander Vanocur, best known as NBC's White House correspondent during the Kennedy and Johnson years, who had been recruited for the job by Roone Arledge, the new ABC News president. Although I had no background in television or Washington reporting, I had doggedly pursued a position there for months, ignoring other, less-interesting opportunities. Finally, in a brief make-or-break meeting with Vanocur—who had already sent me a rejection letter—I pitched half a dozen potential national investigative stories that apparently resonated with him. Days later I joined his staff as its lowest-paid member. I was thrilled—this was my dream job.

As one of the first off-air reporters at ABC News, working around the United States and in a few foreign countries, I was entrusted neither with writing broadcast story scripts nor with assembling written words with the video. Rather, I was at the beck and call of every show and network bureau, at times conducting last-minute on-camera interviews to obtain sound bites for a correspondent's breaking-news piece or accompanying camera crews on occasional early morning stakeouts of officials' homes. Over my six and a half years at ABC, I investigated everything from attempted presidential assassinations to unsolved crimes from the civil rights era, from prospective Supreme Court nominees to FBI misconduct, from Washington corruption scandals such as ABSCAM to the 1980 presidential campaign. I remain proud of my work during these years, which provided my continuing education about the United States and the world, about national and local politics and news gathering, about internal corporate machinations and duplicity, about truth and airbrushed truth (and the best techniques for distinguishing the two).

Yet over time, the work was becoming enormously frustrating. The Vanocur Special Reporting unit was disbanded after a year, and I was reassigned within the ABC Washington Bureau. Independently, I had begun to conclude that, generally speaking, network television news (in that pre-Internet age) was disconcertingly tethered to the front-page news judgment of the nation's most respected newspapers. When I would propose exclusive stories up the ladder, for example, I would frequently receive notes back saying, "I haven't read this in the *New York Times*" as the rationale for not pursuing them.

It became painfully apparent over time that network television news was not especially interested in investigative reporting, certainly not to the extent or the depth of the best national print outlets. In fact, the most trusted man in America around this time, CBS News anchor Walter Cronkite, had told *Time* magazine something in 1966 that still rang true more than a decade later: that "the networks, including my own, do a first-rate job of disseminating the news, but all of them have third-rate news-gathering organizations. We are still basically dependent on the wire services. We have barely dipped our toe into investigative reporting."[12]

Gradually, television's daily editorial insecurity vis-à-vis the older print world and its own tepid commitment to enterprise journalism caused me to conclude that all three major networks were mostly interested in the *illusion* of investigative reporting. Breathless, "exclusive" coverage of the latest government report (preferably ahead of the other networks), replete with "revelations" and "findings"—all unabashedly piggybacking on the investigations of others, official reports by inspectors general or congressional committees, criminal or civil court records—could create the aura of an aggressive news organization, for much less money than actually *doing* the original reporting. I found it sobering to realize that the news organization I worked for didn't consider the work of finding the actual truth about a complicated situation economically efficient or even necessary. Covering the occasional oversight activities of those in government, rather than the behind-the-scenes machinations of the powerful interests actually influencing and often benefiting from the public policy decision-making process, was simpler, cheaper, and less likely to arouse outside controversy or spur libel litigation.

The absurdity of this faux-investigative game reached its nadir for me one day when I was asked to follow up on a wire service report about former president Lyndon Johnson. Someone with personal access to Johnson when he was Senate majority leader in the late 1950s had just asserted under oath that he had on more than one occasion given Johnson envelopes of cash. I was explicitly asked to "check it out" for that evening's news program, and I was also specifically urged to call Pulitzer Prize–winning author Robert Caro, who was in the early stages of crafting his magnificent multivolume biography, *The Years of Lyndon Johnson* (he began writing it in 1975 and, remarkably, continues to this day).

This was just plain silly. I had only a few hours to confirm the veracity of an allegation of misconduct more than two decades earlier, said to have been committed by a president deceased for more than a decade. Plausible or not, allegations this serious and anecdotal would take months, if not years, of archival research and reporting to investigate, and even then the chances of being able to reach a credible conclusion about what had happened were still very low. Furthermore, reporters hate "playing catch up" to other news organizations, and there are few things more demeaning than calling another reporter, even if the reporter in question (Caro) had long ago left *Newsday* to become a distinguished biographer and historian.

Still, an assignment is an assignment. I gritted my teeth and tracked down Caro. He couldn't have been more gracious, but we both immediately realized that this was a fool's errand. In his own meticulous reporting, examining every day of Johnson's adult life, Caro had not yet scrutinized the time period of these sensational allegations. I sheepishly thanked him and handed in some sort of response to the supremely ludicrous challenge I'd been given.

I came away from that poignant, teaching moment vividly aware of the vast difference between fluff and noise masquerading as the serious pursuit of the truth and the real thing.

I still tried hard to carve out a professional space where my investigative instincts could flourish. Between the myriad of daily news-production tasks I handled, I would also write long internal investigative memos, which ABC News Bureau chief Carl Bernstein once dubbed "the Lewis newsletter." After a few years of this, I had become, as once described by ABC News senior vice president Dick Wald, "the eyes and ears of the Washington bureau." But outside of the network and within the profession of journalism, I was virtually unknown, toiling away in what was essentially a dead-end job.

It didn't help matters that I had the temerity to turn down an investigative producer job for correspondent Geraldo Rivera at the prime-time TV newsmagazine *20/20*. The offer was made to me in a one-on-one meeting in New York City by ABC News vice president David Burke, who occupied an office adjacent to that of Roone

Arledge. Taking that position would have immediately more than doubled my salary, but I nevertheless politely declined on the spot. When Burke pressed me to explain my decision, I said that I didn't want to work with Rivera—a controversial showman known for breathless, sensational stories such as (years later) the live unsealing of Al Capone's secret vault (which turned out to be empty).

Burke was flabbergasted and apoplectic with rage; his face turned red, his neck veins popped, he jabbed a finger at me, and he spewed a string of expletives, along with a line I've never forgotten: "You people in [the] Washington [Bureau] are so fucking smug and arrogant. The only reporter at this network with any balls is Geraldo Rivera." What's more, he made it emphatically clear that I would never be offered another job at ABC News, and I've been told that he went out of his way to block any promotions or transfers to other bureaus.

At the same time, to my dismay, I discovered that big-time newspaper editors viewed TV news veterans with great suspicion and distrust. In their view, I had begun my professional journalism career by going to work on the dark side. So with considerable frustration, and with no appealing alternatives, I resigned myself to staying at ABC until a better opportunity came along.

In March 1984, it did. Veteran CBS News correspondent Mike Wallace called me to ask if I might be interested in producing investigative segments for him at *60 Minutes*. I had never met Wallace or spoken with him, and I was floored by his unexpected call. Of course, I had followed his network career for many years and was fully aware that *60 Minutes* was the highest-rated, most honored network news program in the history of television. Wallace had been one of the two original *60 Minutes* correspondents in 1968, earning fame for his unflinchingly aggressive interview style and investigative edge. He'd been assaulted on the floor of the 1968 Democratic National Convention in Chicago, and he'd interviewed the Ayatollah Khomeini in Tehran during the Iran hostage crisis in 1979—just two highlights from an award-winning, sometimes controversial career. At this particular time, Wallace was also under siege from a landmark, multimillion-dollar libel lawsuit over a *CBS Reports* documentary about General William Westmoreland and the Vietnam War. "Westmoreland vs. CBS" was headed to trial later that September. (The suit was eventually withdrawn, but not before Wallace had to be hospitalized following a nervous breakdown.)

I was excited by the opportunity to work with him. I traveled to New York, met Wallace, senior producer Phil Scheffler, and the show's legendary founder, executive producer Don Hewitt, who had been at CBS since 1948. I was hired and began work in New York City weeks later as an associate producer, assigned to Wallace, with the verbal understanding that if things worked out I would soon be promoted and signed to a four-year contract as a full producer.

During my first year at *60 Minutes*, I looked into 150 possible stories and wrote memoranda about a couple dozen of them. Yet only three became broadcast segments on the program. I had been hired explicitly to break big, edgy, investigative stories, but I soon discovered that large, original investigations of my own were generally impractical—even at a show famous for its exposés—because of the intense time pressures. So the challenge was to find important, previously investigated subjects that could be told well and further reported on television.

There were other restrictions as well. The dictum at *60 Minutes*, as often repeated by Don Hewitt, was that "we don't do stories about issues, we do stories about people." Good "characters" were essential for these morality plays, and without a few of them, there simply would be no 13:30 story aired—then considered the "ideal" segment length, I had been told. Stories and interviews were shot on film, the way it had been done since the beginning of television.

Even though I was already very familiar with the glitz and glamour of network television, the *60 Minutes* milieu was another level of exciting: the high-pressure screenings, the Hollywood celebrities occasionally walking the halls, the offices and edit rooms where memorable moments in television news history had occurred. Edward R. Murrow's great *See It Now* producer, Joseph Wershba, who reported the classic Milo Radulovich story that had so infuriated Senator Joseph McCarthy and whom was later played in the film *Good Night and Good Luck* by Robert Downey Jr., sat directly across the hall from me. I'll always remember his affability, insights, sense of humor, humility, and welcoming kindness to a relatively young pup.[13]

During my roughly five years at the program, I investigated and brought to broadcast segments about such diverse subjects as a corrupt public school superintendent in Appalachia; multimillion-dollar Social Security check fraud by postal employees in San Francisco; the controversial appointment of US labor secretary Raymond Donovan; the looting of Empire Savings and Loan in Texas, the first long-form story on prime-time network television about the national savings and loan scandal; art fraud involving Salvador Dali lithographs; murder and other preventable deaths inside the worst hospital in America; Robert Brennan, First Jersey Securities, and the defrauding of thousands of investors; the high-pressure legal tactics of the tobacco industry; the career-ending improprieties of celebrity divorce lawyer Marvin Mitchelson; and the registered foreign-agent lobbyists inside the highest levels of the 1988 Bush and Dukakis presidential campaigns.[14]

Most of these stories, along with others I produced, were of the classic, formulaic, good-versus-evil *60 Minutes* genre. We exposed outrageous betrayals of the public trust, in which some of the victims were handicapped children deprived of a chance to attend public school, emotionally vulnerable women sexually preyed upon, mental health patients subject to abysmal mistreatment, former smokers dying of lung cancer, and elderly citizens fleeced of their life savings and retirement income. Other stories less dramatically exposed government illogic, incompetence, mismanagement, or simply poor judgment.

In a half-dozen segments involving companies or individuals, implicit or explicit legal threats were made against CBS, either before or after the stories aired. In one, a petition was filed in Washington to revoke the network's license to broadcast; in another, Wallace and I were subpoenaed to reveal the identity of a disguised interviewee, whose identity we had carefully concealed even from CBS, not trusting our employer to honor our personal pledge of confidentiality to this key source. Fortunately, these legal threats against us were dismissed.[15]

I served as associate producer on a story called "The Czar of Clinton County," produced by Lowell Bergman, which dealt with the infamous malfeasance of a Kentucky school superintendent who had been investigated earlier by the *Courier Journal* of Louisville. This was a story that required me to become particularly sensitive to the physical environs and my own conspicuous presence on the ground there.[16] Robert Polston, with twenty-three of his relatives on the public payroll in the second-poorest county in the nation and already under investigation by the FBI and the US Department of Education, ruled over the lowest-ranked school system in Kentucky, which was ranked dead last among all fifty states.

I soon realized I was being followed wherever I drove, and I once had to meet some brave but nervous whistleblowers behind a cemetery after midnight, carefully parking my conspicuous rental car far away. These informants were justifiably worried about losing their jobs, or worse; one of them actually offered me a "piece," which I quickly realized was a handgun. I politely declined, joking that I would probably "shoot my foot off" with it. As we talked, a car they recognized kept circling the area; the trackers inside were undoubtedly seeking to learn where I had gone and with whom I was talking. My indelibly etched memory of this town is that the trees and houses almost seemed to have eyes, especially after dark.

After weeks of reporting, on the eve of filming our story, Wallace, Bergman, and I were unexpectedly interrupted at dinner and invited to a large room in the back of the restaurant. There we found at least two dozen citizens of Clinton County who had heard that "*60 Minutes* is in town" and had driven twenty miles to secretly inform us about the conditions they had been living through. Some of them broke down and cried as they told harrowing stories of sexual assault; of arson against people "not with the program"; of federal dollars allocated for handicapped children never being spent for that purpose, their parents told to keep them home because there was simply no money for their educations. This outpouring made a huge impression on Wallace, who had literally just arrived on the scene. Later that night, Kentucky state police officers came to our motel to urge that we leave the area immediately, as they'd received an explicit death threat against us.

But leaving was out of question. The next day, at the last school board meeting before the November elections, we let the cameras roll. (Weeks earlier, Polston had declined our request for an on-air interview.) When Mike confronted Polston with the questions I had written for him—What about those twenty-three relatives on the payroll? What about those handicapped children?—Polston's perspiring face turned red, and he literally started chewing his tie while talking. Mike's piercing public questions before the cameras seemed to embolden some of the citizens to confront Polston directly, all of which we recorded.

Because of the nationwide attention and embarrassment caused by our story, the Kentucky governor removed Superintendent Robert Polston from his position within days. The Polston saga remains the most personally gratifying and inspiring investigative story I've ever worked on. Not only were we shining a light on rampant abuses of power, we were also directly helping the people who had been personally victimized by it for many years.

All of my *60 Minutes* stories were investigative, and two received Emmy nominations. It was clear as I approached my thirty-fifth birthday that I could likely remain a successful—and extremely well-paid—network investigative producer for decades to come.

But I had also seen things at two networks that had troubled me profoundly: nationally important stories not pursued; well-connected, powerful people and companies with questionable policies and practices that were not investigated precisely because of the connections and the power they boasted.

And in developing my last *60 Minutes* segment, entitled "Foreign Agent," I had been pressured by my superiors to take specific information out of the script for reasons entirely unrelated to journalism. The segment, which featured well-known former US officials and presidential campaign aides from both parties who were cashing in on their political connections by working as lobbyists for foreign entities, was time-sensitive and perishable, not likely to be broadcast after the upcoming 1988 election. Holding out on principle would not work, because the piece, which I'd had to fight for long and hard just to get it initially approved, would lose its timeliness and likely never air—to the disappointment of almost no one there but me. I had stubbornly refused to cave and finally broke the tense, weeks-long impasse by making a major eleventh-hour concession: I agreed to remove a famous individual's name from the script, but not his photograph with four other company executives.

That someone was former commerce secretary Pete Peterson, at the time the CEO of the New York–based investment firm Blackstone and, more important, one of Don Hewitt's closest personal friends. The two men were so close that Don would often join Peterson on his company helicopter for Friday-night flights to the Hamptons, thereby avoiding the summertime bumper-to-bumper traffic.

The script we'd written included the line, "For Japan and other foreign interests, finding former US officials to do their bidding is not at all difficult," accompanied by the image of a Japanese newspaper advertisement with five smiling Blackstone officials, extolling their prior US government service and connections. The translation of the ad read, "If you are thinking about developing a new business or an investment strategy . . . that will be effective in the US, by all means, consult us!"

During the production process, working with my brilliant editor, Simon Surowicz, when I showed Mike Wallace the photo I'd had shipped from Tokyo and was screening, Mike said, "That's not our story—you're not filming that. . . ." And I countered, "Mike, what are you talking about? This is the nut of the story—former officials trading on the prestige of their former positions, trying to make a buck with foreign companies and governments." Wallace and I had a huge expletive-filled shouting match, toe to toe, our faces close; I refused to back down, and he stormed out. We put the picture in the piece.

The first time Don screened the piece, he quipped, "I guess I'm not going to get any more rides on Pete's helicopter." But as the days and weeks wore on, with the piece not green-lighted for air—ostensibly because it was "too long"—I realized that I had no choice but to find some sort of ameliorative editorial compromise, which was offensive to me then and, quite frankly, still is.

One day, while I was on the phone, Don walked into my office and asked whether I'd found a way to "fix" the piece.

"Yes," I said, and I suggested that we remove Peterson's name from the script and replace it with the name of another well-known Blackstone official, former Reagan budget director David Stockman. It was a nanosecond shorter—two syllables instead of three—and it solved the unstated, real problem that Don had with the "story." Don smiled, said "Terrific," and left the room, which meant the segment had just been approved for air that Sunday.

I picked up the open phone receiver and resumed my conversation with one of the segment interviewees, Pat Choate, the PhD economist and author who later ran for vice president on the Ross Perot ticket in 1996. I asked Pat, "Did you hear all that?" And he replied, "Every word."[17]

Choate isn't the only contemporaneous witness who still "vividly" recalls my internal censorship situation prior to or just after the segment was broadcast; I have other friends and former *60 Minutes* colleagues who also remember it well, as well as copies of detailed written correspondence from that time further documenting the turmoil.

But the substitution of Stockman for Peterson didn't settle all the problems with the piece. In the days leading up to the broadcast, other prominent people mentioned in the story had been applying personal and legal pressure on Don and Mike, as well as the president of CBS News. So instead of being praised for producing a powerful, important story, I was under siege, being blamed for causing problems. I found myself in an inhospitable environment for original investigative reporting and its occasional consequences— pushback from the powerful (which should be a badge of honor for a reporter), but also spinelessness from my employer about what we had just published. Wallace and I had several venomous arguments that week, none more boisterous or invective-filled than some phone calls in the hours before the Sunday broadcast, in which we literally hung up on each other.

The whole noxious ordeal made something inside me snap. The morning after "Foreign Agent" led the broadcast, in the midst of a four-year contract, with a family to support, a mortgage to pay, and virtually no savings, I quit *60 Minutes*.

Producers there usually retire, voluntarily or involuntarily, or die on the job—hardly anyone just up and quits. In a brief phone call from my Washington office to the show's offices in New York City, I matter-of-factly informed Mike Wallace that I had decided to leave. My announcement came moments after Wallace had called me, somewhat giddy, to say that CBS chairman Laurence Tisch had just phoned him with effusive congratulations about our hard-hitting story the previous evening. It was the best thing he had seen on CBS in years, Tisch had told him, a "real public service."[18]

At first, Mike thought I was joking about quitting but soon realized I was serious. After nearly two months of eighty-hour to one-hundred-hour weeks, I didn't have the energy to attempt to explain why I was leaving, certain that it wouldn't change anything anyway.

Later that morning, I faxed Don Hewitt a three-sentence letter of resignation I'd typed on plain paper, rather than on show stationery. It began: "I have come to the difficult decision that I must leave *60 Minutes*" and it ended with, "It has been exciting and memorable working for you, and I wish you and everyone at *60 Minutes* all the best. Sincerely, Chuck Lewis."

Wallace and others at the program later asked my friends and colleagues if perhaps I was having a nervous breakdown. Don Hewitt wanted to know if "this" was all about money; he indicated that my contract could be substantially renegotiated upward, and then I could get back to work. Of course, my departure had nothing to do with either of these factors.

Nor was it driven by any personal animus on my part toward Mike Wallace. Mike was certainly not the easiest man to work with, but I respected him and his enormous contribution to broadcast journalism, and appreciated the opportunity he had given me. Years after I left the show, we had a cordial if slightly awkward rapprochement. A full decade after my departure, there was even a one-year editorial consulting contract between my new organization and CBS, which neither party chose to renew.

And in 2008, Mike agreed to my request to interview him for my multimedia oral history presentation, *Investigating Power.* Seconds before the interview was set to begin, Mike, who was months away from turning ninety and understandably not as sharp as he had once been, leaned over and said to me earnestly, "You and I, we're okay, right?"

It was an indelible, ironic moment, with television's most feared interviewer worried that his former producer might be planning to turn the tables and skewer him for posterity. I gently reassured Mike that we were okay, and we proceeded with the interview.[19]

Looking back, my departure from *60 Minutes* was not about psychological stress, financial issues, or personal pique. It was a matter of principle. It was simply time for me to leave.[20]

～∂～

Many people, then and since, have asked me what exactly I was thinking—after all, I was walking away from a successful career full of future promise. Certainly, quitting *60 Minutes* was the most impetuous thing I have ever done. But looking back, I realize how I'd changed. Beneath my polite, mild-mannered exterior, I'd developed a bullheaded determination *not* to be denied, misled, or manipulated. And more than at any previous time, I had had a jarring epiphany that the obstacles on the way to publishing the unvarnished truth had become more formidable *internally* than externally. I joked to friends that it had become far easier to investigate the bastards—whoever they are—than to suffer through the reticence, bureaucratic hand-wringing, and internal censorship of my employer.[21]

In a highly collaborative medium, I had found myself working with overseers I felt I could no longer trust journalistically or professionally, especially in the face of public criticism or controversy—

a common occupational hazard for an investigative reporter. My job was to produce compelling investigative journalism for an audience of 30 million to 40 million Americans. But if my stories generated the slightest heat, it was obvious to me who would be expendable. My sense of isolation and vulnerability was palpable.

The best news about this crossroads moment was that after eleven years in the intense, cutthroat world of network television news, I still had some kind of inner compass. I was still unwilling to succumb completely to the lures of career ambition, financial security, peer pressure, or conventional wisdom.

But the bad news was that major investigative reporting did not seem to be particularly valued by national news editors, whether in broadcasting or newspapers. Instead, they seemed satisfied merely to reactively report on the systemic abuses of power, trust, and the law in Washington—from the Iran-Contra scandal to the savings and loan disaster to the first resignation of a House Speaker since 1800. There was very little proactive, original investigative journalism about these or other vitally important subjects, and, equally galling to me, there was smug arrogance and complacency instead of apologetic humility by those in the national press corps, despite their lackluster pursuit of such abuses of power.

There had to be a better way.

8

The Future of Truth

The spirit of truth and the spirit of freedom—
they are the pillars of society.
—HENRIK IBSEN, 1877[1]

W EEKS AFTER I QUIT my job as an investigative producer at *60 Minutes*, in defiance of the overwhelming advice of many respected people inside and outside of CBS and declining job offers from other TV networks and elsewhere, I decided to begin a nonprofit investigative reporting organization. I knew almost nothing about the nonprofit world, had no management, financial, or fund-raising experience, and also understood the bleak reality that most new ventures fail. Illogically, I hoped that mine would somehow succeed.

I saw an opening for an organization dedicated to digging deep beneath the smarminess of Washington's daily-access journalism into the actual records and documents few reporters seemed to be reading, which I knew from experience would reveal broad patterns of cronyism, favoritism, personal enrichment, and outrageous (though mostly legal) corruption. My dream was a kind of journalistic utopia—an investigative milieu in which no one would tell me who or what *not* to investigate and in which the final story would be unfettered by time and space limitations, and untrammeled by the power of corporate or government interests bent on burying the truth.

I recruited two trusted journalist friends, Alejandro Benes and Charles Piller, to serve on the board of directors of this new organization, and I assumed the roles of board chairman and executive director.[2] In part because the words "investigative reporting" had already been used in the names of other nonprofit organizations (including the Center for Investigative Reporting, in California), we named our new group the Center for Public Integrity. Although this title sounded a little odd and somewhat pretentious, we had a definite rationale in mind. It seemed to us that on some level, all investigative reporting focuses on affronts to public integrity—violations of the way things *ought* to be. So our name was intended to emphasize not just the process but the ultimate purpose of investigative journalism: to hold those in power accountable and to inform the public about significant distortions of the truth.

I had no political or ideological agenda. (This differentiated us from cause-oriented nonprofit organizations such as Ralph Nader's Public Citizen and John Gardner's Common Cause, which also had pioneered the release of impressive, substantive, news-making reports about various public issues, beginning approximately two decades earlier.) Then and now, as stated on the Center's website, its mission has been "to serve democracy by revealing abuses of power, corruption and betrayal of public trust by powerful public and private institutions, using the tools of investigative journalism."[3] The modus operandi: to investigate macro, systemic issues of great public relevance, using a "quasi-journalistic, quasi political science" approach, in order to publish broad-based reports about government and public policy distortions of democracy that "name names," specifically identifying those responsible for these distortions.

The Center for Public Integrity was incorporated in Washington, DC, on March 30, 1989, and months later the IRS approved its tax exempt status as a 501 (c)(3) nonprofit educational organization. On October 1, 1989, I began working full-time as the Center's sole employee, from the guest bedroom of my suburban Virginia home.

My first self-assigned project was a fuller version of the *60 Minutes* "Foreign Agent" story, whose partial suppression still stuck in my craw. It became the Center's first report, "America's Frontline Trade Officials," a 201-page study published in December 1990 and presented at a National Press Club news conference covered by C-SPAN, CNN, the ABC News program *20/20*, and many other networks. It disclosed that 47 percent of White House trade officials over a fifteen-year period became paid, registered "foreign agent" lobbyists for countries or overseas corporations after they left government—a vivid illustration of the "revolving door" problem that encouraged government officials to develop cozy relationships with the very organizations they were supposed to be monitoring or regulating, in hopes of landing lucrative private-sector jobs after leaving office.

Our report prompted a Justice Department ruling, a General Accounting Office report, a congressional hearing, and it was partly responsible for an executive order issued by President Bill Clinton in January 1993, placing a lifetime ban on foreign lobbying by former White House trade officials. This response was deeply gratifying to me—it showed that our approach of conducting systematic investigations and announcing our findings to the national news media could actually lead to media coverage and to systemic change.

We were starting to be noticed. At the same time, we had assembled an advisory board of distinguished Americans, including Pulitzer Prize–winning historians Arthur Schlesinger Jr. and James MacGregor Burns, Notre Dame president emeritus Father Theodore Hesburgh, and veteran journalist Hodding Carter. And by May

1990, the Center had secured enough money from a foundation, some companies, and labor unions, and a consulting contract with ABC News to open its first office in downtown Washington, DC. (My home was required as collateral on the lease.)

The issue of perceived financial "purity" and the sources from which the Center should accept money has been an important topic at nearly every board meeting since 1989. The Center bends over backward to avoid even the appearance of a conflict of interest and has never accepted donations from government, political parties, or advocacy organizations.[4] And beginning in 1995, we stopped raising funds from companies and labor unions because of their direct economic interests in influencing public policy. Transparency and accountability have always been core values for us. The Center's major donors are disclosed online, along with annual reports, IRS 990 disclosure forms for at least the past ten years, and brief bios of every employee.

As the Center grew, I had to develop my skills as a leader and manager. I never subscribed to the traditional attitude that working in the nonprofit sector should demand "hair shirt" abstemiousness. Instead, my informal workplace motto was that quality begets quality, which means that top-flight journalism can come only from skilled editorial practitioners who are well paid, given generous benefits, and have sufficient time and the latest technology needed to do their very best work. However, for about the first dozen years, the Center did not assign the title "reporter" to any staff member (although some were designated "editors" and "writers"). The reason: most journalists are reluctant to report on the work of other journalists, so we worried that our reports would go uncovered in the news media if they appeared to be produced by a competing organization. Eventually, as our journalistic reputation grew to the point where we were hard to ignore, we altered the policy, which gratified staff members who were proud to be known as "reporters."

Since 1990, the editorial staff has been augmented by hundreds of undergraduate and graduate student interns; in addition, there are annual paid fellowship arrangements with the University of Delaware Political Science Department (the Soles Fellowship, begun in 1998, honors my distinguished professor and mentor, James R. Soles) and the American University School of Communication (SOC). Interns, who are paid a respectable hourly rate, work side by side with veteran reporters, mixing their youthful exuberance with the wisdom of experience in a way that creates beneficial synergies for the entire staff.

Our editorial approach reflects an investigative methodology combining prodigious research and reporting, "peeling the onion" by extensively consulting secondary and primary written sources, then interviewing several—sometimes hundreds—of people. Center projects usually take at least a few months from idea to publication, and sometimes they have taken years. The writing and editing, optimally by at least two layers of editors, takes weeks and multiple drafts, and the fact-checking and libel review by outside counsel can also be elaborate and time-consuming. No reporting project is initiated or published without the personal approval of the executive director, who functions essentially as both the executive editor and publisher.

This brand of no-stone-unturned journalism, which has been the hallmark of the Center's work since its inception, is increasingly rare in for-profit newsrooms, because today's advertising-supported, major-media journalists are generally expected to run full-speed on "the hamster wheel," as Dean Starkman so insightfully put it in the *Columbia Journalism Review*. The advent of the Internet, which makes publication so much easier and faster from a technical standpoint, is a mixed blessing in this regard. "The online game," Starkman noted, "is a volume game. More content generates more traffic, which hopefully means higher ad rates . . . [and] more posts means less time spent on each . . . [And] less time per piece is, of course, a recipe for lower-quality journalism." In this frenzied environment, deeply reported stories have increasingly become perceived as an economically unjustifiable luxury to be eschewed. That means that, as Starkman explains, the real cost of the hamster wheel "is investigations you will never see, good work left undone, public service not performed . . . [It] is the mainstream media's undoing, in real time, and they're doing it to themselves."[5]

Of course, the Center for Public Integrity has also embraced online distribution, albeit in a different way than commercial news outfits. The Center website went live in 1996, and our first online reports appeared in 1999. That migration online was concurrent with a push to produce commercially published books, the first of which (*Beyond the Hill: A Directory of Congress from 1984 to 1993. Where Have All The Members Gone?*) was released in 1995. Center book exposés were selected as the runner-up finalist in the Investigative Reporters and Editors annual book award competition in 1996, 1997, 1998, and 2000, and in 1999, the Center project *Animal Underworld: Inside America's Black Market for Rare and Exotic Species*, actually won the IRE book award. In 2007, the Center released its sixteenth book, published by Louisiana State University Press, about the aftermath of Hurricane Katrina.

The release of reports on the Web and distribution of major works via the nation's bookstores represented an important change in the amplification and dissemination of the Center's investigative findings. The Center no longer has to depend solely on coverage by the news media to inform the public about its findings; now the organization is reporting directly to citizens, and if mainstream journalists also deem the work newsworthy, all the better.

The Center's investigative reports are probably best known for exposing political influence and its impact on public policy decision-making in Washington, DC, and state capitals. Our early efforts included systematic, unprecedented investigations of the conflicts of interest of national political party chairmen (*Private Parties*, 1992) and unpaid policy advisers to the major presidential candidates (*Under the Influence*, 1992 and 1996).[6]

In 1996, dozens of researchers, writers, and editors amassed and analyzed half a dozen types of federal and state records to produce the first of the Center's three quadrennial *Buying of the President* exposés, published weeks before any primary votes were cast, which methodically examined the powerful special interests closely aligned with each of the major presidential candidates. The first book in the series, serialized in the *New York Times*, provided substantial editorial basis for the 1996 *Frontline* documentary "So You Want to Buy a President?," and the various major candidates' "Top Ten Career Patrons" lists moved worldwide on the wires. In the book's foreword, author Kevin Phillips observed, "In the thirty-five-year cavalcade of presidential campaign books that began with Theodore White's landmark *The Making of the President, 1960*, no one has ever concentrated on the quiet but just as critical influence battles fought with checkbooks . . . Documentation like this has never before been compiled and published in advance of the election being described. *Never*. And the spotlight is scorching."[7] The 2004 edition was on the *New York Times* short or extended best-seller list for approximately three months. Also in 1996, the Center also broke the Clinton Lincoln Bedroom fund-raising scandal ("Fat Cat Hotel"), which detailed how large donors to the president's reelection campaign were rewarded with overnight stays in the White House.

Our first five years of investigating corruption in state legislatures culminated in a national investigation of conflicts of interest by state lawmakers that, in 2000, was discreetly disseminated in embargoed fashion to a consortium of fifty leading newspapers in fifty states.[8] We analyzed and posted online the annual financial disclosure filings of more than 5,700 state lawmakers, exposing literally hundreds of apparent conflicts of interest related to their conduct of official business. That scrutiny continued for the next decade with a series of major reports that generated significant local media coverage and prompted twenty-one states to change their financial disclosure laws, forms, or rules pertaining to lawmakers. Similarly, after the Center exposed the lax disclosure systems regarding lobbying, twenty-four states improved their lobbyist transparency requirements.[9]

Over time, the Center tracked lobbying in all fifty state capitals, as well as monetary transfers between hundreds of political party committees nationwide, trips for public officials paid for by powerful interests, and a host of other such ethics-related subjects. Investigations of this kind were aided by the creation of a computer-assisted reporting "data cave," in which many thousands of government records available in Washington and the state capitals were carefully analyzed by specially trained reporters and editors. All of these documents are accessible online in searchable databases.

Thanks to these exhaustive investigations of dubious government activities, the Center grew steadily in reputation, funding, and size. But one subject we hadn't yet tackled was the media's power and influence, which citizens were increasingly asking me about. So in 2001, we created the "Well-Connected" project, which tracked information about media, technology, and telecommunications corporations. Our watchdog reporting included cumulative, detailed, political-influence information gleaned from government documents about media ownership, as well as media and telecom companies' federal and state lobbying and campaign contribution activities. The project team made news in 2003 when it uncovered that Federal Communications Commission officials had been taken on 2,500 all-expense-paid trips, over an eight-year period, by the media companies they were entrusted to regulate.[10] Within months, Congress curbed all such privately funded travel at the agency.

Other projects that earned widespread public attention included the online publication, in February 2003, of the secret "Patriot II" draft legislation, which the Center revealed against the explicit wishes of the Justice Department.[11] The story caused a bipartisan uproar, as Congress had been told for six months that there was no Bush administration intention to propose sequel legislation to the 2001 Patriot Act. Weeks later, mere days after the US invasion of Iraq, the Center published a new report disclosing that at least nine of the thirty members of the Defense Policy Board, the government-appointed group that advises the secretary of defense, had ties to companies with more than $76 billion in defense contracts in 2001 and 2002.[12]

We like to think that the Center for Public Integrity's publication of thoughtful, in-depth investigative reporting—and the public's growing embrace of that work—provides a potent counterweight to some of the disturbing trends unfolding in American media: the rise of the cable TV shout-fests; talk radio's derisive invective; and the flight to shorter, lighter local and network television news stories, sometimes augmented with cartoonish graphics to make sure the audience actually understands the point of the reporting. At times, it feels as though too many people are becoming benumbed by what Carl Bernstein calls "the spectacle, and the triumph, of the idiot culture."

I once asked Bernstein what precisely had prompted his eloquent 1992 denunciation of that "idiot culture" in our media. He described to me precisely when, for him, the downslide had all begun:

[It started when] not just the *New York Post* and the *New York Daily News* tabloids, but *Newsday*, which was then owned by the *Los Angeles Times* and was probably the best tabloid newspaper in America, did the 'whole front page this day' [in 1990] about the breakup of Donald Trump's first marriage to Ivana Trump and Trump's new relationship with this woman named Marla Maples. And on that same day, the allies of World War II agreed to the re-unification of Germany, and Nelson Mandela was released from the South African gulag that he had been in for all of those years. Those stories were inside *Newsday*, the two other tabloids here, and many other newspapers in America. And [in] every local news broadcast in this town [New York City], television, the Mandela and reunification stories *followed* the Trump marriage stories.

To me, that became a kind of allegory . . . for what was hap-pening. And meanwhile, the following week or two, ABC News, where I had gone to work, premiered its news magazine show called *Primetime Live* with Sam Donaldson, who is a great re-porter, and with Diane Sawyer, who is remarkably talented. And Diane was sent not to the Brandenburg Gate and not to Robben Island in South Africa. She was sent to Marla Maples' apart-ment. And I wrote, "That is the triumph of idiot culture."[13]

Sadly, our political and media idiot culture has continued to de-teriorate even further in the years since then. But it doesn't have to be this way. We've learned at the Center for Public Integrity that there are in fact large audiences interested in long-form, detailed, public-affairs reporting, be it on domestic subjects or on global issues. In fact, the Center's forays into international reporting have demonstrated that the dumbing down of the news by media cor-porations—including the shuttering of numerous overseas news bureaus by American media companies—by no means jibes with the interests of all news consumers.

In October 2003, for example, the Center published "Windfalls of War," which examined the major US government contracts in Afghanistan and Iraq, definitively revealing Halliburton and its subsidiary, Kellogg, Brown and Root, to be the overwhelmingly largest financial beneficiary of our invasions of those countries. For six months, twenty researchers, writers, and editors had worked on the project, filing seventy-three Freedom of Information Act (FOIA) requests and even suing the US Army and the State Department (and ultimately winning the release of key, no-bid contract documents).[14] That report, which won the first George Polk online investigative reporting award, was prepared by the Washington staff of the Center's International Consortium of Investigative Journalists, which I began in 1977 and which is helping to fill the void for aggressive reporting left by the contraction of commercial media.

The idea of investigative reporters working with one another across borders first became a gleam in my eye after an international conference in Moscow in 1992. By 1997, after close consultation with colleagues, including Bill Kovach, then curator of the Nieman Foundation at Harvard, a precise idea had taken shape, and it finally appeared that I would be able to secure sufficient funds. ICIJ was born.

ICIJ is the first working network of some of the world's preeminent investigative reporters collaborating to produce original international enterprise journalism, its ranks now comprising 175 people in over sixty countries on six continents. I've already mentioned "Windfalls of War," which ICIJ helped produce in 2003; that report had been preceded in 2002 by "Making a Killing: The Business of War," which used contributions from thirty-two reporters globally to identify ninety private military companies working for governments, corporations, and even criminal groups around the world.[15]

ICIJ members have also collaborated to produce international reports exposing illegal cigarette smuggling by the major manufacturers; the on-the-ground, human rights impact of US military aid in Latin America; the growing, global role of private military companies; the privatization of water; offshore tax havens; the politics of oil; global climate change lobbying; the international trade in asbestos; the illegal black-market overfishing of the world's oceans; the shadowy global business of buying and selling human body parts; and other essential topics. Indeed, the ICIJ-generated investigative online content transformed the Center for Public Integrity into "the first global website devoted to international exposés," according to the *Encyclopedia of Journalism*.[16]

A vivid example of the international impact and multimedia journalistic possibilities of the ICIJ in the Internet age appeared in April 2002, when the Center posted a report from Washington revealing that Ukrainian president Leonid Kuchma had personally authorized the sale of $100 million worth of sensitive antiaircraft radar technology to Iraq in apparent violation of United Nations sanctions, complete with an audio tape of Kuchma speaking Ukrainian as he made the deals. Within weeks of its release, US aid to the Ukraine was suspended and Kuchma was under criminal investigation in Kiev.[17] Such work has made the Center an international authority on both political corruption and investigative journalism.

Our experience in these two areas has helped us develop some important new initiatives on the global front. In my years of traveling and speaking abroad, I had become concerned that most reporting on global corruption, though extremely dangerous and heroic, was not as effective as it could be because its focus tended to be micro, lacking in context, and therefore limited in its relevance. I remember first noticing this problem back in 1977, while traveling in Tashkent, Uzbekistan, as part of a fact-finding research team sponsored by the Council on Foreign Relations. Those concerned with corruption and governmental abuses in that repressive country—from foreign investors and companies with offices there, to tourists, journalists, and endangered indigenous human rights activists—seemed to lack current, credible information about the quality of governance, rule of law, civility, press freedom, and accountability. There was no satisfactory single source generating such vital insight and making it publicly available.

By the 1990s, a possible solution to this problem was emerging. The Center's national survey investigations into conflicts of interest in Washington and the state legislatures had suggested a more sweeping, objective way of examining cronyism and corruption. I began to wonder: What if our often-macro investigative methodological approach in the United States could be adapted to the rest of the world?

In July 1999, I asked a recent University of Delaware grad, newly arrived in our offices, to help me explore a new way of monitoring and reporting on corruption, government accountability, and openness around the world. That effort culminated in a 750,000-word Center report, published online in 2004, entitled "Global Integrity." The unprecedented undertaking, by far the Center's largest-ever effort, was prepared by two hundred paid social scientists, journalists, and peer review editors in twenty-five countries on six continents.

This massive project spawned Global Integrity, a new nonprofit organization with an academic, social-science orientation and quantitative methodological component, and with greater and more diverse funding and capacity needs than the Center for Public Integrity. To address this situation, in December 2004, I recommended to the board of directors that this new entity be spun off as a global nongovernmental organization, completely separate and independent from the Center for Public Integrity. It was one of my last official acts as executive director of the Center.

Since 2006, Global Integrity has published annual Global Integrity Reports, including a "Global Integrity Index" that illuminates not only "the existence of laws, regulations and institutions designed to curb corruption but also their implementation, as well as access that average citizens have to those mechanisms" in countries around the world.[18] Each authoritative report and slew of news stories about the findings is building public credibility and interest, especially in multilateral institutions such as the World Bank and the United Nations, keen on an independent, comprehensive, credible assessment of the quality of governance and civility in each country, in diagnostic detail.[19]

ꕥ

One mark of an enduring institution is the ability to survive one or more leadership transitions. In 2004, after fifteen years at the helm of the Center for Public Integrity (and having celebrated my fiftieth birthday), I came to the sober realization that at some point, the founder would simply have to leave the building for the long-term health of the enterprise. It was painful for me to watch the ensuing two transition years, but in late 2006, the board of directors chose a fine new executive director. Bill Buzenberg is a veteran journalist who has worked as innovative news executive at newspapers and public radio for more than thirty-five years. As the first NPR managing editor and vice president of news, he launched such programs as *Talk of the Nation* and *Speaking of Faith*.[20]

The Center's work has often had a feisty irreverence, which has excited, amused, or enraged readers, depending on their point of view. Of course, no one at the Center has ever harbored any fantasies about being invited to dinner at the White House, regardless of occupant. Subjects of Center investigations, regardless of ideology or political party, are usually neither pleased nor amused. Indeed, over the years Center reports have generated angry newspaper op-eds, incensed calls to radio programs, and even sneak attacks by public relations people posing as reporters to ask distracting questions at nationally televised Center news conferences. Our advisory board members and donors have been personally pressured, as well.

And yet another occupational hazard of afflicting the powerful with inconvenient truths is that they may decide to sue you. Although the Center did not face a single lawsuit in its first decade of existence, as its public profile rose, three libel lawsuits were brought against the organization within eighteen months, beginning in late 2000. All of them filed during my tenure were eventually dismissed. There were also numerous verbal and written legal threats from companies and individuals in the United States and around the world who ultimately chose not to sue.

But weeks after we had published a story about Dick Cheney's years as the CEO of Halliburton, in August 2000, we found ourselves being sued in US district court in Washington by two Russian billionaire oligarchs represented by the powerful DC law firm of Akin Gump Strauss, Hauer, Feld, LLP. Published within days of the Republican National Convention in which Cheney was nominated to be the party's nominee for vice president of the United States, the story showed that Halliburton had doubled its lobbying, campaign contributions, and federal government contracts/loans during Cheney's five years as CEO, compared to the five years preceding his tenure there—and that among the apparent beneficiaries of Cheney's influence-peddling were the powerful owners of one of Russia's biggest banks.[21]

OAO Alfa Bank v. Center for Public Integrity was one of the largest libel cases brought in the United States in a quarter century. It ultimately entailed five years of discovery, twenty depositions (including my own two-day, videotaped interrogation), and 107,000 pages of documents. To our astonishment, Joel Kaplan, the associate dean of the Syracuse University S.I. Newhouse School of Public Communications and a former board member of Investigative Reporters and Editors, testified under oath that he had been paid at least $400,000 as an expert witness to help the oligarchs. Even more amazing, it was Kaplan's *tenth* libel case as an "expert witness" on behalf of plaintiffs suing journalists.

This David versus Goliath struggle cost each side millions of dollars. My major goal was to shield the Center newsroom and allow our ongoing investigative reporting to be relatively undeterred and undistracted. It worked: during the five-year siege of litigation, we still managed to publish one hundred investigative projects, including four books.[22] The case was finally dismissed in September 2005, upholding the vital principle that public figures cannot prevail in a libel suit against journalists unless they can demonstrate "actual malice" or "reckless disregard" for the truth—an appropriately high standard that clearly exonerated the Center.

Of course, we were delighted that the suit was unsuccessful. But it illuminated the immediate need for an institutional bulkhead protecting the organization from future storms of litigation. To provide such a shield, the Fund for Independence in Journalism, a 509 (a) (3) endowment and legal defense support organization, was created. Initial foundation contributions totaled $4 million, and, in addition, five of the most prestigious law firms in America pledged, on a case-by-case basis, to defend the Center for Public Integrity in any future actions, pro bono.[23]

Journalists and news organizations inevitably make mistakes, and the Center is no different in that regard. The way an organization (or a person, for that matter) stands up, takes responsibility, and perseveres through serious challenges and adversities says as much about its character as its successes and awards.

We once discovered, to our horror, that we had a plagiarist on our staff; he was fired immediately, and after a careful investigation lasting months, we apologized to the public and personally to the individual journalists and their editors who had been victimized. Moreover, very painfully, but appropriately, we returned a prestigious national journalism award for a Center book in which his "unattributed material" unfortunately had been published.

In 2011 and 2012, it became uncomfortably apparent that an extremely ambitious new digital business plan for the Center, including an audacious rebranding as iWatchNews.org, had been wildly unrealistic, causing great internal personnel strife and overall financial hardship.[24] The organization's board of directors (including yours truly) and its senior staff had succumbed to that familiar bane of many institutions: hubris. But the organization subsequently corrected that misstep and recalibrated its focus on the possible.

Today, in its global editorial reach, the Center for Public Integrity is the largest nonprofit investigative reporting organization in the world. In the United States, its work has been recognized in almost every conceivable way: the Pulitzer Prize, the Goldsmith Prize for Investigative Reporting, two George Polk Awards, two Overseas Press Club Awards, a Robert F. Kennedy Award, and a total of more than seventy major journalism awards to date.

In early 2007, Bill Buzenberg and I were invited to Cambridge, Massachusetts, to accept on behalf of the Center a Special Citation for its "superb investigative work in the public interest" by judges for the annual Goldsmith Prize for Investigative Reporting at the Joan Shorenstein Center on the Press, Politics and Public Policy at Harvard University's Kennedy School of Government. In the words of Alex S. Jones, director of the Shorenstein Center,

> At a time when many news organizations are curtailing investigative journalism, The Center for Public Integrity has stepped into the breach by mounting investigations of exemplary quality and then freely sharing its findings with other journalists and the public. The Center has become a model for journalistic nonprofit organizations by performing the complex, expensive work that is essential to our democracy and doing so using the highest journalistic standards.[25]

༄

The Center for Public Integrity isn't the only nonprofit organization leading a rebirth of the practice of investigative journalism. Excluding the partially government-funded National Public Radio, the Public Broadcasting System, and their hundreds of affiliate stations and local-news websites, today there are roughly one hundred professional nonprofit news organizations operating throughout the United States. More than two-thirds of those operations were created since 2004.[26] Eighteen of them operate from university campuses—an attempt to inculcate core journalistic values and technical know-how in new generations of reporters and editors in order for them to continue this essential work. The largest university-based reporting center and the only one in the nation's capital is the Investigative Reporting Workshop, which I proposed to the American University School of Communication in late 2007 and have since led. Its purpose is twofold: to create "significant, original investigative reporting on subjects of national and international importance, combining the talents and energies of preeminent journalists working with graduate students," and to analyze and experiment "with new economic models for creating and delivering investigative reporting" and in general, to find ways to enlarge the public space for this vital work.[27]

In late 2011, when my researchers and I at the Investigative Reporting Workshop examined the relevant IRS tax documents and other materials, we found that the seventy-five journalistic organizations profiled collectively boasted annual funding of $135 million and employed 1,300 full-time, paid staff members.[28] In addition, nonprofit investigative news organizations are now operating from England to Italy, from Peru to South Africa, from Jordan to Southeast Asia, where, in 1990, nine female journalists founded the Philippine Center for Investigative Journalism, the first known such nonprofit outside the United States.[29]

One of the distinguishing characteristics of this new phenomenon has been the migration of top major media editors to this nonprofit environment. The abbreviated roster includes former vice president of news for NPR, Bill Buzenberg, now executive director of the Center for Public Integrity; former assistant managing editor of the *Hartford Courant*, Lynne DeLucia, who cofounded the Connecticut Health Investigative Team; Florence Graves, founder and editor of *Common Cause Magazine*, who started the Schuster Institute for Investigative Journalism at Brandeis University; former senior editor for Metro and Watchdog Journalism at the *San Diego Union-Tribune*, Lorie Hearn, now editor of Investigative Newsource; Joel Kramer, who separately served as editor and publisher of the *Minneapolis Star-Tribune*, and launched MinnPost; former executive editor of the *Philadelphia Inquirer*, Robert Rosenthal, who now directs the Center for Investigative Reporting; Paul Steiger, former managing editor of the *Wall Street Journal*, who became founding executive editor of ProPublica; and Margaret Wolf Freivogel, former assistant managing editor of the *St. Louis Post-Dispatch*, who is the founding editor of the *St. Louis Beacon*.[30]

There is also a slew of former newspaper or network television investigative reporters who now lead such online nonprofit news ventures as the Florida Center for Investigative Reporting, the New England Center for Investigative Reporting at Boston University, Broward Bulldog, the Wisconsin Center for Investigative Journalism, Watchdog New England at Northeastern University, and Voice of Orange County, among others.

One catalyst for the emergence of the new nonprofit journalism movement was the advertising revenue crisis that began to devastate the newspaper industry in 2004. Suddenly, there was a deluge of downsized or unemployed traditional journalists seeking a new, more secure way to do their watchdog work. Concurrently, philanthropic institutions and individuals realized that you can't have communities or democracy without information and accountability about the powers that be. Fortuitously, they combined forces in an extraordinary, historic way.

Admittedly, I am hardly objective about this transformation, having founded or cofounded five nonprofit journalistic enterprises and having proudly served on approximately fifteen nonprofit boards of directors or advisory boards the past two-plus decades.[31] But my biases notwithstanding, the evidence is compelling: when it comes to the pursuit of truth without fear or favor, nonprofit journalism is an integral part of the present and the future.

The two oldest investigative reporting nonprofit organizations in the United States—the Center for Investigative Reporting (CIR) and the Center for Public Integrity (CPI)—were created by investigative reporters in 1977 and 1989, respectively. Lowell Bergman, Dan Noyes, Henry Weinstein, and David Weir, in Northern California, founded CIR; I've already recounted how I launched CPI in Washington, DC.

Early on, the respective models were slightly different. CIR preferred a small staff and low overhead, its staff and freelance journalists directly partnering from the outset on major projects with traditional media outlets. By contrast, CPI built a more traditional full-time newsroom staff (with paid vacation and other benefits), assisted by paid student interns, who prepared exhaustive reports released to the media and later published online and in book form.

A third nonprofit muckraking outfit, best known as *Mother Jones* magazine (but actually published by an organization of a different name), began in Northern California in 1976 and broke national investigative news stories almost immediately, such as Mark Dowie's 1977 exposé of the Ford Pinto's exploding gas tanks.[32]

In recent years, several in the burgeoning array of nonprofit news organizations have distinguished themselves journalistically. For example, in 2011, Jesse Eisinger and Jake Bernstein's investigative reporting for ProPublica into the questionable practices on Wall Street won the Pulitzer Prize for National Reporting, ProPublica's second Pulitzer in two years. (In late 2008, in a nod to this emerging trend, the Pulitzer committee announced that independent, online news sites, including nonprofit news organizations, would henceforth be eligible for the prestigious awards.)

In 2012, the Center for Investigative Reporting–California Watch, with KQED San Francisco, was awarded the IRE Medal, the highest honor bestowed by the organization Investigative Reporters and Editors, for a nineteen-month series ("On Shaky Ground") about shortcomings in the way California protects its schools from the threat of earthquakes. "Flying Cheap," a co-production of PBS *Frontline* and the Investigative Reporting Workshop at American University, won the Society of Professional Journalists' National Documentaries Award for its examination of the safety of regional airlines, which helped prompt a tougher federal safety law. And the Center for Public Integrity and its International Consortium of Investigative Journalists, along with the BBC International News Services, won the IRE Medal for their collaboration "Dangers in the Dust: Inside the Global Asbestos Trade."

Another tremendously exciting development is a move by journalism departments in the nation's colleges and universities to embrace a "teaching hospital" model, creating daily and investigative news stories for mainstream outlets—in some cases year-round, rather than just during academic semesters—through the reporting and writing of upper-class undergrads and graduate students. One notable example is the Carnegie-Knight Initiative on the Future of Journalism Education, whose News21 program has, since 2005, annually recruited university journalism students to produce in-depth reporting on a single subject. Their multipart, multimedia series pieces, edited and coordinated by Arizona State University's Walter Cronkite School of Journalism and Mass Communications, have been co-published with major news media outlets.[33] In 2010, for instance, the *Washington Post* and MSNBC.com were among those that published parts of a twenty-three-story series, produced by eleven student reporters from eleven universities, on shortcomings in US transportation safety.

In the past six years, we've also seen a surge in the number of news services run by university students, which provide either "hyper-local" reporting or coverage of individual state capitals—the sort of bread-and-butter journalism that the Associated Press and other major media outlets have largely abandoned. At Arizona State, for example, the Cronkite News Service provides editorial copy to thirty media clients, including fourteen of the state's largest newspapers. Similarly, Florida International University's South Florida News Service does community-level reporting for the *Miami Herald*, the *South Florida Sun-Sentinel*, and the *Palm Beach Post*; at the University of Alabama, graduate students provide similar coverage for the *Anniston Star*; and the City University of New York Graduate School of Journalism and Columbia University's Graduate School of Journalism have created student-run news services, NY City News Service and New York World, respectively.[34] There are many other examples.

Universities are also collaborating to produce specialized, subject-related journalism, filling the void created by the decimation of mainstream-media newsrooms. For example, the Hechinger Institute on Education and the Media, based at Teachers College at Columbia University, uses staff writers and freelancers to produce *The Hechinger Report*, which focuses on journalism about education.[35] And the John Jay College of Criminal Justice is home to The Crime Report, an enterprising daily news service covering criminal justice issues that is a partnership of criminal justice journalists and John Jay College's Center on Media, Crime and Justice.[36]

The most important public-service journalism will increasingly emanate from partnerships between these new nonprofit journalism entities, which have the time and talent to produce invaluable content, and the shrinking major-media organizations, which have larger audiences but smaller budgets for reporting and want to augment their daily and investigative coverage. The need for journalistic collaboration is mutual and very real, and the opportunities are enormous and growing.

There are clear incentives helping to drive this trend toward partnerships between for-profit and nonprofit journalism organizations. First, there is the familiarity factor: in many cases, the nonprofits are run by people whom news executives already know or know of, credible and respected practitioners with whom they are professionally and editorially comfortable.

Second, those heading up newsrooms recognize that they need to immediately do something smart, ambitious, and constructive to reclaim the important role their organizations once played in community life—a role that, as we've seen, has been gradually disappearing.

Finally, nonprofit organizations that include university faculties and their students can provide additional technical expertise, be it forensic accounting, computer science, multimedia production, or other expertise. And in the increasingly competitive business world of the twenty-first century, who can resist the partnership prospects of innovation, intellectual capital, additional plant and equipment, physical space, and quality journalism at vastly reduced costs of labor and other expenses?

As an example, consider the blossoming relationship between the *Washington Post* and the American University School of Communication (SOC), in Washington, DC. There is a long history of affinity between the two institutions, thanks to the SOC alumni populating the *Post*'s newsroom and such educational services as the newsroom online multimedia convergence training provided by university experts. So in 2011, it was natural for *Washington Post* local editor Vernon Loeb to approach Larry Kirkman, at the time the SOC dean, about a deeper, more innovative partnership. That led to a dinner that included American University president Neil Kerwin,

Post publisher Katharine Weymouth, and *Post* executive editor Marcus Brauchli.

Soon afterward, the annual *Washington Post* Fellow Program was created: the newspaper pays for the master's degree of an incoming journalism student, and the school names five "Dean's Fellows" for annual internships inside the *Post* newsroom. By the end of the 2011–2012 academic year, seven School of Communication students had written more than two hundred bylined articles for the *Post*.[37]

Then, in early 2013, with help from a Ford Foundation grant, the *Post* and SOC announced they were jointly hiring highly respected investigative reporter John Sullivan.[38] Previously, Sullivan had led a five-person team at the *Philadelphia Inquirer* that explored violence in the city's schools, including crimes committed by children against other children. In 2012, the seven-part, multimedia exposé, which prompted reforms to improve safety for both teachers and their students, won for the *Inquirer* the Joseph Pulitzer Gold Medal for Public Service, the most prestigious Pulitzer Prize for journalism.[39]

Sullivan now works as a member of the *Washington Post* investigative team and, simultaneously, as an investigative journalist in residence and senior editor of the Investigative Reporting Workshop at SOC (where I serve as executive editor). As a member of the faculty, he teaches and mentors top students inside the *Post* newsroom, in a new hands-on, investigative reporting "practicum" course—a core curricular component of the new investigative journalism program within the journalism and public affairs master's degree program.

To my knowledge, this level of professional cooperation involving for-profit, philanthropic, and educational institutions is a first for American journalism. This model can be replicated elsewhere, and it should go a long way toward the furtherance of public accountability. At the *Post* and American University, we also believe this is just the beginning of our combined efforts to both create great public-service journalism and instill the values and know-how of investigative reporting in a new generation of truth-tellers. I predict we will see many more such shared arrangements, both in the United States and elsewhere, as other major media outlets and nonprofit news organizations come to see the strategic and professional synergistic advantages of such sharing of finite resources.

In the meantime, the sharing of values, resources, and even content has also been taking place *within* the new nonprofit journalism ecosystem itself. For example, in July 2009, the founders of roughly twenty nonprofit news organizations gathered outside New York City and created the Investigative News Network. Leading philanthropic foundations got behind the historic effort, INN was incorporated, the IRS approved its tax-exempt status, and an executive director was hired. I am proud to say I was present at the creation, proposed the concept and name to the group, and serve as a founding board member and officer. The enterprise is still in its infancy, although membership in this nonprofit news publishers association has already reached nearly one hundred. I hope this is just the beginning and that INN will pioneer the collection and syndication of the best nonprofit investigative reporting content in the United States, and perhaps throughout the world.[40]

And one more exciting component of the new nonprofit journalism ecosystem: in 2001, Brant Houston, then the director of Investigative Reporters and Editors, and Nils Mulvad, a respected Danish investigative journalist, founded what has become known as the Global Investigative Journalism Network (GIJN). It now has more than ninety member organizations in forty countries, and to date has hosted eight international conferences—the first two in Copenhagen, the most recent in Rio de Janeiro—with over 4,000 participating journalists from one hundred countries.[41]

It is abundantly clear, then, that the nonprofit journalism ecosystem is becoming more robust than ever, and that the national and international investigative journalism communities, with authors, freelancers, and reporters from both for-profit and nonprofit news organizations, are vibrant and full of energy and ideas.

But a dose of perspective is also in order. Paul Starr, a two-time Pulitzer Prize–winning author and a longtime Princeton University professor, recently pointed out the discrepancy between the growth of the nonprofit journalism sector and the massive decline in its for-profit counterpart: "It is hard to see how philanthropy can match the resources that are being lost. Since 2000, the [US] newspaper industry alone has lost an estimated '$1.6 billion in annual reporting and editing capacity . . . or roughly 30 percent,' but the new nonprofit money coming into journalism has made up less than one-tenth that amount."[42]

Another valid concern is the issue of long-term funding. How long will private philanthropy remain interested in the state of quality journalism? Is foundation support for investigative journalism a fad that may fade, leaving nonprofits scrambling to find new sources of revenue? If so, where will these revenues come from? Nonprofits have experimented with numerous types of entrepreneurial ideas and approaches for developing so-called earned revenue, including advertising, online sales of content, and paid memberships. None has emerged as a panacea for nonprofit reporting. As for government support, in the United States that is almost certainly a nonstarter. As Starr bluntly puts it, "Most Americans, including those in the news industry, reject out of hand any form of government assistance and say noncommercial support for journalism must come entirely from private, philanthropic sources."

So nonprofit journalism faces some very real challenges in the years ahead. But it seems clear that there is an important role to be played by nonprofit organizations in the quest for truth, sometimes in partnership with and sometimes competing with their counterparts in the for-profit news business.

Imagine a world in which individual researchers, public-interest activists, lawyers, political scientists, government prosecutors and investigators, corporate investigators, forensic accountants, political scientists, computer experts, investigative historians, public anthropologists, and journalists are sometimes looking for truth in all the same places, using the same exciting new data technologies and analytics, exchanging ideas and information, and sometimes working and writing together, whether side by side or across borders and genres.

These collaborative fact-finders, fact-checkers, truth-seekers, and truth-tellers will all come from different perspectives, educational backgrounds, and diverse geographic, cultural, and economic circumstances. But all will share the deep curiosity, patience, determination, and mettle that have always characterized the investigative reporter. They'll be willing to persevere in their quest for answers for months, years, or even decades, when necessary.

Team efforts of this kind on behalf of the truth are already beginning to take shape. They are facilitated by the Internet, mobile telephony, and other new technology tools for disseminating information. And they are driven by the insatiable human demand for truth—a demand that no totalitarian regime has ever succeeded in fully quenching.

When the Iron Curtain fell and the Soviet Union collapsed in 1989, the undying human demand for truth came flooding forth in the countries once known as the Communist bloc. As Pulitzer Prize–winning historian Anne Applebaum put it in her 2012 book, *Iron Curtain: The Crushing of Eastern Europe, 1944–1956*, even after decades of subjugation, "human beings do not acquire 'totalitarian personalities' with such ease. Even when they seem bewitched by the cult of the leader or of the party, appearances can be deceiving. . . . And even when it seems as if they are in full agreement with the most absurd propaganda—even if they are marching in parades, chanting slogans, singing that the party is always right—the spell can suddenly, unexpectedly, dramatically be broken."[43] Civil society communities in the repressed countries sprang to life, aided by the latest communication technologies facilitating the free flow of information—photocopiers, fax machines, mobile phones, and laptop computers made available to them by philanthropic foundations and others in the West. The spell of spoon-fed daily deception was broken because it became impossible for Communist officials to control—or even monitor—the flow of information and censor independent thought, ideas, and, ultimately, truth.[44]

Around the same time, in February 1991, Nelson Mandela was freed after twenty-seven years in a South African prison, thanks in part to a decades-long drumbeat of international pressure directed at the apartheid-based white-minority government led by President F. W. de Klerk. Just over four years later, Mandela was unanimously proclaimed president of South Africa by parliament, and the next day sworn in as the country's first black president.[45]

One of Mandela's earliest official acts was to initiate serious discussions that led to the creation, in mid-1995, of the South African Truth and Reconciliation Commission. Chaired by 1984 Nobel Peace Prize winner Archbishop Desmond Tutu, the commission's mandate was to uncover the facts about crimes and abuses committed during the decades of apartheid. In pursuit of that goal, the panel was given "the power to grant individualized amnesty, search premises and seize evidence, subpoena witnesses, and run a sophisticated witness protection program" as well as a staff of three hundred and an annual budget of roughly $18 million. The commission received testimony from over 21,000 victims and witnesses, one-tenth of whom testified in public hearings, which received massive news media coverage in South Africa.[46]

According to Priscilla Hayner, author of the first comprehensive scholarly work about truth commissions throughout the world, forty similar truth commissions have been created since 1974, which "impact directly on thousands upon thousands of victims, as well as on the possibility of future criminal justice, reforms, reparations and, with luck, perhaps reconciliation and future peaceful community relations." This entire remarkable phenomenon is also symptomatic of "a broader field that has virtually exploded as a field of study and work since 2001," the field of transitional justice. And that involves "a diverse range of disciplines and professions," such as "psychologists, sociologists, anthropologists, political scientists, archive specialists, economists, statisticians, historians, regional specialists and others."[47]

A similarly eclectic, global array of citizens interested in transparency and accountability in government and society in general has coalesced in recent decades, within countries and across borders. Perhaps their biggest adversary is government itself, with its seemingly innate tendency to create ever-expanding zones of secrecy to protect officials from the consequences of their deeds—and misdeeds.

Thanks to authors David Wise and Thomas B. Ross, who in 1964 published *The Invisible Government*, we've long known how seriously out of control our institutional secrecy problem is here in the United States. Unfortunately, the situation has since gotten discernibly worse, which makes whistleblowers and leakers, technologically ingenious hackers and other "idealists, anarchists [and] extremists" seem somewhat heroic as welcome antidotes to our worsening affliction.[48] Consider that in 2001, 8.6 million US government documents were classified; by 2008, 23.8 million were classified, and by 2010, "despite [President] Barack Obama's promises of a more transparent government," 76.7 million documents were classified![49] Today, 4.2 million Americans have some form of security clearance to read classified documents—and of those, 1.2 million have Top Secret clearances.[50] In effect, our citizenry is divided into two tiers—a small elite with access to inside knowledge about our government, and a vast lower echelon that is kept in the dark. There's no reason to believe the situation is better in most other countries.

One partial remedy is laws mandating government transparency. Here in the United States, it took decades of organizing efforts for the idea of such a law to gain traction. Finally, in 1966 President Lyndon Johnson signed into law the Freedom of Information Act, which has since been amended many times.[51] Today, at least ninety countries have established FOIA-style laws and administrative procedures, a potentially invaluable investigative tool for 5.5 billion (out of 7 billion) people in the world attempting to hold those in power accountable.[52]

These laws are imperfect and unevenly implemented, with far too many exemptions to protect entrenched, opaque, frequently venal bureaucratic and other interests; individual citizen requests sometimes take many decades to fulfill, and disclosed documents are sometimes blacked out to a ludicrous extent. Nonetheless, these FOIA laws are part of an overall continuum of progress, especially considering the unacceptable alternative of no such legal requirements, and thus a vastly reduced possibility of disclosure and truth. One hopes that over time the public will more vociferously demand transparency and accountability, and increasingly prevail.

One of the more inspiring and tenacious public-interest organizations that has indeed managed to demand the truth from its government—and then to act on that truth—is Mazdoor Kisan Shakti Sangathan (MKSS), co-founded in the state of Rajasthan, in central India, by a charismatic activist named Aruna Roy whom I met there and interviewed in 2003. A few months later, MKSS leaders confronted and publicly exposed local officials who had falsified government records. In all, twenty-six officials were subsequently prosecuted for systematically making bogus ledger entries regarding government-subsidized wheat, sugar, and kerosene, which they had sold illegally at higher black market prices rather than making it available to the poor. They had also made false register entries for bridges, roads, and other public-works projects that were actually never completed, instead illegally pocketing nearly 5 million rupees. Roy helped lead a local, and then national, campaign for government transparency (their slogan: "The right to information is the right to life"), and in 2005 India formally enacted the Right to Information Act.[53]

Today there is a robust global "right to know" information movement and a related anti-corruption community, which have initiated various cross-border collaborative initiatives, including conferences. Some of the organizations involved, from newest to oldest, are:

- The Sunlight Foundation, founded in Washington, DC, in 2006, which "uses the power of the Internet to catalyze greater government openness and transparency"
- The Open Democracy Advice Centre, based in Cape Town, South Africa, created in 2000 to help with the implementation of the recently enacted access-to-information laws there
- Transparency International, created in 1993 and based in Berlin, best known for publishing a Corruption Perception Index based on annual polling data, ranking the world's most corrupt countries
- Article 19, founded in 1987 and based in London, which promotes "access to information needed to hold the corrupters and the corrupted to account"
- The National Security Archive, located at George Washington University in Washington, DC, founded in 1985 by journalists and scholars "to check rising government secrecy," which, as the foremost nonprofit user of the US Freedom of Information Act, has submitted 40,000 Freedom of Information and declassification requests to over

two hundred US government offices and agencies, in the process prying loose more than 10 million pages of documents

- The Center for Effective Government (formerly OMB Watch), also based in Washington, DC, one of the nation's leading transparency advocacy organizations, established in 1983 to "lift the veil of secrecy shrouding the White House Office of Management and Budget"
- The Center for Responsive Politics, the preeminent research group tracking private campaign money in US political elections, started in Washington in 1983
- The National Institute for Money in State Politics, based in Helena, Montana, which has the only comprehensive and searchable online record of political donations in all fifty states
- The Carter Center, created by former president Jimmy Carter in 1982, in partnership with Emory University, in Atlanta, which seeks to "enhance freedom and information" in the Americas and elsewhere
- The Project on Government Oversight, founded under a different name in 1981, which states that its "investigations into corruption, misconduct, and conflicts of interest achieve a more effective, accountable, open, and ethical federal government"[54]

There are many more such public-interest, good-government, democracy-minded research organizations around the world—including Global Integrity and the Center for Public Integrity, described in depth earlier—just in the fields of tracking corruption and political influence and enhancing government transparency. This community consists of kindred souls in geographically scattered, disparate organizations—serious, well-educated professionals, from lawyers to journalists, from political scientists and other academics to ethicists and data aggregators, from software developers to video producers—in the pursuit and dissemination of truth by many means. No savvy journalist attempting to report about political influence and corruption can do so without consulting and collaborating with these and similarly serious organizations.

In like fashion, professionally diverse researchers in many other public-interest fields are currently publishing their findings online through many hundreds of nonprofit, nonpartisan organizations that focus on the environment, health and safety, human rights, migration, national and international security, and other subjects.

What is particularly fascinating is how many of these relatively new organizations now employ journalists who continue to report, write, and publish, but with different titles, for different audiences, and under different circumstances. Often, their work is now more thoughtful and substantive than in their previous lives as conventional reporters; often, it is equally, if not more, remunerative. Now, major global issues—corruption, human rights, health, security, and so on—are being covered less by the commercial news media than by the surging nonprofit sector.

One of the fastest-growing categories of nongovernmental organizations (NGOs) is that of public policy research organizations, better known as think tanks. According to James McGann at the University of Pennsylvania, who annually tracks their evolution, "Not only have these organizations increased in number, but the scope and impact of their work has also expanded dramatically." There are now 6,603 think tanks operating in 182 countries, nearly 60 percent of them in North America and Western Europe, many based at or affiliated with colleges and universities. In the first decade of this new millennium, think tanks have "witnessed a new phenomenon of global networks and partnerships," which have "become an effective mechanism for transferring knowledge and information internationally." Their high-quality content is released via assorted publishing venues, including websites, blog posts, books, monographs, magazines, newspapers and newsletters, radio, television, web documentaries, and even their own television and radio programs.[55] And for years, think tanks have been aggressively hiring respected print reporters and authors, whether on a full-time or contract basis, as well as researchers, writers, and editors, who operate in much the same fashion as traditional, in-depth journalists. For example, since 2005, Global Integrity has hired more than one hundred journalists as outside writers and editors for its annual Global Integrity Reports.

An outstanding example is New York City–based Human Rights Watch, which has eighteen offices on six continents and publishes online daily in multiple languages. The organization has numerous journalists on its staff—professionals such as award-winning investigative reporter and author Ricardo Sandoval Palos, formerly at the *Dallas Morning News*, Knight Ridder newspapers, the *Sacramento Bee*, and the Center for Public Integrity.[56] No traditional news organization anywhere provides Human Rights Watch's level of both global breadth and substantive thoroughness in its research and reporting on the subject of human rights. Of course, few subjects are also as controversial, and the organization's reports on occasion have upset some of its most dedicated donors and even board members, including founder and chairman emeritus Robert Bernstein, who took the unusual step of rebuking his own organization over its criticism of Israel's human rights policies in a *New York Times* op-ed.[57]

Or take the New America Foundation, based in Washington, DC. It was created in 1999 by founding president Ted Halstead and founding chairman of the board James Fallows, a highly respected author and national correspondent for the *Atlantic Monthly* magazine. New America describes itself as a "nonprofit, nonpartisan public policy institute that invests in new thinkers and new ideas to address the next generation of challenges facing the United States."[58] Today, with an annual budget of about $19 million, it employs 142 people.[59] The director of New America's National Security Studies program is CNN national security analyst Peter Bergen, the author of four books (three of them *New York Times* list bestsellers) who, among other things, interviewed Osama bin Laden prior to 9/11. The foundation has no fewer than thirty-one fellows, including in 2012 such highly regarded journalists and authors as Joel Garreau, a former longtime *Washington Post* reporter and editor; Tim Wu, a professor at Columbia Law School and author of the acclaimed book *The Master Switch: The Rise and Fall of Information Empires*; Brigid Schulte, a veteran reporter for the *Washington Post*; Dr. Sheri Fink, the Pulitzer Prize–winning writer for ProPublica and the *New York Times Magazine*; Mark Hertsgaard, author of *On Bended Knee: The Press and the Reagan Presidency* and five other books; and Jason DeParle, a veteran *New York Times* reporter.[60]

Steve Coll, a former *Washington Post* managing editor and the winner of two Pulitzer Prizes (one for a newspaper series and another for one of his books), served as president of the New America Foundation from 2007 to 2013 and was simultaneously a staff writer for the *New Yorker*.[61] It is unusual for the head of a think tank to also work as an active staff writer for a respected national magazine, but Coll represents an interesting, recent trend—the wearing of two (or more) professional hats representing concurrent cross-platform personas.

None of these nonprofit policy research organizations have paid advertising on their websites, but many are well funded by philanthropic foundations, individuals, and, in some instances, governments. Visibility and public influence are the coin of the realm for such groups, so professional staffers are expected to be quoted, appear on the electronic media, and publish, publish, publish! And there's no more direct way to accomplish the latter than by partnering with newspapers and magazines for the publication of articles or op-eds.

Prolific partnership publishing is regarded as essential to maximizing the impact of these organizations' research findings, policy ideas, and overall public profile. Of course, it is also necessary fodder for their continued funding, not unlike the way readership, listenership, or viewership is closely tethered to advertising revenue at commercial news outlets.

All of this, I would suggest, is a natural, and perhaps even inevitable, evolution. As the need to do more in-depth national and global journalism has increased while traditional news-gathering capacity has dwindled, NGOs have nimbly moved into very important, specialized niches of neglected subject matter, helping to fill glaring information gaps.

～๑๑～

Of course, there are enormous gaps yet to be filled. The growing number of borderless, topic-specific communities of interest will increasingly want access to the most up-to-date and authoritative information, which isn't available today in any coherent form. For example, there are tens of millions of Americans who are environmentally concerned or curious, and many more like them throughout the world, but there is no international broadcast, cable TV, or global video source focused exclusively on this theme.[62] There should be. Global multimedia attention to a topic like the environment—or human rights, education, government corruption, international security, corporate governance, health care, or other similar topics—would provide cross-cultural coherence, as well as vitally important context and information, to interested communities everywhere. One hopes that someday there will be such programming for all these important areas of interest and many more.

In this era of collaboration, globalization, and the Internet, twenty-first-century news gathering must rise above traditional geographic boundaries. At the same time, the concept of public accountability should not be narrowly confined by local or national borders. Inhabitants of the planet are interconnected; so are the immensely complex problems we face and their necessarily collaborative, multi-jurisdictional solutions.

Indeed, I believe we are already moving toward creating what I informally call online knowledge clusters. Why can't there be places where citizens from anywhere can go to find the most authoritative, up-to-date, searchable knowledge about vital issues, combining the best documented information from multiple crowd sources, including academia, journalism, government, and the private and nonprofit sectors? The nearest equivalents today are Wikipedia and perhaps *Encyclopedia Britannica* and other such knowledge compendiums.[63] These online sites are remarkable achievements, but they are often inadequate, inaccurate, or outdated.

We need new ways to amass knowledge across borders and cultures based on documented, reliable sources. Imagine combining the most authoritative information from disparate sectors, including journalism and such academic subject areas as investigative history, forensic accounting, computer science and statistics, political science, economics, public anthropology, human rights, public interest and other law-related fields, court proceedings and their related, unsealed case materials. Imagine an online portal that provides access to all these materials and more—a central clearinghouse for data about the world's worst corporate, financial, and environmental scofflaws; the worst violators of health, safety, and labor rights regulations; companies that have been decertified by one of the world's stock exchanges for fraud or other misbehavior; government agencies that have squandered public funds; and political organizations and lobbying groups that mislead and deceive the citizenry. Creating such a source is mostly a matter of time and money, and I believe it is inevitable.[64]

Technology, then, can play an important role in making vital information available to everyone, everywhere, in real time. Of course, the same technology has made the mission of the truth-teller even more complicated. In today's hyper-evolving Information Age, we have gone from a world with three television networks whose broadcast programs garnered 90 percent of the nation's viewing population to an atomized, twitchy world of thousands of cable channels, the Internet, the World Wide Web, global search engines, and 2 billion Internet users.[65]

Amid this astonishing din of visual and auditory stimuli, the investigative journalist has labored to adapt. Sometimes an important story will strike a public chord and go viral on the web for a few hours. But such broad resonance is exceedingly rare in the overwhelming and distracting deluge of hyped-up information we face every day.

Under these new circumstances, the practice of news gathering itself must also continue to evolve. We journalists need to become less arrogant about our status as filters of information; we need to be more ready to acknowledge the value of authoritative investigative information unearthed by others, from expert specialists to ordinary citizens; and we need to learn to collaborate more closely with one another and with professionals from many fields in our collective search for truth.

For this reason, I have proposed the creation of a new multi-disciplinary academic field called Accountability Studies.[66] Ideally, it would involve professors with different types of accountability knowledge and expertise from throughout the university, and it would enable students to earn a specialized degree in the field. I believe that an array of courses addressing these topics should be offered at every major university. My years of teaching and mentoring hundreds of research interns at three reporting/research centers have shown me that students from widely different academic backgrounds are excited about the prospect of learning exactly how to investigate those in power and hold them accountable. Many thousands would be eager to devote their careers to such work—and not necessarily in traditional journalism.

～∂～

The late James Martin had the sort of credentials that gave him license to authoritatively speculate about the future we face. One of the world's leading authorities on computing and related technology, he had honorary doctorate degrees from all six inhabited continents. The revenue from his one-hundred-plus textbooks—a total unmatched by anyone now living—funded the creation of the Twenty-first Century School (now Oxford Martin School), at Oxford University, which boasts more than thirty institutes and projects concerned with everything from nanotechnology and geo-engineering to stem cell science, cyber security, and a diverse array of other disciplines destined to dramatically shape our future.[67]

In his 2007 book, *The Meaning of the Twenty-first Century*, Martin wrote about the most serious social, economic, environmental, and political challenges facing our world. He concluded:

> Today there are major roadblocks preventing the actions that are needed. There are huge vested interests with massive financial reasons for not changing course . . . There is widespread ignorance . . . For the powerful people who control events, the desire for short-term benefits overwhelms the desire to solve long-term problems. If these roadblocks are not removed, we will steadily head down paths that lead to catastrophe: famines, violence, wars over water, pollution, global pandemics, runaway climate change, terrorism with new types of mass-destruction weapons.[68]

It would be hard for anyone to claim that the problems we face have become any more tractable in the years since Martin wrote those words—or that the "huge vested interests" he described have become any less shortsighted and irresponsible. But who, exactly, is going to hold the powers that be accountable? Who is going to shine the light on the acts of corruption, abuse, despoliation, greed, and oppression that continue to darken our world?

The future of truth and accountability can be great if "we, the people" choose to demand it.

A Note from the Author

WRITING THIS BOOK has been an epic, Sisyphean journey unlike any project I have ever embarked upon. Naturally, I understand this much better today than I did in early 2005 when it began.

Not only am I left with deep humility and respect for this very difficult subject, but what I have written here would not have been remotely possible, certainly, without the millions of words of accumulated wisdom and impeccably gathered information that have preceded and deeply enriched this effort. I am acutely cognizant of the thousands of hours of work that produced the finest newspaper and magazine articles, the most important books, and the most compelling documentaries about these subjects over the past century. My profound thanks and gratitude to all of the preeminent scholars, authors, and reporters whose work cited here has informed me and helped to make this work possible. In addition, I'm not sure I would ever have had the audacity and chutzpah to write about such a profound, imponderable topic had I not hugely benefited from a lifetime of "steeping" from the wisdom and insight of others. Personally, professionally, and intellectually, I have been extraordinarily fortunate to have had many older, more experienced friends, acquaintances, teachers, mentors, and informal advisers throughout my life, many of them unfortunately now deceased. Each made an indelible impression on me and without mentioning them each personally, I will *always* warmly remember their generous spirit, excellent insights, judgment, encouragement, and example.

To give you an idea of the peculiarities of this exploration, consider the important but not-so-simple issue of the book title. Initially, back in late 2004 when I first proposed this book, the title was "The End of Truth: Power, the News Media, and the Public's Right to Know," a play on words inspired by Francis Fukuyama's book *The End of History*. However, "The End of Truth" increasingly seemed too bleak for a potentially interested reader, but also, while somewhat catchy, it was also discordant vis-à-vis my own views. I am neither a philosopher nor a postmodernist who is convinced there is no longer any such thing as truth. In considering an alternative title, I then became enamored of the phrase "If Given the Truth." For years, at the end of speeches and even in some of my earlier books, my favorite quotation was from Abraham Lincoln: "I am a firm believer in the people. If given the truth, they can meet any national crisis. The great point is to give them the real facts." Legendary journalist George Seldes had listed it in his book of quotations, *The Great Thoughts*, cited merely with "Attributed." But when I contacted Dr. Daniel W. Stowell, director of the Papers of Abraham Lincoln at the Lincoln Presidential Library and Museum in Springfield, Illinois, to verify the authenticity of the quotation, he replied, "I'm sorry to report that we have no evidence that Lincoln made this statement." He also referred me to another historian, Dr. Thomas F. Schwartz, at the time the Illinois State Historian and Director of Research and the Lincoln Collection in the Lincoln Presidential Library, who had explicitly called the quotation out as a "misnomer" in an article entitled "Lincoln Never Said That."[1]

Of course, the profound irony of this painful discovery—five years into researching the book—was not lost on me, then or now. Indeed, it is a sobering metaphor for this very difficult, necessarily meticulous undertaking in which very little can be safely assumed. And then, after all of that soul-searching about the use of the word *truth* in the title, my publisher decided that *935 Lies* is a better title, more engaging and reflective of the actual substance of the book. And that new circumstance presented yet another irony for me, because when the Center for Public Integrity and my book researchers and I released *Iraq: The War Card* in January 2008, we very consciously and assiduously had *avoided* using the word *lie*, instead preferring phrases such as "false and erroneous statements."[2] Why? Because whether or not these officials' precise motives can be ascertained or it can even be conclusively established that they had an overt, premeditated *intent* to lie are quite difficult things to determine without unfettered access to the principals and their internal communications—which no journalist or historian has yet been given.

Unfortunately, perhaps more confounding is an even larger, equally unsatisfying issue to ponder: Is there an unequivocal intent to lie, and is that how we should define it, if the presumed prevaricator actually *believes* his or her outright falsehoods? Over the centuries, Homo sapiens has certainly demonstrated a deeply disturbing capacity for self-delusion, as have entire nations occasionally mired in their own mythologies. And along these lines, perhaps the German philosopher Friedrich Nietzsche said it best, that "convictions are more dangerous enemies of truth than lies."[3] Of course, whether Bush and his most senior officials truly *believed* what they said so many times, or they knowingly, unabashedly, were premeditatively making monstrous misrepresentations over and over and over again, the public mind was clearly misled. They—and certainly we—were all victims of the "illusion-of-truth effect," which is that "you are more likely to believe that a statement is true if you have heard it before—whether or not it is actually true." The impact, then, of 935 false statements made by the highest US officials and their exponential reiterations throughout all forms of mass media around the world over a period of more than two years was and remains palpably and painfully discernible.[4]

At the same time, many of the most important, contemporary issues mentioned here—the extent of journalistic truth-telling or laryngitis or mythmaking, presidential misrepresentations leading up to war and what exactly we should call them, the specific uses and abuses of political and corporate power and the related obfuscations, and so on—are highly contentious subjects often seen only through partisan or ideological or financially self-interested lenses. As we've seen, there are few widely accepted truths about the past or the present in these very polarized United States of America, so I fully expect that there will be disagreement or contentiousness about some things that have been written here, irrespective of the sourcing or documentation. C'est la vie.

Having told the story of how the Center for Public Integrity came to be in various venues in the past (but not in as much detail as here) and having written numerous published articles about the state of journalism and in particular nonprofit journalism over the past seven years, in places such as the *Columbia Journalism Review, IRE Journal, Chronicle of Philanthropy*, Harvard *Nieman Reports*, the Shorenstein Center for Press, Politics and Public Policy, the *Princeton Reader*, Oxford University's Reuters Institute, the Investigative Reporting Workshop, and elsewhere, contained herein is some limited material from these ruminations.[5] And finally, though my researchers and I have earnestly attempted to avoid them and considering the long and winding road from word processor to the published page, replete with copyediting changes and the later additions of pagination and source notes, I certainly take full responsibility and also apologize for any inadvertent *factual* errors or omissions that may be contained herein.

This massive project was enriched but also became much more complicated because of two very large detours along the way—the aforementioned, epic *Iraq: The War Card* investigation into the false statements made by President George W. Bush and seven of his top aides for two full years after 9/11, and *Investigating Power*, the online, multimedia presentation of high-definition video interviews I did with two dozen important national journalists, whose pesky questions and independent news coverage exposed and infuriated the powers that be from 1950 to today. The ongoing work-in-progress, www.InvestigatingPower.org, was unveiled publicly on April 25, 2012, at the National Press Club in Washington and on National Public Radio's program *All Things Considered* and elsewhere.[6] Both of these multiyear research efforts produced detailed, historic context and information that has been invaluable to me in terms of editorial steeping, perspective, and so forth, but of course, are also substantial accoutrements to this book for you, the reader.

Both of these projects emanated from the Fund for Independence in Journalism, a nonprofit, legal-defense, and endowment-support organization, now dormant, begun in 2003, of which I was the founding president until stepping down at the end of 2008. No one lived and breathed the two-and-a-half-year, Herculean *War Card* project more than the immensely talented, indefatigable Mark Reading-Smith, the senior researcher/editor there. Imagine culling through *thousands* of national security threat-related statements by the top Bush officials between September 11, 2001, and 2003, affixing those specifically referencing the alleged weapons-of-mass-destruction threat posed by Saddam Hussein's Iraq onto a two-year daily calendar, separately analyzing more than fifty government, journalistic, and other Iraq War–related books and reports written between 2001 and 2008, and then juxtaposing what was said *publicly* each day by officialdom against what was *privately* known and being thought and said inside the government, painstakingly gleaned from those accounts. Special thanks also to Benjamin Turner, Matthew Lewis (no relation), Jeanne Brooks, Stephanie Carnes, Jennifer Spector, Mike Holmes, Julia Dahl, Julie Mañes Bostian, and our web developer Han Nguyen at the Fund for Independence in Journalism, and the excellent folks at the Center for Public Integrity, who also helped ready the final product in the closing days prior to the January 23, 2008, publication and National Press Club news conference—executive director Bill Buzenberg, Helena Bengtsson, Sara Bularzik, Lisa Chiu, Caitlin Ginley, Alan Green, C. Benjamin Haag, Bill Hogan, Josh Israel, Sarah Laskow, Tuan Le, Peter Newbatt Smith, and Devin Varsalona.

In 2007, amid the exhaustive *War Card* research, we also began contacting, scheduling, and shooting high-definition video interviews with twenty-three major national journalists—Christiane Amanpour, Ben Bagdikian, Dean Baquet, Don Barlett, Lowell Bergman, Carl Bernstein, Walt Bogdanich, Ben Bradlee, John Carroll, Florence Graves, Seymour Hersh, Bill Kovach, Murrey Marder, Morton Mintz, Moses Newson, Dana Priest, Gene Roberts, Daniel Schorr, Jim Steele, Barry Sussman, Helen Thomas, Mike Wallace, and Bob Woodward—who each kindly agreed to sit down with me for at least two hours each in Washington, New York, and Berkeley, California. Preparation prior to these interviews was substantial—biographical files and career time lines assembled, the most notable career works gathered and read, and so on—and these interviews were recorded by the end of 2008, transcribed, and from then until late April 2012, over one hundred hours of two-camera (F-900 high-definition cameras, the very best then available) material was screened and distilled into fifty-one produced videos (forty-two conversations and nine short documentaries), totaling approximately four hours and available for reading and viewing online at www.InvestigatingPower.org.

Special thanks to the multimedia project's senior producer and my longtime colleague and friend dating back two decades, Margaret "Mishi" Ebrahim, a former reporter at the Center for Public Integrity, producer for ABC News, *60 Minutes II*, and HDNet's *Dan Rather Reports*, and currently senior producer at the Investigative Reporting Workshop; producer and video editor Ted Roach, a brilliant American University 2011 MFA grad; associate producer Mark Reading-Smith; and our wonderfully creative and infinitely patient website designer and developer, Tarek Anandan. Thanks also to researchers Jeanne Brooks, Dan Ettinger, Vaughn Hillyard, Fritz Kramer, Matthew Lewis, Kate Musselwhite, David Schultz, Allison Terry, Ben Turner, and Valerie Wexler, and to website editor Lynne Perri, copy editor Marcia Kramer, program designer Alissa Scheller, web producers Lydia Beyoud, Yasmine El-Sabawi, and Abbie Kagan. Nearly all of the camera and sound work was done by Ventana Productions—but special thanks also to Investigative Reporting Workshop filmmaker-in-residence, Professor Larry Engel, cameraman and video editor.

Possibly the most important component contained within this book, though, may be the two "Real-Time Truth" charts chronicling some of US history's most heinous government and corporate abuses of power, when they were "officially" recognized as such, and when the first, substantive news reporting about them occurred. The idea for the charts emanated from a creative conversation among Mark Reading-Smith, Matt Lewis, and me—could there be a way to analyze and assess the worst "mortally consequential" deceptions in the United States over the past seventy-five to one hundred years and to gauge precisely *how long* it took the public to actually discover the awful, willfully obscured truths? Over the next five years, at my request, Matt quietly developed long memoranda and compiled files on roughly twenty-five case studies from the most authoritative sourcing, and we refined these charts and entries through multiple drafts into their final form. I am deeply grateful to him for his patience, dedication, and intellectual fortitude; not surprisingly, he is completing two separate master's degrees simultaneously at the University of Minnesota.

A Note from the Author

Other specific, requested research was provided by five Harvard Kennedy School of Government researchers in the spring of 2006, when I was a Shorenstein Fellow there: Tim Coates, Emma Greenman, Rebecca Hummel, Katie Selenski, and Greg Wilson. Their wide-ranging findings were very insightful, as was the research done by Justin Gengler, a doctoral student at the University of Michigan; Sarah Dorsey, my teaching assistant at American University; and former Center for Public Integrity reporter and forensic auditor Derrick Wetherell (asked to very closely scrutinize the Securities and Exchange annual 10K forms of the largest media corporations in America). And at the Investigative Reporting Workshop between 2010 and early 2012, Valerie Wexler provided excellent research, as did Giovanni Russonello, history cum laude grad and former editor in chief of the *Tufts* (University) *Daily* for one full year. The closing months before completing the manuscript were hugely aided by Brandeis University "Washington Semester program" intern Abigail Kagan and especially my yearlong American University School of Communication grad student teaching assistant David Schultz. And my former TA and American University master's alum, Kate Musselwhite, now at the *Washington Post*, was heroic and just plain awesome in the frenetic final days. Thank you.

All of the above people who worked on *Iraq: The War Card*, *Investigating Power*, and *935 Lies* more broadly were, of course, paid. This entire, exceedingly ambitious endeavor simply would not have been possible without the kindness and generosity of individual ($1,000 or more) and foundation donors, many of whom have been very encouraging and supportive of my work for many years. I warmly thank and will always be deeply grateful to: the American Communications Foundation and its founder Cynthia Perry; the Baker-Root Family Foundation; Richard Beattie; Emily Bingham; Jack Block; Geri Mannion and the Carnegie Corporation of New York; Lance Lindblom and the Nathan Cummings Foundation; Mary Stake Hawker and the Deer Creek Foundation; Victor Elmaleh; The Ethics and Excellence in Journalism Foundation; the Ford Foundation; Conrad Martin and the Fund for Constitutional Government; Debby Leff, Larry Hanson, and the Joyce Foundation; the John S. and James L. Knight Foundation; Arthur Lipson; Donna Mae Litowitz and the Litowitz Foundation; Bevis

A Note from the Author

Longstreth; Paula Madison and the Nell Williams Family Foundation; Elspeth Revere and the John D. and Catherine T. MacArthur Foundation; Amy McCombs; the McCormick Foundation; Chico Newman and the John and Florence Newman Foundation; George Soros and the Open Society Foundations; Glen Osterhout; Adelaide Gomer, Bill Bondurant, and the Park Foundation; Sol and Robert Price; Stephen Heintz, Ben Shute, and Rockefeller Brothers Fund; Wade Greene and Rockefeller Family Associates; Lee Wasserman and the Rockefeller Family Foundation; Pamela and George Rohr; Vin Ryan and the Schooner Foundation; Bill Moyers and the Schumann Center for Media and Democracy; Marge Tabankin and the Streisand Foundation; former Fund for Independence in Journalism Board member Paul Volcker; the Public Welfare Foundation; David Haas and the Wyncote Foundation; and the Malcolm H. Wiener Foundation.

These wonderful sponsors have supported my work with my colleagues through the nonprofit organizations I have led, either the Center for Public Integrity (1989–2004), the Fund for Independence in Journalism (2005–2008), and/or the Investigative Reporting Workshop (since 2008) at the American University School of Communication, all in Washington. Barbara Schecter helped me *quintuple* the size of the Center for Public Integrity between 1996 and 2004 as our brilliant development director and has played the same magnificent role at the Investigative Reporting Workshop! To Barbara and all of my colleagues at the workshop—managing editor Lynne Perri, senior producer Mishi Ebrahim, senior editors Wendell Cochran and John Sullivan, and financial operations manager Kris Higgins, thanks very much for your patience and understanding regarding the necessary time away from the office to write this book.

And certainly, I want to thank visionary American University School of Communication dean Larry Kirkman, who encouraged the creation and exciting evolution of the workshop, championed *Iraq: The War Card* and *Investigating Power*, and also gave me a semester off from teaching in early 2008 to allow me time to research and write this book. His talented successor as dean, Jeff Rutenbeck, has been similarly enthusiastic and encouraging. And Center for Public Integrity executive director Bill Buzenberg has also been very encouraging during all facets of this long project, at all times, for which I am very grateful.

A Note from the Author

At a certain point, it became clear to family, friends, and colleagues that I needed to get away for an extended period of quality time, substantially away from daily, non-book responsibilities, travel, speaking, serving on a dozen boards and advisory boards, and to as large an extent as possible, to get off the grid. If I didn't, this book might never get finished.

In the summer of 2011, I was very fortunate to receive an artist-in-residence grant from the Helene Wurlitzer Foundation of New Mexico, and I spent a month in full immersion in a small but perfect casita, sans television or Internet service, in Taos, New Mexico. Although I am a native of Delaware and have lived my entire life in the mid-Atlantic region of the United States, I have always had an indescribable, personal connection with the Land of Enchantment, since hiking fifty miles at Philmont Scout Ranch in Cimarron in July 1969 and hearing Neil Armstrong's first words on a transistor radio as he walked on the moon while my young colleagues and I were camped on the side of a mountain, peering up at the beautiful sky that starry night. Special thanks to the Wurlitzer Foundation, the brilliant and wonderfully supportive artists in residence I befriended while there, and its fine executive director, Michael Knight.

Prior to the New Mexico writing sojourn, back in the spring of 2006, I was honored to be named a Fellow at the Shorenstein Center on the Press, Politics and Public Policy at Harvard University. Its director, Alex Jones, encouraged me to write about "The Growing Importance of Non-profit Journalism," which set me on a track toward publicly encouraging and documenting the evolution of "the new journalism ecosystem" ever since. I am deeply grateful to Alex and everyone at the Shorenstein Center for that extraordinary experience, and separately, back in Washington before and afterward, to Ben Bradlee and Bill Kovach for our indelible ruminations about what has happened to truth, and why.

I want to thank Esther Newberg, of International Creative Management (ICM) in New York, who has been my literary agent for three prior books dating back to the late 1990s. This voyage was much longer and more difficult than any before it, and I deeply appreciate her patience and steadfast support. Special thanks also to Marc Miller, who vetted the Center for Public Integrity's copy its first twenty-one years, to whom I am forever indebted and who also kindly reviewed this manuscript prior to publication. And special thanks, of course, to PublicAffairs founder and editor at large Peter Osnos, publisher Clive Priddle, and gifted and very deft editor Karl Weber.

This book would not have come to fruition without the genius and brilliant sensibilities of my friend and former colleague at the Center for Public Integrity, Alan Green—an incredibly talented reporter, writer, and editor, but more broadly, sage. I will always warmly remember and appreciate the long hours and magnificent dedication and "heart" of every Center for Public Integrity Board and Advisory Board member, staffer, and intern with whom I had the honor of working. Thank you and May the Force Be With You!

Finally, this book is dedicated to my long-suffering wife, Pamela Gilbert. She has endured the long gestation processes of six books during the more than nineteen years of our wonderful marriage. During my work on *The Buying of the President 2004*, our then three-year-old son, Gabriel, pointed at my study and told a visitor, "That's where my Daddy lives." Pamela is one of the leading consumer advocates in the United States today, the former director of Congress Watch (part of Public Citizen), executive director of the U.S. Consumer Product Safety Commission between 1996 and 2001, and today a partner in the Washington law firm Cuneo Gilbert and LaDuca. Her difficult, unsung work on behalf of consumers has saved an incalculable number of lives in this country. I am very proud to be her husband, and her razor-sharp, precise, lawyerly mind and real-world instincts, not to mention her steady, always fair-minded and wise judgment, have been immeasurably helpful to me.

The fact that she happens to be beautiful and is also a magnificent, loving mother to Gabriel and stepmother to my award-winning playwright daughter, Cassie (Cassandra Lewis—see www.BastilleArts.com) seems almost too good to be true—but it is! I could not possibly have a more supportive family, which now also includes a terrific son-in-law, Peter Worrall Slattery. And, as always, encouraging and watching my back from day one, is my mother, Dorothy Cherry Lewis, an American original if ever there was one.

Charles Lewis
Washington, DC
February 4, 2014

Appendix A: Real-Time Truth Charts

A S SHOWN THROUGHOUT THIS BOOK, mortally consequential lies by those in power have often taken months, years, or even decades to discover, a painstaking process in our increasingly impatient and otherwise distracted society. In the easily manipulable information age we live in today, truth delayed is truth (and accountability) denied. And that means the public is often deluded about the most important issues of the day until it's too late to do anything meaningful about them.

The following charts illustrate the painful process by which falsehoods have been finally uncovered and the truth revealed—along with the unconscionable delays forced by those in power who have an interest in keeping the public in the dark.

Some Historic Corporate Abuses and Their Delayed Official Recognition

Abuse of Power	Official Recognition	Reportage
LEAD PAINT POISONING		
1923: Lead paint industry engages in ad campaign focusing on children promising "lead helps to guard your health." For years, industry promoted use in hospitals, classrooms.[1]	1971: President Nixon signs the Lead-Based Paint Poisoning Prevention Act, which capped lead content and started the path toward an eventual ban.[2]	Study of lead paint poisoning among children is reported by *Time* in 1943; *Parade* and CBS reported major stories in 1956.[3]
HEALTH RISKS FROM ASBESTOS		
1934: Internal memos from asbestos industry executives recommend purposeful manipulation of medical findings on asbestos's harm to workers, beginning a pattern stretching multiple decades wherein industry suppressed asbestosis dangers.[4]	1964: Mt. Sinai Medical Center team led by Dr. Irving Selikoff publishes comprehensive, definitive study on asbestos and occupational disease, proving dangers of exposure including links to cancer.[5]	Paul Brodeur begins reporting on asbestos in the *New Yorker* in 1968. His reporting continues through the 1970s and leads to a highly influential series in 1985. Others report on asbestos papers as revealed in trial in 1978.[6]

CONTINUES

249

Abuse of Power	Official Recognition	Reportage
LOVE CANAL		
1942: Hooker Chemical begins dumping more than 20,000 tons of chemicals into the abandoned "Love Canal" on a property later sold to the Niagara Falls School Board. In 1945 a Hooker manufacturing analyst wrote about concerns with health effects and potential lawsuits. Reports would ultimately show toxicity caused chromosomal damage and birth defects.[7]	1978–1995: The New York Department of Health first declares Love Canal "an extremely serious [health] threat" and four months later declares a state of emergency (1978); President Carter declares a national emergency (1980); parent company Occidental Chemical agrees to settlements with residents (1983), New York State (1994), and federal government (1995).[8]	Reporters from the *Niagara Gazette* report on toxic chemicals in 1976, but reporter Mike Brown begins covering the story more aggressively and making public health connections in a series beginning in spring 1978. National media follow with extensive print and television coverage.[9]
BLACK LUNG DISEASE		
1943: British deem black lung a compensable condition; US coal industry and Public Health Service continue on without comprehensive dust standards.[10]	1969: US passes Federal Coal Mine Health and Safety Act.[11]	Media covers West Virginia disaster in 1968 and in 1969 begins to pay more attention to general problems in industry.[12]
CANCER AND SMOKING		
1954: Following landmark health studies in 1950 in the *Journal of the American Medical Association* and *British Medical Journal* linking tobacco use to lung cancer, the Tobacco Industry Research Committee begins public relations campaigns claiming no ill health effects from tobacco smoke.[13]	1964: US surgeon general declares link between smoking and lung cancer in 1957, but definitive recognition comes from comprehensive report on smoking dangers.[14]	*Reader's Digest* stories from 1952–1957 were cause for significant public discussion. Other print publications covered the 1950s medical findings. In 1955 CBS's "See It Now" links cigarette smoking with lung cancer.[15]
THALIDOMIDE AND BIRTH DEFECTS		
1958: German and English drug companies market recently released thalidomide sedatives as safe for pregnant women.[16]	1961–1962: Thalidomide is pulled from markets after physicians made discoveries; US company withdraws FDA application.[17]	German story in 1961; *Washington Post*'s Mintz on FDA in 1962; *Sunday Times* team publish definitive court stories in 1976–1977.[18]
AGENT ORANGE		
1965: Confidential Dow Chemical memo calls Agent Orange "one of the most toxic materials known." Industry leaders secretly meet to discuss contaminant's health threat.[19]	1970: US military stops spraying and surgeon general bans home use; Dow Chemical, Monsanto, other companies settle class-action lawsuit with US veterans for $180 million; Agent Orange Act passes Congress.[20]	A 1970 series in the *New Yorker* by Thomas Whiteside caused the US Senate to hold hearings on Agent Orange.[21]

Abuse of Power	Official Recognition	Reportage
DISEASE FROM PVC		
1966: Confidential internal memo from meeting among B.F. Goodrich Company, Union Carbide, Monsanto, others reveal industry states "there is no question" as to occupational disease caused by PVC.[22]	1974: NIOSH director authors medical report finding a "direct causal relationship" between exposure and "pathological findings." OSHA conducts public hearings, publishes standard for exposure. FDA, EPA, and CPSC take action on bans.[23]	*New York Times* reporter Jane Brody reports ongoing developments in vinyl chloride story throughout 1974; Joe Klein's lengthy 1976 article in *Rolling Stone* also causes broader public awareness.[24]
FORD PINTO		
1971: Confidential internal memo at Ford Motor discloses decision not to make safety improvements to Pinto until "required by law" despite internal "Pricor Report" outlining safety problems.[25]	1978: A National Highway Traffic Safety Administration investigation finds a safety defect existed in 1971–1976 Ford Pintos; Ford announces major recall.[26]	Mark Dowie breaks the story in *Mother Jones* in 1977 revealing internal documents, which leads to NHTSA investigation. *Chicago Tribune* reporters publish more internal documents in 1979.[27]
VIOXX		
2000: Merck trial results show cardiovascular risks from Vioxx research chief says the problems "are clearly there." *New England Journal of Medicine* report altered. [28]	2004: Merck pulls Vioxx from market worldwide due to acknowledgment of cardiovascular risks.[29]	In 2004 the *Wall Street Journal* reports on internal e-mails showing company knowledge of Vioxx dangers.[30]

Some Historic Government Abuses and Their Delayed Official Recognition

Abuse of Power	Official Recognition	Reportage
TUSKEGEE SYPHILIS STUDY		
1932: US Public Health Service launches untreated Tuskegee syphilis study of 600 uninformed black males.[31]	1972: After years of secret complaints, whistleblower steps forward, talks to reporter.[32]	AP reporter passes leak to peer Jean Heller in 1972. Her article breaks open the story.[33]
HUMAN RADIATION EXPERIMENTS		
1944: Federal government sponsors human radiation experiments on Americans that extend for decades and number in the thousands.[34]	1995: Clinton accepts report of commission investigating the experiments, speaks to the American public.[35]	Eileen Welsome series runs in the *Albuquerque Tribune* in 1993.[36]
GUATEMALA SYPHILIS STUDY		
1946: Federal Health Service sponsors syphilis study in Guatemala, infecting nearly 700 unaware prisoners and mental patients.[37]	2010: US government issues a formal apology to the Guatemalan people.[38]	Historian Susan M. Reverby discovers records in 2010, prompting global reportage.[39]

CONTINUES

Abuse of Power	Official Recognition	Reportage
GULF OF TONKIN INCIDENT		
1964: US attacks North Vietnam; LBJ gets Gulf of Tonkin Senate Resolution under false pretenses.[40]	1968, 1971: Sen. Fulbright holds Gulf of Tonkin hearings, apologizes to the nation; Pentagon Papers reveal details of false attack.[41]	Prominent media outlets report on Fulbright investigation in 1968; publish reports on excerpts from Pentagon Papers upon 1971 release.[42]
ELLSBERG BREAK-IN		
1971: Nixon "plumbers" break into Pentagon Papers whistleblower Daniel Ellsberg's psychiatrist's office.[43]	1973: In Ellsberg's trial a federal judge calls the break-in "improper government conduct."[44]	Media covers the eventually dismissed trial of Ellsberg in 1973.[45]
WATERGATE SCANDAL		
1969–1973: Nixon administration sanctions years of various high crimes and misdemeanors capped by the Watergate break-in and cover-up.[46]	1972–1974: DC police arrest burglars; Sen. Ervin and Rep. Rodino lead televised impeachment hearings, issue reports.[47]	The *Washington Post*, *New York Times*, *Time*, and others report the story from 1972 on.[48]
SECRET WAR IN NICARAGUA		
1981: Reagan signs secret finding justifying prior authorization of covert Nicaraguan Contra support, beginning a five-year process of circumventing Congress.[49]	1982: Rep. Edward Boland spearheads first of three amendments to ban covert support, compares action to Gulf of Tonkin.[50]	*Newsweek* cover story in Nov. 1982 takes extensive look at the "secret war for Nicaragua."[51]
IRAN-CONTRA SCANDAL		
1985: US approves arms shipments from Israel to Iran in exchange for hostages; some profits eventually support Nicaraguan Contras.[52]	1986: Following his attorney general's investigation, Reagan announces that weapons sales to Iran assisted the Contras.[53]	Lebanese magazine *Al-Shiraa* breaks the story on arms for hostages Nov. 3, 1986, leading to Western media coverage.[54]
EL MOZOTE MASSACRE		
1981: US-trained Salvadoran battalion slaughters hundreds of its own innocent people in El Mozote.[55]	1993: UN Truth Commission issues definitive war crimes report.[56]	The *New York Times* and *Washington Post* publish within weeks of massacre to cold official reaction.[57]
JUSTIFICATION FOR IRAQ WAR		
2001: Bush administration begins making public case for Iraq War based on WMD possession, link to al Qaeda.[58]	2004: 9/11 Commission finds no notable al Qaeda link and the "Duelfer Report" finds no WMD.[59]	Knight Ridder reporting team challenges admin. assumptions in 2002; numerous authors publish critical books in 2004.[60]

Appendix B: The Iraq War Card

P RESIDENT GEORGE W. BUSH and seven of his administration's top officials, including Vice President Dick Cheney, National Security Adviser Condoleezza Rice, and Defense Secretary Donald Rumsfeld, made at least 935 false statements in the two years following September 11, 2001, about the national security threat posed by Saddam Hussein's Iraq. Nearly five years after the US invasion of Iraq, an exhaustive examination of the record shows that the statements were part of an orchestrated campaign that effectively galvanized public opinion and, in the process, led the nation to war under decidedly false pretenses.

On at least 532 separate occasions (in speeches, briefings, interviews, testimony, and the like), Bush and these three key officials, along with Secretary of State Colin Powell, Deputy Defense Secretary Paul Wolfowitz, and White House Press Secretaries Ari Fleischer and Scott McClellan, stated unequivocally that Iraq had weapons of mass destruction (or was trying to produce or obtain them), links to al Qaeda, or both. This concerted effort was the underpinning of the Bush administration's case for war.

It is now beyond dispute that Iraq did not possess any weapons of mass destruction or have meaningful ties to al Qaeda. This was the conclusion of numerous bipartisan government investigations, including those by the Senate Select Committee on Intelligence (2004 and 2006), the 9/11 Commission, and the multinational Iraq Survey Group, whose "Duelfer Report" established that Saddam Hussein had terminated Iraq's nuclear program in 1991 and made little effort to restart it.

In short, the Bush administration led the nation to war on the basis of erroneous information that it methodically propagated and that culminated in military action against Iraq on March 19, 2003. Not surprisingly, the officials with the most opportunities to make speeches, grant media interviews,

IRAQ: THE WAR CARD

ORCHESTRATED DECEPTION ON THE PATH TO WAR: SEPT. 2001 - SEPT. 2003

935: False Statements by Top Bush Administration Officials on Iraq's Possession of WMD and Links to Al Qaeda

"Simply stated, there is no doubt that Saddam Hussein now has WMD..." – Vice President Dick Cheney, August 26, 2002.

■ False statements about Iraq's possession of weapons of mass destruction

■ False statements about Iraq's links to Al Qaeda

March 19, 2003: The war begins as coalition forces strike Baghdad.

February 5, 2003: Prior to submitting a draft United Nations resolution, Secretary of State Colin Powell tells the U.N. Security Council there is "no doubt" Saddam Hussein has weapons of mass destruction and has the capability to produce more.

September 19, 2002: President Bush sends his war resolution to Congress to authorize the use of force in Iraq. The House and Senate vote in favor on October 10 and 11.

TOTAL **935**

9/11

BUSH **260**

POWELL **254**

RUMSFELD **109**

FLEISCHER **109**

WOLFOWITZ **85**

RICE **56**

CHENEY **48**

McCLELLAN **14**

A project of The Center for Public Integrity • www.publicintegrity.org

and otherwise frame the public debate also made the most false statements, according to this first-ever analysis of the entire body of prewar rhetoric.

President Bush, for example, made 232 false statements about weapons of mass destruction in Iraq and another 28 false statements about Iraq's links to al Qaeda. Secretary of State Powell had the second-highest total in the two-year period, with 244 false statements about weapons of mass destruction in Iraq and 10 about Iraq's links to al Qaeda. Rumsfeld and Fleischer each made 109 false statements, followed by Wolfowitz (with 85), Rice (with 56), Cheney (with 48), and McClellan (with 14).

The massive database at the heart of this project juxtaposes what President Bush and these seven top officials were saying for public consumption against what was known, or should have been known, on a day-to-day basis. This fully searchable database includes the public statements, drawn from both primary sources (such as official transcripts) and secondary sources (chiefly major news organizations) over the two years beginning on September 11, 2001. It also interlaces relevant information from numerous government reports, books, articles, speeches, and interviews.

Consider, for example, these false public statements made in the run-up to war:

+ On August 26, 2002, in an address to the national convention of the Veterans of Foreign Wars, Cheney flatly declared: "Simply stated, there is no doubt that Saddam Hussein now has weapons of mass destruction. There is no doubt he is amassing them to use against our friends, against our allies, and against us." In fact, former CIA director George Tenet later recalled, Cheney's assertions went well beyond his agency's assessments at the time. Another CIA official, referring to the same speech, told journalist Ron Suskind, "Our reaction was, 'Where is he getting this stuff from?'"[1]
+ In the closing days of September 2002, with a congressional vote fast approaching on authorizing the use of military force in Iraq, Bush told the nation in his weekly radio address: "The Iraqi regime possesses biological and chemical weapons, is rebuilding the facilities to make more and, according to the British government, could launch a biological or chemical attack in as little as forty-five minutes after

the order is given. . . . This regime is seeking a nuclear bomb, and with fissile material could build one within a year." A few days later, similar findings were also included in a much-hurried National Intelligence Estimate on Iraq's weapons of mass destruction—an analysis that hadn't been done in years, as the intelligence community had deemed it unnecessary and the White House hadn't requested it.[2]

♦ In July 2002, Rumsfeld had a one-word answer for reporters who asked whether Iraq had relationships with al Qaeda terrorists: "Sure." In fact, an assessment issued that same month by the Defense Intelligence Agency (and confirmed weeks later by CIA director Tenet) found an absence of "compelling evidence demonstrating direct cooperation between the government of Iraq and Al Qaeda." What's more, an earlier DIA assessment said that "the nature of the regime's relationship with al Qaeda is unclear."[3]

♦ On May 29, 2003, in an interview with Polish TV, President Bush declared: "We found the weapons of mass destruction. We found biological laboratories." But as journalist Bob Woodward reported in *State of Denial*, days earlier a team of civilian experts dispatched to examine the two mobile labs found in Iraq had concluded in a field report that the labs were not for biological weapons. The team's final report, completed the following month, concluded that the labs had probably been used to manufacture hydrogen for weather balloons.[4]

♦ On January 28, 2003, in his annual State of the Union address, Bush asserted: "The British government has learned that Saddam Hussein recently sought significant quantities of uranium from Africa. Our intelligence sources tell us that he has attempted to purchase high-strength aluminum tubes suitable for nuclear weapons production." Two weeks earlier, an analyst with the State Department's Bureau of Intelligence and Research had sent an e-mail to colleagues in the intelligence community laying out why he believed the uranium-purchase agreement "probably is a hoax."[5]

♦ On February 5, 2003, in an address to the United Nations Security Council, Powell said: "What we're giving you are facts and conclusions based on solid intelligence. I will cite some examples, and these are from human sources." As it turned out, however, two of the main human sources to which Powell referred had provided false information. One was an Iraqi con artist, code-named "Curveball," whom American intelligence officials were dubious about and in fact had never even spoken to. The other was an al Qaeda detainee, Ibn al-Sheikh al-Libi, who had reportedly been sent to Egypt by the CIA and tortured and who later recanted the information he had provided. Libi told the CIA in January 2004 that he had "decided he would fabricate any information interrogators wanted in order to gain better treatment and avoid being handed over to [a foreign government]."[6]

The false statements dramatically increased in August 2002, with congressional consideration of a war resolution, then escalated through the midterm elections and spiked even higher from January 2003 to the eve of the invasion.

It was during those critical weeks in early 2003 that the president delivered his State of the Union address and Powell delivered his memorable UN presentation.

In addition to their patently false pronouncements, Bush and these seven top officials also made hundreds of other statements in the two years after 9/11, in which they implied that Iraq had weapons of mass destruction or links to al Qaeda. Other administration higher-ups, joined by Pentagon officials and Republican leaders in Congress, also routinely sounded false war alarms in the Washington echo chamber.

The cumulative effect of these false statements—amplified by thousands of news stories and broadcasts—was massive, with the media coverage creating an almost impenetrable din for several critical months in the run-up to war. Some journalists—indeed, even some entire news organizations—have since acknowledged that their coverage during those pre-war months was far too deferential and uncritical. These mea culpas notwithstanding, much of the wall-to-wall media coverage provided additional, "independent" validation of the Bush administration's false statements about Iraq.

The "ground truth" of the Iraq War itself eventually forced the president to backpedal, albeit grudgingly. In a 2004 appearance on NBC's *Meet the Press*, for example, Bush acknowledged that no weapons of mass destruction had been found in Iraq. And on December 18, 2005, with his approval ratings on the decline, Bush told the nation in a Sunday-night address from the Oval Office: "It is true that Saddam Hussein had a history of pursuing and using weapons of mass destruction. It is true that he systematically concealed those programs, and blocked the work of U.N. weapons inspectors. It is true that many nations believed that Saddam had weapons of mass destruction. But much of the intelligence turned out to be wrong. As your president, I am responsible for the decision to go into Iraq. Yet it was right to remove Saddam Hussein from power."

Bush stopped short, however, of admitting error or poor judgment; instead, his administration repeatedly attributed the stark disparity between its prewar public statements and the actual "ground truth" regarding the threat posed by Iraq to poor intelligence from a Who's Who of domestic agencies.

On the other hand, a growing number of critics, including a parade of former government officials, have publicly—and in some cases vociferously—accused the president and his inner circle of ignoring or distorting the available intelligence. In the end, these critics say, it was the calculated drumbeat of false information and public pronouncements that ultimately misled the American people and this nation's allies on their way to war.

Bush and the top officials of his administration have so far largely avoided the harsh, sustained glare of formal scrutiny about their personal responsibility for the litany of repeated, false statements in the run-up to the war in Iraq. There has been no congressional investigation, for example, into what exactly was going on inside the Bush White House in that period. Congressional oversight has focused almost entirely on the quality of the US government's pre-war intelligence—not the judgment, public statements, or public accountability of its highest officials. And, of course, only four of the officials—Powell, Rice, Rumsfeld, and Wolfowitz—have testified before Congress about Iraq.

Short of such review, this project provides a heretofore unavailable framework for examining how the US war in Iraq came to pass. Clearly, it calls into question the repeated assertions of Bush administration officials that they were the unwitting victims of bad intelligence.

Appendix B: The Iraq War Card

Above all, the 935 false statements painstakingly presented here finally help to answer two all-too-familiar questions as they apply to Bush and his top advisers: What did they know, and when did they know it?

This section is reprinted with permission from Charles Lewis and Mark Reading-Smith, "False Pretenses" in Iraq: The War Card *(Washington, DC: The Center for Public Integrity, January 23, 2008), http://www .publicintegrity.org/2008/01/23/5641/false-pretenses, accessed March 9, 2014.*

Notes

EPIGRAPHS

1. William Shakespeare, *The Rape of Lucrece* (1593–1594), l. 29, cited in John Bartlett, *Bartlett's Familiar Quotations*, 16th ed. (New York: Little, Brown, 1992), gen. ed. Justin Kaplan, p. 167.

2. Thomas Jefferson, letter to Colonel Charles Yancey, January 6, 1816, cited in ibid., p. 344.

PROLOGUE: 935 LIES

1. Quoted in Sissela Bok, *Lying: Moral Choice in Public and Private Life* (New York: Pantheon Books, 1978), p. xv, cited from Augustine, "Lying," in *Treatises on Various Subjects*, Fathers of the Church, vol. 14, chap. 14 (New York: Catholic University of America Press, 1952), ed. R. J. Deferrari. See also writings about Augustine and his work in the Christian Classics Ethereal Library, at www.ccel.org.

2. Hannah Arendt, "Truth and Politics," in *The Portable Hannah Arendt*, ed., with an introduction by Peter Baehr (New York: Penguin Books, 2003), p. 568. Originally published in the *New Yorker*, February 25, 1967.

3. See ABC News/*Washington Post* poll, March 13, 2005: "Shortly before the war, do you think Iraq did have weapons of mass destruction that have not been found, or do you think Iraq did not have any weapons of mass destruction?" The response: 56 percent of the respondents answered yes, did have; 40 percent said did not have; 4 percent had no opinion. See also NBC News/*Wall Street Journal* poll, January 19, 2005: "Do you think that Iraq did or did not have weapons of mass destruction before the war began?" The response: 54 percent answered yes, did have; 40 percent said no, did not have, and 6 percent were "not sure." These and scores of other Iraq-related polls in the United States can be found at http://poll.orspub.com.proxyau.wrlc.org/. In a Dartmouth University survey of 1,056

respondents developed by Associate Professor Benjamin Valentino and conducted by YouGov (formerly Polimetrix) between April 26 and May 2, 2012, 63 percent of Republicans said they believed that Saddam Hussein's Iraq had weapons of mass destruction when the United States invaded it in 2003. See http://www.dartmouth .edu/~benv/files/poll%20responses%20by%20party%20ID.pdf.

4. The phrase "of the people, by the people and for the people" was in the last sentence in Lincoln's momentous Gettysburg Address, November 19, 1863. See Garry Wills, *Lincoln at Gettysburg: The Words That Remade America* (New York: Touchstone/Simon and Schuster, 2002), p. 263.

5. George Orwell, "Politics and the English Language," in *George Orwell: Volume 4, In Front of Your Nose, 1946–1950* (Boston: Nonpareil Books, 2000), ed. Sonia Orwell and Ian Angus, pp. 136, 139. This iconic essay was published in 1946.

6. "Methodology: A Look Inside the Center's Reporting Process for 'Iraq: The War Card,'" January 23, 2008, at http://www.publicintegrity.org/2008/01/23/5649 /methodology, accessed December 23, 2013.

7. Charles Lewis and Mark Reading-Smith, "False Pretenses," in *Iraq: The War Card* (Washington, DC: The Center for Public Integrity, January 23, 2008), at http://www.publicintegrity.org/politics/white-house/iraq-war-card, accessed December 23, 2013. See also John H. Cushman Jr., "Web Site Assembles U.S. Prewar Claims," *New York Times*, January 23, 2008, at http://www.nytimes.com/2008/01/23 /washington/23database.html, accessed January 23, 2013. Along with the overview narrative and chart, the two-year daily chronology includes every public, Iraq-related utterance by eight top officials, juxtaposed against the more than fifty books and commission and other government reports published between 2003 and 2008, retrospectively illuminating what was actually known inside the US government, versus what was said publicly. Earlier, in October 2003, six months after the Iraq War began, the Center had posted online all of the known US war contracts in Iraq and Afghanistan. "Windfalls of War" first identified that the corporation formerly run by Vice President Dick Cheney—Halliburton and its subsidiary Kellogg Brown and Root—had received by far the most taxpayer money from those contracts, and this investigative report won the first George Polk Award for Internet Reporting.

8. John H. Cushman, "An Online Scavenger Hunt on Prewar Claims: What Did You Find?" *New York Times*, January 23, 2008, *The Lede* blog, "Update," 4:29 p.m., http://thelede.blogs.nytimes.com/2008/01/23/an-online-scavenger -hunt-on-prewar-claims-what-did-you-find/, accessed January 3, 2013.

9. "Iraq War Illegal, Says Annan," BBC News, September 16, 2004, at http:// news.bbc.co.uk/2/hi/middle_east/3661134.stm, accessed December 23, 2013. Secretary General Kofi Annan, in reference to the invasion, said on September 16, 2004, that "it was not in conformity with the UN Charter. From our point of view, from the charter point of view, it was illegal." Six of the most insightful books about this critical period in US history, in alphabetical order by the author's name, are: Richard Bonin, *Arrows of the Night* (New York: Doubleday, 2011); Richard A. Clarke, *Against All Enemies* (New York: Free Press/Simon and Schuster, 2004);

Michael Isikoff and David Corn, *Hubris* (New York: Crown, 2006); James Mann, *Rise of the Vulcans* (New York: Viking, 2004); George Packer, *The Assassin's Gate* (New York: Farrar, Straus and Giroux, 2005); and Bob Woodward, *Plan of Attack* (New York: Simon and Schuster, 2004).

10. David Barstow, "Message Machine: Behind TV Analysts, Pentagon's Hidden Hand," *New York Times*, April 20, 2008, at http://www.pulitzer.org/archives/8338, accessed December 23, 2013. Barstow and the *Times* successfully sued the Department of Defense and gained Freedom of Information Act access to 8,000 pages of e-mail messages, transcripts, and other records detailing the years of hundreds of private briefings, shepherded trips to Iraq and Guantanamo, and the thousands of talking points provided to the retired officials-turned-commentators. Barstow was awarded the 2009 Pulitzer Prize for Investigative Reporting.

11. David Barstow and Robin Stein, "Under Bush, a New Age of Prepackaged TV News," *New York Times*, March 13, 2005, at http://www.nytimes .com/2005/03/13/politics/13covert.html, accessed December 23, 2013. Also see Christopher Lee, "Administration Rejects Ruling on PR Videos," *Washington Post*, March 15, 2005, at http://www.washingtonpost.com/wp-dyn/articles/A35010 -2005Mar14.html, accessed December 23, 2013.

12. Mike Allen, "Exclusive: McClellan Whacks Bush, White House," *Politico*, May 27, 2008, at http://dyn.politico.com/printstory.cfm?uuid=2C2AD8E6–3048 –5C12–00DD5B339097C9F9, accessed December 23, 2013. Also see Scott McClellan, *What Happened: Inside the Bush White House and Washington's Culture of Deception* (New York: PublicAffairs, 2008).

13. Priest and Risen/Lichtblau each won the Pulitzer Prize in 2006, for Beat Reporting and National Reporting, respectively. To read their stories, go to www .pulitzer.org. Nervous *Times* editors had sat on the domestic surveillance exposé for a year, under intense pressure from the White House, in the name of "national security," including by President Bush directly. But knowing Risen's book, *State of Siege: The Secret History of the CIA and the Bush Administration* (New York: Free Press/Simon and Schuster, 2006), would be published imminently, which would hugely embarrass the newspaper for having blocked the story, the *Times* finally decided to publish it in December 2005. For more about the internal *Times* angst and drama and related issues, read the PBS *Frontline* interview with then executive editor of the *New York Times*, Bill Keller, based on three interviews conducted on July 10, October 18, and November 30, 2006, as part of "Newswar," its four-part investigation based on more than fifty interviews. At http://www.pbs.org/wgbh /pages/frontline/newswar/interviews/keller.html, accessed December 23, 2013.

14. Daniel Trotta, "Iraq War Costs U.S. More Than $2 Trillion: Study," Reuters, March 14, 2013, at http://www.reuters.com/article/2013/03/14/us-iraq-war -anniversary-idUSBRE92D0PG20130314, accessed December 23, 2013. It is based upon a study by the Costs of War Project by the Watson Institute for International Studies at Brown University and the work of approximately thirty academics and experts, who estimated at least 134,000 Iraq civilians have been killed in the conflict. The number of US military and contractor personnel who

incurred "wounds, injuries and medical problems" in Iraq through 2012 was between "60,933–80,484" people. Catherine Lutz, "U.S. and Coalition Casualties in Iraq and Afghanistan," February 21, 2013, at http://costsofwar.org/sites/default /files/articles/11/attachments/USandCoalition.pdf, accessed February 1, 2014. But in light of various issues such as post-traumatic stress disorder (PTSD) and other complex and difficult medical problems, the number of living but suffering Americans from the US-led Iraq War may actually be much higher.

15. I previously expressed this sentiment in a similarly worded passage on the five-year anniversary of the invasion of Iraq, in: Charles Lewis, "Seeking New Ways to Nurture the Capacity to Report," *Nieman Reports* (Spring 2008), published by the Nieman Foundation for Journalism at Harvard University, at http://www .nieman.harvard.edu/reportsitem.aspx?id=100060, accessed December 23, 2013.

16. Tara McKelvey, "The Drone Wars: Administration Chooses Selective Silence," Investigative Reporting Workshop, August 2, 2013, at http://investigative reportingworkshop.org/investigations/obamas-drones/story/analysis_selective _silence/, accessed February 5, 2014; Declan Walsh and Ihsanullah Tipu Mehsud, "Civilian Deaths in Drone Strikes Cited in Report," *New York Times*, October 22, 2013, at http://www.nytimes.com/2013/10/22/world/asia/civilian-deaths-in -drone-strikes-cited-in-report.html?_r=0, accessed February 5, 2014. The report cited was an Amnesty International study. "Drone Wars Pakistan: Analysis," New America Foundation, Washington, DC, at http://natsec.newamerica.net/drones /pakistan/analysis, accessed February 5, 2014. Also see "Get the Data: Drone Wars," Bureau of Investigative Journalism, London, England, at http://www .thebureauinvestigates.com/category/projects/drones/, accessed February 5, 2014.

17. Angie Drobnic Holan, "Lie of the Year: 'If You Like Your Health Care Plan, You Can Keep It,'" *PolitiFact*, December 12, 2013, at http://www.politifact.com /truth-o-meter/article/2013/dec/12/lie-year-if-you-like-your-health-care-plan -keep-it/, accessed February 5, 2014.

18. Ben Kiernan, *Blood and Soil: A World History of Genocide and Extermination from Sparta to Darfur* (New Haven: Yale University Press, 2009), pp. 416–454, 503–511. See also pp. 536–538, where the phrase "China's holocaust" is attributed to Lynn T. White III. According to Kiernan, estimates of deaths from the Cultural Revolution (1966–1976) range from "250,000 to as many as 7–8 million people killed or driven to suicide." Pol Pot's Khmer Rouge slaughter occurred in Cambodia between 1975 and 1979. The Rwanda genocide occurred in 1994. For more information about Cambodia and Rwanda, see Kiernan, pp. 539–554 and 554–569, respectively. The Kiernan book may be "the first global history of genocide," but, of course, each horrific instance of mass extermination has its own body of original research and acclaimed histories. For a bibliography of some of the most respected books about humanity's worst atrocities and how the news media was manipulated or worse, shamelessly complicit, see: www.935Lies.com.

19. Kiernan, *Blood and Soil*, pp. 588–589. The "malignant disease" and "infect" references are from Norman Cigar, *Genocide in Bosnia: The Policy of "Ethnic Cleansing"* (College Station: Texas A&M University Press, 1985), p. 78.

20. Kiernan, *Blood and Soil*, pp. 594–596. See also Lee Feinstein, "Darfur and Beyond: What Is Needed to Prevent Mass Atrocities," CSR No. 22, January 2007, Council on Foreign Relations (www.cfr.org). In 2010, the 194th country, Southern Sudan, declared its independence.

21. Hannah Arendt, *The Origins of Totalitarianism* (New York: Shocken Books/Random House, 2004), p. xv (introduction by Samantha Power, quoting Arendt). This classic book was first published in 1951 by Harcourt.

22. Benjamin C. Bradlee, *Nieman Reports* special issue (Winter 1990).

23. The court-appointed bankruptcy examiner, former federal prosecutor Anton R. Valukas, went through 35 million records and produced a nine-volume, 2,200-page report with 8,000 source notes. He determined that "Lehman's failure to disclose the use of an accounting device to significantly and temporarily lower leverage, at the same time that it affirmatively represented those 'low' leverage numbers to investors as positive news, created a misleading portrayal of Lehman's true financial health. Colorable claims exist against the senior officers who were responsible for balance sheet management and financial disclosure, who signed and certified Lehman's financial statements and who failed to disclose Lehman's use and extent of Repo 105 transactions to manage its balance sheet." In late 2007, when Lehman accountant Matthew Lee refused to sign off on the Repo shenanigan, he was fired *within a week*. Four years after the company's collapse, there have been no federal prosecutions of either Lehman Brothers executives or the accounting firm involved, Ernst and Young. Both Valukas and Lee were interviewed by CBS News *60 Minutes*. See "Report of Anton R. Valukas, Examiner," United States Bankruptcy Court, Southern District of New York, Chapter 11 Case No. 08–13555 (JMP) March 11, 2010, p. 20, http://www.jenner.com/lehman/lehman/VOLUME%201.pdf, accessed August 26, 2012; Michael J. de la Merced and Andrew Ross Sorkin, "Report Details How Lehman Hid Its Woes," *New York Times*, March 11, 2010, at http://www.nytimes.com/2010/03/12/business/12lehman.html?pagewanted=all, accessed August 26, 2012; Steve Kroft, correspondent, James Jacoby and Michael Karzis, producers, "The Case Against Lehman Brothers," CBS News *60 Minutes*, originally broadcast April 22, 2012, rebroadcast August 19, 2012, at http://www.cbsnews.com/video/watch/?id=7418634n&tag=contentBody;storyMediaBox, accessed August 26, 2012.

24. Dean Starkman, "Power Problem: The Business Press Did Everything but Take On the Institutions That Brought Down the Financial System," *Columbia Journalism Review* (May–June 2009). See also Dean Starkman, "A Narrowed Gaze: How the Business Press Forgot the Rest of Us," *Columbia Journalism Review* (January–February 2012), and Anya Schiffrin, ed., *Bad News: How America's Business Press Missed the Story of the Century* (New York: New Press, 2011). Some of the best financial investigative journalism in recent years has been in books; see Bethany McLean and Joe Nocera, *All the Devils Are Here: The Hidden History of the Financial Crisis* (New York: Portfolio/Penguin, 2010); Vicky Ward, *Devil's Casino: Friendship, Betrayal and the High Stakes Games Played Inside Lehman Brothers* (New York: Wiley, 2010); Gretchen Morgenson and Joshua Rosner, *Reckles$ Endangerment:*

How Outsized Ambition, Greed, and Corruption Led to Economic Armageddon (New York: Times Books/Henry Holt, 2011); Michael W. Hudson, *The Monster: How a Gang of Predatory Lenders and Wall Street Bankers Fleeced America—and Spawned a Global Crisis* (New York: Times Books/Henry Holt, 2010); Andrew Ross Sorkin, *Too Big to Fail: The Inside Story of How Wall Street and Washington Fought to Save the Financial System—and Themselves* (New York: Viking, 2009). See also the Academy Award–winning documentary, *Inside Job*, directed by Charles Ferguson (2011), and Charles H. Ferguson, *Predator Nation: Corporate Criminals, Political Corruption, and the Hijacking of America* (New York: Crown Business, 2012).

25. By 1997, the Center for Public Integrity was the largest nonprofit investigative reporting organization in the world (excluding government-funded organizations or general audience/commercially available magazines), its annual budget reaching $8 million by 2010. It also became, and remains, the only news organization in the world with an International Consortium of Investigative Journalists, now composed of 175 premier reporters in nearly 70 countries on six continents, available on a contract or otherwise joint partnership basis, committed to doing *global* enterprise stories about the most important issues of our time. However, in 2008, with the launching of ProPublica in New York and a $10 million annual budget funded for three years by a single donor, and in 2012, with the merger of San Francisco-based Bay Citizen with the Center for Investigative Reporting, bringing CIR's overall budget to $11.5 million and 70+ employees, financially the Center for Public Integrity became the *third* largest nonprofit investigative reporting organization in the world. See Andrew Beaujon, "It's official: Bay Citizen, Center for Investigative Reporting will merge," The Poynter Institute, March 27, 2012, http://www.poynter.org/latest-news/mediawire/167907/its-official-bay-citizen -center-for-investigative-reporting-will-merge/, accessed July 2, 2012.

26. Fred R. Shapiro, ed., *The Yale Book of Quotations*, foreword by Joseph Epstein (New Haven: Yale University Press, 2006), p. 851. From *Le Figaro*, November 25, 1897.

CHAPTER 1: OUR FIRST CASUALTY

1. Ralph Waldo Emerson, "Intellect," Essays 1 (1841), vol. 2, in *The Complete Works of Ralph Waldo Emerson*, at www.rwe.org, published by the Ralph Waldo Emerson Institute.

2. Tim Weiner, *Legacy of Ashes: The History of the CIA* (New York: Doubleday, 2007), p. 240.

3. David Halberstam, *The Powers That Be* (New York: Ballantine, 1993), pp. 413–414 (first published in hardcover by New York: Random House, 1972).

4. Michael R. Beschloss, ed., *Taking Charge: The Johnson White House Tapes, 1963–1964* (New York: Simon and Schuster, 1997), p. 505, and Michael Maclear, *The Ten Thousand Day War: Vietnam, 1945–1975* (New York: St. Martin's Press, 1981), p. 112.

5. Beschloss, *Taking Charge*, p. 506, n. 3.

6. Ibid., p. 508, and Maclear, *Ten Thousand Day War*, p. 115.

7. William Manchester, *The Glory and the Dream: A Narrative History of America, 1932–1972* (New York: Bantam, 1975), p. 1019. See United States Senate, *The Senate Debates the Tonkin Resolution*, August 6–7, 1964, 88th Cong., 2nd Sess., *Congressional Record*, 1964, pp. 18132–18133.

8. George Ball, *The Past Has Another Pattern* (New York: W. W. Norton, 1982), p. 380.

9. Manchester, *The Glory and the Dream*, p. 1019.

10. Eric Alterman, *When Presidents Lie: A History of Official Deception and Its Consequences* (New York: Viking, 2004), pp. 161–163.

11. E. W. Kenworthy, Fox Butterfield, Hedrick Smith, and Neil Sheehan, *The Pentagon Papers: The Secret History of the Vietnam War, as Published by the New York Times* (New York: Quadrangle Books, 1971), chap. 5, "The Covert War and Tonkin Gulf: February–August, 1964," pp. 234–306.

12. Beschloss, *Taking Charge*, p. 493. In early 1964, Johnson had also signed National Security Action Memorandum 288, authorizing South Vietnamese troops to conduct operations in and along the border of Laos. See A. J. Langguth, *Our Vietnam: The War, 1954–1975* (New York: Simon and Schuster, 2000), pp. 296, 299. Daniel Ellsberg, *Secrets: A Memoir of Vietnam and the Pentagon Papers* (New York: Viking, 2002), p. 14.

13. Ellsberg, *Secrets*, p. 14.

14. Halberstam, *The Powers That Be*, pp. 413–414.

15. Ball, *The Past Has Another Pattern*, p. 379.

16. *Chicago Tribune*, April 27, 1990, cited in Norman Solomon, *War Made Easy: How Presidents and Pundits Keep Spinning Us to Death* (Hoboken, NJ: Wiley and Sons, 2005), p. 104. See also Jim and Sybil Stockdale, *In Love and War* (New York: Harper and Row, 1984), pp. 3–36.

17. Robert McNamara, *In Retrospect* (New York: Times Books/Random House, 1995), pp. 132–136.

18. Beschloss, *Taking Charge*, p. 504, citing McNamara's quotation in the *Washington Post*, November 11, 1995.

19. Ellsberg, *Secrets*, p. 10. Ellsberg describes precisely how the truth dribbled out about the nonexistent second attack in 1966, 1970, and 1981 in various important pieces of "new" information.

20. "Tonkin Gulf Intelligence 'Skewed' According to Official History and Intercepts," National Security Archive, Electronic Briefing Book No. 132—Update (John Prados), citing Hanyok's article, "Skunks, Bogies, Silent Hounds, and the Flying Fish: The Gulf of Tonkin Mystery, 2–4 August 1964," *Cryptologic Quarterly* 19 (4) (Winter 2000) and 20 (1) (Spring 2001), declassified November 2005.

21. Weiner, *Legacy of Ashes*, p. 240.

22. Halberstam, *The Powers That Be*, pp. 413–414.

23. The unlikely messenger delivering Johnson's secret warning was a man named Blair Seaborn, the Canadian member of the International Control Commission (ICC), which had been established to oversee implementation of the 1954 and 1962 Geneva Accords. Seaborn met privately on June 18, 1964, in Hanoi with

the prime minister of North Vietnam, Pham Van Dong, and relayed the carefully written message prepared by US officials. It said, in part, that the "U.S. public and official patience with North Vietnamese aggression is growing extremely thin" and, should the conflict escalate, "the greatest devastation would of course result for the DRV (North Vietnam) itself." In the spring, the Joint Chiefs of Staff had secretly been told to draw up precise plans for direct air attacks on North Vietnam, and by the end of May, they had recommended ninety-four specific bombing targets. And on August 10, 1964, just days after the Gulf of Tonkin US military actions and the US Congress's lightning-fast passage of the war-support resolution, Seaborn repeated the American warning in another secret meeting with Pham Van Dong, adding, "If the DRV persists in its present course, it can expect to continue to suffer the consequences." The North Vietnamese prime minister's reaction was "extremely angry." See Ellsberg, *Secrets*, pp. 17–19, quoting from *The Pentagon Papers: The Defense Department History of United States Decision-making on Vietnam*, The Senator Gravel Edition (Boston: Beacon Press, 1971), vol. 3, p. 520; George C. Herring, ed., *The Secret Diplomacy of the Vietnam War: The Negotiating Volumes of the Pentagon Papers* (Austin: University of Texas Press, 1983), p. 32.

24. Ellsberg, *Secrets*, pp. 17–18.

25. David Wise, *The Politics of Lying: Government Deception, Secrecy and Power* (New York: Random House, 1973).

26. *Pentagon Papers*, vol. 3, p. 557.

27. Ibid., p. 558.

28. Ibid., p. 559.

29. Wise, *Politics of Lying*, p. 49.

30. Sissela Bok, *Lying: Moral Choice in Public and Private Life* (New York: Pantheon Books, 1978), p. 172.

31. Fred W. Friendly, "TV at the Turning Point," *Columbia Journalism Review* (Winter 1970–1971), p. 14.

32. William Prochnau, *Once Upon a Distant War: Young War Correspondents and the Early Vietnam Battles* (New York: Times Books, 1995). Also Morley Safer, *Flashbacks: On Returning to Vietnam* (New York: Random House, 1990); John Laurence, *The Cat from Hué: A Vietnam War Story* (New York: PublicAffairs, 2002), p. 136. David Halberstam declared Safer and Laurence "the two best television reporters of the war" in *The Best and the Brightest*, 20th anniv. ed., with a new introduction (New York: Ballantine Books, 1992), p. 509.

33. George C. Herring, *America's Longest War: The United States and Vietnam, 1950–1975*, 4th ed. (New York: McGraw-Hill, 2001), p. 206.

34. Walter Cronkite, *A Reporter's Life* (New York: Knopf, 1996), p. 255. Schlesinger followed Clark Clifford as defense secretary, who replaced McNamara, who had grown disillusioned with the war and was nominated by Johnson to become the president of the World Bank.

35. Halberstam, *The Powers That Be*, p. 512.

36. Gary Paul Gates, *Air Time: The Inside Story of CBS News* (New York: Berkley, 1979), p. 210.

37. Ibid., pp. 210–211.

38. Todd Gitlin, *The Sixties: Years of Hope, Days of Rage* (New York: Bantam, 1993), p. 304, and Herring, *America's Longest War*, pp. 211–227.

39. Interview with Murrey Marder, April 26, 2007, Washington, DC.

40. Clarence R. Wyatt, *Paper Soldiers: The American Press and the Vietnam War* (New York: Norton, 1993), p. 131.

41. See http://www.niemanwatchdog.org/index.cfm?fuseaction=about.Mission_Statement, accessed January 5, 2014. Marder died in 2013 at the age of ninety-three. Also see Charles Lewis, "Murrey Marder: Utterly Tenacious About the Truth," *Nieman Reports* (March 2013), at http://nieman.harvard.edu/reports/article/102857/Murrey-Marder-Utterly-Tenacious-About-the-Truth.aspx.

42. A. J. Langguth, *Our Vietnam: The War, 1954–1975* (New York: Simon and Schuster, 2001), pp. 304–305.

43. For the entire August 24, 1964, Stone essay, "What Few Know About the Tonkin Bay Incidents," see *The Best of I. F. Stone* (New York: PublicAffairs, 2006), ed. Karl Weber, introduction by Peter Osnos, pp. 247–255.

44. Ibid., p. 254. And see also Myra MacPherson, *All Governments Lie! The Life and Times of Rebel Journalist I. F. Stone* (New York: Scribner, 2006), p. 396.

45. Halberstam, *The Powers That Be*, pp. 413–414.

46. Phillip Knightley, *The First Casualty: From the Crimea to Vietnam. The War Correspondent as Hero, Propagandist, and Myth Maker* (New York: Harcourt Brace Jovanovich, 1975), p. 412.

47. Maj. Cass D. Howell, "War, Television and Public Opinion," *Military Review* (February 1987), p. 72, as cited in Jacqueline Sharkey, *Under Fire: Military Restrictions on the Media from Grenada to the Persian Gulf* (Washington, DC: The Center for Public Integrity, 1991), p. 58.

48. John E. Mueller, *War, Presidents and Public Opinion* (New York: Wiley, 1973), p. 167, cited in Sharkey, *Under Fire*, p. 58.

49. Mueller, *War, Presidents and Public Opinion*, pp. 60, 154–156, cited in Sharkey, *Under Fire*, p. 56.

50. Clarence R. Wyatt, *Paper Soldiers: The American Press and the Vietnam War* (New York: Norton, 1993), pp. 7, 219.

51. Ibid., pp. 206–208. Full disclosure: from the late 1990s until 2012, I was a member of the board of directors for the Fund for Investigative Journalism, and I currently serve on the fund's advisory board.

52. Ibid., citing "Hip-Pocket AP," *Newsweek*, December 8, 1969, p. 83.

53. Neil Sheehan, *A Bright Shining Lie* (New York: Vintage Books, 1989), p. 271.

54. Knightley, *The First Casualty*, p. 376.

55. Halberstam, *The Best and the Brightest*, p. viii; interview with Johnson White House press secretary George Christian by David Culbert, September 17, 1979, p. 13 of transcript provided by the Lyndon Baines Johnson Library.

56. Arthur M. Schlesinger Jr., *The Imperial Presidency* (Boston: Houghton Mifflin, 1973), p. ix, citing a letter from Madison to Jefferson, May 13, 1798, in S. K. Padover, ed., *The Complete Madison* (New York: Harper, 1953), p. 258.

57. J. William Fulbright, *The Arrogance of Power* (New York: Random House, 1966), pp. 3–4.

58. Wise, *Politics of Lying*, pp. 62–65, citing Senate Foreign Relations Committee, *The Gulf of Tonkin Incidents Hearings*, February 20, 1968, pp. 35–39.

59. Wise, *Politics of Lying*, p. 17.

60. Email correspondence and subsequent interview with Randy LaSalle, July 12 and 14, 2007, respectively; he is today a popular professor at John Jay College of Criminal Justice in New York, teaching forensic accounting. Date of death and rank from "www.NO-QUARTER.org—Vietnam Casualty Search Page" compiled from government records. Also see "2 Area Marines Killed in Vietnam," *Wilmington Evening Journal*, March 21, 1967, evening edition.

CHAPTER 2: THE PUBLIC'S RIGHT TO KNOW: THE PENTAGON PAPERS, WATERGATE, AND A TRIUMPH FOR TRUTH

1. Investigative reporting by Neil Sheehan. Written by E. W. Kenworthy, Fox Butterfield, Hedrick Smith, and Neil Sheehan, *The Pentagon Papers: The Secret History of the Vietnam War, as published by the New York Times* (New York: Quadrangle Books, 1971), pp. 725–727.

2. Daniel Ellsberg, *Secrets: A Memoir of Vietnam and the Pentagon Papers* (New York: Viking, 2002), pp. 372–375.

3. Interview with Bill Kovach, June 28, 2007, Washington, DC.

4. Susan E. Tifft and Alex S. Jones, *The Trust: The Private and Powerful Family Behind the New York Times* (New York: Little, Brown, 1999), p. 483.

5. Ibid.

6. Ibid., pp. 482–483.

7. Ibid., p. 485.

8. Ibid., pp. 483–484.

9. Ibid., p. 486.

10. Ellsberg, *Secrets*, p. 385, quoting Tony Austin, then an editor at the *New York Times*.

11. Interview with Bill Kovach, June 28, 2007.

12. Tifft and Jones, *The Trust*, p. 489.

13. Ibid., p. 490; Sanford J. Ungar, *The Papers and the Papers: An Account of the Legal and Political Battle over the Pentagon Papers* (New York: Columbia University Press, 1989), pp. 120–123; Geoffrey R. Stone, *Perilous Times: Free Speech in Wartime, from the Sedition Act of 1798 to the War on Terrorism* (New York: W. W. Norton, 2005), pp. 504–505.

14. Ungar, *The Papers and the Papers*, pp. 123–124.

15. Ibid., p. 122.

16. Ibid.

17. Ellsberg, *Secrets*, p. 387.

18. Ibid., pp. 383, 387–390.

19. Interview with Benjamin Bradlee, April 25, 2007, Washington, DC.

20. Interview with Ben Bagdikian, June 19, 2007, Berkeley, California.

21. Ibid.

22. Ibid.; Ungar, *The Papers and the Papers*, p. 138.

23. Ungar, *The Papers and the Papers*, p. 140.

24. Ben H. Bagdikian, *Double Vision: Reflections on My Heritage, Life, and Profession* (Boston: Beacon Press, 1995), p. 17.

25. Ibid., p. 18.

26. Ibid.

27. Ibid.; interview with Ben Bagdikian, June 19, 2007.

28. Ungar, *The Papers and the Papers*, pp. 144–145.

29. Bagdikian, *Double Vision*, p. 19.

30. Ben Bradlee, *A Good Life: Newspapering and Other Adventures* (New York: Touchstone, 1996), p. 315.

31. Ibid., pp. 315–316.

32. Ibid.

33. Katharine Graham, *Personal History* (New York: Knopf, 1997), p. 450.

34. David Halberstam, *The Powers That Be*, pp. 512–513.

35. Bradlee, *A Good Life*, p. 316.

36. Stone, *Perilous Times*, p. 508; Ungar, *The Papers and the Papers*, pp. 155–158.

37. Stone, *Perilous Times*, p. 508; Ungar, *The Papers and the Papers*, pp. 164–169.

38. Stone, *Perilous Times*, p. 509; Ungar, *The Papers and the Papers*, pp. 224–249.

39. Ungar, *The Papers and the Papers*, pp. 242–243.

40. Bradlee, *A Good Life*, p. 322. To read "The Complete Pentagon Papers," see http://www.nytimes.com/interactive/us/2011_PENTAGON_PAPERS.html?ref=pentagonpapers&_r=0, accessed February 2, 2014.

41. Ellsberg, *Secrets*, pp. 400–402.

42. Ibid., pp. 403–408.

43. Stanley I. Kutler, *Abuse of Power: The New Nixon Tapes* (New York: Touchstone, 1998), p. 6.

44. Ibid.; Ellsberg, *Secrets*, pp. 432–437.

45. Kutler, *Abuse of Power*, p. 10; Ellsberg, *Secrets*, p. 435.

46. Barry Sussman, *The Great Cover-Up: Nixon and the Scandal of Watergate*, 3rd ed. (Arlington, VA: Seven Locks Press, 1992), p. 198.

47. Kutler, *Abuse of Power*, p. 20.

48. Ibid., p. 14.

49. Keith W. Olson, *Watergate: The Presidential Scandal That Shook America* (Lawrence: University Press of Kansas, 2003), pp. 18–19. The phone bill was sent to Kathy Chenow, the plumbers' unit secretary, and paid by the White House.

50. Fred Emery, *Watergate: The Corruption of American Politics and the Fall of Richard Nixon* (New York: Touchstone, 1995), pp. 60–61.

51. Ibid., p. 66.

52. Ibid., pp. 69–70.

53. Ellsberg, *Secrets*, pp. 440–441.

54. Richard M. Nixon, *The Memoirs of Richard Nixon* (New York: Grosset and Dunlap, 1978), p. 515.

55. Stone, *Perilous Times*, pp. 456–457; Ungar, *The Papers and the Papers*, pp. 8–9; Ellsberg, *Secrets*, pp. 455–457.

56. Sam Ervin Jr., *The Whole Truth: The Watergate Conspiracy* (New York: Random House, 1980), p. 106.

57. Stone, *Perilous Times*, p. 515; Ellsberg, *Secrets*, p. 457.

58. Nixon, *Memoirs*, p. 515.

59. Quoted in Fred R. Shapiro, *The Yale Book of Quotations* (New Haven: Yale University Press, 2006), p. 515.

60. For the definitive account of this bizarre episode, see Mark Feldstein, *Poisoning the Press: Richard Nixon, Jack Anderson, and the Rise of Washington's Scandal Culture* (New York: Farrar, Straus and Giroux: 2010), pp. 268–290.

61. Ungar, *The Papers and the Papers*, pp. 117–118.

62. Stone, *Perilous Times*, pp. 492–493, citing J. Anthony Lukas, *Nightmare: The Underside of the Nixon Years* (New York: Viking, 1976), pp. 12–13, cited in n. 216. See also Mark Feldstein, "Watergate Revisited," *American Journalism Review* (August–September 2004), at ajrarchive.org/article.asp?id=3735, accessed February 6, 2014.

63. Interview with Daniel Schorr, May 9, 2007, Washington, DC. Schorr died on July 23, 2010. See Patricia Sullivan, "Daniel Schorr, Veteran CBS and CNN Reporter and CNN News Analyst, Dead at Ninety-Three," *Washington Post*, July 24, 2010, at http://www.washingtonpost.com/wp-dyn/content/article/2010/07/23 /AR2010072303146_pf.html, accessed on September 12, 2001; and Robert D. Hershey Jr., "Daniel Schorr, Journalist, Dies at Ninety-Three," *New York Times*, July 23, 2010, at http://www.nytimes.com/2010/07/24/business/media/24schorr .html, accessed on September 12, 2011.

64. Interview with Daniel Schorr, May 9, 2007.

65. Ibid.

66. Ibid.

67. Stone, *Perilous Times*, pp. 492–493.

68. Kutler, *Abuse of Power*, p. 29.

69. The idea of a traditional nonfiction book account of the Washington scandal was discarded by Woodward and Bernstein after a conversation with actor Robert Redford, who suggested they write their own reporting story, which they did in third person. Redford and Dustin Hoffman produced and starred in the movie, Alan Pakula directed, William Goldman wrote the screenplay (and coined the phrase "follow the money"), and Jason Robards won an Academy Award for his portrayal of Ben Bradlee. Several key people in the *Washington Post*'s Watergate coverage were not portrayed in the film, including Watergate editor Barry Sussman, who recommended that Woodward and Bernstein be assigned to cover the story and oversaw their work daily for seventeen months, and owner Katharine Graham, who stood behind all the newspaper's reporting.

70. Bradlee, *A Good Life*, p. 324.

71. Interview with Barry Sussman, May 18, 2007, Washington DC.

72. Bradlee, *A Good Life*, p. 325.

73. The *Post* could not have had a more gifted, highly regarded editor scrutinizing the myriad pieces of the Watergate puzzle. As Halberstam described it, "almost from the start, before anyone else at the *Post*, Sussman saw Watergate as a larger pattern, the result of hidden decisions from somewhere in the top of government which sent smaller men to run dirty errands . . . he sensed the President's role earlier than almost anyone else" (Halberstam, *Powers*, p. 616).

74. Interview with Barry Sussman, May 18, 2007.

75. Interview with Bob Woodward, May 18, 2007, Washington, DC. Of course, much has been written about Woodward's source "Deep Throat" (Mark Felt), his real motivation for leaking, and so forth. See Bob Woodward, with a reporter's assessment by Carl Bernstein, *The Secret Man: The Story of Watergate's Deep Throat* (New York: Simon and Schuster, 2005); Mark Felt and John O'Connor, *A G-Man's Life: The FBI, Being 'Deep Throat,' and the Struggle for Honor in Washington* (New York: PublicAffairs, 2006); Max Holland, *Leak: Why Mark Felt Became Deep Throat* (Lawrence: University Press of Kansas, 2012).

76. Feldstein, "Watergate Revisited."

77. Theodore H. White, *Breach of Faith: The Fall of Richard Nixon* (New York: Atheneum, 1975), p. 322.

78. Interview with Bob Woodward, May 18, 2007.

79. Leonard Downie Jr., *The New Muckrakers* (New York: Mentor/New American Library, 1976), p. 10. There was no separate Pulitzer Prize category for "investigative reporting" until 1985.

80. Carl Bernstein and Bob Woodward, *All the President's Men* (New York: Warner, 1975), p. 9

81. Roy J. Harris Jr., *Pulitzer's Gold: Behind the Prize for Public Service Journalism* (Columbia: University of Missouri Press, 2007), p. 233.

82. Alicia C. Shepard, *Woodward and Bernstein: Life in the Shadow of Watergate* (Hoboken, NJ: John Wiley and Sons, 2007), p. 15.

83. Interview with Carl Bernstein, September 6, 2007.

84. Adam Liptak, "Time Inc. to Yield Files on Sources, Relenting to U.S.," *New York Times*, July 1, 2005, p. 1. For the then-*Time* editor-in-chief's rationale for turning over reporter Cooper's notes to prosecutors, see Norman Pearlstine, *Off the Record: The Press, the Government, and the War over Anonymous Sources* (New York: Farrar, Straus and Giroux, 2007). Also, Interview with Walt Bogdanich, May 31, 2007, New York City.

85. Halberstam, *The Powers That Be* (New York: Ballantine, 1993), p. 616.

86. Interview (e-mail) with Jane E. Kirtley, March 31, 2008. Reportage that the Bush administration found infuriating included Dana Priest's *Washington Post* stories about the CIA's secret prisons overseas (http://www.pulitzer.org/works/2006-Beat -Reporting) and Eric Lichtblau and James Risen's *New York Times* story about the federal government's secret eavesdropping surveillance program (http://www .pulitzer.org/works/2006-Beat-Reporting), both published in 2005 and winners of Pulitzer Prizes. In 2010, the *New York Times* (in partnership with the *Guardian* in England, *Der Spiegel* in Germany and the international, nonprofit organization

WikiLeaks, http://wikileaks.org/) published numerous news stories based upon half a million secret Iraq and Afghanistan battlefield reports and roughly 250,000 State Department embassy cables obtained and posted online by WikiLeaks. See Bill Keller, "Dealing with Assange and the WikiLeaks Secrets," *New York Times Magazine*, January 26, 2011, www.nytimes.com. According to James Goodale, the *New York Times* counsel during the Pentagon Papers period, the hyperactivity by the Obama administration prosecuting "leakers" in six separate cases and invoking the Espionage Act is unprecedented and essentially criminalizes investigative journalism.

87. Interview with Jane E. Kirtley, March 31, 2008.

88. Government clearance and classification information is from James Goodale, *Fighting for the Press: The Inside Story of the Pentagon Papers and Other Battles* (New York: CUNY Journalism Press, 2013), p. 208, citing an editorial, "Why Is That a Secret?" *New York Times*, August 24, 2011; see also Jennifer Lynch and Trevor Timm, "The Dangers in Classifying the News," Electronic Frontier Foundation, October 18, 2011, at https://www.eff.org/deeplinks/2011/10/dangers-classifying-news.

89. Charlie Savage and Leslie Kaufman, "Phone Records of Journalists Seized by U.S.," *New York Times*, May 13, 2013, at http://www.nytimes.com/2013/05/14/us/phone-records-of-journalists-of-the-associated-press-seized-by-us.html, accessed June 24, 2013.

CHAPTER 3: RACE: THE AMERICAN DELUSION

1. Peter Baehr, *The Portable Hannah Arendt* (New York: Penguin Books, 2003), p. 548, citing her essay originally published in the *New Yorker*, February 25, 1967.

2. Matthew Wald, "William V. Roth Jr., Veteran of U.S. Senate, Dies at Eighty-Two," *New York Times*, December 15, 2003.

3. Philip B. Kunhardt Jr., ed., *Life in Camelot* (Boston: Little, Brown, 1988), p. 310.

4. Interview with former US Trade Representative, former secretary of labor and former RNC chairman Bill Brock, July 14, 1992, noted in *Private Parties: Political Party Leadership in Washington Mercenary Culture* (Washington, DC: The Center for Public Integrity, 1992), p. 55.

5. See Stanley I. Kutler, *The Wars of Watergate: The Last Crisis of Richard Nixon* (New York: Knopf, 2013), pp. 498–505, for a discussion of the House Judiciary Committee "gang of seven" GOP congressmen who voted in late July 1974 to impeach Nixon.

6. Howell Raines, "Federal Report Says Hoover Barred Trial for Klansmen in '63 Bombing," *New York Times*, February 18, 1980 (as quoted in ibid.). Also see Cynthia Wesley, "Birmingham Church Bomber Guilty, Gets Four Life Terms," CNN, at http://articles.cnn.com/2001–05–01/justice/church.bombing.05_1_cynthia-wesley-carole-robertson-whites-and-four-blacks?_s=PM:LAW, accessed September 2, 2011.

7. Gary May, *The Informant: The FBI, the Ku Klux Klan, and the Murder of Viola Liuzzo* (New Haven: Yale University Press, 2005), pp. 103–104.

8. Wesley, "Birmingham Church Bomber Guilty."

9. In 2007, FBI director Robert Mueller said the Bureau will focus on investigating about one hundred cases, at http://www.usatoday.com/news/nation /2007–02–27–murder-cases_x.htm. According to the *Clarion-Ledger*, the Southern Poverty Law Center has estimated that between 1954 and 1968, there were 126 unsolved civil rights–related murders, but the organization acknowledges this number is not comprehensive. See http://www.clarionledger.com/apps/pbcs .dll/article?AID=/20070227/NEWS/702270388/0/NEWS. See also the FBI press release on its partnership with the SPLC regarding these murders: http://www .fbi.gov/pressrel/pressrel07/coldcase022707.htm.

10. Mitchell received the 2005 Tom Renner Award at the annual IRE conference, which was held that year in Denver, Colorado. See www.ire.org/contest /05winners.html.

11. *SPLC Report* (Southern Poverty Law Center), at www.southernplc.org, Spring 2007 (from a panel discussion after the screening of the movie *Mississippi Burning*). In 2009, Mitchell was awarded a MacArthur Fellowship. See http://www .macfound.org/fellows/58/; accessed March 16, 2014.

12. E-mail exchange with Jerry Mitchell, May 5, 2008. The *Clarion-Ledger* has been owned by Gannett since 1982. Mitchell singled out executive editor Ronnie Agnew, managing editor Don Hudson, and "especially assistant managing editor Debbie Skipper, who has been my boss for more than a decade and a half." Mitchell and Hank Klibanoff (the Pulitzer Prize–winning co-author with Gene Roberts of *The Race Beat: The Press, the Civil Rights Struggle, and the Awakening of a Nation* [New York: Vintage, 2008]) are also part of a stellar national team of journalists investigating civil rights "cold cases," organized and overseen by the California-based Center for Investigative Reporting, with Paperny Films. The project URL is http://coldcases.org/, accessed September 2, 2011.

13. E-mail exchange with Jerry Mitchell, May 27, 2008.

14. Elliot Jaspin, *Buried in the Bitter Waters: The Hidden History of Racial Cleansing in America* (New York: Basic Books, 2007). The founder of the National Institute for Computer Assisted Reporting (NICAR), for nearly a decade Jaspin computer-analyzed US Census data, analyzed microfilm news stories, and interviewed local historians and others throughout the two-hundred-county region.

15. Douglas A. Blackmon, *Slavery by Another Name: The Re-Enslavement of Black Americans from the Civil War to World War II* (New York: Anchor Books, 2008).

16. Jaspin, *Buried in the Bitter Waters*, p. 10.

17. Gunnar Myrdal, *An American Dilemma: The Negro Problem and Modern Democracy* (Piscataway, NJ: Transaction, 1995), p. 205, cited in Roberts and Klibanoff, *The Race Beat*, p. 8.

18. Myrdal, *An American Dilemma*, p. 548.

19. Ibid., p. 554.

20. Ibid., p. 48.

21. Roberts and Klibanoff, *The Race Beat*, p. 10.

22. Ibid., p. 24, pp. 73–74 and 204–205. Hodding Carter Jr., through his writing in his *Greenville Delta Democrat-Times*, bluntly criticized the enraged, white Citizens Councils and the Ku Klux Klan in Mississippi, almost unheard of for a white person or a newspaper editor in the South. Carter won a Pulitzer Prize for editorials on racial tolerance in 1946 and wrote over twenty books focused on the South and its history.

23. Ibid., p. 13, citing on p. 415, Armistead Scott Pride, "Negro Newspapers: Yesterday, Today and Tomorrow," *Journalism Quarterly* 28 (2) (Spring 1951): 179.

24. Myrdal, *An American Dilemma*, pp. 908–909.

25. Ibid., p. 924, citing on p. 1425, Edwin Mims, *The Advancing South*, (Port Washington, NY: Kennikat Press, 1969), p. 268.

26. Interview with Gene Roberts, June 13, 2007, New York City. During his eighteen years as executive editor of the *Philadelphia Inquirer*, his staff won seventeen Pulitzer Prizes. He later became the managing editor of the *New York Times*.

27. Roberts and Klibanoff, *The Race Beat*, pp. 86–108.

28. Ibid. As *The Race Beat* brilliantly details, an accomplished Alabama journalist named William Bradford Huie, whose books had sold 40 million copies, paid the law firm that defended Bryant and Milam $4,410 and got exclusive interviews with Bryant and his wife, Carolyn, and Milam, as well as their signed releases. The *Look* story, published in January 1956, was headlined "The Shocking Story of Approved Killing in Mississippi."

29. Interview with Moses Newson, June 27, 2007, Washington, DC.

30. Ibid.

31. Roberts and Klibanoff, *The Race Beat*, pp. 180–183.

32. Interview with Moses Newson, June 27, 2007.

33. Ibid.

34. Interview with Gene Roberts, June 13, 2007.

35. Nick Kotz, *Judgment Days: Lyndon Baines Johnson, Martin Luther King Jr., and the Laws That Changed America* (New York: Mariner/Houghton Mifflin, 2006), p. xv. Kotz is a renowned Pulitzer Prize–winning journalist and the author of five previous books. See also David J. Garrow, *Bearing the Cross: Martin Luther King, Jr., and the Southern Christian Leadership Conference* (New York: Quill/William Morrow, 1986). And of course the remarkable trilogy of books produced over nearly a quarter century by Taylor Branch: *At Canaan's Edge* (New York: Simon and Schuster, 2006); *Parting the Waters* (New York: Simon and Schuster, 1989); *Pillar of Fire* (New York: Simon and Schuster, 1999).

36. Kotz, *Judgment Days*, pp. 50–59.

37. David Halberstam, *The Children* (New York: Fawcett/Random House, 1999), pp. 435–443, and Kotz, *Judgment Days*, pp. 57–58. For the full text of the letter, see Clayborne Carson, ed., *The Autobiography of Martin Luther King, Jr.* (New York: Warner Books, 1998), pp. 188–204.

38. Halberstam, *The Children*, pp. 435–443.

39. Diane McWhorter, *Carry Me Home: Birmingham, Alabama, the Climactic Battle of the Civil Rights Revolution* (New York: Simon and Schuster, 2001), p. 367.

40. Halberstam, *The Children*, pp. 435–443.

41. Ibid., and Kotz, *Judgment Days*, pp. 58–59.

42. Ibid., and Arthur M. Schlesinger Jr., *A Thousand Days: John F. Kennedy in the White House* (Boston: Houghton Mifflin, 1965), pp. 950–977.

43. Kotz, *Judgment Days*, pp. 60–62, and Schlesinger, *A Thousand Days*, p. 964.

44. Ibid.

45. Kotz, *Judgment Days*, p. 62; Schlesinger, *A Thousand Days*, p. 966.

46. Adam Liptak, "Supreme Court Invalidates Key Part of Voting Rights Act," *New York Times*, June 25, 2013, at http://www.nytimes.com/2013/06/26/us/supreme-court-ruling.html?pagewanted=all&_r=0, accessed February 4, 2014. See also Gary May, *Bending Toward Justice: The Voting Rights Act and the Transformation of American Democracy* (New York: Basic Books, 2013).

47. Roberts and Klibanoff, *The Race Beat*, pp. 375–384. Also see David J. Garrow, *Protest at Selma: Martin Luther King, Jr., and the Voting Rights Act of 1965* (New Haven: Yale University Press, 1978), pp. 60–68. Almost half a century after his murder had prompted the great Selma march, Jackson's killer, Alabama state trooper James Bonard Fowler, pled guilty to manslaughter on November 15, 2010. He was sentenced to six months in prison. The light sentence was dubbed "a slap in the face to the people of this country" by Perry County commissioner Albert Turner Jr. (Robbie Brown, "Forty-Five Years Later, an Apology and Six Months," *New York Times*, November 15, 2010, accessed July 27, 2011, at http://www.nytimes.com/2010/11/16/us/16fowler.html?_r=1&hpw.

48. Interview with Eugene Roberts, June 13, 2007, New York. Schulke was working on contract for *Life* magazine through his agent, Black Star, according to Roberts and Klibanoff, *The Race Beat*, p. 285.

49. Garrow, *Protest at Selma*, pp. 60–68, and Kotz, *Judgment Days*, pp. 281–285, citing in n. 13, "Five Hundred and Twenty-five in Selma Defy Ban of Governor," *New York Times*, March 8, 1965 (Wallace's statement).

50. John Lewis, with Michael D'Orso, *Walking with the Wind: A Memoir of the Movement* (New York: Simon and Schuster, 1998), p. 326.

51. Ibid., pp. 325–331. Roy Reed, "Alabama Police Use Gas and Clubs to Route Negroes," *New York Times*, March 8, 1965.

52. Lewis, *Walking with the Wind*, p. 331.

53. Ibid., pp. 336–338; Roberts and Klibanoff, *The Race Beat*, p. 388.

54. Kotz, *Judgment Days*, pp. 308–314, and Lewis, *Walking with the Wind*, pp. 339–340.

55. May, *The Informant*, chap. 13, "Digging In," pp. 287–315.

56. Ibid.

57. For the best public description of the entire saga and our own investigative ten-state efforts (the *Washington Post* called the *20/20* stories "dynamite journalism"), see ibid.

58. Ibid.

59. Without Rowe's testimony, to be fair, there almost certainly would have been no successful federal prosecution of Thomas and Wilkins, who were convicted

and served time in separate federal prisons for violating Viola Liuzzo's civil rights. But without Rowe's noisy presence and participation with them that fateful night, directly or even indirectly through racially charged bravado and atmospherics, would Viola Liuzzo have been killed at all? That he was a provocateur of violence is beyond dispute. Four years earlier, for example, the *Birmingham Post-Herald* had published an infamous photograph of Rowe physically beating Freedom Riders in the Birmingham bus station in 1961. And as historian Gary May detailed in his 2005 book, *The Informant*, Alabama attorney general William Baxley and his investigators in 1977 had also found Rowe's accounts not credible, regarding not just his own conduct and involvement in the Liuzzo murder but also the earlier Sixteenth Street Birmingham church bombing they were successfully investigating and prosecuting at the time. The night of Viola Liuzzo's death, Rowe hours later had bragged to two close Birmingham friends, one of them a policeman, that he had "smoked a whore" in Selma, which was later recalled to a racially mixed grand jury along with other, under oath, firsthand testimony, and in 1978 Rowe was indicted on Alabama state charges for the murder of Viola Liuzzo. A federal judge later blocked the prosecution of Rowe, ruling not about his actual criminal culpability for the crime, but instead determining that the informant in 1965 had been granted immunity from any prosecution. And even the FBI headquarters had its own internal concerns about Rowe's credibility regarding the Liuzzo murder and the manner in which it had been investigated internally. For instance, as we found at ABC and years later Diane McWhorter also noted in *Carry Me Home*, why had its field investigation into the slaying somehow, curiously and inexplicably, neglected to do a paraffin test on Rowe's gun to see if it had been recently fired, or to take fingerprints from the murder weapon, for which Director J. Edgar Hoover later had demanded an explanation?

60. For more information, see Lewis, *Walking with the Wind*.

61. Adam Nagourney, "A Busy Weekend for Big Names," *New York Times*, February 27, 2007, at http://query.nytimes.com/gst/fullpage.html?res=9503EFDB1E 3EF934A15751C0A9619C8B63, accessed February 5, 2014. Nagourney noted, "Senator Barack Obama of Illinois agreed weeks ago to attend and to speak at a Sunday morning church service. Mr. Obama had hoped to have the stage to himself. But as things turn out, Senator Hillary Rodham Clinton of New York decided last week that she would go, too, speaking at a different church service."

62. David Remnick, *The Bridge: The Life and Rise of Barack Obama* (New York: Knopf, 2010), pp. 16–21. See also Patrick Healy and Jeff Zeleny, "Clinton and Obama Unite, Briefly, in Pleas to Blacks," *New York Times*, March 5, 2007.

63. For example, unemployment among blacks is *twice* what it is for whites. See Office of Applied Studies, Substance Abuse and Mental Health Services Administration, *National Survey on Drug Use and Health Report: Illicit Drug Use, by Race/ Ethnicity, in Metropolitan and Non-Metropolitan Counties: 2004 and 2005* (Washington, DC: Government Printing Office, 2007), accessed July 25, 2011, at http:// www.oas.samhsa.gov/2k7/popDensity/popDensity.htm; Office of Applied Studies, Substance Abuse and Mental Health Services Administration, *Results from the 2008*

National Survey on Drug Use and Health: National Findings (Washington, DC: Government Printing Office, 2009), accessed July 25, 2011, at http://www.oas.samhsa .gov/nsduh/2k8nsduh/2k8Results.pdf.

June 2011 unemployment numbers: White, 8.1 percent (10,135,000); Black, 16.2 percent (2,877,000); Hispanic (any race), 11.6 percent (2,653,000). Source: Bureau of Labor Statistics, *Household Data*, "Table A-4. Employment Status of the Civilian Non-Institutional Population by Race, Hispanic or Latino Ethnicity, Sex, and Age, Seasonally Adjusted," accessed July 27, 2011, at http://bls.gov/web/empsit /cpseea04.htm.

As recently as 2004, white family median net worth was *seven times* higher than that of a median black family, $140,700 to $20,700, with Latino median net worth at $18,600. Source: Survey of Consumer Finances, Federal Reserve Bank, 2006.

Of the children living in poverty in the United States, 33 percent are black, compared to 9 percent who are white. Sources: Poverty rates in 2009 among those under 18: White, 11.9 percent (1,850,000); Black, 35.4 percent (4,480,000), Hispanic (any race), 33.1 percent (5,610,000). See Carmen DeNavas-Walt, Bernadette D. Proctor, and Jessica C. Smith, U.S. Census Bureau, *Income, Poverty, and Health Insurance Coverage in the United States: 2009*, (Washington, DC: Government Printing Office, 2010), accessed July 27, 2011, at http://www.census.gov /prod/2010pubs/p60–238.pdf.

The Great Recession hit Hispanic, Asian and African American families much harder than whites, their median net worth falling 66 percent, 54 percent, and 53 percent, respectively, compared to only a 16 percent drop for whites between 2005 and 2009, according to the Pew Research Center using Census data. In 2009, 39.4 percent of those incarcerated in federal prisons were black, 34.2 percent were white, and 20.6 percent were Hispanic. Sources: Marie Gottschalk, "Two Separate Societies: One in Prison, One Not," *Washington Post*, April 15, 2008. See also Marie Gottschalk, *The Prison and the Gallows: The Politics of Mass Incarceration in America* (New York: Cambridge University Press, 2006), and Heather C. West, Bureau of Justice Statistics, *Prison Inmates at Midyear 2009*, accessed July 27, 2011, at http:// bjs.ojp.usdoj.gov/index.cfm?ty=pbdetail&iid=2200.

According to a 2009 study, blacks accounted for 44.8 percent of those serving time in state prisons for drug crimes, whereas the vastly larger white population composed only 28.5 percent of those serving time. Source: 20.2 percent of those serving in state prison on drug crimes, meanwhile, are Hispanic. Marc Mauer, "The Changing Racial Dynamics of the War on Drugs," The Sentencing Project, Washington, DC, 2009, accessed July 28, 2011, at http://sentencingproject.org /doc/dp_raceanddrugs.pdf.

Meanwhile, our public schools are growing increasingly re-segregated by redistricting and tiered education systems that are supposedly designed to separate high and low achievers. Sources: Gary Orfield and John T. Yun, "Resegregation in American Schools," Harvard: The Civil Rights Project, 1999, at http://course .cas.sc.edu/germanyk/post1945/materials/orfield_Resegregation_American _Schools99.pdf. Also see John Iceland, Daniel H. Weinberg, and Erika Steinmetz,

U.S. Census Bureau, "Racial and Ethnic Segregation in the United States, 1980–2000," presented at the annual meetings of the Population Association of America, Atlanta, 2002, accessed July 27, 2011, at http://www.tsjugephd.com/PCC_Courses /Articles_files/Iceland%20et%20al.pdf.

64. Lee Atwater and Todd Brewster, "Lee Atwater's Last Campaign," *Life* 14 (2) (February 1991): 58–67.

65. Ibid.

66. Bernard Weinraub, "Campaign Trail: A Beloved Mug Shot for the Bush Forces," *New York Times*, October 3, 1988.

67. Kathleen Hall Jamieson, *Dirty Politics: Deception, Distraction, and Democracy* (New York: Oxford University Press, 1992), pp. 16, 42. See also Drew Westen, *The Political Brain* (New York: PublicAffairs, 2007), pp. 63–68: "The Willie Horton ad was well attuned to the primate brain, and particularly to the amygdala, which is highly responsive to both facial expressions and fear-evoking stimuli. The ad was packed with both . . . The mug shot of Horton was obviously the most emotionally powerful image in the ad, playing on every white person's fears of the dangerous, lawless, violent, dark black male." From p. 65, citing N. A. Valentino, V. L. Hutchings, and I. White, "Cues That Matter: How Political Ads Prime Racial Attitudes During Campaigns," *American Political Science Review* 96 (1) (March 2002): 75–90.

68. John McQuaid and Mark Schleifstein, "Washing Away" (five-part series), New Orleans *Times-Picayune*, June 23–27, 2002, accessed July 26, at 2011, http:// www.nola.com/washingaway/. The *Times-Picayune* and the Biloxi-Gulfport (Mississippi) *Sun Herald* each won the 2006 Pulitzer Prize for Public Service. The *Times-Picayune* was cited "for its heroic, multi-faceted coverage of Hurricane Katrina and its aftermath, making exceptional use of the newspaper's resources to serve an inundated city even after the evacuation of the newspaper plant." The newspaper also won the George Polk award, which noted, "With only a skeleton staff whose members themselves were displaced from their homes, the paper persevered, covering the disaster and serving as a critical and accurate source of information for the battered New Orleans community and the world. Although the paper's offices were forced to move from its headquarters in the flooded city, its reporters remained on the streets working. Without access to its printing presses, the nearly 170-year-old paper stepped up its online editions and blogs, generating more than 30 million hits a day. Literally, the reporters and editors astonishingly kept reporting and the newspaper kept publishing even though their building was underwater." Curtis Brainard, "Calling Katrina," The Observatory, *CJR*, April 6, 2010, accessed July 26, 2011, at http://www.cjr.org/the_observatory/calling _katrina.php. See also: "The 2006 Pulitzer Prize Winners, Public Service," The Pulitzer Prize, accessed July 27, 2011, at http://www.pulitzer.org/citation/2006 -Public-Service; and "George Polk Award Winners Honored for Excellence in 14 Categories," *Long Island University Magazine* 17 (Spring 2006), accessed July 27, 2011, at www.liu.edu/About/News/~/media/Files/ . . . /LIUMag_Spring2006 .ashx. Two of the best books about Hurricane Katrina are: John McQuaid and

Mark Schleifstein, *Path of Destruction: The Devastation of New Orleans and the Coming Age of Superstorms* (New York: Little Brown, 2006) and Douglas Brinkley, *The Great Deluge: Hurricane Katrina, New Orleans, and the Mississippi Gulf Coast* (New York: William Morrow, 2006).

69. John Solomon and Margaret Ebrahim, "Video Shows Bush Clearly Warned Before Katrina Struck," Associated Press, March 2, 2006, at http://www.concordmonitor.com/article/video-shows-bush-clearly-warned-before-Katrina-struck.

70. On September 6, 2005, a Federal Emergency Management Agency spokeswoman in an e-mail to Reuters denied the news agency's request to accompany FEMA personnel on rescue boats and also stated, "We have requested that no photographs of the deceased be made by the media." From "Taking Journalists by Storm," in Corinna Zarek, "Katrina Clampdown," *The News Media and the Law* 29 (4) (Fall 2005): 7–8, published by The Reporters Committee for Freedom of the Press, Arlington, Virginia, at www.rcfp.org. On September 9, 2005, reporters were "barred from covering the collection of dead bodies," and Lieutenant General Russel Honoré of the US Army, overseeing the federal relief effort in New Orleans, declared a "zero access" policy for the news media there. CNN immediately filed a First Amendment lawsuit against FEMA, and US district court judge Keith Ellison in Houston granted CNN's request for a temporary restraining order against FEMA. In the initial hearing, Ellison said, "based on the facts as pleaded, that's all I have, it looks like a prior restraint to me. I cannot authorize that." After he formally issued an order against FEMA that he called "unambiguous," the government caved and on September 10, 2005, the Bush Justice Department (specifically US attorney Keith Wyatt) acknowledged in court that it had "no plans to bar, impede, or prevent news media from their news gathering and reporting activities. . . ." Melanie Marquez, "Zero Access Adds Up to Prior Restraint: CNN Wins a Court Order After Military Officials Overseeing Katrina Relief Efforts Attempt to Muzzle the Press," *The News Media and the Law* 29 (4) (Fall 2005): 8–9. See also "CNN Strikes a Blow for First Amendment," *Television Week* 24 (38) (September 19, 2005): p. 10. Deborah Zabarenko, Reuters, "U.S. Censoring Katrina Coverage, Groups Say," *Washington Post*, September 8, 2005, at http://www.washingtonpost.com/wp-dyn/content/article/2005/09/07/AR2005090702126_pf.html, accessed September 3, 2011.

71. David K. Shipler, "Monkey See, Monkey Do: If Pols Ignore Poverty, the Press Does, Too," *Columbia Journalism Review* (November–December 2005): 11–12.

72. Kotz, *Judgment Days*, p. 434.

73. Statement by Representative John Lewis, U.S. House of Representatives, *Congressional Record*, p. E1813, September 8, 2005, at http://www.gpo.gov/fdsys/pkg/CREC-2005-09-08/pdf/CREC-2005-09-08-extensions.pdf, accessed July 28, 2011.

CHAPTER 4: AMERICA'S SECRET FOREIGN POLICY AND THE ARROGANCE OF POWER

1. Fred R. Shapiro, ed., *The Yale Book of Quotations* (New Haven: Yale University Press, 2006), p. 570.

2. There have been numerous books on this overall subject or parts thereof over the years, but an excellent recent one is by veteran foreign correspondent Stephen Kinzer, *Overthrown: America's Century of Regime Change from Hawaii to Iraq* (New York: Times Books/Henry Holt, 2006).

3. The "desolate" quotation is from Peter Kornbluh, *The Pinochet File: A Declassified Dossier on Atrocity and Accountability* (New York: New Press, 2003), p. 341; "cold and barren" is from John Dinges and Saul Landau, *Assassination on Embassy Row* (London: Writers and Readers, 1981, first published New York: Pantheon/Random House, 1980), p. 8.

4. Dinges and Landau, *Assassination on Embassy Row*, p. 8.

5. Kornbluh, *The Pinochet File*, pp. 341–342.

6. Seymour Hersh, *The Price of Power: Kissinger in the Nixon White House* (New York: Summit, 1983), p. 332.

7. Henry Kissinger, *White House Years* (New York: Little, Brown, 1979) and *Years of Upheaval* (New York: Little, Brown, 1982).

8. Charles Lewis, "The Destabilization of Chile by the United States, 1970–73," unpublished senior thesis, University of Delaware, May 1975, p. 173, which cites Tad Szulc, "How Kissinger Runs Our 'Other Government,'" *New York Times*, September 30, 1974.

9. Tim Weiner, "In Tapes, Nixon Muses About Break-Ins at Foreign Embassies," *New York Times*, February 26, 1999, at http://www.nytimes.com/1999/02/26/us/in-tapes-nixon-muses-about-break-ins-at-foreign-embassies.html?pagewanted=all&src=pm, accessed January 5, 2012.

10. Ibid.

11. Hersh, *The Price of Power*, p. 333.

12. Taylor Branch and Eugene M. Propper, *Labyrinth; How a Stubborn U.S. Prosecutor Penetrated a Shadowland of Covert Operations on Three Continents to Find the Assassins of Orlando Letelier* (New York: Viking, 1982), pp. 15–26; Kornbluh, *The Pinochet File*, pp. 341–346.

13. Townley was allowed to plead guilty to one count of conspiracy to murder a foreign official, in order to become the prosecution's "star witness" against the others, who were convicted largely based on Townley's testimony at US District Court in Washington, DC, on February 14, 1979. Judge Barrington Parker sentenced Alvin Ross and Guillermo Novo to two consecutive life sentences each for the murders of Letelier and Moffitt. Each would serve a minimum of forty years before being eligible for parole. Ignacio Novo was sentenced to eight years on the lesser charges of false declarations. However, on September 15, 1980, the US Court of Appeals (Judges Howard F. Corcoran, George E. MacKinnon, and Roger Robb) overturned the convictions of all three men, on the basis of legal technicalities. Months later, the new Reagan/William French Smith Justice Department decided not to appeal that decision to the US Supreme Court. On May 31, 1981, following a new trial, a federal jury acquitted Alvin Ross and Guillermo Novo of all murder charges and convicted Ignacio Novo of making false declarations before a grand jury; he pled guilty to a single charge in October 1981. Regarding the initial

trial, see Dinges and Landau, *Assassination on Embassy Row*, pp. 344–377. For "the continuing aftermath," see Branch and Propper, *Labyrinth*, pp. 572–610.

14. Kornbluh, *The Pinochet File*, pp. 422–428 and 457–469.

15. Kinzer, *Overthrown*, p. 213. See also Larry Rohter, "A Torture Report Compels Chile to Reassess Its Past," *New York Times*, November 28, 2004, at http:// www.nytimes.com/2004/11/28/international/americas/28chile.html?_r=1 &ref=recardolagos, accessed on August 8, 2011. See also Jonathan Kandell, "Augusto Pinochet, Ninety-one, Ex-Dictator of Chile, Dies," December 10, 2006, at http://www.nytimes.com/2006/12/10/world/americas/10cnd-pinochet-obit.html, accessed August 8, 2011.

16. "Covert Action in Chile, 1963–1973," Staff Report of the Select Committee to Study Government Operations with Respect to Intelligence Activities, United States Senate, December 18, 1975, pp. 2–4, at http://foia.state.gov/reports /churchreport.asp.

17. That aid included loans and grants. Ibid.

18. Ibid., pp. 8–10. Dollars/inflation conversion from: http://www/bls.gov /data/inflation_calculator.htm.

19. Kornbluh, *The Pinochet File*, pp. 4–5. The memorandum was dated August 14, 1964.

20. Ibid., pp. 8–10.

21. Ibid.

22. Ibid., pp. 10 and 82. Also see Roger Morris, with Shelley Mueller and William Jelin, "Through the Looking Glass in Chile: Coverage of Allende's Regime," *Columbia Journalism Review* (November–December 1974): 20. As Stephen Kinzer has vividly described, when Kennecott, Anaconda, and the Cerro Mining Corporation were nationalized with the approval of a constitutional amendment in July 1971, Allende decried the "immoral high profits" made for years by Anaconda and Kennecott. He declared an annual profit of up to 12 percent per year to be "rightful" and anything beyond to be "excessive." According to his formulation, Kennecott and Anaconda had made $774 million in excess profits the preceding fifteen years, which exceeded the "book value" of their mines. The Chilean comptroller agreed, and the companies thus were not "awarded a cent." A top Kennecott official in Santiago said, "Nationalization was inevitable. It was only a question of time!" One of Anaconda's lawyers lamented, "We used to be the fuckor. Now we're the fuckee." Kinzer, *Overthrown*, pp. 186–187, citing Theodore H. Moran, *Multinational Corporations and the Politics of Dependence: Copper in Chile* (Princeton: Princeton University Press, 1974), p. 153.

23. Ibid., p. 7. Anthony Sampson, *The Sovereign State of ITT* (New York: Stein and Day, 1973), pp. 264–265 and 276–277, and Terry Sanford et al., "Report of the Special Review Committee of the Board of Directors," *International Telephone and Telegraph Supplementary Report* (New York, n.d.), pp. 48–49, both cited in Nathaniel Davis, *The Last Two Years of Salvador Allende* (Ithaca: Cornell University, 1985), p. 12.

24. In 1860, Lincoln received 39.8 percent of the US popular vote, defeating Southern Democrat John C. Breckinridge, Democrat Stephen Douglas, and

Constitutional Union candidate John Bell to win the presidency. In 1970, Popular Unity candidate Allende received 36.3 percent of the Chilean popular vote, defeating National Party candidate Jorge Alessandri and Christian Democratic candidate Radomiro Tomic.

25. Kornbluh, *The Pinochet File*, pp. 1–2, 17, 37.

26. "Covert Action in Chile," p. 13, citing "Multinational Corporations and United States Foreign Policy," *Hearings Before the Subcommittee on Multinational Corporations, of the Committee on Foreign Relations*, United States Senate, 93rd Cong. (Washington, DC: GPO, 1973), Part 2, pp. 542–543. See also Tad Szulc, "Trying to Read Meaning of Allende Victory," *New York Times*, September 20, 1970, and Lawrence Roberts, "US Again Denies Anti-Allende Policy," *Washington Post*, September 10, 1974.

27. Kornbluh, *The Pinochet File*, p. 10.

28. "Covert Action in Chile," p. 12.

29. Kornbluh, *The Pinochet File*, pp. 27–28, citing Chilean police reports and Seymour Hersh, who first reported the details of the Schneider assassination in *The Price of Power*, p. 290.

30. Kornbluh, *The Pinochet File*, p. 29.

31. Robert Dallek, *Nixon and Kissinger: Partners in Power* (New York: Harper-Collins, 2007), p. 238.

32. Ibid., pp. 29–35; see also "Document 16. CIA, SECRET Memorandum from John Horton on Conversation with False Flagger, Conversation with Bruce MacMaster—Chile Operations," February 18, 1971, pp. 74–76. According to Kornbluh, the reference to the $35,000 payment was released "in a short paragraph" in a September 2000 report to Congress in "CIA Activities in Chile" (from *Pinochet File*, p. 34).

33. Ibid., p. 31. There are numerous reasons for serious skepticism about Kissinger's emphatic under-oath claim that on October 15 he had told the CIA to "stand down" regarding the encouragement of a military coup that required Schneider's removal. For one thing, just over a week earlier, on October 6, 1970, Kissinger had asked CIA director Helms to come to the White House, and hours later, on October 7, Helms had sent an "urgent directive" to the CIA Station in Santiago that said, "Contact the military and let them know that the USG [U.S. government–ed.] wants a military solution and that we will support them now and later . . . create at least some sort of coup climate . . . sponsor a military move." On October 16, with Helms traveling in Southeast Asia, the deputy director of the CIA, Tom Karamessines, following a White House meeting with Kissinger on October 13, had sent another military-coup-encouraging cable to Santiago, "It is firm and continuing policy that Allende be overthrown by a coup . . . encourage [them] to amplify their planning . . . [and] join forces with other coup planners . . . we wish them optimum good fortune." And four days after Kissinger's supposed "stand down" directive regarding any Chilean military coup instigation, on October 19, Karamessines received a "comprehensive plan" from CIA Santiago regarding the Schneider kidnapping and coup plot. He met that afternoon with Kissinger's dep-

uty Alexander Haig. Karamessines later testified before Congress that he would have "very promptly" informed Kissinger and/or Haig of such serious information, and separately, Kissinger's deputy Haig later told Congress that regarding any such information he would have received, "I would consider I had no degree of latitude, other than to convey to him what had been given to me." See Kornbluh, *The Pinochet File*, pp. 29–32, n. 45 on p. 512, referencing "Alleged Assassination Plots," p. 250; and pp. 58–59 (Document 9. CIA, SECRET Cable [Urgent Directive from Director Helms to Stimulate a Military Solution], October 7, 1970); and pp. 68–69 (Document 13, CIA, SECRET Cable from Santiago Station [Report on Plan to Kidnap Gen. Rene Schneider and Initiate a Military Coup], October 19, 1970). See also Tim Weiner, *Legacy of Ashes: The History of the CIA* (New York: Doubleday, 2007), pp. 306–313. And see Hersh, *The Price of Power*, pp. 278–294. According to Hersh, information provided by then former president Nixon via interrogatories, and Kissinger and Haig in secret testimony, was that after October 15, 1970, the CIA "had been operating on its own," up to and after the Schneider assassination, and the Senate Intelligence Committee "made no effort to investigate" the contradiction between their account and the CIA's.

34. Dallek, *Nixon and Kissinger*, pp. 236–237, citing a Richard Nixon–Henry Kissinger telephone conversation on September 15, 1970, from the Richard Nixon Presidential Materials at National Archives II, College Park, Maryland. The Karamessines bottle quote is from Kornbluh, *The Pinochet File*, pp. 25–26 and 62–63, quoting "Document 11. CIA, SECRET Memorandum of Conversation, 'Dr. Kissinger, Mr. Karamessines, Gen. Haig at the White House'—October 15, 1970."

35. Richard M. Nixon, *The Memoirs of Richard Nixon* (New York: Grosset and Dunlap, 1978), pp. 489–490. There is no mention of the Schneider assassination or the human rights carnage that followed the September 1973 military coup d'état in Chile. See also Kissinger, *White House Years*, pp. 653–683, and his statement that the military coup "effort was terminated by me on October 15, 1970" (p. 674). And from Kissinger, *Years of Upheaval*, chap. 9, "Chile: The Fall of Salvador Allende," pp. 374–413: "In the Senate Committee's investigation of US *government* plots to *assassinate* foreign leaders . . . amid all of its insinuation the Senate Committee did find that there was no US plot to assassinate General Schneider. Indeed, no one intended assassination" (italics in original, p. 677). See Henry Kissinger, *Years of Renewal* (New York: Simon and Schuster, 1999), pp. 749–760: "Though we had had no hand in the military coup, we thought it saved Chile from totalitarianism and the Southern Cone from collapse into radicalism. We did not approve of Pinochet's methods. . . ." At the same time, Kissinger wrote, "We were also highly conscious of the double standard that was applied to post-coup Chile. No radical anti-American revolution suffered the vituperation launched against the clumsy authoritarians in Santiago" (pp. 753–754).

36. "A Conversation with the President," January 4, 1971, John T. Woolley and Gerhard Peters, The American Presidency Project [online] (Santa Barbara, CA), at http://www.presidency.ucsb.edu/ws/?pid=3307/.

37. "Covert Action in Chile," p. 13.

38. "Panel Interview at the Annual Convention of the American Society of Newspaper Editors," April 16, 1971, Woolley and Peters, The American Presidency Project [online], at http://www.presidency.ucsb.edu/ws/?pid=2982.

39. "Covert Action in Chile," p. 15.

40. Kornbluh, *The Pinochet File*, pp. 86–94. See also "Covert Action in Chile," pp. 13–18.

41. The nearly forty-year controversy over whether Allende was murdered or committed suicide appears to have been resolved recently by a team of Chilean and international forensic experts. A judge investigating 726 human rights cases related to the Pinochet era ordered Allende's remains exhumed, and in 2011 the experts concluded "that the head injuries he sustained were consistent with bullets fired from a single AK-47 assault rifle" known to be in his possession at the time of the coup. See Alexei Barrionuevo and Pascale Bonnefoy, "Allende Was a Suicide, an Autopsy Concludes," *New York Times*, July 20, 2011.

42. *The Report on the Chilean National Commission on Truth and Reconciliation*, also known as the Rettig Commission Report, English Edition (Notre Dame, IN: Notre Dame University Press, 1993), noted in Peter Kornbluh, *The Pinochet File*, p. 154, with footnote on p. 517. The Pinochet quote is from Kornbluh, p. 113. The two Americans killed in the immediate aftermath of the coup were named Charles Horman and Frank Teruggi; also killed were Ronni Moffitt in Washington in 1974 and Boris Weisfeiler in southern Chile in early 1985. Horman's murder received by far the most news coverage—reporting by Frank Manitzas of CBS News, and two stories in the *Washington Post* about Horman (Joanne Omang, "Chilean Charges General Ordered American's Death," *Washington Post*, June 10, 1976; Lewis H. Diuguid, "The Man Who 'Knew Too Much,'" *Washington Post*, June 20, 1976). There was a subsequent book by Thomas Hauser, *The Execution of Charles Horman: An American Sacrifice* (New York: Harcourt, Brace, Jovanovich, 1978), which was later reissued in paperback under the title *Missing*. The movie *Missing* was released in February 1982 and later nominated for a Best Picture Academy Award, and it won the Oscar for best screenplay. The movie starred Jack Lemmon and Sissy Spacek and was directed by Costa-Gavras. In January 1983, former US ambassador to Chile Nathaniel Davis, US consul Frederick Purdy, and US naval attaché Ray Davis sued Hauser, Costa-Gavras, and Universal Pictures for $150 million for defamation. The case was dismissed in July 1987, and Universal and Costa-Gavras and the plaintiffs issued a joint statement that *Missing* was "not intended to suggest that Nathaniel Davis, Ray Davis or Frederick Purdy ordered or approved the order for the murder of Charles Horman—and would not wish viewers of the film to interpret it this way." See Kornbluh, *The Pinochet File*, chap. 5, "American Casualties," pp. 268–322 and nn. 1 and 2. See also Davis, *The Last Two Years of Salvador Allende*, pp. 378–382.

43. Kornbluh, *The Pinochet File*, p. 202. Pinochet requested the meeting with Urrutia. For more information, Kornbluh cites Ambassador Nathaniel Davis's memcon on the Pinochet-Urrutia meeting, "Gen. Pinochet's Request for Meeting with MILGP Officer," September 12, 1973.

44. Ibid., pp. 202–206. See also "Document 3. Department of State, SECRET Meeting Minutes of the Washington Special Action Group, 'Chile,' September 20, 1973, p. 236.

45. Kornbluh, *The Pinochet File*, pp. 203–206. See also "Covert Action in 'Chile,'" p. 15, Table II, Foreign Aid to Chile from U.S. Government Agencies and International Institutions—Total of Loans and Grants (in millions of dollars), 1953 through 1974.

46. Mark Feldstein, *Poisoning the Press: Richard Nixon, Jack Anderson, and the Rise of Washington's Scandal Culture* (New York: Picador, 2011), p. 277, from Dallek, *Kissinger and Nixon*, pp. 511–512, citing Nixon White House tapes.

47. "Alleged Assassination Plots Involving Foreign Leaders," *An Interim Report of the Select Committee to Study Governmental Operations with Respect to Intelligence Activities,* United States Senate (Washington, DC: Government Printing Office, 1975; reprinted by Ipswich, MA: Mary Ferrell Foundation Press), p. 1. For a complete online archive of all of the Church Committee reports, see http://www .aarclibrary.org/publib/contents/church/contents_church_reports.htm, accessed September 16, 2011.

48. Kornbluh, *The Pinochet File*, pp. 217–222.

49. Ibid.

50. Kornbluh, *The Pinochet File*, op. cit., pp. 217–222; see Seymour M. Hersh, *The Price of Power: Kissinger in the Nixon White House* (New York: Summit Books, 1983), pp. 258–296 (Chapters 21 and 22). Hersh's reporting hugely influenced the rest of the news media, including the CBS News Washington bureau. Schorr was assigned to "develop what, in effect, would be a television version of Hersh's stories." Transcript of the *CBS Evening News with Walter Cronkite*, February 28, 1975, in which Schorr begins, "President Ford has reportedly warned associates that if current investigations go too far, they could uncover several assassinations of foreign officials in which the CIA was involved . . . " Schorr and others reported the details of these CIA activities in the summer and fall of 1975, as "an unbelievable array of witnesses" began parading before closed hearings of the Church Committee. Daniel Schorr, *Clearing the Air* (Boston: Houghton Mifflin, 1977), pp. 153–155. See also Daniel Schorr, *Staying Tuned: A Life in Journalism* (New York: Pocket Books/ Simon & Schuster, 2001), pp. 261–272. Schorr also reported closely on the House of Representatives Pike Committee's findings and he managed to obtain a leaked copy of its unpublished final report. Remembering how the *New York Times* published the Pentagon Papers in their entirety in book form, he asked his employer, CBS News, to publish the report via one of its two book companies. But CBS declined. Schorr gave the leaked report to the *Village Voice*, where it was published, and he was subsequently investigated for months by the House ethics committee, which eventually voted 6–5 *not* to recommend a contempt citation over his refusal to reveal his source. Schorr left CBS, twenty-three years after being hired by Edward R. Murrow.

51. For more information about this whole complicated First Amendment episode, see Schorr's *Clearing the Air*, pp. 179–284, and *Staying Tuned*, pp. 277–300;

assault on the intelligence community quote from Kissinger's memoir, *Years of Upheaval*, p. 313. For his recollections and perspective of the "Intelligence Investigations," see pp. 310–343. For a discussion of how Kissinger misled Ford, see Kornbluh, *The Pinochet File*, pp. 219–222.

52. I had only been "on the job" at ABC News for a few weeks before Helms was indicted, and I was fortunate to be in the courtroom that day, the only time a CIA director was ever prosecuted for a crime. The Helms false statements were made to the full Senate Foreign Relations Committee on March 6, 1973, in executive session. In response to Senator Frank Church's question, "Mr. Helms, did the CIA attempt at any time to prevent Salvador Allende Gossens from being elected President of Chile in 1970?" Helms replied "No, sir." And so on. From Kornbluh, *The Pinochet File*, pp. 103–104, citing Richard Harris, "Secrets," *New Yorker*, April 10, 1978. See also Thomas Powers, *The Man Who Kept the Secrets* (New York: Knopf, 1979), pp. 7–11 and 253–275 (including the footnotes on pp. 413–419), 345–353. See Anthony Marro, "Helms, Ex-C.I.A. Chief, Pleads No Contest to Two Misdemeanors," *New York Times*, November 1, 1977; Anthony Marro, "Helms Is Fined $2,000 and Given Two-Year Suspended Prison Term," *New York Times*, November 5, 1977; Dick Clark, "That Helms 'Badge of Honor,'" *New York Times*, November 13, 1977.

53. Richard Helms, with William Hood, *A Look over My Shoulder: A Life in the Central Intelligence Agency* (New York: Random House, 2003), pp. 393–408 and 339–346, for his recollections about being prosecuted by the Justice Department.

54. Robert Schakne, letter to the editor, "An Exchange on Chile: Robert Schakne and Roger Morris," *Columbia Journalism Review* 13 (5) (January–February 1975): 56–58; and Robert Schakne, "Chile: Why We Missed the Story," *Columbia Journalism Review* 14 (6) (March–April 1976): 60–62. Schakne died in 1989, "Robert Schakne, Sixty-three, a CBS News Reporter," *New York Times*, September 1, 1989, at http://www.nytimes.com/1989/09/01/obituaries/robert-schakne -63-a-cbs-news-reporter.html. His letter to the editor was in response to a long, eloquent, hard-hitting article by Roger Morris, author and former National Security Council staff assistant to Henry Kissinger. See Morris, with Shelly Mueller and William Jelin, "Through the Looking Glass in Chile: Coverage of Allende's Regime," *Columbia Journalism Review* 13 (4) (November–December 1974): 15–26. "The unwritten, untelevised story of U.S. policy toward Allende's Chile was in part another casualty of the continuing failure of independent, inquiring reporting . . . But the failures of journalism—in covering the policy made in Washington and the events on the scene—were also failures to understand and to report the reality of a very different culture" (p. 24). The lowest point journalistically in the whole Allende-Nixon episode was when the CIA, in a period of two weeks, brought twenty-three reporters into Chile from ten countries prior to the 1970 election: "They combined with the CIA 'assets' already in place to produce more than 700 articles before the congressional election—a staggering total whose ultimate influence cannot be measured," according to Hersh in *The Price of Power*, pp. 272–273, citing the Senate Intelligence Committee.

55. *Hearings Before the Select Committee to Study Governmental Operations with Respect to Intelligence Activities of the United States Senate*, 94th Cong., 1st Sess., Vol. 7, Covert Action, December 4 and 5, 1975, p. 15, at http://www.scribd.com /doc/37274519/Church-Committee-Hearings-Volume-7, accessed on August 9, 2011.

56. Raymond W. Baker, *Capitalism's Achilles Heel: Dirty Money and How to Renew the Free-Market System* (New York: Wiley and Sons, 2005), pp. 54–55, 387; citing two reports issued by the U.S. Senate Committee on Governmental Affairs, Permanent Subcommittee on Investigations, "Money Laundering and Foreign Corruption: Enforcement and Effectiveness of the Patriot Act, Case Study Involving Riggs Bank," July 15, 2004, p. 18, and "Money Laundering and Foreign Corruption: Enforcement and Effectiveness of the Patriot Act, Supplemental Staff Report on U.S. Accounts Used by Augusto Pinochet," March 16, 2005, p. 7.

57. John Dinges, *The Condor Years: How Pinochet and His Allies Brought Terrorism to Three Continents* (New York: New Press, 2004), pp. 197–198, citing an interview of Hewson Ryan: The Association for Diplomatic Studies and Training, Foreign Affairs Oral History Project, interviewed by Richard Nethercut, April 27, 1988 (Dinges notes; p. 291; the interview accessed online September 24, 2011, at http://www.gwu.edu/~nsarchiv/NSAEBB/NSAEBB125/condor15.pdf. Ryan died in 1991 ("Hewson A. Ryan, Sixty-nine, Professor and Envoy," *New York Times*, October 1, 1991, at http://www.nytimes.com/1991/10/01/obituaries/hewson-a-ryan-69 -professor-and-envoy.html, accessed September 24, 2011). Dinges, an award-winning, former *Washington Post* and *Time* reporter has written in *The Condor Years* (pp. 247–253), "It is a major conclusion of this book that U.S. officials knew enough to have stopped the [Letelier] assassination, and that they launched a flawed and foreshortened effort to do so, then covered up their failure after Letelier and an American woman [Ronni Moffitt] were murdered."

58. Peter Kornbluh, ed., "Kissinger Blocked Demarche on International Assassinations to Condor States; Rescinded Orders to Warn Military Regimes Days Before Letelier Bombing in Washington, D.C.; Overruled Aides Who Wanted to 'Head Off' a 'Series of International Murders,'" at http://www.gwu.edu/~nsarchiv /NSAEBB/NSAEBB312/index.htm. Kissinger, through his assistant Tara Butzbaugh, declined my written request for an interview on October 31, 2011, citing "his heavy travel schedule at this time," and I was told to "check back with me in the Spring of next year" (e-mail exchange). For the record, I did not check back with Kissinger's office half a year later.

59. Chalmers Johnson, *Nemesis: The Last Days of the American Republic* (New York: Metropolitan Books/Henry Holt, 2006), p. 109. See also Dinges and Landau, *Assassination on Embassy Row*, pp. 240–244; Dinges, *The Condor Years*, pp. 68–71. See David Binder, "F.B.I. Gets Tip in the Letelier Bombing Case That High Chilean Secret Policeman Flew to U.S. Last Month," *New York Times*, September 23, 1976, p. 8; Stephen J. Lynton and Timothy S. Robinson, "No New Leads Uncovered in Letelier Probe," *Washington Post*, November 1, 1976; John A. Conway, "Murder Mystery," Newsweek Periscope Column, *Newsweek*, October 11, 1976.

60. See John B. Judis, *William F. Buckley, Jr.; Patron Saint of the Conservatives* (New York: Simon and Schuster, 1988), pp. 89–92, 98, 359, 405–406, and p. 494, n. 23. See the original court records: *Attorney General of the United States of America, United States Department of Justice v. American-Chilean Council, Marvin Liebman, Incorporated, and Marvin Liebman*, Civil Action 78–2379, Complaint filed December 18, 1978. Final Judgment of Permanent Injunction against the ACC and Liebman, filed November 8, 1979; See also Godfrey Hodgson, "I Don't Stoop. I Merely Conquer," *New York Times*, May 15, 1988, at http://www.nytimes.com /books/00/07/16/specials/buckley-judis.html, accessed January 7, 2012.

61. Kornbluh, *The Pinochet File*, pp. 473–479. Regarding the practice of public officials hoarding and hiding government records after they leave government, see Steven Weinberg, "For Their Eyes Only," July 1992, The Center for Public Integrity, Washington, DC, at http://www.publicintegrity.org/assets/pdf/FORTHEIR EYESONLY.pdf, accessed September 12, 2011.

62. For more information, see Eric Alterman, *When Presidents Lie: A History of Official Deception and Its Consequences* (New York: Viking, 2004); Piero Gleijeses, *The Dominican Crisis: The 1965 Constitutionalist Revolt and American Intervention* (Baltimore: Johns Hopkins University Press, 1978); Kinzer, *Overthrown*; Jacqueline Sharkey, *Under Fire: Military Restrictions on the Media from Grenada to the Persian Gulf* (Washington, DC: The Center for Public Integrity, 1991); *The Panama Deception*, a documentary film directed by Barbara Trent, written and edited by David Kasper, narrated by Elizabeth Montgomery, which won the 1992 Academy Award for Best Documentary Feature.

63. Two interesting ruminations on this fascinating subject by iconic thinkers are Reinhold Niebuhr, *The Irony of American History* (New York: Scribners, 1952) and George F. Kennan, "Morality and Foreign Policy," *Foreign Affairs* (Winter 1985–1986): 205–218.

64. Cynthia Arnson, *Crossroads: Congress, the President, and Central America, 1976–1992* (New York: Pantheon, 1989), pp. 36–38. The Special Central American and Caribbean Security Assistance Act was sent to Congress on November 9, 1979, and not approved until September 1980. The House authorization vote was very close: 202–197. For a detailed discussion of US policy toward Nicaragua in the last year of Somoza's regime and the eighteen months of the Sandinistas, see Robert A. Pastor, *Condemned to Repetition: The United States and Nicaragua* (Princeton: Princeton University Press, 1988), pp. 140–229.

65. Ronald Reagan, *Reagan in His Own Hand: The Writings of Ronald Reagan That Reveal His Revolutionary Vision for America*, ed. Kiron K. Skinner et al. (New York: Free Press, 2001), p. 159. The March 6, 1979, broadcast was entitled, "Cuba."

66. Walter LaFeber, *Inevitable Revolutions: The United States in Central America*, 2nd ed. (New York: W. W. Norton, 1993), p. 5.

67. "Secret wars" quote from Haynes Johnson, *Sleepwalking Through History: America in the Reagan Years* (New York: Norton, 1991), pp. 257–258. Reagan comments are from William M. LeoGrande, *Our Own Backyard: The United States in Central America, 1977–1992* (Chapel Hill: University of North Carolina Press,

2000), p. 201, citing "Remarks at the Annual Washington Conference of the American Legion," February 22, 1983, *Reagan Papers, 1983*, book 1, pp. 264–267.

68. LaFeber, *Inevitable Revolutions*, p. 362.

69. Ibid., pp. 362–363. The $30 billion in losses number and rich-poor gap are from the Center for Latin American Monetary Studies, cited in *Excelsior*, December 15, 1987, in *Central America NewsPak*, December 21, 1987–January 3, 1988, pp. 1–2; *Washington Post*, March 19, 1986.

70. *Guatemala: Memory of Silence* (Guatemala: Memoria del Silencio), Commission for Historical Clarification (Comisión para el Esclarecimiento Histórico), at http://www.usip.org/publications/truth-commission-guatemala; for the report in English, see http://shr.aaas.org/guatemala/ceh/report/english/toc.html, both accessed January 30, 2012. See also "The Atrocity Findings: 'The Historic Facts Must Be Recognized,'" *New York Times*, February 26, 1999; Larry Rohter, "Searing Indictment," *New York Times*, February 27, 1999; "Guatemala's Nightmare Past," *New York Times*, February 28, 1999; Adam Jones, *Genocide: A Comprehensive Introduction*, 2nd ed. (New York: Routledge, 2011), pp. 139–148.

71. Kate Doyle, "Helping Guatemala Find the Truth," *New York Times*, March 1, 1999; Charles Babington, "Clinton: Support for Guatemala Was Wrong," *Washington Post*, March 11, 1999; Douglas Farah, "Papers Show U.S. Role in Guatemalan Abuses," *Washington Post*, March 11, 1999. See the Guatemala Documentation Project, directed by Kate Doyle, National Security Archive, at http://www.gwu.edu/~nsarchiv/latin_america/guatemala.html, accessed January 30, 2012. "Report of New Developments," Restoration of the National Police Archive Project, Procuraduria de los Derechos Humanos, PDH, December 2006, at http://www.d.dccam.org/Projects/Affinity/Restoration_of_the_National_Police_Archive_Project.pdf, accessed January 30, 2012; Emily Willard, "Former Senior Guatemalan Officials Arrested for Genocide and Forced Disappearance," National Security Archive, June 30, 2011, at http://nsarchive.wordpress.com/2011/06/30/former-senior-guatemalan-officials-arrested-for-genocide-and-forced-disappearance/, accessed January 30, 2012. See also Archivo Histórico de la Policía Nacional, at http://www.archivohistoricopn.org/, accessed January 30, 2012. For an excellent analysis of the military, see Jennifer Schirmer, *The Guatemalan Military Project: A Violence Called Democracy* (Philadelphia: University of Pennsylvania Press, 1998).

72. Alma Guillermoprieto, "Salvadoran Peasants Describe Mass Killing: Woman Tells of Children's Death," *Washington Post*, January 27, 1982. See also Raymond Bonner, "Massacre of Hundreds Reported in Salvador Village," *New York Times*, January 27, 1982; Raymond Bonner, *Weakness and Deceit: U.S. Policy and El Salvador* (New York: Times Books, 1984); Mark Danner, *The Massacre at El Mozote* (New York: Vintage/Random House, 1994); Tom Rosenstiel and Amy S. Mitchell, eds., *Thinking Clearly: Cases in Journalistic Decision-Making* (New York: Columbia University Press, 2003), chap. 5, Stanley Meisler, "The Massacre in El Mozote" (also available online at http://www.journalism.org/node/1786, accessed January 30, 2012).

73. Ed Bradley, correspondent; David Gelber, producer; "Massacre at El Mozote; U.S. Government Beginning to Release Facts of 1981 Massacre by El

Salvador Troops," CBS News *60 Minutes* transcript, March 14, 1993. See also Report of the Secretary of State's Panel on El Salvador, July 1993, p. 58.

74. Mark Danner, "The Truth of El Mozote," *New Yorker*, December 6, 1993, at http://www.markdanner.com/articles/show/the_truth_of_el_mozote, accessed February 4, 2012. Also see U.S. Senate, Committee on Foreign Relations, *Certification Concerning Military Aid to El Salvador: Hearing Before the Committee on Foreign Relations*, 97th Cong., 2nd Sess., February 8, 1982, pp. 20–22; Stanley Meisler, "The Massacre in El Mozote," pp. 119–122; John A. Kirch, "Raymond Bonner and the Salvadoran Civil War 1980 to 1983," paper presented at the Association for Education in Journalism and Mass Communication (AEJMC), Toronto, Canada, August 2004, citing William A. Henry III and Harry Kelly, "Press: War as a Media Event," *Time*, March 29, 1982. *Time*'s Henry called Bonner "the most controversial journalist on the scene" and also observed, "An even more crucial if common oversight is the fact that women and children, generally presumed to be civilians, can be active participants in guerrilla war. *New York Times* correspondent Raymond Bonner underplayed that possibility." See Mike Hoyt, "The Mozote Massacre: It Was the Reporters' Word Against the Government's," *Columbia Journalism Review* (January–February 1993); Joseph C. Goulden, *Fit to Print: A. M. Rosenthal and His Times* (Secaucus, NJ: Lyle Stuart, 1988), pp. 327–345.

75. Interview with Bill Kovach, July 27, 2010, Washington, DC.

76. Ibid.; Joseph C. Goulden, *Fit to Print*, pp. 327–345; Michael Massing, "About-Face on El Salvador," *Columbia Journalism Review* (November–December 1982), pp. 42–48. See also Mark Hertsgaard, *On Bended Knee: The Press and the Reagan Presidency* (New York: Farrar Straus Giroux, 1988), pp. 186–203. Hertsgaard concluded about the effects of Bonner's forced departure from El Salvador: "El Salvador was whisked from the U.S. news agenda; a nasty thorn was removed from the paw of the administration; other journalists were warned against reporting too frankly about U.S. policy in Central America; and the American public was deprived of a full and accurate accounting of exactly what was being done in its name in the troubled lands south of the border." It should be noted that years later, Bonner did eventually return to the *New York Times* as a contract writer.

77. Interview with Raymond Bonner, March 1, 2012, Washington, DC.

78. Danner, "The Truth of El Mozote"; Tim Golden, "Salvador Skeletons Confirm Reports of Massacre in 1981," *New York Times*, October 22, 1992, at http://www.nytimes.com/1992/10/22/world/salvador-skeletons-confirm-reports-of-massacre-in-1981.html?pagewanted=all, accessed on February 6, 2012. "From Madness to Hope: The Twelve-Year War in El Salvador: Report of the Commission on the Truth for El Salvador," The El Salvador Truth Commission, posted by the U.S. Institute of Peace from the UN Security Council, Annex, at http://www.usip.org/files/file/ElSalvador-Report.pdf, accessed April 29, 2012. See also "El Salvador: War, Peace, and Human Rights, 1980–1994," the National Security Archive's collection of declassified U.S. government records, at www.gwu.edu/~nsarchiv/nsa/publication/elsalvador2/. See also http://nsarchive.chadwyck.com/nsa/documents/EL/01324/all.pdf.

79. *60 Minutes* transcript, March 1993, and Bonner interview, March 1, 2012.

80. In March 1993, five days after the El Salvador Truth Commission report was published, the Salvadoran legislature astonishingly passed a blanket amnesty *prohibiting* the prosecution of anyone responsible for the El Mozote massacre or any other war-related crimes against humanity. See Danner, "The Truth of El Mozote"; George S. Vest, Richard W. Murphy, and I. M. Destler, U.S. Department of State, "Report of the Secretary of State's Panel on El Salvador" (Washington, DC: Government Printing Office, July 15, 1993).

81. Three articles by Clifford Krauss, "Christopher Picks El Salvador Panel," *New York Times*, March 25, 1993; "Clinton Vows Full Review of U.S. Role in Salvador," *New York Times*, July 13, 1993; and "Testimony in '82 on Salvador Criticized," *New York Times*, July 16, 1993, at http://www.nytimes.com/1993/07/16/world /testimony-in-82-on-salvador-criticized.html?pagewanted=all, accessed February 6, 2012.

82. Theodore Draper, *A Very Thin Line: The Iran-Contra Affairs* (New York: Hill and Wang, 1992), pp. 27–28 and 71–93.

83. Quoted material is from Executive Summary of the *Report of the Congressional Committees Investigating the Iran-Contra Affair, with Supplemental, Minority, and Additional Views*, November 1987; *U.S. House of Representatives Select Committee to Investigate Covert Arms Transactions with Iran, U.S. Senate Select Committee on Secret Military Assistance to Iran and the Nicaraguan Opposition* (Washington, DC: Government Printing Office, 1987), pp. 3–22.

84. See Draper, *A Very Thin Line*; Peter Kornbluh and Malcolm Byrne, *The Iran-Contra Scandal: The Declassified History*, foreword by Theodore Draper (New York: A National Security Archive Documents Reader/The New Press, 1993). See "Document 90, Office of the Independent Counsel, Fact Sheet, December 1992," pp. 342–343, detailing the precise outcomes of Walsh's Iran-Contra prosecutions up to that time, eleven convictions with two of them dismissed on appeal, on the eve of the President George H. W. Bush pardons. According to historian Draper's foreword, "Dozens of officials, including the highest, testified publicly or privately for hours and even days under oath about what they knew and did . . . Nothing comparable on this scale has ever opened the national security branches of government to such scrutiny." "Report of the Congressional Committees Investigating the Iran-Contra Affair"; *The Tower Commission Report: The Full Text of the President's Special Review Board*, a *New York Times* Special, introduction by R. W. Apple Jr. (New York: Bantam, 1987).

85. Seymour M. Hersh, "The Iran-Contra Committees: Did They Protect Reagan?" *New York Times Magazine*, April 29, 1990. It should be noted that predictably, the Iran-Contra Republican minority report (the ranking House Republican was Representative Richard B. Cheney) forcefully disagreed with the conclusions of the committee: "The mistakes of the Iran-Contra Affair were just that—mistakes in judgment, and nothing more. There was no constitutional crisis, no systematic disrespect for the 'rule of law,' no grand conspiracy, and no Administration-wide dishonesty or coverup." It was Cheney who had helped shepherd Oliver North's

final televised testimony, and he later received an appreciative call on a Saturday soon afterward from First Lady Nancy Reagan and President Reagan, who thanked him "for the role I had played in the investigation." Dick Cheney with Liz Cheney, *In My Time* (New York: Threshold Editions/Simon and Schuster, 2011), pp. 143–148.

86. Eleanor Randolph, "Press Blunders: How Newshounds Blew the Iran-Contra Story," *Washington Post* (Outlook), November 15, 1987; and www.pulitzer .org and http://www.liu.edu/About/News/Polk/Previous.aspx, both accessed on February 13, 2012. See also Mark Hertsgaard's chapter, "In Front of Their Noses," *On Bended Knee*, pp. 299–316.

87. Anthony Lewis, "Why Not Watergate?" *New York Times*, May 11, 1990, at http://www.nytimes.com/1990/05/11/opinion/abroad-at-home-why-not-watergate .html, accessed February 13, 2012.

88. Lawrence E. Walsh, *Firewall: The Iran-Contra Conspiracy and Cover-Up* (New York: Norton, 1997), pp. 531. See also Lawrence E. Walsh, *The Gift of Insecurity: A Lawyer's Life* foreword by Nina Totenberg (Chicago: American Bar Association/ ABA Publishing, 2003), pp. 267–279. See also Bob Woodward, *Shadow: Five Presidents and the Legacy of Watergate* (New York: Simon and Schuster, 1998), pp. 91–170; George P. Shultz, *Turmoil and Triumph: My Years as Secretary of State* (New York: Scribner's, 1993), pp. 783–859; Ronald Reagan, *The Reagan Diaries*, ed. Douglas Brinkley (New York: HarperCollins, 2007), pp. 453–462 and 512–518.

89. Charles Lewis, "Freedom of Information Under Attack," The Center for Public Integrity, Washington, DC, June 26, 2002. Also "Executive Order 13233 of November 1, 2001," *Federal Register* 66 (214) (Monday, November 5, 2001), at http://frwebgate.access.gpo.gov/cgi-bin/getpage.cgi?dbname=2001_register &position=all&page=56025, accessed February 16, 2012; "Executive Order 13489—Presidential Records," National Archives, January 21, 2009, at http:// www.archives.gov/about/laws/appendix/13489.html, accessed February 16, 2012; e-mail exchange with Peter Kornbluh of the National Security Archive, February 13, 2012; Steven L. Henson, "The President's Papers Are the People's Business," *Washington Post*, December 16, 2001.

CHAPTER 5: DOUBT IS THEIR PRODUCT: THE CORPORATE WAR ON TRUTH

1. Walter Lippmann, *Liberty and the News* (New Brunswick, NJ: Transaction Publishers, 1995; Harcourt, Brace and Howe, 1920), p. 13.

2. Transcript of recorded remarks of Bob Woodward, speaking at the third members' meeting of the Center for Public Integrity International Consortium of Investigative Journalists, at the Freedom Forum, Arlington, Virginia, June 28, 2001.

3. Alicia C. Shepard, *Woodward and Bernstein: Life in the Shadow of Watergate* (Hoboken, NJ: Wiley and Sons, 2007), pp. 194–204.

4. Florence George Graves, "Enshrining Investigative Reporting," *American Journalism Review* (April 1998), at http://www.ajr.org/article.asp?id=164, accessed June 24, 2012.

5. Shepard, *Woodward and Bernstein*, pp. 199–200. According to Shepard, even more complicating, Woodward's then girlfriend and now wife, Elsa Walsh, whom he had actually hired, was sharing an apartment with Janet Cooke.

6. E-mail exchange with Morton Mintz, March 20, 2010.

7. Ibid., August 5, 2008.

8. Morton Mintz profile and career time line, "Investigating Power," at www.investigatingpower.org, accessed June 22, 2012.

9. John F. Kennedy: "Remarks upon Presenting the President's Awards for Distinguished Federal Civilian Service," August 7, 1962, available online by Gerhard Peters and John T. Woolley, The American Presidency Project, at http://www.presidency.ucsb.edu/ws/?pid=8807, accessed June 23, 2012.

10. Wallace F. Janssen, FDA historian, "The Story of the Laws Behind the Labels," *FDA Consumer* (June 1981), at www.fda.gov/AboutFDA/WhatWeDo/History/Overviews/ucm056044.htm, accessed June 23, 2012.

11. Morton Mintz, *The Therapeutic Nightmare: A Report on Prescription Drugs, the Men Who Make Them, and the Agency That Controls Them* (Boston: Houghton Mifflin, 1965).

12. Interview with Morton Mintz, April 27, 2007, Washington, DC. In subsequent digging into FDA records, Mintz found that to try to get thalidomide approved, the William S. Merrell Company had "made 50 contacts with Dr. Kelsey and FDA officials." Morton Mintz, "FDA, with New Power, Faces Call for Reform," *Washington Post*, August 26, 1962.

13. See http://www.mortonmintz.com/work2.htm, accessed June 23, 2012. Book information is from www.johnemossfoundation.org/bio/mintz.htm, accessed June 26, 2012. See Morton Mintz, *At Any Cost: Corporate Greed, Women, and the Dalkon Shield* (New York: Pantheon, 1985).

14. E-mail exchange with Morton Mintz, August 5, 2008.

15. Carol Felsenthal, *Power, Privilege, and the Post: The Katharine Graham Story* (New York: Putnam, 1993), p. 356.

16. Interview/e-mail exchange with John Hanrahan, June 25, 2012.

17. Interview/e-mail exchange with Barry Sussman, June 27, 2012.

18. Larry Tye, *The Father of Spin: Edward L. Bernays and the Birth of Public Relations* (New York: Picador, 2002), p. 9.

19. Edward Bernays, *Propaganda* (New York: Liveright, 1928; reprint New York: Ig Publishing, 2005), pp. 37–38.

20. Scott M. Cutlip, *The Unseen Power: Public Relations, a History* (Hillsdale, N.J.: Lawrence Erlbaum Associates: 1994), p. 151; John Stauber and Sheldon Rampton, *Toxic Sludge Is Good for You! Lies, Damn Lies and the Public Relations Industry*, introduction by Mark Dowie (Monroe, ME: Common Courage Press, 1995), p. 22; Brendan I. Koerner, "Who Must Register as a Foreign Agent?" at www.slate.com, July 10, 2003. I.G. Farben, which no longer exists, is most notorious for its participation, fully and knowingly, in the medical experimentation and mass extermination at Auschwitz, actually producing the poison gas used to kill Jews (*United States of America v. Carl Krauch et al.*, Records of the United States Nuremberg War

Crimes Trials, National Archives Microfilm Publications, August 14, 1947–July 30, 1948). Lee denied that his work for Farben in the early years of the Third Reich was essentially a ruse and that he was actually assisting the Nazi government, but prior to his congressional testimony, in a private letter to his son James, who was working in Germany on the Farben account, he had acknowledged that they in fact were there "to advise Berlin how to state its own case to the American people." Separately, James once wrote home to his mother: "The muscles of my right arm are still swollen from saluting. I'm getting to be a pretty good Nazi." He also told his mother in private correspondence that he (James) had "friends . . . in the Propaganda Ministerium" (Ivy Ledbetter Lee Papers: Public Policy Papers, Department of Rare Books and Special Collections, Princeton University Library).

21. Richard Kluger, *Ashes to Ashes: America's Hundred-Year Cigarette War, the Public Health, and the Unabashed Triumph of Philip Morris* (New York: Vintage, 1997), pp. 78–79, quoting from Edward L. Bernays, *Biography of an Idea: Memoirs of Public Relations Counsel Edward L. Bernays* (New York: Simon and Schuster, 1965), pp. 386–387.

22. Ibid.

23. Ibid.

24. Tye, *The Father of Spin*, p. 33.

25. *Annals of the American Academy of Political and Social Science* 250 (March 1947): 113–120, the basis for "The Engineering of Consent" chapter in Edward Bernays, *Public Relations* (Norman: University of Oklahoma Press, 1952), p. 168.

26. Kluger, *Ashes to Ashes*, p. 136, and David Michaels, *Doubt Is Their Product: How Industry's Assault on Science Threatens Your Health* (New York: Oxford University Press, 2008), p. 5.

27. Michaels, *Doubt Is Their Product*, p. 5.

28. Ibid., p. 6.

29. Allan M. Brandt, *The Cigarette Century: The Rise, Fall, and Deadly Persistence of the Product That Defined America* (New York: Basic Books, 2007), pp. 165–166.

30. Ibid., pp. 170–171, citing http://legacy.library.ucsf.edu/tid/qxp91e00.

31. Ibid., p. 233, from Addison Yeaman, "Implications of Battelle Hippo I & II and the Griffith Filter," July 17, 1963, Bates No. 2074459290/9294, at http://legacy.library.ucsf.edu/tid/ari52c00.

32. Michaels, *Doubt Is Their Product*, p. 9.

33. Ibid., p. 11, from "Smoking and Health Proposal," Brown and Williamson document no. 680561778–1786, 1969, at http://legacy.library.ucsf.edu/tid/nvs40f00.

34. Ibid., p. 11, from Panzer F. letter to Kornegay HR, "Subject: The Roper Proposal," American Tobacco document no. 963012260–2263, May 1, 1972, at http://legacy.library.ucsf.edu/tid/crn15f00.

35. Philip J. Hilts, "Seven Tobacco Executives Deny Cigarettes Are Addictive," *New York Times*, April 14, 1994. See also "Nicotine and Cigarettes," Waxman hearing transcript, at http://www.pbs.org/wgbh/pages/frontline/shows/settlement/timelines/april94.html.

36. Ibid.

37. "Blowing Smoke," *Baltimore Sun*, April 16, 1994. Myron Levin, "All Seven Tobacco Executives in Perjury Probe Have Quit the Industry," *Los Angeles Times*, June 1, 1996. Ultimately, no CEO was personally prosecuted for perjury. Regarding Congress's scrutiny of major US corporations, that hearing was and remains unprecedented, for its extraordinary public accountability and educational importance. And the role of an awakened national news media was significant, too. Waxman, who in 2014 announced his retirement after forty years in Congress, told me: "A lot of industries are eager to maintain their economic well-being and to enhance it. That's why they have lobbyists; that's why they have lawyers. If they have a lot of money, they can do that and give out campaign contributions. The special interests do have a lot of influence in Congress. But I think it is important to note that if you keep at it and get to the truth, after a while, it erodes the position of those special interests . . . If there's no press there—if an independent press is not there—then our country is in real danger. Because it's hard to communicate to the American people when the news is being not only manipulated by those who stand to benefit from it, but the sources of how they get the news are manipulated as well" (interview with Representative Henry Waxman, May 9, 2011, Washington, DC).

38. Interview with Richard Carmona, April 5, 2011. According to his congressional testimony, besides tobacco issues, Carmona was also pressured not to speak publicly about "the scientific and medical aspects of stem cell research, emergency contraception, comprehensive sex education and prison or mental health issues." See "Unhealthy Interference," *New York Times*, July 12, 2007; *The Surgeon General's Vital Mission: Challenges for the Future*, Hearing Before the Committee on Oversight and Government Reform, House of Representatives, July 10, 2007, p. 48; Gardiner Harris and Robert Pear, "Ex-Officials Tell of Conflict over Science and Politics," *New York Times*, July 12, 2007; and *Health Consequences of Involuntary Exposure to Tobacco Smoke: A Report of the Surgeon General*, July 27, 2006, at http://www.surgeongeneral.gov/library/secondhandsmoke/.

39. C. Everett Koop, Foreword to Stanton A. Glantz, John Slade, Lisa A. Bero, Peter Hanauer, and Deborah E. Barnes, *The Cigarette Papers* (Berkeley/Los Angeles: University of California Press, 1996), p. xiv. The electronic version of *The Cigarette Papers* and 8,000 pages of source documents are available at http://www.library.ucsf.edu/tobacco.

40. Brandt, *The Cigarette Century*, p. 487. See also Robert N. Proctor, "Tobacco and the Global Lung Cancer Epidemic," *Nature Reviews Cancer* 1 (2001): 82–88; and World Health Organization, *The Tobacco Atlas* (Geneva: WHO: 2002), at http://www.who.int/tobacco/en/atlas11.pdf. And also see Robert N. Proctor, *Golden Holocaust: Origins of the Cigarette Catastrophe and the Case for Abolition* (Berkeley and Los Angeles: University of California Press, 2011). Beginning in the late 1970s, with Americans smoking less, the industry began an aggressive export strategy, supported by US trade officials in both Democratic and Republican administrations, from Jimmy Carter to Barack Obama, prying open foreign markets

of younger, replacement smokers. President Bill Clinton's US trade representative, Mickey Kantor, who as an attorney had previously assisted the tobacco industry in its opposition to no-smoking bans and whose law firm had represented Philip Morris, told me in 1994 that the tobacco industry "has every right to engage in exports, and to the degree that I'm charged with the responsibility of opening markets, I will continue to do so for all legal products" (Margaret Ebrahim and Charles Lewis, "Will Washington Kick Tobacco?" *Nation*, April 25, 1994, pp. 555–557). Barack Obama's first US trade representative, Ronald Kirk, who had previously worked as a consultant for Philip Morris, signed on with other countries in 2010 in challenging a new Canadian law aimed at preventing the sale of candy-flavored cigarettes that are popular among child smokers (interview with Matthew Myers, president, Campaign for Tobacco Free Kids, March 28, 2011, Washington, DC); "Lobbyist Record of Texas Democratic Senate Hopeful Kirk Draws Scrutiny," April 4, 2002, at http://www.highbeam.com/doc/1G1–84407491.html (accessed February 7, 2014). Also, http://legacy.library.ucsf.edu/tid/tyy42c00/pdf and http://legacy.library.ucsf.edu/tid/jch81a00/pdf?search=%22ronald%20kirk%22, accessed February 7, 2014. Regarding the Kirk/USTR challenge to Canada law preventing the sale of candy-flavored cigarettes that are popular among child smokers, see http://www.wto.org/english/news_e/news10_e/tbt_24mar10_e.htm (accessed February 7, 2014).

41. William Dicke, "George Seldes Is Dead at 104; an Early, Fervent Press Critic," *New York Times*, July 3, 1995, at http://www.nytimes.com/1995/07/03/obituaries/george-seldes-is-dead-at-104-an-early-fervent-press-critic.html, accessed June 1, 2012.

42. Randolph T. Holhut, *The George Seldes Reader: An Anthology of the Writings of America's Foremost Journalistic Gadfly* (New York: Barricade Books, 1994), p. 11. See George Seldes, *You Can't Print That!* (New York: Payson and Clarke, 1929).

43. Seldes, *You Can't Print That!* pp. 81–82. *In Fact* lasted until 1950, when it was "red-baited to death by the McCarthyites," according to Jensen. Seldes's newsletter inspired I. F. Stone to begin publishing I. F. Stone's *Weekly* in 1953; Seldes gave Stone his valuable subscription list to get started. When George Seldes, then ninety-one years old, received a George Polk career award in 1982, I. F. Stone said, "I'm very proud to acknowledge that George was the model for my weekly . . . He soared above the conventions of his time, a lone eagle, unafraid and indestructible." From Myra MacPherson, *All Governments Lie! The Life and Times of Rebel Journalist I. F. Stone* (New York: Scribner, 2006), pp. 346–347. See George Seldes, *Freedom of the Press* (Garden City, NY: Garden City Publishing Company, 1937) and *Lords of the Press* (New York: Julian Messner, 1938).

44. Rick Goldsmith, "George Seldes on Tobacco: Fifty Years Ahead of His Time: More Than Fifty Articles from Seldes's Newsletter *In Fact* (1940–1950)," at http://www.brasscheck.com/seldes/tobac.html, accessed June 3, 2012. See also the documentary film produced and directed by Goldsmith, *Tell the Truth and Run: George Seldes and the American Press*, at http://www.newday.com/films/Tell_the_Truth_and_Run.html. It was nominated for a Best Documentary Feature Academy Award in 1996.

45. Goldsmith, "George Seldes on Tobacco," and Carl Jensen, *Stories That Changed America: Muckrakers of the Twentieth Century* (New York: Seven Stories Press, 2002), p. 82.

46. Judith Serrin and William Serrin, eds., *Muckraking! The Journalism That Changed America* (New York: New Press, 2002), pp. 54–56.

47. Ibid., citing Kluger, *Ashes to Ashes*, p. 152.

48. Goldsmith, "George Seldes on Tobacco," p. 1.

49. "Edward R. Murrow, Broadcaster and Ex-Chief of U.S.I.A., Dies," *New York Times*, April 28, 1965, at www.nytimes.com/learning/general/onthisday/bday /0425.html, accessed on June 19, 2012.

50. Joseph Ben-David, ed., "Big News: Ed Murrow—Victim of Smokers' Cancer," *Reporter on Smoking and Health* 1 (4) (October–November 1963): 1–2, at http://archive.tobacco.org/Documents/reporter4.html, accessed June 4, 2012. See also Sally Bedell Smith, *In All His Glory: The Life of William S. Paley, the Legendary Tycoon and His Brilliant Circle* (New York: Simon and Schuster, 1990), pp. 386–387.

51. Smith, *In All His Glory*, pp. 70–71.

52. Thomas Whiteside, "Annals of Advertising: Cutting Down," *New Yorker*, December 19, 1970.

53. Kluger, *Ashes to Ashes*, p. 327.

54. Brandt, *The Cigarette Century*, p. 271, citing Jack Gould, "Networks Look for Lean Season," *New York Times*, November 16, 1970.

55. Whiteside, "Annals of Advertising." The dual alliance between the broadcasters and big tobacco frayed badly later that year, under the pressure of the impending legislation and regulation. Regarding Wasilewski's misleading assertions, see Kluger, *Ashes to Ashes*, pp. 330–331.

56. Whiteside, "Annals of Advertising."

57. UPI, "Senate, 75–9, Votes a Cigarette Ad Ban," *New York Times*, March 11, 1970; AP, "Nixon Signs Bill Banning Radio-TV Cigarette Ads," *New York Times*, April 2, 1970. The tobacco industry had shrewdly ensured that the new law was a *total* smoking-related radio-television advertising ban, including a prohibition on the increasingly effective anti-smoking commercials that had been airing for a few years.

58. "Table 3, Domestic Cigarette Advertising Expenditures by Media for Years 1963–1974 (millions of dollars)," *Federal Trade Commission Cigarette Report for 2007 and 2008*, issued 2011, at http://www.ftc.gov/os/2011/07/110729cigarettereport .pdf, accessed June 21, 2012.

59. Brandt, *The Cigarette Century*, p. 272, citing Thomas Whiteside, *Selling Death: Cigarette Advertising and Public Health* (New York: Liveright, 1971), pp. 120–122.

60. *Federal Trade Commission Cigarette Report for 2007 and 2008*, Tables 2, 2a, 2b, 2c, 2d, and 3. The exact cumulative cigarette-advertising revenue figure is $10,943,996,000, broken down into $7,758,820,000 spent in magazines and $3,185,176,000 in newspapers. The last year such figures are available is 2008, and in recent years, cigarette advertising in newspapers and magazines has substantially diminished.

61. Estimated number of tobacco-attributable deaths from 1976–2008: 12,075,515. Based upon US Centers for Disease Control mortality data.

62. Brandt, *The Cigarette Century*, pp. 272–275. The US Food and Drug Administration, which began operating as a federal regulatory agency in 1906 and took its current name in 1930, did not get the statutory authority to regulate the tobacco industry until 2009, with the passage of the Family Smoking Prevention and Tobacco Control Act. See http://www.fda.gov/AboutFDA/WhatWeDo/History /default.htm, accessed June 22, 2012.

63. Gilbert Cranberg, Randall Bezanson, and John Soloski, *Taking Stock: Journalism and the Publicly Traded Newspaper Company* (Ames: Iowa State University Press, 2001), pp. 27–33.

64. Steven Waldman, et. al., *The Information Needs of Communities*, op. cit., p. 10, citing the Pew Research Center Project for Excellence in Journalism, *State of the News Media* 2010, http://stateofthemedia.org/2010/overview-3/, accessed July 5, 2012.

65. Douglas Gomery, "Tisch, Laurence, U.S. Media Mogul," Chicago, Illinois, Museum of Broadcast Communications, at http://www.museum.tv/eotvsection .php?entrycode=tischlauren.

66. At the time of our *60 Minutes* tobacco story, there were 125 pending civil lawsuits in the United States brought by smokers or their families against the tobacco companies. For our segment, we interviewed New Jersey attorney Marc Edell and his colleague Alan Darnell, but we focused not on the Cipollone lawsuit but on another of their tobacco cases and plaintiffs, Doris and Roy Smith, and their daughter Pam, whom we interviewed. Richard Bonin and Charles Lewis, co-producers and writers, Mike Wallace, senior correspondent, "Tobacco on Trial," CBS News *60 Minutes* (transcript), January 3, 1988.

67. "Tobacco on Trial" (transcript).

68. Brandt, *The Cigarette Century*, pp. 323–355. See also Donald Janson, "Cigarette Maker Assessed Damages in Smoker's Death," *New York Times*, June 14, 1988. To clarify, the jury exonerated Philip Morris and Lorillard of the charges against them, conspiracy and fraud. It also assessed Mrs. Cipollone with 80 percent of the blame for her death and 20 percent to Liggett, which meant that under the law, Mr. Cipollone was not entitled to compensatory damages. The jury also decided not to award any punitive damages to Mr. Cipollone.

69. Brandt, *The Cigarette Century*, pp. 323–355, and Richard Kluger, *Ashes to Ashes*, pp. 639–677. One of the reasons the anti-tobacco industry plaintiff litigation slowed to a trickle is because the Supreme Court had ruled that the Public Health Cigarette Smoking Act of 1969 effectively preempted plaintiff claims against the industry that they hadn't been sufficiently warned about the dangers of smoking. In other words, the number of potential litigants had just been dramatically decreased to the pre-1969 pool of aging smokers.

70. David Kessler, *A Question of Intent: A Great American Battle with a Deadly Industry* (New York: PublicAffairs, 2001), pp. 72–84. By the time Kessler left the FDA in 1997, his agency "tobacco team" consisted of eighty-nine people. The fact that Deep Cough is a woman and that she has a doctorate in engineering is from Dan

Zegart, *Civil Warriors: The Legal Siege on the Tobacco Industry* (New York: Random House/Delacourt Press, 2000), pp. 100–119.

71. Kessler, *A Question of Intent*, p. 104.

72. Ibid., pp. 104–106. See also Alicia C. Shepard, "Up in Smoke," *American Journalism Review* (November 1995), at http://www.ajr.org/article_printable.asp?id =1594, accessed on July 7, 2012.

73. Interview with Walt Bogdanich, May 31, 2007, New York City.

74. Martin Koughan (producer for ABC News *Turning Point*), ABC News letterhead letter, August 9, 1993, to Michael Miles, Chairman and CEO, Philip Morris Companies, describing the project that will explore, among other things, "the aggressive expansion and promotion of tobacco exports to other countries in Eastern Europe, Russia and Asia." Koughan requested an on-camera interview. Barry Holt, Vice President of Corporate Communications, Philip Morris, replied to Koughan on company letterhead on behalf of Michael Miles, dated August 17, 1993, "Unfortunately, Mr. Miles will be unable to participate in an on-camera interview with you. However, as you get further along in the development of your story, I would be pleased to speak with you. In the meantime, I'd welcome any additional details you could provide about this show: i.e., what kinds of companies/ people you are talking to; how you are developing some of the themes you mentioned in your letter; etc. I'm sorry we can't move ahead at this time. I do wish you the best of luck with the preparation of your piece."

75. Roone Arledge personal papers, including his daily appointments calendar, Rare Book and Manuscript Library, Butler Library, Columbia University, New York, New York. Editorial and legal approval information is from Martin Koughan and undisputed by the ABC News top producers and executives with whom I spoke.

76. Interview with Martin Koughan, June 21, 2010, Sonoma, California.

77. Interview with Walt Bogdanich, May 31, 2007.

78. Michael Janofsky, "Philip Morris Accuses ABC of Libel," *New York Times*, March 25, 1994. For a full transcript of the first Waxman hearing, involving the testimony of David Kessler and others, see *Regulation of Tobacco Products: Hearings Before the Subcommittee on Health and the Environment of the Committee on Energy and Commerce*, U.S. House of Representatives, 103rd Cong., 2nd Sess., March 25, 1994, at http://www.archive.org/stream/regulationoftoba01unit /regulationoftoba01unit_djvu.txt, accessed on July 8, 2012. At the beginning of the hearing, Waxman said, "We will not hear, however, from individuals at the center of this controversy because they have declined to testify at this hearing. These individuals set the standards for industry conduct. They set the limits on company practices. They know how much nicotine is added to cigarettes and why. The subcommittee extended an invitation to Michael Miles, the chairman and CEO of Philip Morris and other top tobacco company officials . . . Mr. Miles had the time to hold a press conference and announce a lawsuit yesterday, but he wouldn't find the time to come before the Congress of the United States and talk about this very issue. Without objection I would ask that letters from Mr. Miles,

James Johnson of RJ Reynolds, and T.E. Sandefur, Jr. of Brown and Williamson be printed in the record at the conclusion of my opening statement." Separately, veteran journalist Steve Weinberg made an interesting observation in the *Columbia Journalism Review* (November–December 1995, p. 34), unnoticed by other reporters and editors, that regarding the $10 billion lawsuit, "Virginia law limits punitive damage awards to $350,000 and that the largest libel award ever upheld in court was less than 1 percent of Philip Morris' demand."

79. Interview with Martin Koughan, June 21, 2010.

80. Howard Kurtz, "Long-Term Effect of ABC Settlement Concerns Critics," *Washington Post*, August 23, 1995, at http://legacy.library.vcsf.edu/tid/shr37d00/pdf, accessed February 7, 2014.

81. Ibid.

82. Following an undercover investigation in 1992 by the ABC News program *Primetime Live* of unsanitary food handling and conditions in Food Lion supermarkets, the company filed a highly publicized $2.47 billion lawsuit alleging fraud and other charges against ABC. In 1997, a federal district court jury in Greensboro, North Carolina, awarded the supermarket chain $5.5 million "after finding that ABC had engaged in fraud, though that was later reduced to $315,000. The case had been closely followed by news organizations that feared that plaintiffs could win crippling damage awards without having to prove that the news reports in question were false or malicious." In 1999, a federal court of appeals in Richmond, Virginia, reduced all but $2 of the damages that a jury had ordered ABC News to pay to the Food Lion supermarket chain and ruled that "Food Lion's attempt to win a multimillion-dollar fraud verdict because two ABC employees had lied their way into jobs in Food Lion stores was 'an end-run' around First Amendment protections for journalists." Felicity Barringer, "Appeals Court Rejects Damages Against ABC in Food Lion Case," *New York Times*, October 21, 1999, at http://www.nytimes.com/1999/10/21/us/appeals-court-rejects-damages-against-abc-in-food-lion-case.html?pagewanted=all&src=pm, accessed on July 9, 2012; Jane Kirtley, "Getting Mauled in Food Lion's Den," *American Journalism Review* (March 1997), at http://www.ajr.org/Article.asp?id=1769, accessed July 9, 2012.

83. Telephone conversation with Murphy's ABC assistant, Annie, June 18, 2012.

84. Roone Arledge, *Roone: A Memoir* (New York: HarperCollins, 2003).

85. Telephone interview with Paul Friedman, July 3, 2012. In a subsequent e-mail exchange on July 8, 2012, he added, "This was hardly the first time hundreds of thousands of dollars were spent on a project that didn't air. There was always a lot of wastage on the magazine programs and in documentaries—having nothing to do with orders to suppress a controversial story. I want to repeat that I only remember thinking the producers hadn't presented a great hour. Apparently what I said in public reflected that . . . Most important: in 40 years at three network news divisions, as both an executive producer and the creator/supervisor of two investigative units, I was *never* asked by anyone above me in the ranks (either news division or corporate) to soften a story or stay away from any subject."

86. E-mail interview/exchange with Alan Wurtzel, June 19, 2012. Follow-up e-mails to Wurtzel on June 20 and July 3 were not answered, nor was my telephone call on July 16 returned.

87. Interview/e-mail exchange with Richard "Dick" Wald, August 3, 2012. I interacted with Dick Wald during my years (1977–1984) at ABC News; today, he is the Fred W. Friendly Professor of Professional Practice in Media and Society, Columbia University Graduate School of Journalism. Lower-level ABC News officials downstream below Wald and Wurtzel were not particularly helpful. Phyllis McGrady, the program executive producer at the time, never answered my e-mail questions. And *Turning Point* senior producer Betsy West, whom I worked with briefly at ABC in the early 1980s, recalled, "I was told that Roone Arledge and Paul Friedman did not find the story compelling enough to sustain a prime-time hour on *Turning Point*. After trying to work with the producer to improve the story, I agreed with them. The [Philip Morris] lawsuit played no role in my thinking. I have no way of knowing if the lawsuit played a role in the thinking of my bosses." E-mail sent to Phyllis McGrady, June 18, 2012, but never answered. Interview/e-mail exchange with Betsy West, July 14, 2012.

88. *Turning Point* programming information is from http://www.tvguide .com/detail/tv-show.aspx?tvobjectid=205190&more=ucepisodelist&episodeid =840288.

89. Around the time of the internal constraints Bogdanich was facing vis-à-vis the ABC lawyers, which ended up in the *Wall Street Journal*, he got a gruff telephone call one night at home. He said "Hello," and the other person said, "You are a fucking asshole if you don't hire your own lawyer." Bogdanich said, "Who is this?" And the voice answered, "Sy Hersh." Bogdanich in fact did retain his own lawyer, someone Hersh had recommended: "Best move I ever made." Interview with Walt Bogdanich, May 31, 2007. See also Stanton A. Glantz, John Slade, Lisa A. Bero, Peter Hanauer, and Deborah E. Barnes, *The Cigarette Papers*, foreword by C. Everett Koop (Berkeley/Los Angeles: University of California Press, 1996), p. xiv. The electronic version of *The Cigarette Papers* and 8,000 pages of source documents are available at http://www.library.ucsf.edu/tobacco.

90. Interview with Walt Bogdanich, May 31, 2007.

91. Ibid.

92. Ibid.

93. Interview with Paul Friedman, July 3, 2012. Roone Arledge, in his memoir, wrote, "I often wondered if he [Murphy] would have said the same thing to me, as opposed to my second in command. Probably. But I was outraged when I got back and found a distraught Paul in my office" (Arledge, *Roone*, pp. 394–396). This is a somewhat curious passage to me, because in Arledge's personal papers is a "priviledged & confidential" [*sic*] memo dated June 28, 1996 (and another, similar one five days earlier) from ABC lawyer Alan Braverman, to Arledge, with draft lawsuit settlement language: "we plan to send out this morning. Thank you for your help in this process." He may have been outraged, but could hardly have been surprised. In an earlier "priviledged and confidential" [*sic*] missive, this one from Walt

Bogdanich to Braverman, with copies to Roone Arledge, Paul Friedman, Richard Wald, Tom Yellin, and Forrest Sawyer, dated February 2, 1995, Bogdanich wrote, "Thank you for asking for my opinion on your latest settlement proposal . . . I cannot support the current settlement proposal as written, and I strongly urge you not to send it. The statement is at best misleading, and at worst factually inaccurate . . . I believe your settlement proposal is unfair and unwarranted." From the Roone Arledge personal papers.

94. For the complete apology, see Mark Landler, "ABC News Settles Suits on Tobacco," *New York Times*, August 22, 1995, at http://www.nytimes .com/1995/08/22/us/the-media-business-abc-news-settles-suits-on-tobacco .html?pagewanted=all&src=pm, accessed on July 9, 2012.

95. Alicia Shepard, "Up in Smoke," *American Journalism Review* (November 1995). See also Benjamin Weiser, "ABC and Tobacco: The Anatomy of a Network News Mistake," *Washington Post*, January 7, 1996; Geraldine Fabrikant, "The Media Business: The Merger; Walt Disney to Acquire ABC in $19 Billion Deal To Build A Giant For Entertainment," *New York Times*, August 1, 1995, at http:// www.nytimes.com/1995/08/01/business/media-business-merger-walt-disney -acquire-abc-19-billion-deal-build-giant-for.html?pagewanted=all&src=pm, accessed on July 9, 2012.

96. Weiser, "ABC and Tobacco." See also Jonathan Alter, "The Cave on Tobacco Road," *Newsweek*, September 3, 1995, at http://www.thedailybeast.com/newsweek /1995/09/03/the-cave-on-tobacco-road.html, accessed on July 9, 2012.

97. Interview with Walt Bogdanich, May 31, 2007.

98. Peter Jennings, anchor; Tom Yellin and David Gelber, executive producers; Walt Bogdanich, Jeanmarie Condon, Producers, "Never Say Die, How the Cigarette Companies Keep on Winning," ABC-TV Special, June 27, 1996, at http:// archive.org/details/tobacco_xsy27a00, accessed on July 9, 2012. See Jacques Steinberg, "Peter Jennings, Urbane News Anchor, Dies at Sixty-Seven," *New York Times*, August 8, 2005, at http://www.nytimes.com/2005/08/08/business/media /08jennings_obit.html?pagewanted=all, accessed on July 9, 2012.

99. Geraldine Fabrikant, "CBS Accepts Bid from Westinghouse; $5.4 Billion Deal," *New York Times*, August 2, 1995, at http://www.nytimes.com/1995/08/02 /business/cbs-accepts-bid-by-westinghouse-5.4-billion-deal.html?pagewanted =all&src=pm, accessed July 9, 2012. Also see Marie Brenner, "The Man Who Knew Too Much," *Vanity Fair* (May 1996), at http://www.vanityfair.com/magazine /archive/1996/05/wigand199605, accessed July 9, 2012.

100. Bill Carter, "'60 Minutes' Ordered to Pull Interview in Tobacco Report," *New York Times*, November 9, 1995, at http://www.nytimes.com/1995/11/09/us /60-minutes-ordered-to-pull-interview-in-tobacco-report.html?pagewanted =all&src=pm, accessed on July 9, 2012.

101. "Self-Censorship at CBS," *New York Times*, November 12, 1995, at http:// www.nytimes.com/1995/11/12/opinion/self-censorship-at-cbs.html, accessed on July 9, 2012.

102. Daniel Schorr, correspondent; Neil Docherty, Jim Gilmore, producers;

David Fanning, executive producer, "Smoke in the Eye," *Frontline*, April 2, 1996, at http://www.pbs.org/wgbh/pages/frontline/smoke/smokescript.html, accessed on July 9, 2012.

103. Interview with Lowell Bergman, June 19, 2007, Berkeley, California.

104. Ibid.

105. Geraldine Fabrikant, "CBS Accepts Bid from Westinghouse; $5.4 Billion Deal. Also Marie Brenner, "The Man Who Knew Too Much."

106. Interview with Lowell Bergman, June 19, 2007.

107. Don Hewitt, *Tell Me a Story: Fifty Years and 60 Minutes in Television* (New York: PublicAffairs, 2001), p. 199 (see pp. 186–206 for his reflections about the entire tobacco-Wigand-*60 Minutes* saga).

108. Ibid.

109. Interview with Martin Koughan, June 21, 2010.

110. E-mail with Clifford Douglas, July 10, 2012. Interview with him, July 12, 2012.

111. Paul Brodeur, *Outrageous Misconduct: The Asbestos Industry on Trial* (New York: Pantheon, 1985); Alan Derickson, *Black Lung: Anatomy of a Public Health Disaster* (Ithaca: Cornell University Press, 1998); Gerald Markowitz and David Rosner, *Deceit and Denial: The Deadly Politics of Industrial Pollution* (Berkeley: University of California Press, 2002); Michaels, *Doubt Is Their Product*, pp. 19–28, 91–94 (beta-Naphthylamine); pp. 34–37 (vinyl chloride); pp. 124–141, 221–224, 227–229 (beryllium); p. 50 (ephedra); pp. 146–149, 153–155, 255–256 (Vioxx); Sherry Jones, Bill Moyers, "Trade Secrets: A Moyers Report" (PBS documentary and website produced by Public Affairs Television, Inc., in association with Washington Media Associates, Inc.), at http://www.pbs.org/tradesecrets/; Gina Kolata, "The Sad Legacy of the Dalkon Shield," *New York Times*, December 6, 1987, at www .nytimes.com/1987/12/06/magazine/the-sad-legacy-of-the-dalkon-shield.html. Regarding Rezulin and other deadly drugs, see David Willman's Pulitzer Prize–winning articles in 2000 in the *Los Angeles Times*, at http://www.pulitzer.org/works /2001-Investigative-Reporting.

112. Frank Graham Jr., *Since Silent Spring* (New York: Houghton Mifflin, 1970), pp. 1–68. Rachel Carson, *Silent Spring: The Classic That Launched the Environmental Movement*, 40th Anniversary Edition, introduction by Linda Lear, afterword by Edward O. Wilson (New York: Houghton Mifflin, 1962/2002). Stauber and Rampton, *Toxic Sludge Is Good For You!* pp. 123–125; E. Bruce Harrison, *Going Green: How to Communicate Your Company's Environment Commitment* (Burr Ridge, IL and New York: Irwin, 1993), pp. xiv–xv.

113. Stauber and Rampton, *Toxic Sludge*, pp. 123-125; Harrison, *Going Green*, pp. xiv-xi.

114. Interview with E. Bruce Harrison, November 30, 2011, and follow-up e-mail exchange December 1, 2011.

115. "Harrison Named CEO of CPB," *O'Dwyer's PR Daily*, June 24, 2005. See also Harrison, *Going Green*, pp. xiv–xv. And interview and follow-up e-mail exchange with Harrison, December 1, 2011.

116. Graham, *Since Silent Spring*, pp. 74–79. See also David A. Fahrenthold, "Bill to Honor Rachel Carson on Hold," *Washington Post*, May 23, 2007; "Dr. Coburn Stands for Science—Rachel Carson and the Death of Millions," press release issued by the senator's office June 7, 2007, at http://coburn.senate.gov /public/index.cfm/rightnow?ContentRecord_id=16EA56F1–5C06–4E30–965E -CA7E91034178, accessed October 5, 2011, with "Click here to read more about why Rachel Carson's science was wrong," which links to http://rachelwaswrong .org/, accessed October 5, 2011. In 2010, Senator Tom Coburn had a perfect 100 "Defenders of Liberty" American Conservative Union rating and the ACU's third-highest lifetime rating in the US Senate, 98.17 out of 100 (http://www.conservative .org/congress-ratings/, accessed October 5, 2011).

117. Peter Overby, "Billionaire Brothers in Spotlight in Wis[consin] Union Battle," February 25, 2011, http://www.npr.org/2011/02/25/134040226/in-wis -union-battle-focus-on-billionaire-brothers. See also the important and comprehensive article by Jane Mayer, "Covert Operations," *New Yorker*, August 30, 2010. The Center for Public Integrity and I first investigated Koch Industries in 1995, results of which were published in Charles Lewis and the Center for Public Integrity, *The Buying of the President* (New York: Avon, 1996), pp. 127–131. Interestingly, Harrison said he was not aware of the Coburn action against Carson or the RachelWasWrong.org website; in the interview, he described Coburn as "very conservative," and the continued smear effort by a polluter-funded nonprofit as an atypical "outlier" example of corporate conduct.

118. See Charles Lewis, Eric Holmberg, Alexia Campbell, and Lydia Beyoud, "The Koch Club: Koch Millions Spread Influence Through Nonprofits, Colleges," Investigative Reporting Workshop, July 1, 2013, at http:// investigativereportingworkshop.org/investigations/the_koch_club/story/Koch _millions_spread_influence_through_nonprofits/, accessed December 17, 2013. See also http://www.newyorker.com/online/blogs/newsdesk/2013/07/the-kochs -and-the-action-on-global-warming.html, accessed December 17, 2013.

119. Frank Rich, "The Billionaires Bankrolling the Tea Party," *New York Times*, August 28, 2010, at http://www.nytimes.com/2010/08/29/opinion/29rich.html, accessed October 22, 2011.

CHAPTER 6: WHERE HAVE YOU GONE, EDWARD R. MURROW?

1. Edward R. Murrow speech before the Radio, Television and News Directors Association, Chicago, Illinois, October 15, 1958, at http://www.rtnda.org/pages /media_items/edward-r.-murrow-speech998.php, accessed February 19, 2012. For the atmospherics before and after the speech, see A. M. Sperber, *Murrow: His Life and Times* (New York: Freundlich Books, 1986), pp. 529–542; David Halberstam, *The Powers That Be* (New York: Knopf, 1979), pp. 147–152. See also Val Adams, "News of TV and Radio: Texaco Loses Interest in $4,500,000 Deal as Hiken Keeps 'Principles,'" *New York Times*, October 19, 1958. This famous speech also opens and ends the 2005 film, *Good Night and Good Luck*, which received six Academy Award nominations.

2. Sperber, *Murrow*, pp. 79–156; Gary Paul Gates, *Air Time: The Inside Story of CBS News* (New York: Berkley, 1979), pp. 16–17; Murrow's comment about the CBS bureau offices is from Morley Safer, "Foreword," in Ralph Engelman, *Friendlyvision: Fred Friendly and the Rise and Fall of Television Journalism* (New York: Columbia University Press, 2009), pp. vii–viii. Also see Denis Richards, *The Fight at Odds: Royal Air Force 1939–45* (London: Her Majesty's Stationery Office, 1974; first published in 1953), p. 217, and Juliet Gardiner, *The Blitz: The British Under Attack* (London: Harper, 2010), pp. 174–176. According to Gardiner, following the dramatic US media coverage of the German Blitz and its "uncritical portrait of Britain's united and steadfast defiance," there had been, declared the British ambassador in Washington, Lord Lothian, an "almost miraculous change of opinion," in the United States. By December 1940, 60 percent of those Americans polled were "now prepared to risk war." Philip Seib, *Broadcasts from the Blitz: How Edward R. Murrow Helped Lead America into War* (Dulles, VA: Potomac Books, 2006).

3. Sperber, *Murrow*, pp. 210, 232–234.

4. Ibid., pp. 248–252, citing Edward R. Murrow, CBS Radio, April 15, 1945.

5. Murrow and his wife, Janet, dined with Eleanor Roosevelt while "a steady stream of officials went past to the Oval Office"; hours later, after Janet had returned to their hotel, Murrow met and had sandwiches and beer with FDR shortly after midnight. See Sperber, *Murrow*, pp. 200–208; the White House part is cited from the White House usher's diary, noted in Anthony Cave Brown, *The Last Hero: Wild Bill Donovan* (Times Books: New York: 1983).

6. Nicholas Lemann, "The Wayward Press: The Murrow Doctrine," *New Yorker*, January 23, 2006, at http://www.newyorker.com/archive/2006/01/23/060123fa_fact1, accessed March 12, 2012.

7. Sperber, *Murrow*, p. 210, n. 24, citing Hopkins to Murrow telegram, January 10, 1942 (caps in original), p. 718. Prior to the Hopkins telegram, playwright, author, and Roosevelt speechwriter Robert Sherwood, who was setting up the propagandistic Office of War Information, had tried unsuccessfully to convince Murrow to lead the radio effort. He had then urged Hopkins to send the imploring telegram. See Robert E. Sherwood, *Roosevelt and Hopkins: An Intimate History* (New York: Harper and Brothers, 1948).

8. Sperber, *Murrow*, pp. 221–222. The Paley wartime position is from Sally Bedell Smith, *In All His Glory: The Life of William S. Paley* (New York: Simon and Schuster, 1990), pp. 206–215.

9. Smith, *In All His* Glory, pp. 291–300.

10. Robert L. Hilliard and Michael C. Keith, *The Broadcast Century and Beyond*, 5th ed. (Burlington, MA: Elsevier/Focal Press, 2010), pp. 115–116. The first network evening news program was NBC's *Camel News Caravan*, sponsored by the R.J. Reynolds Tobacco Company and anchored by John Cameron Swayze. It began at the end of the summer of 1948, and CBS soon followed with *Douglas Edwards with the News*, which was sponsored by Oldsmobile (General Motors). See Sig Mickelson, *The Decade That Shaped Television News: CBS in the 1950s* (Westport, CT: Praeger, 1998), pp. 10–11.

11. Gary Paul Gates, "Sig Mickelson—An Early Visionary," at www.cbsnews
.com/2102–201_162–176772.html?tag=contentMain;contentBody, accessed July
27, 2012.

12. Mickelson, *The Decade That Shaped Television News*, p. 49. The show had an
odd, initial time slot, 3:30 p.m. on a Sunday, but the half-hour program, sponsored
by Alcoa, was soon moved to Tuesday nights at 10:30 p.m., where it would reside
until it went off the air in 1958.

13. Jack Gould, "Radio and Television: Edward R. Murrow's News Review, 'See
It Now,' Demonstrates Journalistic Power of Video," *New York Times*, November
19, 1951.

14. Bob Edwards, *Edward R. Murrow and the Birth of Broadcast Journalism*
(Hoboken, NJ: John Wiley and Sons, 2004), p. 107. Although Edwards, the host
for many years of NPR's *Morning Edition*, had never met or worked with Murrow,
his mentor was Ed Bliss, Murrow's longtime producer and writer, who began the
broadcast journalism program at the American University School of Communication after his retirement. And his slender but comprehensive biography of Murrow
is informed by "thirty years of conversation" with Bliss, who died in 2002.

15. Ibid. See also Fred W. Friendly, *Due to Circumstances Beyond Our Control . . .*
(New York: Random House, 1967), pp. 68–69.

16. Smith, *In All His* Glory, pp. 300–304, and p. 676, citing an article by Bryce
Oliver in *New Republic*, January 13, 1947.

17. Ibid. The *Variety* quote is from August 14, 1949.

18. Sperber, *Murrow*, pp. 338–339.

19. Smith, *In All His Glory*, pp. 300–304, 676.

20. Edward Alwood, *Dark Days in the Newsroom: McCarthyism Aimed at the Press*
(Philadelphia: Temple University Press, 2007), p. 3.

21. Ibid., pp. 64 and 170 (nn. 96 and 97). Folk singer and former CBS executive producer Tony Kraber, publicly accused by film director Elia Kazan along
with seven others of Communist activities, invoked the Fifth Amendment in a
1955 HUAC hearing but also acknowledged that he had been asked to resign from
CBS in 1951. See House Committee on Un-American Activities, *Investigation of
Communist Activities, New York Area*, 84th Cong., 1st Sess., August 17–18, 1955,
pt. 7 (Washington, DC: Government Printing Office, 1955), pp. 2435–2447. And
in 1954, the Federal Communications Commission did not renew the license of a
television station in Erie, Pennsylvania, after its owner, Edward Lamb, was accused
of being a member of the Communist Party. See "TV License Held Up on New
Red Charge," *New York Times*, March 13, 1954. See also David Everitt, *A Shadow
of Red: Communism and the Blacklist in Radio and Television* (Chicago: Ivan R. Dee,
2007), pp. 199–203; Susan L. Brinson, *The Red Scare, Politics, and the Federal Communications Commission, 1941–1960* (Westport, CT: Greenwood/Praeger, 2004),
pp. 159–220; Hilliard and Keith, *The Broadcast Century and Beyond*, p. 126; and
Victor S. Navasky, *Naming Names* (New York: Viking, 1980).

22. Smith, *In All His Glory*, pp. 305–307 and p. 677, citing William S. Paley,

As It Happened: A Memoir (Garden City, NJ: Doubleday, 1979), pp. 286. See also Daniel Schorr, *Clearing the Air* (Boston: Houghton Mifflin, 1977), pp. 274–284.

23. Smith, *In All His Glory*, pp. 302–304; Sperber, *Murrow*, pp. 346–349. "Unwarranted criticism" quote is from Smith; "blacked out" quote is from Sperber. The *Newsweek* article she cited was published September 25, 1950.

24. Glenn Collins, "Celebrating the Memory and Art of Paul Robeson," *New York Times*, October 30, 1988, at http://www.nytimes.com/1988/10/30/arts /celebrating-the-memory-and-art-of-paul-robeson.html, accessed December 29, 2012.

25. Douglas Martin, "Milo Radulovich, Eighty-one, Dies; Symbol of '50s Red Scare," *New York Times*, November 21, 2007. Radulovich became a heroic, defiant symbol of the guilt-by-association excesses of the McCarthy, anti-communism period, and in 2005, he was a consultant for the feature film, *Good Night and Good Luck*. See also Sperber, *Murrow*, pp. 416–420.

26. Edwards, *Edward R. Murrow*, pp. 110–112. Also see "A Brief History of IIE," Institute of International Education website, at http://www.iie.org/en/Who-We -Are/History, accessed December 29, 2012. The third co-founder of IIE was Stephen Duggan Sr., professor of political science at the College of the City of New York and IIE's first president (Sperber, *Murrow*, pp. 414–416).

27. Gates, *Air Time*, pp. 24–25 (emphasis in original).

28. Hilliard and Keith, *The Broadcast Century and Beyond*, p. 146. See also Friendly, *Due to Circumstances*, pp. 22–67. One week after taking on McCarthy directly, Murrow followed with another program critical of McCarthy and the conduct of his committee, profiling Annie Lee Moss, an employee of the Department of the Army mistakenly accused of being a member of the Communist Party, harassed under the lights by McCarthy and committee counsel Roy Cohn. "See It Now: Annie Lee Moss Before the McCarthy Committee," March 16, 1954, The Paley Center for Media, New York, New York, at http://www .paleycenter.org/collection/item/?q=edward+r.+murrow+and+Joseph+McCarthy &p=1&item=T76:0023, accessed December 30, 2012.

29. Halberstam, *The Powers That Be*, pp. 144–145.

30. Ibid., p. 147.

31. Ibid. Edwin R. Bayley, *Joe McCarthy and the Press* (Madison: University of Wisconsin Press, 1981), pp. 202–210. See also Thomas C. Reeves, *The Life and Times of Joe McCarthy: A Biography* (New York: Stein and Day, 1982), p. 526. The official cause of death was cirrhosis of the liver, but it is the accepted wisdom of many historians and biographers that McCarthy drank himself to death. See Haynes Johnson, *The Age of Anxiety: McCarthyism to Terrorism* (New York: Harcourt, 2005), pp. 452–455.

32. Halberstam, *The Powers That Be*, pp. 146–151.

33. Ibid., pp. 146–152. See also Smith, *In All His Glory*, pp. 371–387.

34. Halberstam, *The Powers That Be*, pp. 503–505. See also Friendly, *Due to Circumstances*, pp. 212–264.

35. Chad Raphael, *Investigated Reporting: Muckrakers, Regulators, and the Struggle over Television Documentary* (Urbana: University of Illinois Press, 2005), p. 3, citing Raymond L. Carroll, "Economic Influences on Commercial Network Television Documentary Scheduling," *Journal of Broadcasting* 23 (1979): 415.

36. Ibid.

37. Don Hewitt, "Filling Time with Second-Rate News Magazines," Twenty-First Annual Frank E. Gannett Lecture, Media Studies Center, New York (Arlington, VA: Freedom Forum World Center, 1998), pp. i–ii, 9.

38. Ibid., p. 238, citing Markus Prior, *Post-Broadcast Democracy: How Media Choice Increases Inequality in Political Involvement and Polarizes Elections* (New York: Cambridge University Press, 2007).

39. Robert Picard, "Tremors, Structural Damage and Some Casualties, but No Cataclysm: The News About News Provision," background paper to the presentation by the author at the US Federal Trade Commission Workshop, "From Town Crier to Bloggers: How Will Journalism Survive the Internet Age?" December 1–2, 2009, at http://www.robertpicard.net/files/PicardFTCbackgroundpaper.pdf, accessed January 4, 2013.

40. Paul Starr, "An Unexpected Crisis: The News Media in Postindustrial Democracies," *International Journal of Press/Politics* 17 (2) (April 2012): 234–242, citing Alicia Adserà, Carles Boix, and Mark Payne, "Are You Being Served? Political Accountability and the Quality of Government," *Journal of Law, Economics and Organization* 19 (2003): 445–489; Aymo Brunettia and Beatrice Weder, "A Free Press Is Bad News for Corruption," *Journal of Public Economics* 87 (2003): 1801–1824; Sam Schulhofer-Wohl and Miguel Garrido, "Do Newspapers Matter? Evidence from the Closure of the *Cincinnati Post*," NBER Working Paper No. 1487 (2009); James M. Snyder Jr., and David Stromberg, "Press Coverage and Political Accountability," NBER Working Paper No. 13878 (2008).

41. Steven Waldman and others, "The Information Needs of Communities," Federal Communications Commission, at http://www.fcc.gov/info-needs-communities, Overview, p. 13.

42. Ibid., p. 10, with citations on pp. 366–367 in Overview, nn. 14 and 15; Network news staff statistic is from "Overview" in Pew, "The State of the News Media 2010," at http://stateofthemedia.org/2010/overview-3/; the newsmagazine number is from "Magazines: News Investment" in Pew, "The State of News Media 2010," at http://stateofthemedia.org/2010/magazines-summary-essay/news-investment/, both accessed January 1, 2013.

43. Interview with Matthew Zelkind, news director and station manager, WKRN-TV, by Steven Waldman, in Waldman, "The Information Needs of Communities," Overview, p. 13 and n. 44, p. 367.

44. Ibid., p. 10, with citations on pp. 366–367 in Overview, nn. 17 and 18; local all-news cable channel number is from Adam Lynn, Mark Cooper, and S. Derek Turner, "National Owners Dominate Local Cable News; Local Cable News Channels Do Not Significantly Contribute to Source or Viewpoint Diversity," *Free*

Press 1 (5) (2006), at http://www.freepress.net/files/study_4_cable_local_news.pdf, accessed January 1, 2013.

45. The marketing consultant widely credited with "inventing" the happy talk, friendly anchor studio banter, and related stylistic approaches, his clients including the major TV networks and over one hundred local TV stations, was Frank N. Magid, once called by *Time* magazine "the nation's leading television news doctor." Nationally, he helped ABC develop *Good Morning America*. See Margalit Fox, "Frank Magid, Creator of 'Action News,' Dies at Seventy-Eight," *New York Times*, February 10, 2010, at http://www.nytimes.com/2010/02/10/arts/television/10magid.html, accessed January 1, 2013. See also "Move Over Water-Skiing Squirrel—Here's a Snowboarding Opossum," KUSA-TV (Gannett owned, NBC affiliate in Denver, Colorado), March 14, 2012, at http://www.9news.com/rss/story.aspx?storyid=256249, accessed January 1, 2013.

46. Edward R. Murrow speech before the Radio, Television and News Directors Association, Chicago, Illinois, October 15, 1958, at http://www.rtnda.org/pages/media_items/edward-r.-murrow-speech998.php, accessed February 19, 2012; http://www.americanrhetoric.comspeeches/newtonminow.html.

47. Leonard Downie Jr. and Michael Schudson, "The Reconstruction of American Journalism," Columbia University Graduate School of Journalism, October 20, 2009, at http://www.journalism.columbia.edu/cs/ContentServer?pagename=JRN/Render/DocURL&binaryid=1212611716626, p. 17.

48. Waldman, "The Information Needs of Communities," p. 10, at www.fcc.gov/infoneedsreport, citing Advertising Expenditures, Newspaper Association of America, http://www.naa.org/trends-and-numbers.aspx, accessed July 4, 2012, and "Newspapers: News Investment," in Pew Research Center's Project for Excellence in Journalism, "The State of the News Media 2010," at http://www.stateofthemedia.org/2010/newspapers_news_investment.php, accessed July 4, 2012.

49. Waldman, "The Information Needs of Communities," at http://www.fcc.gov/info-needs-communities, Overview, p. 10, with related citations in the footnotes section, p. 366, nn. 11, 13, 14. Advertising revenue drop is from "Advertising Expenditures," Newspaper Association of America (last updated March 2010), at http://www.naa.org/TrendsandNumbers/Advertising-Expenditures.aspx. Regarding the 25 percent figure and Watergate comparison, the number of editorial employees in newspaper newsrooms in 1971 was estimated to be 38,000 (John W. C. Johnstone, Edward J. Slawski, and William M. Bowman, *The News People: A Sociological Portrait of American Journalists and Their Work* [Chicago: University of Illinois Press, 1976]). In 2010, the American Society of Newspaper Editors found "total newsroom employment" to be at 41,600 ("Newsroom Employment up Slightly, Minority Numbers Plunge for Third Year," American Society of News Editors, April 7, 2011, at http://asne.org/article_view/articleid/1788/newsroom-employment-up-slightly-minority-numbers-plunge-for-third-year.aspx). Population comparison data come from: *Population, Housing Units, Area*

Measurements, and Density: 1790–1990, U.S. Census Bureau, at http://www.census
.gov/population/www.censusdata/files/table-2.pdf; press release, "U.S. Census
Bureau Announces 2010 Census Population Counts—Apportionment Counts
Delivered to President," U.S. Census Bureau, December 21, 2010, at http://2010
.census.gov/news/releases/operations/cb10-cn93.html. Network news staff number is from "Overview" in Pew, "The State of the News Media 2010," at http://
stateofthemedia.org/2010/overview-3/.

50. Twenty-seven states with no reporters in Washington is from: "The New
Washington Press Corps: As Mainstream Media Decline, Niche and Foreign
Outlets Grow," Pew Research Center's Project for Excellence in Journalism,
Feb. 11, 2009, at http://www.journalism.org/analysis_report/new_washington
_press_corps; 22,000 laws passed in state capitals figure is from the National
Conference of State Legislatures; number of registered lobbyists in state capitals
versus Washington is from the National Institute on Money in State Politics, at
http://www.followthemoney.org/database/graphs/lobbyistlink/lobbymap.phtml
?p=0&y=2011&l=0 and OpenSecrets.org (http://www.opensecrets.org/lobby/);
number of reporters in state capitals is from Waldman, "The Information Needs
of Communities," Overview, p. 11, n. 23, citing in part Jennifer Dorroh, "Statehouse Exodus," *American Journalism Review* (April–May 2009), at http://www
.ajr.org/article.asp?id=4721. The number of statehouse reporters fell from 524
in 2003 to 355 in 2009. The foreign correspondent number is from Priya Kumar,
"Foreign Correspondents: Who Covers What," *American Journalism Review* (December–January 2011), at http://www.ajr.org/article.asp?id=4997. It should be noted
that the actual number of eliminated foreign correspondent positions is really much
worse; according to the article, "The current list includes a combination of staffers
and contract writers, who were not included in 2003. They were counted this time
to reflect changes in the industry. If only full-time correspondents were listed, the
current number would be far lower. Stringers are not included in the tally."

51. Mary Walton, "Investigative Shortfall," *American Journalism Review* (September 2010).

52. Waldman, "The Information Needs of Communities," Overview, p. 11, n.
28, citing interview with Mark Horvit (executive director of IRE) by M. K. Guzda
Struck, FCC, August 16, 2010. By 2014, IRE membership had rebounded to 5,000.

53. Daniel J. Boorstin, *The Image: A Guide to Pseudo-Events in America,* 25th
anniv. ed. (New York: Vintage, 1992), p. 6.

54. John Nichols and Robert W. McChesney, *Dollarocracy: How the Money and
Media Election Complex Is Destroying America* (New York: Nation Books/Perseus,
2013), pp. 194 and 311 (n.), citing their earlier book, *The Death and Life of American Journalism* (New York: Nation Books, 2010), appendix 3, pp. 264–265 and the
preface, "written specifically for the paperback edition." They estimate that in a
few years, the public relations spinners to journalists ratio will become 6:1.

55. Martin Moore, "Churnalism Exposed," *Columbia Journalism Review,* March
3, 2011, at http://www.cjr.org/the_news_frontier/churnalism_exposed.php7page
=all&print=true.

56. Nick Davies, *Flat Earth News* (London: Chatto and Windus, 2008), pp. 52–53. Also, e-mail interview with Nick Davies, November 16, 2010.

57. Ibid., quoting from Justin Lewis, Andrew Williams, Bob Franklin, James Thomas, and Nick Mosdell, "The Quality and Independence of British Journalism," Cardiff School of Journalism, Media and Cultural Studies, pp. 1–64. Of course, evidence of how low the everyday practices of news judgment in Britain had fallen could not have been any more stark or sensational than the phone and e-mail hacking scandal that resulted in the 2011 closing of the *News of the World*, owned by conservative media mogul Rupert Murdoch's News Corporation. See Lowell Bergman, correspondent, Neil Docherty and Lowell Bergman, producers, "Murdoch's Scandal," PBS *Frontline*, March 27, 2012, at http://www.pbs.org /wgbh/pages/frontline/murdochs-scandal/, accessed June 27, 2012.

58. Wendy Bacon, Michelle Loh, Alex Taylor, and Sasha Pavey, "Spinning the Media: Key Findings in a Week in the Life of the Media," University of Technology Sydney/Australian Centre for Independent Journalism, at http://www.crikey .com.au/2010/03/15/spinning-the-media-key-findings-in-a-week-in-the-life-of -the-media/.

59. Davies, *Flat Earth News*, p. 97.

60. Paul Farhi, "Is It News, or Is It Product Placement?" *Washington Post*, December 7, 2011. See also James Rainey, "The News Is, That Pitch Was Paid For: When Spokespersons for Hire Promote Products on Local TV News Shows," *Los Angeles Times*, September 15, 2010, at http://articles.latimes.com/2010/sep/15 /entertainment/la-et-onthemedia-20100915, accessed March 3, 2012.

61. Waldman, "The Information Needs of Communities," at http://www.fcc .gov/info-needs-communities, June 9, 2011, chap. 3, Television, Broadcast TV, pp. 91–94.

62. Interview with Eugene Roberts, June 13, 2007, New York City.

63. Felicity Barringer, "Newspaper Publisher Quits to Protest Profit Goals," *New York Times*, March 20, 2001, at http://www.nytimes.com/2001/03/20/business /newspaper-publisher-quits-to-protest-profit-goals.html, accessed January 4, 2013.

64. Comments by Jay Harris, former publisher, *San Jose Mercury News*, IRE national conference, Chicago, Illinois, June 2001. And he used a marvelous phrase, about how journalists in a difficult financial climate too often exercise self-censorship, for fear their publishers and their editors will block time-consuming or controversial investigative stories, and thus during their own reporting process, stop, exercising what he called "anticipatory self-restraint." I've seen and heard this happen myself, many times unfortunately, in the United States and around the world. Today, Jay holds the Wallis Annenberg Chair in Journalism and Democracy at the Annenberg School for Communication at the University of Southern California.

65. "2006 Annual Report on the State of the News Media," Executive Summary, 2, The Pew Research Center's Project for Excellence in Journalism, Washington, D.C. (accessible online at www.pej.org).

66. Charles Layton, "Sherman's March," *American Journalism Review* (February–March 2006), at http://www.ajr.org/article.asp?id=4037, accessed January 4, 2013.

Shown in late 2013 and early 2014 on PBS stations WNET, WHYY, and other US stations, the film's website, http://www.blackandwhiteanddeadallover .net, includes a trailer and other information. Several journalists (including the author) were interviewed for the documentary, produced by Lenny Feinberg and directed by Chris Foster.

67. Mary Walton, "The Selling of Small-Town America," chap. 2 in Gene Roberts, ed. in chief, Thomas Kunkel and Charles Layton, gen. eds., *Leaving Readers Behind: The Age of Corporate Newspapering* (Fayetteville: University of Arkansas Press: 2001), pp. 19–21.

68. Ibid.

69. Jack Bass, "Newspaper Monopoly," chap. 4 in Roberts, *Leaving Readers Behind,* pp. 109–156. The two newspapers referenced are the *Morning News* in Springdale, Arkansas, and the aforementioned *Northwest Arkansas Times* in Fayetteville.

70. Gilbert Cranberg, Randall Bezanson, and John Soloski, *Taking Stock: Journalism and the Publicly Traded Newspaper Company* (Ames: Iowa State University Press, 2001), p. 154.

71. Jack Fuller, *What Is Happening to News: The Information Explosion and the Crisis in Journalism* (Chicago: University of Chicago Press, 2010), pp. 10–11.

72. Rick Edmonds of the Poynter Institute, Emily Guskin, Tom Rosenstiel, and Amy Mitchell, Project on Excellence in Journalism, "Newspapers: Building Digital Revenues Proves Painfully Slow," "The State of the News Media 2012," April 11, 2012, at http://stateofthemedia.org/2012/newspapers-building-digital -revenues-proves-painfully-slow/, accessed July 4, 2012.

CHAPTER 7: A WATCHDOG IN THE CORRIDORS OF POWER

1. This is one of three marble-engraved quotations of the great scientist at the Albert Einstein Memorial Statue, sculpted by Robert Berks and unveiled in 1979, on the grounds of the National Academy of Sciences in Washington, DC (www.nasonline.org). It is a shorter version of Einstein's statement about academic freedom for a conference of the Emergency Civil Liberties Committee, March 3, 1954, from the Einstein Archive 28–1025, as quoted in Alice Calaprice (collected and edited by), *The New Quotable Einstein* (Princeton: Princeton University Press, 2005), p. 69.

2. Fred R. Shapiro, ed., *The Yale Book of Quotations* (New Haven: Yale University Press, 2006), p. 145 (from the *Paris Review,* Spring 1958).

3. The phrase "watchdog in the corridors of power" comes from the title of the first national news story written about the author and the Center for Public Integrity, written by Peter H. Stone, "A Watchdog in the Corridors of Power," *National Journal* 25 (11) (March 13, 1993): 641.

4. Interview with Florence Graves, June 27, 2007, Washington, DC. Nellie Bly, whose real name was Elizabeth Cochrane, got herself temporarily committed and later wrote "Ten Days in a Mad-House" in the *New York World,* October 16, 1887; it caused a public uproar and some much-needed reforms. Ida M.

Tarbell worked for S. S. McClure at *McClure's* magazine and between late 1902 and 1904, wrote a seminal nineteen-part series and later book, *The History of the Standard Oil Company*. It helped lead to the 1911 Supreme Court decision to break up Standard Oil. For more, see Judith and William Serrin, *Muckraking! The Journalism That Changed America* (New York: New Press, 2002), pp. 142–146 and 151–154, respectively. See also Ann Bausum, *Muckrakers: How Ida Tarbell, Upton Sinclair, and Lincoln Steffens Helped Expose Scandal, Inspire Reform, and Invent Investigative Journalism*, foreword by Daniel Schorr (Washington, DC: National Geographic, 2007).

5. Ibid.

6. Florence Graves and Charles E. Shepard, "Packwood Accused of Sexual Advances," *Washington Post*, November 22, 1992, at http://www.brandeis.edu /investigate/selectedwork/docs/PackwoodAccusedofSexualAdvances.pdf, accessed January 25, 2014. For more information about Florence Graves and her work, see http://www.investigatingpower.org/journalist/florence-graves/, accessed January 25, 2014.

7. Interview with Bill Kovach, June 28, 2007, Washington, DC. For more information about Bill Kovach and his career, see http://www.investigatingpower .org/journalist/bill-kovach/, accessed January 26, 2014.

8. Ibid.

9. Ibid.

10. Interview with Daniel Schorr, May 9, 2007, Washington, DC. For more information, see http://www.investigatingpower.org/journalist/daniel-schorr/, accessed January 26, 2014. Three years before his death, Schorr received the 2007 Goldsmith Career Award for his distinguished sixty years in journalism; to see and hear the recorded presentation of that award and his speech, see http://forum.iop .harvard.edu/content/2007-goldsmith-awards-ceremony (52:00 into the program), accessed January 26, 2014.

11. Patricia Sullivan, "Daniel Schorr, Veteran CBS and CNN Reporter and CNN News Analyst, Dead at 93," *Washington Post*, July 24, 2010, at http://www .washingtonpost.com/wp-dyn/content/article/2010/07/23/AR2010072303146 _pf.html, accessed January 26, 2014.

12. Howard Kurtz, "Anchors in an Unmoored World," *Washington Post*, July 27, 2009, citing "Television: The Most Intimate Medium," October 14, 1966 (cover story, Cronkite on the cover), at http://www.time.com/time/magazine /article/0,9171,840700,00.html, accessed September 3, 2011.

13. Joe Wershba died in May 2011. Dennis Hevesi, "Joseph Wershba, a Journalist Who Helped Take On McCarthy, Dies at Ninety," May 17, 2011, at http:// www.nytimes.com/2011/05/18/business/media/18wershba.html, accessed Jan. 6, 2012.

14. For more description of the Kentucky school story reporting, see The Center for Public Integrity, *Citizen Muckraking: How to Investigate and Right Wrongs in Your Community* (Monroe, ME: Common Courage Press, 2000), pp. 2–5. On the Kentucky story and the Social Security check–postal fraud story, I was

the associate producer, and I co-wrote and co-produced the tobacco lawyers segment with Richard Bonin. I wrote and produced the rest of the stories referenced, among others. For more information about the travails of Marvin Mitchelson, including my reporting efforts, see John A. Jenkins, *Ladies Man: The Life and Trials of Marvin Mitchelson* (New York: St. Martin's Press, 1992), pp. 227–236.

15. It was a reassuring pleasure to work pre-publication with exceptionally competent CBS lawyers Rick Altobeth and Jonathan Sternberg during these years.

16. The *Courier-Journal* reporter who had first investigated the Clinton County story was Richard Whitt. He had a "poor, rural upbringing" and practiced what he called "redneck journalism," as explained in the obituary by the Institute for Rural Journalism and Community Issues at the University of Kentucky in Lexington, which established a Richard Whitt Memorial Fund for Rural Journalists after he died suddenly of a heart attack at age sixty-four. "It's the kind of journalism that when you read the paper in the morning you say, 'Damn, that makes me mad,' and it makes your neck red. That motivates people to do things." He won the Pulitzer Prize for his reporting in 1978. See "Richard Whitt, 'Redneck Journalist,' Sixty-Four," Institute for Rural Journalism and Community Issues, January 28, 2009, at http://www.uky.edu/CommInfoStudies/IRJCI/RichWhitt.htm. See also Paula Burba, "Former C-J Reporter Richard Whitt Dies," *Courier-Journal* (Louisville, Kentucky), January 28, 2009.

17. E-mail exchange with Dr. Pat Choate, December 3, 2011. Twenty-three years later, Pat recalled: "I remember the event vividly, and that is the way it happened."

18. The story later received an Emmy nomination in 1988 in the "Outstanding Investigative Journalism" category by the National Academy of Arts and Sciences.

19. For my personal remembrance of him, see Charles Lewis, "'Honor and Privilege' to Work with Mike Wallace," Investigative Reporting Workshop, April 9, 2012, at http://investigativereportingworkshop.org/blogs/shop-notes/posts/2012/apr/09/mike-wallace/.

20. Don Hewitt, who conceived and led *60 Minutes* from 1968 until he was forced out in 2004, died in August 2009. See Jacques Steinberg, "Don Hewitt, Creator of '60 Minutes,' Dies at Eighty-Six," *New York Times*, August 20, 2009, at http://www.nytimes.com/2009/08/20/business/media/20hewitt.html?pagewanted=all, accessed January 6, 2012. Mike Wallace's last segment was broadcast in early 2008, and he died on April 7, 2012. Tim Weiner, "Mike Wallace, CBS Pioneer of '60 Minutes,' Dies at Ninety-Three," *New York Times*, April 8, 2012, at http://www.nytimes.com/2012/04/09/business/media/mike-wallace-cbs-pioneer-of-60-minutes-dead-at-93.html?pagewanted=all. For my personal remembrance of him, see Lewis, "'Honor and Privilege.'"

21. Before my problems in October 1988 or the infamous 1995 CBS Inc. decision to block producer Lowell Bergman's tobacco story, immortalized in the movie *The Insider*, it was quietly understood by the program's few investigative producers that over the years a few sensitive subjects had been avoided, or segments even killed in midproduction.

1. Henrik Ibsen, *Pillars of Society*, Act III (1877), cited in John Bartlett, *Bartlett's Familiar Quotations*, 16th ed., Justin Kaplan, gen. ed. (New York: Little, Brown, 1992), p. 507. The Norwegian playwright died in 1906. See "Henrik Ibsen Dead: Norway in Mourning," *New York Times*, May 23, 1906, at http://query.nytimes .com/mem/archive-free/pdf?res=F20612F73A5A12738DDDAD0A94DD405 B868CF1D3, accessed November 25, 2012.

2. Alex Benes had directed ABC News's Central American war coverage in the 1980s; we had met on an exciting story we investigated in Panama, Miami, and Washington in 1979 while both working at ABC. At the time the Center began, in 1989, he had not yet become the director of news for NBC News in New York. Charlie Piller and I met in 1984, when we realized we were both investigating the US Army's secretive and controversial biological warfare research program at Dugway Proving Grounds in Utah and elsewhere. The author of two books, including *Gene Wars*, a longtime reporter for the *Los Angeles Times*, today he is an investigative reporter for the *Sacramento Bee*. He attended every Center board meeting for eighteen years and served as the chairman of the board from 2000 to mid-2007 before deciding to step down; marking the first time a Lewis, Benes, or Piller was not on the board or staff of the organization. In June 2009, I was invited to return to the board after a five-year hiatus, around the time of the twentieth anniversary, and I agreed to serve one three-year term.

3. See http://www.publicintegrity.org/about, accessed January 27, 2014.

4. For more information about how the Center for Public Integrity is funded, including the names of specific donors, see http://www.publicintegrity.org/about /our-work/supporters, accessed March 16, 2004.

5. Dean Starkman, "The Hamster Wheel," *Columbia Journalism Review* (September–October 2010), at www.cjr.org/cover_story/the_hamster_wheel.php, accessed September 15, 2012. Dean Starkman, "The Hamster Wheel vs. the Quality Imperative," *Columbia Journalism Review* (September 14, 2012), at www.cjr.org /the_audit/jrc_low-quality_is_baked_into.php, accessed September 15, 2012. One of many revealing statistics in this important article: the *Wall Street Journal* published just over 26,000 articles in 2000, and by 2008, the number had risen to 38,000, an increase of roughly 50 percent accomplished with fewer newsroom employees—and not counting "Web-only material, blogs, NewsHub, etc., which the staff also produces."

6. In the first 1992 "Under the Influence" report, we discovered that the deputy chairman of President George H. W. Bush's reelection campaign, James Lake, was also a registered lobbyist for the Bank of Credit and Commerce International, his firm receiving over $1 million while under several federal grand jury and other investigations for criminal misconduct. BCCI was eventually found to have defrauded 50,000 depositors around the world. When I mentioned this startling factoid to a well-known reporter in the Washington bureau of the *New York Times*, hoping the newspaper might find our forthcoming report newsworthy, he figuratively

yawned and told me that it wasn't a news story, because "it isn't illegal." I looked at him in disbelief. When I held the news conference at the National Press Club days later in the midst of presidential election season, sixty reporters came and this item received good national news coverage. See some description of this and other major reports from 1990 to 2000 in the 2000 Annual Report, p. 15, at http://www.iwatchnews.org/files/manual/pdf/corporate/2000_CPI_Annual_Report.pdf, accessed September 3, 2011. See also Charles Lewis, "Commentary: Under the Influence: Why This Series?" The Center for Public Integrity, Washington, DC, March 2, 2000, at http://www.iwatchnews.org/2000/03/02/3306/commentary -under-influence-why-series, accessed September 3, 2011.

7. Foreword by Kevin Phillips, in Charles Lewis and the Center for Public Integrity, *The Buying of the President* (New York: HarperCollins/Avon, 1996), p. 1.

8. "Our Private Legislatures: Public Service, Personal Gain," The Center for Public Integrity, May 21, 2000, at http://projects.publicintegrity.org/oi/report .aspx?aid=614. Led by director Diane Renzulli, Center researchers found that, according to an analysis of financial disclosure reports filed in 1999 by 5,716 state legislators, more than one in five sat on a legislative committee that regulated their professional or business interest; at least 18 percent had financial ties to businesses or organizations that lobby state government; and nearly one in four received income from a government agency other than the state legislature, in many cases working for agencies the legislature funds. "The Center for Public Integrity: Investigative Journalism in the Public Interest," 2010 Annual Report, p. 24.

9. Unpublished memo from former Center director of state projects Leah Rush to Chuck Lewis, July 27, 2010.

10. Bob Williams and Morgan Jindrich, "On the Road Again—and Again; FCC Officials Rack Up $2.8 Million Travel Tab with Industries They Regulate," The Center for Public Integrity, May 22, 2003, at http://projects.publicintegrity.org /telecom/report.aspx?aid=15#. The Washington bureau of ABC News was preparing a potential *World News Tonight* piece based on these dramatic Center findings involving the political influence of the broadcast industry, and in the eleventh hour, one of the show's top producers "on the rim" in New York told the correspondent (we later learned), "Are you out of your fucking mind?" and the produced segment was abruptly killed.

11. After days of foraging around Washington, discreetly trying to ascertain the authenticity of the extraordinary leaked document, and when satisfied that it was genuine, we then called a very senior George W. Bush/Attorney General John Ashcroft Justice Department official about the document. We were ominously told we would be "very sorry" if we published it. We asked that person to spell his/her name and we immediately posted the story and the one-hundred-plus-page document on the Center website. See Charles Lewis and Adam Mayle, "Justice Depart. Drafts Sweeping Expansion of Anti-Terrorism Act," The Center for Public Integrity, February 7, 2003, at http://www.publicintegrity.org/articles/entry/377/.

12. To our surprise, the Defense Policy Board would not provide the financial disclosure information regarding former secretary of state Henry Kissinger and

the other members, and my staff thought we would not be able to proceed. I disagreed, saying that just because some of those people don't want us to know of their financial entanglements doesn't mean we can't find them out ourselves through other means. So we cobbled together information about their financial ties and awarded contracts to their employers from corporate and government press releases and various commercial databases such as Lexis-Nexis. See André Verlöy and Daniel Politi, data by Aron Pilhofer, "Advisors of Influence: Nine Members of the Defense Policy Board Have Ties to Defense Contractors," The Center for Public Integrity, March 28, 2003, at http://www.publicintegrity.org /articles/entry/374/#printThis.

13. Interview with Carl Bernstein, September 6, 2007, New York, New York. See the "idiot culture" video interview segment at http://www.investigatingpower .org/journalist/carl-bernstein/. See also Carl Bernstein, "The Idiot Culture," *New Republic* (July 8, 1992), pp. 22–28, at http://www.carlbernstein.com/magazines_the _idiot_culture.pdf, accessed January 27, 2014.

14. Kevin Baron, Maud Beelman, Neil Gordon, Laura Peterson, Aron Pilhofer, Daniel Politi, André Verlöy, Bob Williams, and Brooke Williams contributed to this report, which was written by Ms. Beelman, "Windfalls of War," The Center for Public Integrity, October 30, 2003. Research editor and attorney Peter Newbatt Smith handled the FOIA litigation, working with the Center's outstanding attorney for twenty-one years, Marc Miller of MacLeod, Watkinson and Miller. See http://projects.publicintegrity.org/wow/report.aspx?aid=65.

15. This eleven-part series/book won the Society of Professional Journalists online investigative reporting award. See http://projects.publicintegrity.org /bow/.

16. Mark Feldstein, "Investigative Reporters," in Christopher H. Sterling, gen. ed., *Encyclopedia of Journalism* (Thousand Oaks, CA: Sage Publications, 2009), vol. 2, p. 801. See also Mark Feldstein, "Muckraking Goes Global," *American Journalism Review* (April–May 2012), at http://www.ajr.org/Article .asp?id=5294. For all of the ICIJ investigations since 1998, see http://www.icij .org/projects, accessed January 27, 2014. For the first six years, the director of ICIJ was Maud Beelman; since 2001, it has been Gerard Ryle.

17. Phillip van Niekirk and André Verlöy, "Special Report: Kuchma Approved Sale of Weapons System to Iraq," The Center for Public Integrity, April 15, 2002, at http://www.publicintegrity.org/2002/04/15/3197/special-report-kuchma -approved-sale-weapons-system-iraq, accessed January 27, 2014.

18. See http://www.globalintegrity.org.

19. For a description of the unique approach, see http://www.globalintegrity .org/aboutus/approach.cfm. My co-founders of Global Integrity are its managing director, Nathaniel Heller, and international director, Marianne Camerer, based in Washington, DC, and Cape Town, South Africa, respectively.

20. See www.publicintegrity.org, "About Us" and under "Board of Directors."

21. Knut Royce and Nathaniel Heller, "Cheney Led Halliburton to Feast at Federal Trough," *Public i* (The Center for Public Integrity), August 2, 2000.

22. See Charles Lewis, "Colin Powell's Critique: Part II," *New York Times*, August 3, 2000, at www.nytimes.com/2000/08/03/opinion/colin-powell-s-critique -part-ii.html, accessed August 18, 2012. See Edward B. Colby, "The Russians, the Reporters, and a Hired Gun," *Columbia Journalism Review* (May–June 2005): 20. During these intense years, the Center for Public Integrity was magnificently served by our retained, Washington-based outside attorneys—Marc Miller of Mc-Leod, Watkinson and Miller, Michael Sullivan of Levine, Sullivan, Koch and Schulz (who defended us against Akin Gump and the Russians), and Pat Carome of Wilmer Cutler (now Wilmer Hale, who handled all Center international legal issues).

23. The fund was created because the Center could no longer obtain affordable libel insurance after the Russian lawsuit was filed and was thus more vulnerable to external legal threats. Three years after the litigation was dismissed, I resigned from the fund as president and the organization became dormant (but there to fight another day, if needed). And today, the Center once again has libel insurance. However, after nearly seven years of no libel litigation directed against the Center, since 2012 two new lawsuits have been filed. For more about the history of the fund and "the circumstances pertaining to these decisions," see my letter posted on the organization's website at http://web.archive.org/web/20110202064549/http://www.tfij .org/about/status/, accessed January 28, 2014. For a more detailed description of the human dimension of the lawsuit, see: "Under Siege: The Personal Toll of Media Lawsuits," on p. 29 of Drew Sullivan's "Libel Tourism: Silencing the Press Through Transnational Legal Threats" (Center for International Media Assistance/National Endowment for Democracy), January 6, 2010, at http://cima.ned.org/sites/default /files/CIMA-Libel_Tourism-Report.pdf, accessed on August 18, 2012.

24. Mariah Blake, "Something Fishy?" *Columbia Journalism Review* (July–August 2012): 24–29, at http://www.cjr.org/feature/something_fishy.php. In August 2012, the Center for Public Integrity returned to its original website URL, www.Public Integrity.org.

25. Transcript, 2007 Goldsmith Award ceremonies, p. 16; also http://www .hks.harvard.edu/presspol/prizes_lectures/goldsmith_awards/transcripts/2007 _goldsmith_awards.pdf.

26. Brad Plumer, "Why Exactly Should the Government Fund PBS and NPR?" *Washington Post* (blog), October 10, 2012, at http://www.washingtonpost.com/blogs /wonkblog/wp/2012/10/10/why-exactly-should-the-government-fund-pbs-and-npr, accessed January 28, 2014. Public television and radio stations received $445 million from the government in 2012. A recent Zogby survey found that 55 percent of Americans polled "flatly opposed" any cuts in government funding for PBS and NPR, "while only 35 percent agreed that 'the government cannot afford to subsidize public television.'" As to the number of privately (nongovernment) funded, nonprofit news organizations, there has been substantial recent research about this, with various numbers and findings, depending upon the methodology, the historic time frame examined, and so on. But the Investigative News Network alone, begun in 2009, today has roughly one hundred nonprofit news member organizations throughout the United States. See www.investigativenewsnetwork.org, accessed January 28, 2014.

27. After being hired as a "Distinguished Journalist in Residence" in 2006, I first proposed the idea for the workshop to Associate Professor Wendell Cochran, a former reporter and the journalism division director at the time, and to then Dean Larry Kirkman in October 2007, and it was approved by the university president, Neil Kerwin, and the Board of Trustees in March 2008. For more about the award-winning workshop, what it has done to date, the more than sixty investigative multimedia projects it has published in partnership with the *Washington Post*, the *New York Times*, and many other respected news organizations (including helping to incubate two books, co-producing six documentaries with PBS *Frontline* and *Showtime*), involving more than seventy-five students from various universities and seven professors, see http://www.investigativereportingworkshop.org/about/.

28. Details, including website URL links, about seventy-five profiled nonprofits can be found at: Charles Lewis, Brittney Butts, and Kate Musselwhite, "A Second Look: The New Journalism Ecosystem," Investigative Reporting Workshop (iLab), August 31, 2012, at http://investigativereportingworkshop.org/ilab/story/second-look/, accessed January 2, 2013. For more detail about how the "nonprofit journalism ecosystem" has evolved historically, see Charles Lewis, "The Growing Importance of Nonprofit Journalism," Joan Shorenstein Center on the Press, Politics and Public Policy, Harvard University, April 2007, at http://shorensteincenter.org/wp-content/uploads/2012/03/2007_03_lewis.pdf, accessed January 2, 2013. To be clear, some of the nonprofits at or very near universities are 501 (c) (3) separately incorporated, tax-exempt, nonprofit companies, and some are projects or "centers" within a university and also not incorporated. Either status can involve free rent, student interns, teaching/mentoring, access to library databases, and other resources, and so forth.

29. Sheila Coronel and eight other women began the Philippine Center, which has published some of the most important, courageous reporting in that nation. Today, Sheila is a professor of journalism at the Columbia University Graduate School of Journalism and the director of the Stabile Center for Investigative Journalism. For more about her work, see http://www.journalism.columbia.edu/profile/31, accessed January 29, 2014. The fearless motto of the Philippine Center today is: "We tell it like it is. No matter who. No matter what." See http://pcij.org/, accessed January 29, 2014.

30. In late 2013, the *St. Louis Beacon* merged with St. Louis Public Radio—see https://www.stlbeacon.org/#!/content/33800/editors_weekly_merger_112213?coverpage=4427, accessed January 29, 2014. An unfolding nonprofit journalism phenomenon nationwide is the somewhat logical confluence of interests between public television and radio stations and investigative reporting centers. For example, in Denver, Laura Frank, formerly an investigative reporter for the now shuttered *Rocky Mountain News* newspaper, is the founder and executive director of I-News Network and the vice president of news for the Denver-based PBS station. In San Diego, the relationship between Investigative Newsource and KPBS is less formalized or entwined (http://inewsource.org/, accessed January 29, 2014). Its founder, former *San Diego Union-Tribune* reporter and senior editor Lorie Hearn,

has no joint position with San Diego's longtime PBS station, and her organization, though its offices are located inside the KPBS newsroom, is also separately incorporated with its own tax-exempt status and also operates closely with San Diego State University. These and other public media entities in the United States are becoming more symbiotic, in varying degrees. Why? Local public broadcasting/online media stations rarely do enterprise journalism, but they do have a loyal following of "listeners/viewers like you." And recently created local investigative reporting centers have generally not yet had the time or resources to develop either a major public audience or dedicated annual support.

31. Full disclosure: over the past quarter century, I have served on numerous nonprofit journalism–related organization boards and advisory boards in the United States—the Center for Public Integrity, the Center for Responsive Politics, the Fund for Independence in Journalism, the Fund for Investigative Journalism, the Investigative News Network, Investigative Newsource, the National Institute for Money in State Politics, the New England Center for Investigative Reporting, the News Literacy Project, the Sunlight Foundation, and the Wisconsin Center for Investigative Journalism.

32. Published by the Foundation for National Progress, *Mother Jones* was founded in 1976 by Adam Hochschild, Paul Jacobs, Jeffrey Klein, Richard Parker, and others, and to date it has won six National Magazine Awards. See http://www.motherjones.com/about, accessed January 2, 2013. See also Mark Dowie, "Pinto Madness," *Mother Jones*, August 31, 1977, at http://www.motherjones.com/politics/1977/09/pinto-madness, accessed January 3, 2013.

33. Tim Francisco, Alyssa Lenhoff, and Michael Schudson, "The Classroom as Newsroom: Leveraging University Resources for Public Affairs Reporting," *International Journal of Communication* 6 (2012), Feature 2677–2697, at http://ijoc.org, accessed January 2, 2013.

34. Ibid., see also Jan Schaffer, "Journalism Schools as Startup Accelerators," Nieman Journalism Lab ("Predictions for Journalism 2013: A Nieman Lab Series"), at http://www.niemanlab.org/2012/12/journalism-schools-as-startup-accelerators/, accessed January 3, 2013.

35. See http://hechingerreport.org/about/, accessed January 30, 2014.

36. See http://www.thecrimereport.org/about-us/about, accessed January 20, 2014.

37. American University 2011–2012 Annual Report, at http://www.american.edu/finance/loader.cfm?csModule=security/getfile&pageid=3364568, accessed January 3, 2013.

38. Charles Lewis, "Workshop, American, Washington Post Jointly Hire Investigative Reporter," Investigative Reporting Workshop, April 4, 2013, at http://investigativereportingworkshop.org/ilab/story/workshop-au-post-jointly-hire-top-journalist/, accessed June 27, 2013.

39. See http://www.pulitzer.org/citation/2012-Public-Service, accessed January 3, 2013. At the time of the Sullivan announcement, the *Washington Post* and the American University School of Communication were led by new executive editor

Marty Baron and new Dean Jeffrey Rutenbeck, respectively. And it all began with a phone-call conversation between Vernon Loeb and yours truly, and of course, my subsequent conversations with Sullivan. Regarding the Pulitzer Prize for Public Service Journalism and its history, see Roy J. Harris Jr., *Pulitzer's Gold: Behind the Prize for Public Service Journalism* (Columbia: University of Missouri Press, 2007).

40. The three-day conference was held at the Pocantico Conference Center at the John D. Rockefeller estate outside New York City, sponsored by the Rockefeller Brothers Foundation. Given that, a century earlier, an intrepid investigative reporter, Ida Tarbell, had written one of the most important exposés in US history, which eventually led to the breakup of Rockefeller's Standard Oil, this was a historic meeting in an ironic setting. (For the only dual biography of Tarbell and Rockefeller, see Steve Weinberg, *Taking on the Trust: The Epic Battle of Ida Tarbell and John D. Rockefeller* [New York: Norton, 2008].) I was the original draftsman of the "Pocantico Declaration" before it was collectively debated and edited at the conference. For more information, see Charles Lewis, "Great Expectations," *Columbia Journalism Review* (September–October 2009): 17–18, at www.investigativenewsnetwork.org, accessed December 16, 2012. For the text of the Pocantico Declaration, see http://www.investigativenewsnetwork.org/about/pocantico-declaration, accessed December 16, 2012.

41. For more information about the Global Investigative Journalism Network, see www.gijn.org/about/, accessed January 30, 2014.

42. Paul Starr, "An Unexpected Crisis: The News Media in Postindustrial Democracies," *International Journal of Press/Politics* (SAGE) 17 (March 2012): 234, citing Project for Excellence in Journalism, "Overview," in "State of the News Media 2010," at http://www.stateofthemedia.org/2010/overview_intro.php, accessed January 4, 2013.

43. Quoted material is from Anne Applebaum, *Iron Curtain: The Crushing of Eastern Europe, 1944–1956* (New York: Doubleday, 2012), p. 461.

44. Evgeny Morozov and others have credibly chided journalists and philanthropic foundations and others for overstating the significance of these Western efforts, which Morozov refers to as the "Cold War triumphalism" of "cyberutopians." However, it is also not prudent to dismiss these efforts or their long-term democratic impact on local civil-society citizens. See Evgeny Morozov, *The Net Delusion: The Dark Side of Internet Freedom* (New York: PublicAffairs, 2011), pp. xiv–xv, 6–7, 47–50.

45. Bill Keller, "Mandela Is Named President, Closing the Era of Apartheid," *New York Times*, May 10, 1994, at http://www.nytimes.com/1994/05/10/world/mandela-is-named-president-closing-the-era-of-apartheid.html, accessed December 2, 2012; Bill Keller, "South Africa's New Era: The Overview; South Africans Hail President Mandela; First Black Leader Pledges Racial Unity," *New York Times*, May 11, 1994, at http://www.nytimes.com/1994/05/11/world/south-africa-s-new-era-overview-south-africans-hail-president-mandela-first.html, accessed December 2, 2012. Mandela died in December 2013. See Bill Keller, "Nelson Mandela, South Africa's Liberator as Prisoner and President, Dies at Ninety-Five," *New*

York Times, at http://www.nytimes.com/2013/12/06/world/africa/nelson-mandela _obit.html?ref=international-home, accessed January 30, 2014.

46. Priscilla B. Hayner, *Unspeakable Truths: Transitional Justice and the Challenge of Truth Commissions*, 2nd ed., foreword by Kofi Annan, (New York: Routledge, 2011), pp. 27–32 and 237. According to Hayner (p. 29), "the "greatest innovation of the commission and the most controversial of its powers, was its ability to grant individual amnesty for "politically motivated crimes committed between 1960 and April 1994." See also Nelson Mandela, *Long Walk to Freedom: The Autobiography of Nelson Mandela* (New York: Back Bay Books/Little Brown, 1994); Anthony Sampson, *Mandela: The Authorized Biography* (New York: Knopf, 1999); Allister Sparks and Mpho Tutu, *Desmond Tutu, Authorized* (New York: HarperOne/HarperCollins, 2011).

47. Hayner, *Unspeakable Truths*, p. 237.

48. I met WikiLeaks co-founder Julian Assange in April 2010 when we both found ourselves on the same panel at a conference at the University of California Graduate School of Journalism in Berkeley. For the video recording of this panel, see Logan Symposium: The New Initiatives, moderated by veteran journalist Lowell Bergman, at http://fora.tv/2010/04/18/Logan_Symposium_The_New _Initiatives, accessed December 16, 2012. For the best single book, among many, about WikiLeaks and its significance, see Andy Greenberg, *This Machine Kills Secrets: How WikiLeakers, Cypherpunks, and Hacktivists Aim to Free the World's Information* (New York: Dutton/Penguin, 2012). The "idealists, anarchists, extremists" quote is from the book jacket. See also David Leigh and Luke Harding, *The Guardian, WikiLeaks: Inside Julian Assange's War on Secrecy* (London: PublicAffairs, 2011).

49. Greenberg, *This Machine Kills Secrets*, pp. 5, 327; "76.7 million documents . . . " cited from Information Security Oversight Office Annual Report, April 15, 2011.

50. Greenberg, *This Machine Kills Secrets*, p. 5, citing Greg Miller, "How many security clearances have been issued? Nearly enough for everyone in the Washington area," WashingtonPost.com, September 20, 2011, at http://www .washingtonpost.com/blogs/checkpoint-washington/post/how-many-security -clearances-has-the-government-issued-nearly-enough-for-everyone-in-the -washington-area/2011/09/20/gIQAMW3OiK_blog.html, accessed December 17, 2012.

51. "The Universal Declaration of Human Rights, United Nations, at www .un.org/en/documents/udhr/index.shtml, accessed December 13, 2012. See also Michael Lemov, *People's Warrior: John Moss and the Fight for Freedom of Information and Consumer Rights* (Madison, NJ: Fairleigh Dickinson Press, 2011), pp. 41–69.

52. Toby McIntosh, "FOI Laws: Vary Depending on Definitions," at http:// www.freedominfo.org/2011/10/foi-laws-counts-vary-slightly-depending-on -definitions/, accessed September 21, 2012. See also Alasdair Roberts, *Blacked Out: Government Secrecy in the Information Age* (New York: Cambridge University Press, 2006), pp. 14–15. It should be noted that Sweden and Finland had the first laws, adopted in 1766. Gustav Bjorkstrand and Juha Mustonen, "Introduction: Anders Chydenius' Legacy Today," in Juha Mustonen, ed., *The World's First Freedom of*

Information Act (Kokkola, Sweden: Anders Chydenius Foundation, 2006), p. 4, at http://www.access-info.org/documents/Access_Docs/Thinking/Get_Connected /worlds_first_foia.pdf, accessed September 21, 2012.

53. Roberts, *Blacked Out*, pp. 1–4; Mazdoor Kisan Shakti Sangathan, at www .mkssindiz.org/about-us/, accessed December 13, 2012. For information about India's Right to Information Act, see www.freedominfo.org/regions/east-asia /india/, accessed December 13, 2012.

54. For more information, see http://www.globalintegrity.org/about/story; www .sunlightfoundation.com/about/; www.opendemocracy.org.za/about/background/; http://www.transparency.org/whoweare/organisation; http://www.publicintegrity .org/about; www.article19.org/pages/en/freedom-of-information.html; http://www .gwu.edu/~nsarchiv/nsa/the_archive.html; www.ombwatch.org/25th; http://www .opensecrets.org/about/index.php; http://www.followthemoney.org/Institute/index .phtml; https://www.cartercenter.org/peace/americas/index.html; www.pogo.org /about/, all accessed December 14, 2012. Full disclosure: I am on the board of the Center for Responsive Politics; practically since its inception, I have served on the Sunlight Foundation Advisory Board; I am on the advisory board (an "International Associate") of the Open Democracy Advice Centre; in the period of 2005–2007, I was a paid consultant to the Carter Center about access to information and accountability issues in Latin America, in particular Jamaica and Bolivia.

55. Numbers cited in the text come from James G. McGann, "The Global 'Go-To Think Tanks,' 2010," United Nations University Edition (Philadelphia: University of Pennsylvania, January 2011), pp. 5–16, at http://gotothinktank.com /dev1/wp-content/uploads/2013/07/2012_Global_Go_To_Think_Tank_Report _-_FINAL-1.28.13.pdf, accessed January 30, 2014.

56. See http://www.hrw.org/bios/ricardo-sandoval-palos, accessed December 15, 2012.

57. The issue was about Israel's human rights record vis-à-vis its neighboring Arab countries. See Robert L. Bernstein, "Rights Watchdog, Lost in the Mideast," *New York Times*, October 20, 2009, at www.nytimes.com/2009/10/20/opinion /20bernstein.html, accessed September 26, 2012. See also Ben Birnbaum, "Minority Report: Human Rights Watch Fights a Civil War over Israel," *New Republic*, April 27, 2010, at www.tnr.com/article/minority-report-2, accessed September 26, 2002. Kathleen Peratis, "Correspondence: We're Actually Good for Israel," *New Republic*, April 26, 2010, at www.tnr.com/article/politics/correspondence-were -actually-good-israel, accessed September 26, 2012.

58. See http://newamerica.net/about, accessed December 17, 2012.

59. E-mail exchange with Clara Hogan of the New America Foundation, September 28, 2012.

60. See http://newamerica.net/, accessed December 17, 2012.

61. "Steve Coll to Step Down as New America Foundation President," June 25, 2012, at http://newamerica.net/pressroom/2012/steve_coll_to_step_down_as_new _america_foundation_president, accessed December 17, 2012. He transitioned into

a senior fellow position in the National Security Studies Program at the foundation, "I am thrilled by the opportunity to remain as a researcher and writer."

62. Roughly 70 percent of Americans are "either an active participant in the movement or sympathetic towards it," according to Gallup polling data. Riley E. Dunlap, "The State of Environmentalism in the U.S.," Gallup News Service, April 19, 2007, at http://www.gallup.com/poll/27256/state-environmentalism -us.aspx, accessed December 15, 2012. John W. Wright (with editors and reporters of the *Times*), *The New York Times Almanac 2011* (New York: Penguin, 2010), p. 505. Over half the world's countries, 107 to be exact, speak Chinese, Hindi, English, Spanish, or Arabic.

63. See www.wikipedia.org and http://www.britannica.com/, each accessed December 18, 2012.

64. I described such a source in my article "A Social-Network Solution," *Columbia Journalism Review* (March–April 2009): 26–29, at http://www.cjr.org /feature/a_socialnetwork_solution_1.php?page=all, accessed December 18, 2012.

65. Neal Gabler, *Life: The Movie* (New York: Knopf, 1998). Two billion Internet users estimate is based on data compiled by the World Bank through 2010: http:// search.worldbank.org/all?qterm=number+of+internet+users+in+the+world &Search=go.

66. In 2013, I formally proposed this concept within American University in Washington, in an evening lecture at the University of Australia in Melbourne, and in a chapter ("The Rise of the NGOs") of a new book, *Transparency in Politics and the Media*, published in October 2013 by the Reuters Institute for the Study of Journalism at the University of Oxford and edited by Nigel Bowles, James T. Hamilton, and David A. L. Levy.

67. Guardian, June 28, 2013, at http://www.guardian.co.uk/technology/2013 /jun/28/james-martin, published an obituary of Martin.

68. James Martin, *The Meaning of the Twenty-first Century* (New York: Riverhead Books, 2006, 2007), pp. 6–7 and "About the Author," on the last page.

A NOTE FROM THE AUTHOR

1. The quote is from an e-mail exchange with Daniel W. Stowell, August 29, 2010. See Thomas F. Schwartz, "Lincoln Never Said That," Illinois Historic Preservation Agency, at http://www.state.il.us/hpa/facsimiles.htm. See also the late Pulitzer Prize–winning historian Don E. Fehrenbacher's book, compiled and edited with his wife, Virginia Fehrenbacher, *Recollected Works of Abraham Lincoln* (Stanford, California: Stanford University Press, 1996).

2. My extreme reluctance to use the "L-word" regarding the "935 false statements" about the national security threat posed by Saddam Hussein's Iraq, as documented by the Center for Public Integrity's *Iraq: The War Card* report, actually became a public issue in the *New York Times*. Its longtime reporter John Cushman interviewed and quoted me later on the day the report was released, in a blog post. I had complained about the wording he had used, as it strongly implied I had said the word "lies" in my conversations with him. I had sent him a long e-mail,

in which I said, "I am not using the 'L' word in any interviews or comments to-day, nor will I in the weeks and months ahead. Short on sleep and very tired, if I actually said that to you, it was a mistake on my part. No one knows what these officials actually believed. And as someone not involved in 'access journalism' here in Washington—quite the contrary—I sure as hell don't know what these or any administration's folks actually believe or want to believe. We actually, as a peo-ple, still don't know the full story about that." Cushman's response—all of this published in the *Times* digital edition—was: "Fair enough. False statements they may be, but contrary to the reference in the earlier version of this post, until Mr. Lewis is able to read the speakers' minds and hearts, he says he is not prepared to call them lies." John Cushman, "An Online Scavenger Hunt on Prewar Claims: What Did You Find?" and "The 'L' Word," in the blog feature "The Lede," *New York Times*, January 23, 2008, at http://thelede.blogs.nytimes.com/2008/01/23/an-online-scavenger-hunt-on-prewar-claims-what-did-you-find/?.

3. Fred R. Shapiro, ed., *The Yale Book of Quotations*, foreword by Joseph Epstein (New Haven: Yale University Press, 2006), p. 551.

4. David Eagleman, *Incognito: The Secret Lives of the Brain* (New York: Pantheon Books, 2011), p. 65. See also I. M. Beggs, A. Anas, and S. Farinacci, "Dissociation of Processes in Belief: Source Recollection, Statement Familiarity, and the Illusion of Truth," *Journal of Experimental Psychology* 121 (1991): 446–458.

5. To read some of this prior writing, see http://investigativereportingworkshop .org/people/editors/charles-lewis/ and also go to http://investigativereporting workshop.org/ilab/charles_lewis_bibliography/ and www.charles-lewis.com.

6. Other news coverage about *Investigating Power* included Associated Press (in www.washingtonpost.com), *Huffington Post*, and YouTube, which featured on its homepage three produced video segments from *Investigating Power* (McCar-thyism, the Vietnam My Lai massacre, and Watergate) on World Press Freedom Day, May 3, 2012. See also Charles Lewis, "Reporting That Changed History: A Journalist Mines the Past to Inform the Future," *Columbia Journalism Review*, April 25, 2012, at http://www.cjr.org/behind_the_news/reporting_that_changed _history.php?page=all. Charles Lewis, "A Tribute to Reporting National 'Mo-ments of Truth,'" Nieman Watchdog, Nieman Foundation for Journalism at Harvard University, April 25, 2012, at http://www.niemanwatchdog.org/index .cfm/blog/%E2%80%9Dhttp:/index.cfm?fuseaction=Showcase.view&showcaseid =173.

APPENDIX A: REAL-TIME TRUTH CHARTS

1. Gerald Markowitz and David Rosner, "'Cater to the Children': The Role of the Lead Industry in a Public Health Tragedy, 1900–1955," *American Journal of Public Health* 90 (1) (January 2000): 40, at http://www.ncbi.nlm.nih.gov/pmc/articles /PMC1446124/pdf/10630135.pdf (see footnotes in the article for primary source, *National Geographic* advertisement). Additional information and documentation avail-able at Cincinnati Children's Environmental Health Center, at http://www.cincinnati childrens.org/research/project/enviro/hazard/lead/lead-advertising/default.htm.

The aforementioned *National Geographic* was published in 1923. The authors make reference to such advertisements throughout the 1920s.

2. US Department of Housing and Urban Development, "History of Lead-Based Paint Legislation," accessed May 13, 2010, at http://www.hud.gov/offices /cpd/affordablehousing/training/web/leadsafe/ruleoverview/legislationhistory. cfm. Some states did pass laws regulating the industry beginning in the 1950s. The industry also took steps to reduce lead content voluntarily beginning in 1955, which critics argue served to delay federal action on the issue. More on the legislation can be found at Gerald Markowitz and David Rosner, *Deceit and Denial: The Deadly Politics of Industrial Pollution* (Berkeley: University of California Press, 2002), p. 44.

3. Markowitz and Rosner, *Deceit and Denial*, pp. 58 and 331. The authors cite the CBS coverage as part of the Lead Industry Association's quarterly report of the secretary on October 1, 1956, accessed in LIA Papers. No story title is listed for the CBS story. Also see "Don't Let *Your* Child Get Lead Poisoning," *Parade* (July 1956).

4. Environmental Working Group, "Asbestos: Think Again," 2004, at http:// www.ewg.org/sites/asbestos/about.php; Paul Brodeur, *Outrageous Misconduct: The Asbestos Industry on Trial* (New York: Pantheon Books, 1985), pp. 107–117; David E. Lilienfeld, "The Silence: The Asbestos Industry and Early Occupational Cancer Research—a Case Study," *American Journal of Public Health* 81 (1991): 791–800; Jock McCulloch and Geoffrey Tweedale, *Defending the Indefensible: The Global Asbestos Industry and Its Fight for Survival* (Oxford: Oxford University Press, 2008), p. 267; Bill Richards, "New Data on Asbestos Indicate Cover-Up of Effects on Workers," *Washington Post*, November 12, 1978, (retrieved via LEXIS-NEXIS); David Wessel, "Asbestos: Who Knew What When?" *Boston Globe*, October 26, 1982.

5. Irving J. Selikoff, Jacob Churg, and E. Cuyler Hammond, "Asbestos Exposure and Neoplasia," *Journal of the American Medical Association* 188 (1) (1964): 22–26, at http://jama.ama-assn.org/cgi/content/abstract/188/1/22; Burt A. Folkart, "Irving Selikoff; Found Asbestos Link to Cancer," *Los Angeles Times*, May 21, 1992; Brodeur, *Outrageous Misconduct*.

6. Brodeur, *Outrageous Misconduct*; Charles E. Claffey, "Taking on the Asbestos Industry," *Boston Globe*, December 26, 1985; Geraldine Fabrikant, "Cash vs. Cachet at New Yorker," *New York Times*, June 2, 1986; Barry Meier, "The Toxic Journalist," *Wall Street Journal*, April 16, 1986; Lawrence Martin. "Asbestos Workers Not Told of Hazards, Papers Indicate," *Globe and Mail*, November 23, 1978; Richards, "New Data on Asbestos Indicate Cover-Up."

7. Michael H. Brown, "Love Canal and the Poisoning of America," *Atlantic Monthly* (December 1979), at http://www.theatlantic.com/past/docs/issues/79dec /lovecanal1.htm; Michael H. Brown, "A Toxic Ghost Town," *Atlantic Monthly* (July 1989), at http://www.theatlantic.com/magazine/archive/1989/07/a-toxic-ghost -town/3360/; Michael H. Brown. *Laying Waste: The Poisoning of America by Toxic Chemicals* (New York: Pocket Books, 1981); William Glaberson, "Suit Focuses on Records from 1940's," *New York Times*, October 22, 1990; New York Department of Health, "Love Canal Follow-up Health Study," October 2008, at http://www

.health.ny.gov/environmental/investigations/love_canal/docs/report_public
_comment_final.pdf; Sam Howe Verhovek, "After Ten Years, the Trauma of Love
Canal Continues," August 5, 1988, at http://www.nytimes.com/1988/08/05/nyre-
gion/after-10-years-the-trauma-of-love-canal-continues.html; Anthony DePalma
and David Staba, "Love Canal Declared Clean, Ending Toxic Horror," *New York
Times*, March 18, 2004; Lynn R. Goldman, Beverly Paigen, Mary M. Magnant,
and Joseph H. Highland; "Low Birth Weight, Prematurity, and Birth Defects in
Children Living near the Hazardous Waste Site, Love Canal," *Hazardous Waste and
Hazardous Materials* 2 (2) (1985): 209–223. Additional documents and "an introduction to the history and background of the events that occurred at Love Canal"
can be found at: "Love Canal Collections: A University Archives Collection," University at Buffalo, at http://library.buffalo.edu/specialcollections/lovecanal/.

8. Matthew L. Wald, "Out-of-Court Settlement Reached over Love Canal,"
New York Times, June 22, 1994, at http://www.nytimes.com/1994/06/22/nyregion
/out-of-court-settlement-reached-over-love-canal.html?pagewanted=all
&src=pm; US Department of Justice, "Occidental to Pay $129 Million in Love
Canal Settlement," press release, December 21, 1995, at http://www.justice.gov
/opa/pr/Pre_96/December95/638.txt.html.

9. "Love Canal Timeline," *Niagara Gazette*, July 26, 2006, at http://niagara
-gazette.com/local/x681250975/HEADLINE-NO-1-Love-Canal-timeline/print.

10. Alan Derickson, *Black Lung: Anatomy of a Public Health Disaster* (Ithaca:
Cornell University Press, 1998), p. 121. Also see *Coal Mining and the Black Lung
Movement* (2008), a US government DVD with three separate films: "Black Lung:
A History"; news coverage of the 1960s black lung movement; and "Reflections,"
a history of the US Mining Safety and Health Administration and federal government agency efforts to help the miners, at http://laborfilms.com/2012/02/21
/coal-mining-and-the-black-lung-movement-2008/.

11. US Department of Labor, "History of Mine Safety and Health Legislation,"
at http://www.msha.gov/mshainfo/mshainf2.htm, accessed December 15, 2010.

12. "Coal Mining and the Black Lung Movement," DVD.

13. Tobacco Industry Research Committee press conference, June 15, 1954,
University Club, New York, at http://legacy.library.ucsf.edu/tid/ryd6aa00/pdf;
memorandum of understanding covering Services for Tobacco Industry Research
Committee by Hill & Knowlton, January 8, 1954, at http://legacy.library.ucsf.edu
/tid/eax60e00/pdf?search=%22tobacco%20industry%20research%20council
%20hill%20knowlton%22. Also see Allen Brandt, *The Cigarette Century: The Rise,
Fall, and Deadly Persistence of the Product That Defined America* (New York: Basic
Books, 2007).

14. US Surgeon General's Advisory Committee on Smoking and Health, and
US Public Health Service, Office of the Surgeon General, "Smoking and Health";
US Public Health Service, Office of the Surgeon General, 1964, Official Report, at
http://profiles.nlm.nih.gov/NN/B/B/M/Q/_/nnbbmq.pdf.

15. Kenneth E. Warner, "Cigarette Advertising and Media Coverage of
Smoking and Health," *New England Journal of Medicine* 312 (February 1985):

384–388; *Reader's Digest* articles referenced include: R. Norr, "Cancer by the Carton," *Reader's Digest* 61 (December 1952): 7–8, C. Lieb, "Can the Poisons in Cigarettes Be Avoided?" *Reader's Digest* 63 (December 1953): 45–47, L. Miller and J. Monahan, "The Facts Behind the Cigarette Controversy," *Reader's Digest* 65 (July 1954): 1–6. Also see Stanton A. Glantz, John Slade, Lisa A. Bero, Peter Hanauer, and Deborah E. Barnes, eds., *The Cigarette Papers* (Berkeley: University of California Press, 1996). Coverage at http://ark.cdlib.org/ark:/13030 /ft8489p25j/ includes the *New York Times*, May 27, 1950, and *Life*, December 21, 1953. Veteran freelance reporter George Seldes published roughly one hundred revelatory tobacco-related articles for the *In Fact* newsletter, but they were largely ignored by major US publications.

16. Rock Brynner and Trent Stephens, *Dark Remedy: The Impact of Thalidomide and Its Revival as a Vital Medicine* (Cambridge, MA: Perseus Publishing, 2001).

17. Ibid.; Bridget M. Kuehn, "Francis Kelley Honored for FDA Legacy: Award Notes Her Work on Thalidomide, Clinical Trials," *Journal of the American Medical Association* 304 (19) (2010): 2109–2112.

18. Brynner and Stephens, *Dark Remedy*. See also William A. Silverman, "The Schizophrenic Career of a 'Monster Drug,'" *Pediatrics* 110 (2) (August 2002): 404–406, at http://pediatrics.aappublications.org/cgi/content/full/110/2/404; Morton Mintz, "Heroine of FDA," *Washington Post*, July 15, 1962; The Insight Team of the *Sunday Times* of London, *Suffer the Children: The Story of Thalidomide* (New York: Viking, 1979).

19. Jason Grotto and Tim Jones, "Agent Orange's Lethal Legacy: Defoliants More Dangerous Than They Had to Be," *Chicago Tribune*, December 17, 2009, at http://www.chicagotribune.com/health/agentorange/chi-agent-orange-dioxindec 17,0,2121785,full.story.

20. "Tentative Agent Orange Settlement Reached," *Science* 224 (4651) (May 25, 1984): 849–850, at http://www.sciencemag.org/content/224/4651/849.short. Companies involved in the class action suit include: Dow, Monsanto, Diamond Shamrock, Uniroyal, T.H. Agricultural and Nutrition, Hercules, Thompson Chemical. The Monsanto website also makes reference to these seven companies, at http://www.monsanto.com/newsviews/Pages/agent-orange-background -monsanto-involvement.aspx; Jason Grotto and Tim Jones. "Agent Orange's Lethal Legacy: For U.S., a Record of Neglect," *Chicago Tribune*, December 4, 2009, at http://www.chicagotribune.com/health/agentorange/chi-agent-orange1-dec04 ,0,6366546,full.story.

21. Douglas Martin, "Thomas Whiteside, 79, Dies; Writer Exposed Agent Orange," *New York Times*, October 12, 1997, at http://www.nytimes.com/1997/10/12 /nyregion/thomas-whiteside-79-dies-writer-exposed-agent-orange.html. Thomas Whiteside's Agent Orange works included: "Defoliation," *New Yorker*, February 7, 1970, and articles in "Department of Amplification," *New Yorker*, on June 20 and July 4, 1970.

22. The memo from B.F. Goodrich Company came from Department of Industrial Hygiene and Toxicology Manager W. E. McCormick and is addressed to medi-

cal representatives from Union Carbide Corporation, Imperial Chemical Industries, Ltd., Monsanto Company, Solvay & Cle., and The Distillers Company, Ltd.; "Trade Secrets: A Moyers Report," Public Affairs Television, 2001, accessed May 4, 2012, at http://www.pbs.org/tradesecrets/docs/pdf/BOB_20010215_162533.pdf.

23. Paul D. Blanc, *How Everyday Products Make People Sick: Toxins at Home and in the Workplace* (Berkeley: University of California Press, 2007); Markowitz and Rosner, *Deceit and Denial.*

24. Blanc, *How Everyday Products Make People Sick,* pp. 73–74. More than a dozen articles were published in the *New York Times* between January and October 1974. Also see Joe Klein, "The Plastic Coffin of Charlie Arthur," *Rolling Stone,* January 15, 1976; Bill Moyers and Sherry Jones, writers, and Sherry Jones, producer, "Trade Secrets: A Moyers Report," a production of Public Affairs Television, Inc., in association with Washington Media Associates, Inc., 2001, at http://www.pbs .org/tradesecrets/program/overview.html.

25. Lee Patrick Strobel, *Reckless Homicide? Ford Pinto's Trial* (South Bend, IN: And Books, 1980); Douglas Birsch and John H. Fielder, eds., *The Ford Pinto Case: A Study in Applied Ethics, Business, and Technology* (Albany: State University of New York Press, 1994). Also by Lee Strobel: "Ford Ignored Pinto Fire Peril, Secret Memos Show," *Chicago Tribune,* October 13, 1979; "Girls' Death Car Among Pintos Recalled by Ford," *Chicago Tribune,* October 14, 1979; "Pinto Trial: Ford Versus an 'Army,'" *Chicago Tribune,* October 21, 1979.

26. National Highway Traffic Safety Administration, "Investigation Report: Alleged Fuel Tank and Filler Neck Damage in Rear-End Collision of Subcompact Passenger Cars," May 1978, at http://www.autosafety.org/ODIPinto.pdf; Associated Press, "Fuel Tank Defects Prompt Recall of Pintos, Bobcats," June 10, 1978; Birsch and Fielder, *The Ford Pinto Case;* and Strobel, "Ford Ignored Pinto Fire Peril," "Girls' Death Car," and "Pinto Trial."

27. Mark Dowie, "Pinto Madness," *Mother Jones* (September–October 1977), at http://www.motherjones.com/politics/1977/09/pinto-madness; Strobel, "Ford Ignored Pinto Fire Peril," "Girls' Death Car," and "Pinto Trial."

28. Anna Wilde Mathews and Barbara Martinez, "E-Mails Suggest Merck Knew Vioxx's Dangers at Early Stage," *Wall Street Journal,* November 1, 2004, at http://boardingschoolsettlement.ca/Press/2004_11_01_WSJ.htm; Rita Rubin, "How Did Vioxx Debacle Happen?" *USA Today,* October 12, 2004, at http://www .usatoday.com/news/health/2004–10–12-vioxx-cover_x.htm.

29. Snigdha Prakash and Vikki Valentine, "Timeline: The Rise and Fall of Vioxx," National Public Radio, November 10, 2007, at http://www.npr.org/templates /story/story.php?storyId=5470430.

30. Mathews and Martinez, "E-Mails Suggest Merck Knew," at http:// boardingschoolsettlement.ca/Press/2004_11_01_WSJ.htm. NPR reporter Snigdha Prakash wrote a comprehensive, award-winning account of the Vioxx trials: Snigdha Prakash, *All the Justice Money Can Buy: Corporate Greed on Trial* (New York: Kaplan Publishing, 2011). A team of researchers from the Cleveland Clinic also published a harshly critical analysis of the dangers of Vioxx in the *Journal of the*

American Medical Association in 2001: Debabrata Mukherjee, Steven E. Nissen, and Eric J. Topol, "Risk of Cardiovascular Events Associated with Selective COX-2 Inhibitors," *Journal of the American Medical Association* 286 (8) (August 22–29, 2001), at http://jama.jamanetwork.com/article.aspx?articleid=194132.

31. Tuskegee Syphilis Study Legacy Committee, "Final Report of the Tuskegee Syphilis Study Legacy Committee," May 20, 1996, at http://www.hsl.virginia.edu /historical/medical_history/bad_blood/report.cfm; James H. Jones, *Bad Blood: The Tuskegee Syphilis Experiment* (Free Press: New York: 1981).

32. Jones, *Bad Blood*; Susan M. Reverby, "Examining Tuskegee: The Infamous Syphilis Study and Its Legacy," at http://www.examiningtuskegee.com/aboutbook .html.

33. Jones, *Bad Blood*.

34. US Department of Energy, "Advisory Committee on Human Radiation Experiments—Final Report: Executive Summary," at http://www.hss.energy.gov /HealthSafety/ohre/roadmap/achre/summary.html; *Final Report of the Advisory Committee on Human Radiation Experiments* (New York: Oxford University Press, 1996).

35. US Department of Energy report and website, "Appendix A: Remarks by President William J. Clinton in Acceptance of Human Radiation Final Report," October 3, 1995, at Document2http://www.hss.energy.gov/healthsafety/ohre /roadmap/whitehouse/appa.html; *Final Report of the Advisory Committee on Human Radiation Experiments*.

36. US Department of Energy report and website, "Why the Committee Was Created," at http://www.hss.energy.gov/healthsafety/ohre/roadmap/achre/preface _2.html.

37. Susan M. Reverby, "'Normal Exposure' and Inoculation Syphilis: A PHS 'Tuskegee' Doctor in Guatemala, 1946–1948," *Journal of Policy History* (January 2011), at http://www.wellesley.edu/WomenSt/Reverby,%20Normal,%20JPH.pdf.

38. "Joint Statement by Secretaries Clinton and Sebelius on a 1946–1948 Study," US Department of State, October 1, 2010, at http://www.state.gov /secretary/rm/2010/10/148464.htm.

39. Reverby, "'Normal Exposure.'"

40. John Prados, "The Gulf of Tonkin Incident, Forty Years Later," National Security Archive, August 2004, at http://www.gwu.edu/~nsarchiv/NSAEBB /NSAEBB132/index.htm; Walter Cronkite,. "Gulf of Tonkin's Phantom Attack," National Public Radio, August 2, 2004, http://www.npr.org/templates/story/story .php?storyId=3810724.

41. John Prados, "Essay: Fortieth Anniversary of the Gulf of Tonkin Incident," National Security Archive, August 4, 2004, at http://www.gwu.edu/~nsarchiv/ NSAEBB/NSAEBB132/essay.htm; I. F. Stone, "McNamara and Tonka Bay: The Unanswered Questions," *New York Review of Books*, March 28, 1968, at http://www. nybooks.com/articles/archives/1968/mar/28/mcnamara-and-tonkin-bay-the-un-answered-questions/?pagination=false; US Senate Historical Office, Execu- tive Sessions of the Senate Foreign Relations Committee (Historical Series),

vol. 20, 90th Cong., 2nd Sess., 1968, released 2010, at http://www.scribd.com /doc/34439771/US-Senate-Releases-Vietnam-Gulf-Of-Tonkin-Testimony-From-1968; Daniel Ellsberg, *Secrets: A Memoir of Vietnam and the Pentagon Papers* (New York: Viking Adult, 2002); National Archives, "Pentagon Papers," online archives, released 2011, accessed 2012, at http://www.archives.gov/research/pentagon-papers/; John Prados, ed., "The Gulf of Tonkin Incident, Forty Years Later," National Security Archive, August 4, 2004, at http://www.gwu.edu/~nsarchiv/ NSAEBB/NSAEBB132/index.htm.

42. John W. Finney, "Fulbright Is Building His Tonkin Case," *New York Times*, January 8, 1968; John W. Finney, "Fulbright Says McNamara Deceives Public on Tonkin," *New York Times*, February 22, 1968; Neil Sheehan, Hedrick Smith, E. W. Kenworthy, and Fox Butterfield, "The Covert War," *New York Times*, June 13, 1971; Neil Sheehan, "Secret Pentagon Study on Viet Nam," *Chicago Tribune*, June 20, 1971.

43. "The Pentagon Papers: Secrets, Lies, and Audiotapes," National Security Archive, at http://www.gwu.edu/~nsarchiv/NSAEBB/NSAEBB48/nixon.html.

Martin Arnold, "Pentagon Papers Charges Are Dismissed: Judge Byrne Frees Ellsberg and Russo, Assails 'Improper Government Conduct,'" *New York Times*, May 11, 1973, at http://www.nytimes.com/learning/general/onthisday/big/0511 .html#article.

44. Ibid.

45. Louis Liebovich, *Richard Nixon, Watergate, and the Press* (Praeger Publishers: Westport, CT: 2003).

46. Daniel Schorr, *The Senate Watergate Report: The Historic Ervin Committee Report, Which Initiated the Fall of a President* (New York: Carroll and Graf, 2005).

47. US House, House Committee on the Judiciary. Impeachment of Richard M. Nixon, President of the United States, 93rd Cong., 2nd Sess., 1974, H. Rept. 93–1305.

48. Liebovich, *Richard Nixon, Watergate, and the Press*.

49. Bob Woodward, *Veil: The Secret Wars of the CIA, 1981–1987* (New York: Simon and Schuster, 1987).

50. "The Iran-Contra Affair Twenty Years On," National Security Archive, November 24, 2006, at http://www.gwu.edu/~nsarchiv/NSAEBB/NSAEBB210 /index.htm.

51. John Breecher et al., "A Secret War for Nicaragua," *Newsweek*, November 8, 1982.

52. "*Under*standing the Iran-Contra Affairs," Brown University, at http://www .brown.edu/Research/Understanding_the_Iran_Contra_Affair/index.php; Theodore Draper, *A Very Thin Line: The Iran-Contra Affairs* (New York: Hill and Wang, 1992); "An Iran-Contra Guide: What Happened and When," *New York Times*, March 17, 1988, at http://www.nytimes.com/1988/03/17/world/an-iran-contra -guide-what-happened-and-when.html.

53. "The Iran-Contra Affair Twenty Years On."

54. "Report of the Congressional Committees Investigating the Iran-Contra Affair," U Congress, November 1987, p. xv.

55. "From Madness to Hope: The Twelve-Year War in El Salvador," report of the Commission on Truth in El Salvador, United Nations Security Council, Document S/25500, April 1, 1993, at http://www.usip.org/publications /truth-commission-el-salvador; Mark Danner, *The Massacre at El Mozote* (New York: Vintage Books, 1994).

56. "From Madness to Hope"; Danner, *The Massacre at El Mozote*.

57. Mike Hoyt, "The Mozote Massacre," *Columbia Journalism Review* (January–February 1993), at http://web.archive.org/web/20071116142355/http:// backissues.cjrarchives.org/year/93/1/mozote.asp; Raymond Bonner, "Massacre of Hundreds Reported in Salvador Village," *New York Times*, January 27, 1982.

58. Charles Lewis and Mark Reading-Smith, "Iraq: The War Card," Center for Public Integrity, January 23, 2008, http://projects.publicintegrity.org/WarCard/.

59. 9/11 Commission, *The 9/11 Commission Report: Final Report of the National Commission on Terrorist Attacks upon the United States* (New York: W. W. Norton and Company, 2004), at http://www.gpoaccess.gov/911/pdf/fullreport.pdf; "Comprehensive Report of the Special Advisor to the DCI on Iraq's WMD," Central Intelligence Agency, September 30, 2004, at https://www.cia.gov/library/reports /general-reports-1/iraq_wmd_2004/index.html.

60. "Iraq Intelligence," *McClatchy Newspapers*, at http://www.mcclatchydc.com /reports/intelligence/. Information on the John Walcott–led Knight Ridder team can be found at the Nieman Foundation on Journalism at Harvard University, at http://www.niemanwatchdog.org/index.cfm?fuseaction=showcase.view &showcaseid=89. See also: Ron Suskind, *The Price of Loyalty: George W. Bush, the White House, and the Education of Paul O'Neill* (New York: Simon and Schuster, 2004); James Banford, *A Pretext for War: 9/11, Iraq, and the Abuse of America's Intelligence Agencies* (New York: Doubleday, 2004); Richard A. Clarke, *Against All Enemies: Inside America's War on Terror* (New York: Free Press, 2004); Bob Woodward, *Plan of Attack: The Definitive Account of the Decision to Invade Iraq* (New York: Simon and Schuster, 2004); Michael Iskikoff and David Corn, *Hubris: The Inside Story of Spin, Scandal, and the Selling of the Iraq War* (New York: Crown, 2006).

APPENDIX B: THE IRAQ WAR CARD

1. "Vice President Speaks at VFW 193rd National Convention," August 26, 2002, Office of the Press Secretary, White House website, at http://georgewbush -whitehouse.archives.gov/news/releases/2002/08/20020826.html, accessed February 6, 2014.

2. "Radio Address by the President to the Nation," September 28, 2002, Office of the Press Secretary, White House website, at http://georgewbush-whitehouse .archives.gov/news/releases/2002/09/20020928.html, accessed February 6, 2014; "Key Judgments [from October 2002 NIE]: Iraq's Continuing Programs for Weapons of Mass Destruction," declassified July 18, 2003, Federation of American

Scientists website, at http://www.fas.org/irp/cia/product/iraq-wmd.html, accessed February 6, 2014.

3. "DoD News Briefing—Secretary Rumsfeld and General Pace," July 30, 2002, news transcript, US Department of Defense website, http://www.defense .gov/transcripts/transcript.aspx?transcriptid=3624, accessed February 6, 2014.

410. "Interview of the President by TVP, Poland," May 29, 2003, Office of the Press Secretary, White House website, at http://georgewbush-whitehouse.ar-chives.gov/g8/interview5.html, accessed February 6, 2014; Bob Woodward, *State of Denial: Bush at War, Part 3* (New York: Simon and Schuster, 2007).

5. "President Delivers 'State of the Union,'" January 28, 2003, Office of the Press Secretary, White House website, at http://georgewbush-whitehouse.archives .gov/news/releases/2003/01/20030128-19.html, accessed February 6, 2014.

6. "A Policy of Evasion and Deception," the full text of US Secretary of State Colin Powell's speech to the United Nations on Iraq, Washington Post, February 5, 2003, at http://www.washingtonpost.com/wp-srv/nation/transcripts/powelltext _020503.html, accessed February 6, 2014.

Bibliography

Alterman, Eric. *When Presidents Lie: A History of Official Deception and Its Consequences*. New York: Viking, 2004.

Alwood, Edward. *Dark Days in the Newsroom: McCarthyism Aimed at the Press*. Philadelphia: Temple University Press, 2007.

Applebaum, Anne. *Iron Curtain: The Crushing of Eastern Europe, 1944–1956*. New York: Doubleday, 2012.

Arendt, Hannah. *The Origins of Totalitarianism*. New York: Shocken Books/Random House, 2004.

———. *The Portable Hannah Arendt*. Edited and with an introduction by Peter Baehr. New York: Penguin Books, 2003.

Arledge, Roone. *Roone: A Memoir*. New York: HarperCollins, 2003.

Arnson, Cynthia J. *Crossroads: Congress, the President, and Central America, 1976–1992*. New York: Pantheon, 1989.

Bagdikian, Ben H. *Double Vision: Reflections on My Heritage, Life, and Profession*. Boston: Beacon Press, 1995.

Baker, Raymond W. *Capitalism's Achilles Heel: Dirty Money and How to Renew the Free-Market System*. New York: John Wiley and Sons, 2005.

Ball, George. *The Past Has Another Pattern*. New York: W. W. Norton, 1982.

Bamford, James. *A Pretext for War: 9/11, Iraq, and the Abuse of America's Intelligence Agencies*. New York: Doubleday, 2004.

Bausum, Ann. *Muckrakers: How Ida Tarbell, Upton Sinclair, and Lincoln Steffens Helped Expose Scandal, Inspire Reform, and Invent Investigative Journalism*. Foreword by Daniel Schorr. Washington, DC: National Geographic, 2007.

Bayley, Edwin R. *Joe McCarthy and the Press*. Madison: University of Wisconsin Press, 1981.

337

Bibliography

Bernays, Edward L. *Biography of an Idea: Memoirs of Public Relations Counsel Edward L. Bernays*. New York: Simon and Schuster, 1965.

———. *Propaganda*. New York: Liveright, 1928. Reprint, New York: Ig Publishing, 2005.

Beschloss, Michael, ed. *Taking Charge: The Johnson White House Tapes, 1963–1964*. New York: Simon and Schuster, 1997.

Birsch, Douglas, and John H. Fielder, eds. *The Ford Pinto Case: A Study in Applied Ethics, Business, and Technology*. Albany: State University of New York Press, 1994.

Blackmon, Douglas A. *Slavery by Another Name: The Re-Enslavement of Black Americans from the Civil War to World War II*. New York: Anchor Books, 2008.

Bok, Sissela. *Lying: Moral Choice in Public and Private Life*. New York: Pantheon Books, 1978.

Bonin, Richard. *Arrows of the Night*. New York: Doubleday, 2011.

Bonner, Raymond. *Weakness and Deceit: U.S. Policy and El Salvador*. New York: Times Books, 1984.

Boorstin, Daniel J. *The Image: A Guide to Pseudo-Events in America*. 25th anniv. ed. New York: Vintage, 1992.

Bradlee, Ben. *A Good Life: Newspapering and Other Adventures*. New York: Simon and Schuster, 1995.

Branch, Taylor. *At Canaan's Edge*. New York: Simon and Schuster, 2006.

———. *Parting the Waters*. New York: Simon and Schuster, 1989.

———. *Pillar of Fire*. New York: Simon and Schuster, 1999.

———, and Eugene M. Propper. *Labyrinth; How a Stubborn U.S. Prosecutor Penetrated a Shadowland of Covert Operations on Three Continents to Find the Assassins of Orlando Letelier*. New York: Viking, 1982.

Brandt, Allan M. *The Cigarette Century: The Rise, Fall, and Deadly Persistence of the Product That Defined America*. New York: Basic Books, 2007.

Brinkley, Douglas. *Cronkite*. New York: HarperCollins, 2012.

Brinson, Susan L. *The Red Scare, Politics, and the Federal Communications Commission, 1941–1960*. Westport, CT: Greenwood/Praeger, 2004.

Brodeur, Paul. *Outrageous Misconduct: The Asbestos Industry on Trial*. New York: Pantheon, 1985.

Brown, Anthony Cave. *The Last Hero: Wild Bill Donovan*. New York: Times Books, 1983.

Brown, Michael H. *Laying Waste: The Poisoning of America by Toxic Chemicals*. New York: Pocket Books, 1981.

Brynner, Rock, and Trent Stephens. *Dark Remedy: The Impact of Thalidomide and Its Revival as a Vital Medicine*. Cambridge, MA: Perseus Publishing, 2001.

Carson, Clayborne, ed. *The Autobiography of Martin Luther King, Jr.* New York: Warner Books, 1998.

Carson, Rachel. *Silent Spring: The Classic That Launched the Environmental Movement*. 40th anniv. ed, with an introduction by Linda Lear and an afterword by Edward O. Wilson. New York: Houghton Mifflin, 2002.

Bibliography

The Center for Public Integrity. *Citizen Muckraking: How to Investigate and Right Wrongs in Your Community*. Monroe, ME: Common Courage Press, 2000.

Cheney, Dick, with Liz Cheney. *In My Time*. New York: Threshold Editions/Simon and Schuster, 2011.

Cigar, Norman. *Genocide in Bosnia: The Policy of "Ethnic Cleansing."* College Station: Texas A&M University Press, 1985.

Clarke, Richard A. *Against All Enemies: Inside America's War on Terror*. New York: Free Press/Simon and Schuster, 2004.

Cranberg, Gilbert, Randall Bezanson, and John Soloski. *Taking Stock: Journalism and the Publicly Traded Newspaper Company*. Ames: Iowa State University Press, 2001.

Cronkite, Walter. *A Reporter's Life*. New York: Knopf, 1996.

Cutlip, Scott M. *The Unseen Power: Public Relations, a History*. Hillsdale, NJ: Lawrence Erlbaum Associates, 1994.

Dallek, Robert. *Nixon and Kissinger: Partners in Power*. New York: HarperCollins, 2007.

Danner, Mark. *The Massacre at El Mozote*. New York: Vintage/Random House, 1994.

Davies, Nick. *Flat Earth News*. London: Chatto and Windus, 2008.

Davis, Nathaniel. *The Last Two Years of Salvador Allende*. Ithaca: Cornell University, 1985.

Derickson, Alan. *Black Lung: Anatomy of a Public Health Disaster*. Ithaca: Cornell University Press, 1998.

Dinges, John. *The Condor Years: How Pinochet and His Allies Brought Terrorism to Three Continents*. New York: New Press, 2004.

———, and Saul Landau. *Assassination on Embassy Row*. London: Writers and Readers, 1981.

Downie, Leonard, Jr. *The New Muckrakers*. New York: Mentor/New American Library, 1976.

Draper, Theodore. *A Very Thin Line: The Iran-Contra Affairs*. New York: Hill and Wang, 1992.

Edwards, Bob. *Edward R. Murrow and the Birth of Broadcast Journalism*. Hoboken, NJ: John Wiley and Sons, 2004.

Ellsberg, Daniel. *Secrets: A Memoir of Vietnam and the Pentagon Papers*. New York: Viking, 2002.

Emery, Fred. *Watergate: The Corruption of American Politics and the Fall of Richard Nixon*. New York: Touchstone, 1995.

Engelman, Ralph. *Friendlyvision: Fred Friendly and the Rise and Fall of Television Journalism*. New York: Columbia University Press, 2009.

Ervin, Sam, Jr. *The Whole Truth: The Watergate Conspiracy*. New York: Random House, 1980.

Everitt, David. *A Shadow of Red: Communism and the Blacklist in Radio and Television*. Chicago: Ivan R. Dee, 2007.

Feldstein, Mark. *Poisoning the Press: Richard Nixon, Jack Anderson, and the Rise of Washington's Scandal Culture*. New York: Picador, 2011.

Felsenthal, Carol. *Power, Privilege, and the Post: The Katharine Graham Story*. New York: Putnam, 1993.

Felt, Mark, and John O'Connor. *A G-Man's Life: The FBI, Being "Deep Throat," and the Struggle for Honor in Washington*. New York: PublicAffairs, 2006.

Final Report of the Advisory Committee on Human Radiation Experiments. New York: Oxford University Press, 1996.

Friendly, Fred W. *Due to Circumstances Beyond Our Control . . .* New York: Random House, 1967.

Fulbright, J. William. *The Arrogance of Power*. New York: Random House, 1966.

Fuller, Jack. *What Is Happening to News: The Information Explosion and the Crisis in Journalism*. Chicago: University of Chicago Press, 2010.

Gabler, Neal. *Life: The Movie. How Entertainment Conquered Reality*. New York: Knopf, 1998.

Gardiner, Juliet. *The Blitz: The British Under Attack*. London: Harper, 2010.

Gardner, Howard, Mihaly Csikszentmihalyi, and William Damon. *Good Work: When Excellence and Ethics Meet*. New York: Basic Books/Perseus, 2001.

Garrow, David J. *Bearing the Cross: Martin Luther King, Jr., and the Southern Christian Leadership Conference*. New York: Quill/William Morrow, 1986.

———. *Protest at Selma: Martin Luther King, Jr., and the Voting Rights Act of 1965*. New Haven: Yale University Press, 1978.

Gates, Gary Paul. *Air Time: The Inside Story of CBS News*. New York: Berkley, 1979.

Gitlin, Todd. *The Sixties: Years of Hope, Days of Rage*. New York: Bantam, 1993.

Glantz, Stanton A., John Slade, Lisa A. Bero, Peter Hanauer, and Deborah E. Barnes. *The Cigarette Papers*. Berkeley/Los Angeles: University of California Press, 1996.

Gleijeses, Piero. *The Dominican Crisis: The 1965 Constitutionalist Revolt and American Intervention*. Baltimore: Johns Hopkins University Press, 1978.

Goodale, James. *Fighting for the Press: The Inside Story of the Pentagon Papers and Other Battles*. New York: CUNY Journalism Press, 2013.

Graham, Frank, Jr. *Since Silent Spring*. New York: Houghton Mifflin, 1970.

Graham, Katharine. *Personal History*. New York: Knopf, 1997.

Greenberg, Andy. *This Machine Kills Secrets: How WikiLeakers, Cypherpunks, and Hacktivists Aim to Free the World's Information*. New York: Dutton/Penguin, 2012.

Halberstam, David. *The Best and the Brightest*. 20th anniv. ed., with a new introduction. New York: Ballantine Books, 1992.

———. *The Children*. New York: Fawcett/Random House, 1999.

———. *The Powers That Be*. New York: Ballantine, 1993.

Harris, Roy J., Jr. *Pulitzer's Gold: Behind the Prize for Public Service Journalism*. Columbia: University of Missouri Press, 2007.

Harrison, E. Bruce. *Going Green: How to Communicate Your Company's Environment Commitment*. Burr Ridge, IL, and New York: Irwin, 1993.

Bibliography

Helms, Richard, with William Hood. *A Look over My Shoulder: A Life in the Central Intelligence Agency*. New York: Random House, 2003.

Herring, George C. *America's Longest War: The United States and Vietnam, 1950–1975*. 4th ed. New York: McGraw-Hill, 2001.

Hersh, Seymour M. *Cover-Up: The Army's Secret Investigation of the Massacre at My Lai 4*. New York: Random House, 1972.

———. *The Price of Power: Kissinger in the Nixon White House*. New York: Summit, 1983.

Hertsgaard, Mark. *On Bended Knee: The Press and the Reagan Presidency*. New York: Farrar Straus Giroux, 1988.

Hewitt, Don. *Tell Me a Story: Fifty Years and 60 Minutes in Television*. New York: PublicAffairs, 2001.

Hilliard, Robert L., and Michael C. Keith. *The Broadcast Century and Beyond*. 5th ed. Burlington, MA: Elsevier/Focal Press, 2010.

Holhut, Randolph T. *The George Seldes Reader: An Anthology of the Writings of America's Foremost Journalistic Gadfly*. New York: Barricade Books, 1994.

Holland, Max. *Leak: Why Mark Felt Became Deep Throat*. Lawrence: University Press of Kansas, 2012.

Hudson, Michael W. *The Monster: How a Gang of Predatory Lenders and Wall Street Bankers Fleeced America—and Spawned a Global Crisis*. New York: Times Books/Henry Holt, 2010.

The Insight Team of the *Sunday Times* of London. *Suffer the Children: The Story of Thalidomide*. New York: Viking, 1979.

Iraq: The War Card. Washington, DC: The Center for Public Integrity, 2008.

Isikoff, Michael, and David Corn. *Hubris: The Inside Story of Spin, Scandal, and the Selling of the Iraq War*. New York: Crown, 2006.

Jamieson, Kathleen Hall. *Dirty Politics: Deception, Distraction, and Democracy*. New York: Oxford University Press, 1992.

Jaspin, Elliot. *Buried in the Bitter Waters: The Hidden History of Racial Cleansing in America*. New York: Basic Books, 2007.

Jensen, Carl. *Stories That Changed America: Muckrakers of the Twentieth Century*. New York: Seven Stories Press, 2002.

Johnson, Chalmers. *Nemesis: The Last Days of the American Republic*. New York: Metropolitan Books/Henry Holt, 2006.

Johnson, Haynes. *The Age of Anxiety: McCarthyism to Terrorism*. New York: Harcourt, 2005.

———. *Sleepwalking Through History: America in the Reagan Years*. New York: W. W. Norton, 1991.

Johnstone, John W. C., Edward J. Slawski, and William M. Bowman. *The News People: A Sociological Portrait of American Journalists and Their Work*. Champaign: University of Illinois Press, 1976.

Jones, James H. *Bad Blood: The Tuskegee Syphilis Experiment*. New York: Free Press, 1981.

Judis, John B. *William F. Buckley, Jr., Patron Saint of the Conservatives.* New York: Simon and Schuster, 1988.

Kenworthy, E. W., Fox Butterfield, Hedrick Smith, and Neil Sheehan. *The Pentagon Papers: The Secret History of the Vietnam War, as published by the New York Times.* New York: Quadrangle Books, 1971.

Kessler, David. *A Question of Intent: A Great American Battle with a Deadly Industry.* New York: PublicAffairs, 2001.

Kiernan, Ben. *Blood and Soil: A World History of Genocide and Extermination from Sparta to Darfur.* New Haven: Yale University Press, 2009.

Kinzer, Stephen. *Overthrown: America's Century of Regime Change from Hawaii to Iraq.* New York: Times Books/Henry Holt and Company, 2006.

Kissinger, Henry. *White House Years.* New York: Little, Brown, 1979.

———. *Years of Renewal.* New York: Simon and Schuster, 1999.

———. *Years of Upheaval.* New York: Little, Brown, 1982.

Kluger, Richard. *Ashes to Ashes: America's Hundred-Year Cigarette War, the Public Health, and the Unabashed Triumph of Philip Morris.* New York: Vintage Books, 1997.

Knightley, Phillip. *The First Casualty: From the Crimea to Vietnam. The War Correspondent as Hero, Propagandist, and Myth Maker.* New York: Harcourt Brace Jovanovich, 1975.

Kornbluh, Peter. *The Pinochet File: A Declassified Dossier on Atrocity and Accountability.* New York: New Press, 2003.

———, and Malcolm Byrne. *The Iran-Contra Scandal: The Declassified History.* Foreword by Theodore Draper. New York: New Press, 1993.

Kotz, Nick. *Judgment Days: Lyndon Baines Johnson, Martin Luther King Jr., and the Laws That Changed America.* New York: Mariner/Houghton Mifflin, 2006.

Kunhardt, Philip B., Jr., ed. *Life in Camelot: The Kennedy Years.* Boston: Little, Brown, 1988.

Kutler, Stanley I. *Abuse of Power: The New Nixon Tapes.* New York: Touchstone, 1998.

———. *The Wars of Watergate: The Last Crisis of Richard Nixon.* New York: Knopf, 2013.

LaFeber, Walter. *Inevitable Revolutions: The United States in Central America.* 2nd ed. New York: W. W. Norton, 1993.

Langguth, A. J. *Our Vietnam: The War, 1954–1975.* New York: Simon and Schuster, 2001.

Laurence, John. *The Cat from Hué: A Vietnam War Story.* New York: PublicAffairs, 2002.

Leigh, David, and Luke Harding. *WikiLeaks: Inside Julian Assange's War on Secrecy.* London: Guardian Books, 2011.

Lemov, Michael. *People's Warrior: John Moss and the Fight for Freedom of Information and Consumer Rights.* Madison, NJ: Fairleigh Dickinson Press, 2011.

LeoGrande, William M. *Our Own Backyard: The United States in Central America, 1977–1992.* Chapel Hill: University of North Carolina Press, 2000.

Bibliography

Lewis, Charles. "The Destabilization of Chile by the United States, 1970–73." Unpublished senior thesis, University of Delaware, May 1975.

———, and the Center for Public Integrity. *The Buying of the President*. New York: HarperCollins/Avon, 1996.

Lewis, John, with Michael D'Orso. *Walking with the Wind: A Memoir of the Movement*. New York: Simon and Schuster, 1998.

Liebovich, Louis. *Richard Nixon, Watergate, and the Press*. Westport, CT: Praeger Publishers, 2003.

Lippmann, Walter. *Liberty and the News*. New Brunswick, NJ: Transaction Publishers, 1995. Originally published by Harcourt, Brace and Howe, 1920.

Lukas, J. Anthony. *Nightmare: The Underside of the Nixon Years*. New York: Viking, 1976.

Maclear, Michael. *The Ten Thousand Day War: Vietnam, 1945–1975*. New York: St. Martin's Press, 1981.

MacPherson, Myra. *All Governments Lie! The Life and Times of Rebel Journalist I. F. Stone*. New York: Scribner, 2006.

Manchester, William. *The Glory and the Dream: A Narrative History of America 1932–1972*. New York: Bantam, 1975.

Mandela, Nelson. *Long Walk to Freedom: The Autobiography of Nelson Mandela*. New York: Back Bay Books/Little Brown, 1994.

Mann, James. *Rise of the Vulcans*. New York: Viking, 2004.

Markowitz, Gerald, and David Rosner. *Deceit and Denial: The Deadly Politics of Industrial Pollution*. Berkeley: University of California Press, 2002.

Martin, James. *The Meaning of the Twenty-first Century*. New York: Riverhead Books, 2006, 2007.

May, Gary. *Bending Toward Justice: The Voting Rights Act and the Transformation of American Democracy*. New York: Basic Books, 2013.

———. *The Informant: The FBI, the Ku Klux Klan, and the Murder of Viola Liuzzo*. New Haven: Yale University Press, 2005.

McChesney, Robert W., and John Nichols. *The Death and Life of American Journalism*. New York: Nation Books, 2010.

McClellan, Scott. *What Happened: Inside the Bush White House and Washington's Culture of Deception*. New York: PublicAffairs, 2008.

McCulloch, Jock, and Geoffrey Tweedale. *Defending the Indefensible: The Global Asbestos Industry and Its Fight for Survival*. Oxford: Oxford University Press, 2008.

McLean, Bethany, and Joe Nocera. *All the Devils Are Here: The Hidden History of the Financial Crisis*. New York: Portfolio/Penguin, 2010.

McNamara, Robert. *In Retrospect*. New York: Times Books/Random House, 1995.

McWhorter, Diane. *Carry Me Home: Birmingham, Alabama, the Climactic Battle of the Civil Rights Revolution*. New York: Simon and Schuster, 2001.

Michaels, David. *Doubt Is Their Product: How Industry's Assault on Science Threatens Your Health*. New York: Oxford University Press, 2008.

Mickelson, Sig. *The Decade That Shaped Television News: CBS in the 1950s*. Westport, CT: Praeger, 1998.

Mintz, Morton. *At Any Cost: Corporate Greed, Women, and the Dalkon Shield*. New York: Pantheon, 1985.

———. *The Therapeutic Nightmare: A Report on Prescription Drugs, the Men Who Make Them, and the Agency That Controls Them*. Boston: Houghton Mifflin, 1965.

Morgenson, Gretchen, and Joshua Rosner. *Reckle$$ Endangerment: How Outsized Ambition, Greed, and Corruption Led to Economic Armageddon*. New York: Times Books/Henry Holt, 2011.

Morozov, Evgeny. *The Net Delusion: The Dark Side of Internet Freedom*. New York: PublicAffairs, 2011.

Mueller, John E. *War, Presidents and Public Opinion*. New York: John Wiley and Sons, 1973.

Mustonen, Juha, ed. *The World's First Freedom of Information Act*. Kokkola, Sweden: Anders Chydenius Foundation, 2006.

Myrdal, Gunnar. *An American Dilemma: The Negro Problem and Modern Democracy*. Piscataway, NJ: Transaction, 1995.

Nichols, John, and Robert W. McChesney. *Dollarocracy: How the Money and Media Election Complex Is Destroying America*. New York: Nation Books/Perseus, 2013.

Nixon, Richard M. *The Memoirs of Richard Nixon*. New York: Grosset and Dunlap, 1978.

Olson, Keith W. *Watergate: The Presidential Scandal That Shook America*. Lawrence: University Press of Kansas, 2003.

Orwell, George. "Politics and the English Language." In *George Orwell: Volume 4, In Front of Your Nose, 1946–1950*. Edited by Sonia Orwell and Ian Angus. Boston: Nonpareil Books, 2000.

Packer, George. *The Assassin's Gate*. New York: Farrar, Straus and Giroux, 2005.

Paley, William S. *As It Happened: A Memoir*. Garden City, NJ: Doubleday, 1979.

Pastor, Robert A. *Condemned to Repetition: The United States and Nicaragua*. Princeton: Princeton University Press, 1988.

Powers, Thomas. *The Man Who Kept the Secrets*. New York: Knopf, 1979.

Prakash, Snigdha. *All the Justice Money Can Buy: Corporate Greed on Trial*. New York: Kaplan Publishing, 2011.

Prior, Markus. *Post-Broadcast Democracy: How Media Choice Increases Inequality in Political Involvement and Polarizes Elections*. New York: Cambridge University Press, 2007.

Prochnau, William. *Once Upon a Distant War: Young War Correspondents and the Early Vietnam Battles*. New York: Times Books, 1995.

Raphael, Chad. *Investigated Reporting: Muckrakers, Regulators, and the Struggle over Television Documentary*. Urbana: University of Illinois Press, 2005.

Reagan, Ronald. *The Reagan Diaries*. Edited by Douglas Brinkley. New York: HarperCollins, 2007.

———. *Reagan in His Own Hand: The Writings of Ronald Reagan That Reveal His Revolutionary Vision for America*. Edited by Kiron K. Skinner, et al. New York: Free Press, 2001.

Bibliography

Reeves, Thomas C. *The Life and Times of Joe McCarthy: A Biography*. New York: Stein and Day, 1982.

Remnick, David. *The Bridge: The Life and Rise of Barack Obama*. New York: Knopf, 2010.

Richards, Denis. *The Fight at Odds: Royal Air Force 1939–45*. London: Her Majesty's Stationery Office, 1974; first published in 1953.

Risen, James. *State of Siege: The Secret History of the CIA and the Bush Administration*. New York: Free Press/Simon and Schuster, 2006.

Roberts, Alasdair. *Blacked Out: Government Secrecy in the Information Age*. New York: Cambridge University Press, 2006.

Roberts, Gene, and Hank Klibanoff. *The Race Beat: The Press, the Civil Rights Struggle, and the Awakening of a Nation*. New York: Vintage, 2008.

Roberts, Gene, editor in chief, and Thomas Kunkel and Charles Layton, general editors. *Leaving Readers Behind: The Age of Corporate Newspapering*. Fayetteville: University of Arkansas Press, 2001.

Rosenstiel, Tom, and Amy S. Mitchell, eds. *Thinking Clearly: Cases in Journalistic Decision-Making*. New York: Columbia University Press, 2003.

Safer, Morley. *Flashbacks: On Returning to Vietnam*. New York: Random House, 1990.

Sampson, Anthony. *Mandela: The Authorized Biography*. New York: Knopf, 1999.

———. *The Sovereign State of ITT*. New York: Stein and Day, 1973.

Schirmer, Jennifer. *The Guatemalan Military Project: A Violence Called Democracy*. Philadelphia: University of Pennsylvania Press, 1998.

Schlesinger, Arthur M., Jr. *The Imperial Presidency*. Boston: Houghton Mifflin, 1973.

———. *A Thousand Days: John F. Kennedy in the White House*. Boston: Houghton Mifflin, 1965.

Schorr, Daniel. *Clearing the Air*. Boston: Houghton Mifflin, 1977.

———. *The Senate Watergate Report: The Historic Ervin Committee Report, Which Initiated the Fall of a President*. New York: Carroll and Graf, 2005.

———. *Staying Tuned: A Life in Journalism*. New York: Pocket Books/Simon and Schuster, 2001.

Seib, Philip. *Broadcasts from the Blitz: How Edward R. Murrow Helped Lead America into War*. Dulles, VA: Potomac Books, 2006.

Seldes, George. *Freedom of the Press*. Garden City, NY: Garden City Publishing Company, 1937.

———. *Lords of the Press*. New York: Julian Messner, 1938.

———. *You Can't Print That!* New York: Payson and Clarke, 1929.

Serrin, Judith, and William Serrin, eds. *Muckraking! The Journalism That Changed America*. New York: New Press, 2002.

Sharkey, Jacqueline. *Under Fire: Military Restrictions on the Media from Grenada to the Persian Gulf*. Washington, DC: The Center for Public Integrity, 1991.

Sheehan, Neil. *A Bright Shining Lie*. New York: Vintage Books, 1989.

Shepard, Alicia C. *Woodward and Bernstein: Life in the Shadow of Watergate*. Hoboken, NJ: John Wiley and Sons, 2007.

Sherwood, Robert E. *Roosevelt and Hopkins: An Intimate History*. New York: Harper and Brothers, 1948.

Shultz, George P. *Turmoil and Triumph: My Years as Secretary of State*. New York: Scribner's, 1993.

Smith, Sally Bedell. *In All His Glory: The Life of William S. Paley, the Legendary Tycoon and His Brilliant Circle*. New York: Simon and Schuster, 1990.

Sorkin, Andrew Ross. *Too Big to Fail: The Inside Story of How Wall Street and Washington Fought to Save the Financial System—and Themselves*. New York: Viking, 2009.

Sparks, Allister, and Mpho Tutu. *Desmond Tutu, Authorized*. New York: HarperOne/HarperCollins, 2011.

Sperber, A. M. *Murrow: His Life and Times*. New York: Freundlich Books, 1986.

Stauber, John, and Sheldon Rampton. *Toxic Sludge Is Good for You! Lies, Damn Lies and the Public Relations Industry*. Introduction by Mark Dowie. Monroe, ME: Common Courage Press, 1995.

Stone, Geoffrey R. *Perilous Times: Free Speech in Wartime, from the Sedition Act of 1798 to the War on Terrorism*. New York: W. W. Norton, 2005.

Strobel, Lee Patrick. *Reckless Homicide? Ford Pinto's Trial*. South Bend, IN: And Books, 1980.

Suskind, Ron. *The Price of Loyalty: George W. Bush, the White House, and the Education of Paul O'Neill*. New York: Simon and Schuster, 2004.

Sussman, Barry. *The Great Cover-Up: Nixon and the Scandal of Watergate*. Digital edition. Catapulter Books, 2010.

Tifft, Susan E., and Alex S. Jones. *The Trust: The Private and Powerful Family Behind the New York Times*. New York: Little, Brown, 1999.

The Tower Commission Report: The Full Text of the President's Special Review Board. A New York Times Special. Introduction by R. W. Apple Jr. New York: Bantam, 1987.

Tye, Larry. *The Father of Spin: Edward L. Bernays and the Birth of Public Relations*. New York: Picador, 2002.

Ungar, Sanford J. *The Papers and the Papers: An Account of the Legal and Political Battle over the Pentagon Papers*. New York: Columbia University Press, 1989.

Walsh, Lawrence E. *Firewall: The Iran-Contra Conspiracy and Cover-Up*. New York: W. W. Norton, 1997.

———. *The Gift of Insecurity: A Lawyer's Life*. Foreword by Nina Totenberg. Chicago: American Bar Association/ABA Publishing, 2003.

Ward, Vicky. *Devil's Casino: Friendship, Betrayal and the High Stakes Games Played Inside Lehman Brothers*. New York: Wiley, 2010.

Weber, Karl, ed. *The Best of I. F. Stone*. New York: PublicAffairs, 2009.

Weinberg, Steve. *Taking on the Trust: The Epic Battle of Ida Tarbell and John D. Rockefeller*. New York: Norton, 2008.

Weiner, Tim. *Legacy of Ashes: The History of the CIA*. New York: Doubleday, 2007.

Westen, Drew. *The Political Brain*. New York: PublicAffairs, 2007.

Bibliography

White, Theodore H. *Breach of Faith: The Fall of Richard Nixon*. New York: Atheneum, 1975.

Whiteside, Thomas. *Selling Death: Cigarette Advertising and Public Health*. New York: Liveright, 1971.

Wills, Garry. *Lincoln at Gettysburg: The Words That Remade America*. New York: Touchstone/Simon and Schuster, 2002.

Wise, David. *The Politics of Lying: Government Deception, Secrecy and Power.* New York: Random House, 1973.

Woodward, Bob. *Plan of Attack: The Definitive Account of the Decision to Invade Iraq*. New York: Simon and Schuster, 2004.

———. *Shadow: Five Presidents and the Legacy of Watergate*. New York: Simon and Schuster, 1998.

———. *State of Denial: Bush at War, Part 3*. New York: Simon and Schuster, 2007.

———. *Veil: The Secret Wars of the CIA, 1981–1987*. New York: Simon and Schuster, 1987.

———, with a reporter's assessment by Carl Bernstein. *The Secret Man: The Story of Watergate's Deep Throat*. New York: Simon and Schuster, 2005.

Wyatt, Clarence R. *Paper Soldiers: The American Press and the Vietnam War*. New York: W. W. Norton, 1993.

Zegart, Dan. *Civil Warriors: The Legal Siege on the Tobacco Industry*. New York: Random House/Delacourt Press, 2000.

Index

ABC News, 20, 52, 58, 139
  Liuzzo investigation, 74–76
  tobacco industry and, 141–143
  See also Day One
Abrams, Elliott, 108, 113
Abrams, Floyd, 31
ABSCAM, 145, 185
ACC. *See* American-Chilean Council
Accountability Studies, 236–237
Agnew, Spiro, 25
Alessandri, Jorge, 89–90
All the President's Men (movie), 47
All the President's Men (Woodward,
  Bernstein), 47
Allende, Salvador, 84–85, 89–91, 95
Alliance for Progress, 88
Alter, Jonathan, 143
Alternative media, 177
Alwood, Edward, 158
American Brands, 200
American Journalism Review, 173–174
*An American Dilemma: The Negro
  Problem and Modern Democracy*
  (Myrdal), 62–63, 82
American-Chilean Council (ACC), 102

American University, 151, 203, 216,
  219, 221, 222
Americans for Prosperity Foundation,
  152
Anderson, Jack, 43–44
Anniston Star, 220
AP. *See* Associated Press
Applebaum, Anne, 225
Arendt, Hannah, 55
Arledge, Roone, 139–140, 142–143,
  184, 187–188
Arlington National Cemetery, 3, 24
Arnett, Peter, 12
The Arrogance of Power (Fulbright), 23
Article 19, 229
Ashes to Ashes (Kluger), 128
Ashmore, Harry, 63
Associated Press (AP), 16, 112
Atlanta Journal-Constitution, 182
Atwater, Lee, 79
Aylwin Patricio, 87

Baby boomers, 1
Bagdikian, Ben, 32
Ball, George, 5–6, 8

Baltimore Afro-American, 66
Baltimore Sun, 125
Bancroft, Harding, 28, 31
Bass, Jack, 174
Beebe, Frederick R. ("Fritz"), 34
Benes, Alejandro, 200
Bergen, Peter, 233
Bergman, Lowell, 143, 145–147, 191, 218
Bernays, Edward, 120–123, 128
Bernstein, Carl, 47, 180, 187
    fading of, 131
    on idiot culture, 207–208
    international celebrity, 50
    warnings to, 51
    as watchdog, 55
    Watergate reporter, 48, 115
Bernstein, Jake, 218
Bevel, James, 68
Bezanson, Randall, 175–176
Bickel, Alexander M., 31
Big media, 53
Big Six, 76
Black, Hugo, 27
Blackmon, Douglas A., 61
Blakeslee, Carol, 75
Blanton, Thomas, 59
Bogdanich, Walt, 52, 136–138, 141–143
Bok, Sissela, 11
Bonin, Richard, 132–133
Bonner, Raymond, 107–109
Booker, Simeon, 66
Boorstin, Daniel, 169–170
Bradlee, Ben, 33, 35–36, 47, 51, 98
    on El Mozote massacre, 109
    on Graham, 52
    on legal fees, 117
Brauchli, Marcus, 222
A Bright Shining Lie (Sheehan), 20–21

Brill, A. A., 121
Brock, Bill, 57
Brown and Williamson, 200
Brown v. Board of Education, 58, 60, 62, 64, 156–157
Browne, Malcolm, 12
Brownell, Herbert, 29, 31
Bryant, Roy, 65
Buckley, William F., Jr., 101–102
Buried in the Bitter Waters (Jaspin), 61
Burke, David, 187–188
Burns, James MacGregor, 201
Bush, George H. W., 79, 80, 113, 114
Bush, George W., 53, 80, 103, 114
Butler, Nicholas Murray, 160
"Buying of the President," 205
Buzenberg, Bill, 212, 217
Buzhardt, J. Fred, 85
Byrne, William Matthew, Jr., 42

Califano, Joseph, 47
Calley, William, 19–20
Capone, Al, 188
Carmona, Richard, 125
Carnegie-Knight Initiative on the Future of Journalism Education, 219
Caro, Robert, 186–187
Carson, Rachel, 149–151
Carter, Hodding, Jr., 63, 201
Carter, Jimmy, 104, 126
Carter Center, 230
Castro, Fidel, 88, 104
Catledge, Turner, 29
CBS, 132, 183
    tobacco industry and, 143–149
Center for Effective Government, 230
Center for Public Integrity, 115
    awards, 215, 219

board of directors, 201–202
book publication, 204
"Buying of the President"
    publication, 205
digital business plan, 215
dismissals, 214
editorial staff, 203
financial purity, 202
founding, 200
Fund for Independence in
    Journalism, 214
on global corruption, 210–211
Global Integrity project, 211–212, 232
incorporation, 201
interns, 203, 218
investigative reporting, 201, 204–209,
    212, 216
lawsuit, 213–214
online distribution, 204
reporters, 202–203, 218
"Windfalls of War" publication,
    208–209
Center for Responsive Politics, 230
Central America
Cold War and, 105
El Mozote massacre cover-up,
    107–110
history and background of wars,
    103–110
secret wars, 103–110
Central Intelligence Agency (CIA)
Chilean politics and, 88–93, 98–99
covert actions, 7
domestic-surveillance activities,
    45–46
Guatemala and, 106
Chardy, Alfonso, 112
Cheney, Dick, 52, 213
Chicago Tribune, 8, 30

The Children (Halberstam), 68
Chilean politics, 84
assassinations, 86–87
Buckley and, 101–102
Chile Declassification Project,
    102–103
Church Committee investigation,
    96–97, 100
CIA and, 88–93, 98–99
embassy break-in, 85–86
FUBELT project, 91, 93
history, 85–96
investigative reporting, 97–98
kidnapping and murder, 92
Kissinger domino theory, 91
Kissinger on, 95–96
Nixon and, 90–96, 99
Operation Condor, 87, 100
torture, 87–88
US bilateral aid, 94–95
Choate, Pat, 195
Christian, George, 21
Christopher, Warren, 109
Church, Frank, 96
Church Committee investigation,
    96–97, 100
Churchill, Winston, 155
Churnalism, 170
CIA. *See* Central Intelligence Agency
Cipollone, Rose, 132–135
Civil Rights Act of 1964, 69
Civil-rights movement, 64–65
murders, 60–61
Clarion-Ledger, 60–61
Clark, Roger, 34, 36
Clinton, Bill, 77
Clinton, Hillary, 77
CNN, 131, 183, 201, 233
Cohen, William, 57

Cold War, 23, 157
  Central America and, 105
  rights, 32
Collingwood, Charles, 156
Colson, Charles, 38, 39, 41, 44
Columbia Journalism Review, 99, 203
Common Cause, 200
Common Cause Magazine, 181
The Condor Years (Dinges), 101
Connor, Eugene ("Bull"), 67–68
Consciousness-raising, 65
Contreras, Manuel, 87, 101
Cooke, Janet, 117–118
Cooper, Matt, 52
Corporate war on truth
  green-washing, 151
  Koch Industries and, 151–152
  overview, 115–120
  Silent Spring and, 149–151
  tobacco industry, 120–149
Counterattack newsletter, 157
Courier Journal, 191
Cox, Archibald, 49, 57
Cranberg, Gilbert, 175–176
Cronkite, Walter, 99, 220
  on news-gathering, 185
  on patriotism, 13
  on *60 Minutes*, 144–145
  on Vietnam War, 14–15
Cronkite News Service, 220
CropLife America, 150

Dalkon Shield, 119
Dallek, Robert, 93–94
Daughters of the American
  Revolution, 1
Davies, Nick, 170
Day One (television show), 136–137
DDT, 149–151

Dean, John, 44
Deep Cough, 136–137, 141
Defense Policy Board, 207
deKlerk, F. W., 226
DeLucia, Lynne, 217
DeParle, Jason, 233
Digital revolution, 166
Dinges, John, 84, 101
Dispatch News Service, 20
Doll, Richard, 122
Donaldson, Sam, 208
Donovan, Raymond, 190
Douglas, Cliff, 136–137, 148
Dow, 150
Dowie, Mark, 218
Downey, Robert, Jr., 190
Downie, Leonard, Jr., 168
Doyle, Tom, 135–136
Dukakis, Michael, 79
DuPont, 150

Eagle Scout, 1
Eaton, William, 74
Ebony, 66
Edell, Marc, 133, 135
Edwards, Bob, 156
Ehrlichman, John, 39, 40, 46
Einstein, Albert, 179
Eisenhower, Dwight D., 65, 96
Eisinger, Jesse, 218
El Mozote massacre cover-up, 107–110
Ellsberg, Daniel, 8
  charges dismissed, 42–43
  Nixon on, 38–39
  Nixon plotting against, 39–42
  Pentagon Papers and, 30, 32–33, 38
  psychiatrist office break-in, 40–42
Emerson, Ralph Waldo, 1
Encyclopedia Britannica, 235

Enders, Thomas, 107
Enemies List, 44
Environment global attention, 234
Ervin, Sam, 48
Espionage Act of 1917, 30, 36, 54
Essaye, Anthony, 34, 36
Evening News with Walter Cronkite
    (television show), 13, 99
Evers, Medgar, 60–61, 69

Fallows, James, 232
FBI. *See* Federal Bureau of Investigation
FDA. *See* Food and Drug Administration
Federal Bureau of Investigation (FBI),
    30, 38–40, 44–46, 59–60, 74–75,
    145
    See also Hoover, J. Edgar
Federal Trade Commission, 128–129
Felt, Mark, 48
Fielding, Lewis, 40–41
Fink, Sheri, 233
First Amendment, 37, 52–53, 98, 149
The First Casualty (Knightley), 20
Fish, Hamilton, 57
Flat Earth News (Davies), 170
FOIA. *See* Freedom of Information Act
Food and Drug Administration (FDA),
    135–137
Ford Pinto, 218
Foreign Agents Registration Act, 121
Foreign policy, secret
    Central America secret wars,
        103–110
    Chilean politics, 84–103
    Iran-Contra scandal, 110–114
    Iraq War, 103
    overview, 83–84
    See also Vietnam War
Frankel, Max, 31

Freedom of Information Act (FOIA),
    228
Freedom Riders, 66–67
Freedom Works, 152
Frei, Eduardo, 89, 92
Freivogel, Margaret Wolf, 217
Friedman, Paul, 139, 140, 142
Friendly, Fred, 160, 162
    resignation, 163–164
Frontline (television show), 205, 219
Frost, David, 43
FUBELT project, 91
Fulbright, J. William, 23–24, 164
Fuller, Jack, 176
Fund for Independence in Journalism,
    214

Gannett, 174, 176
Gardner, John, 200
Garreau, Joel, 233
Gates, Gary Paul, 156
Genocide, 106
Gesell, Gerhard, 36, 41
Geyelin, Phil, 33, 36
GIJN. *See* Global Investigative
    Journalism Network
Global corruption, 210–211
Global data clearinghouse, 235
Global Integrity project, 211–212, 232
Global Investigative Journalism
    Network (GIJN), 223
Global right to know, 229–230
God's work, 23
Golden Rule, 1
Goldenson, Leonard, 129
Goldwater, Barry, 10
Good Night and Good Luck (movie), 190
Goodale, James, 28–29, 31, 54
Goodrich-Gulf, 150

Government activities
  disregard for public, 22
  dubious, 206
  transparency, 227–228
Graham, Katherine, 33–34, 36, 47
  Bradlee on, 52
  on Mintz, 119
  threats to, 51
Graham, Philip, 16
Graves, Florence, 181, 217
Great Depression, 2
The Great Cover-Up (Sussman), 39
Greenfield, Meg, 33–34
Green-washing, 151
Gruening, Ernest, 5
Guatemala, 105–106
Guillermoprieto, Alma, 107–108, 109
Gulf of Tonkin Resolution, 4–6, 9,
  16–17
  Fulbright hearings, 23–24
Gurfein, Murray, 32

Haeberle, Ronald, 20
Haig, Alexander, 85
Halberstam, David, 12, 14, 18, 20, 68
  on Murrow, 161–163
  on self-deception, 21
Haldeman, H. R., 39, 43, 44
Halstead, Ted, 232
Hanrahan, John, 119–120
Hanyok, Robert, 9
Hard work, 2
Harris, Jay T., 172–173
Harrison, E. Bruce, 150–151
Harrison, Patricia, 150–151
"Harvest of Shame," 163, 165
Hayner, Priscilla, 226
Hearn, Lorie, 217
Hechinger Report, 220

Helms, Richard, 90, 92, 98, 101
Hemingway, Ernest, 179
Hersh, Seymour, 19–20, 85, 97–98, 112
Hertsgaard, Mark, 233
Hesburgh, Theodore, 201
Hewitt, Don, 134, 144–147, 165, 189
  60 Minutes and, 193–195
Hill, A. Bradford, 122
Hill, John W., 122–123
Hilliard, Robert L., 158
Hinton, Deane, 108–109
Ho Chi Minh, 8, 10
Hoover, J. Edgar, 44–45, 59
Hopkins, Harry, 155
Horton, William, 79
House Foreign Affairs Committees, 4
Houston, Brant, 223
Hoyt, Tom, 123
Human Rights Watch, 232
Humphrey, Hubert, 46
Hunt, E. Howard, 40, 48, 50, 101
Huntley, Chet, 12
Huntley-Brinkley Report, 12
Hurricane Katrina, 80–81
Hyper-local reporting, 220

ICIJ. *See* International Consortium of
  Investigative Journalists
Idiot culture, 207–208
IIE. *See* Institute of International
  Education
*The Image: A Guide to Pseudo-Events in
  America* (Boorstin), 169
In Fact newsletter, 126–127
In Retrospect (McNamara), 8
The Informant (May), 59
INN. *See* Investigative News Network
The Insider (movie), 146–147
Institute for Policy Studies (IPS), 84

Institute of International Education
(IIE), 160–161
Inter-American Development Bank, 84
Internal Revenue Service (IRS), 40,
46, 201
International Consortium of
Investigative Journalists (ICIJ),
115–117, 209–210
Internet search engines, 236
Investigative News Network (INN),
223
Investigative Reporters and Editors
(IRE), 61
Investigative reporting
Center for Public Integrity, 201,
204–209, 212, 216
Chilean politics, 97–98
ICIJ, 115–117
IRE, 61
losing value, 198
pursuing hidden truth, 179–180
teaching hospital model, 219
television and, 185–186
tobacco industry, 126–129, 136–141
tools, 200
Vietnam War, 17–20
Investigative Reporting Workshop, 151,
216, 219, 222
The Invisible Government (Wise, Ross),
227
IPS (Institute for Policy Studies), 84
Iran-Contra scandal
Bush, G. H. W. papers, 114
Central America wars background
and history, 103–110
cover-up, 113–114
defying Congress, 110–111
investigation, 111–112
reporting, 112

Iraq War, 103
IRE. *See* Investigative Reporters and
Editors
*Iron Curtain: The Crushing of Eastern
Europe, 1944–1956* (Applebaum),
225
IRS. *See* Internal Revenue Service

Jackson, Jimmie Lee, 71
Jamieson, Kathleen Hall, 79
Jaspin, Elliot, 61–62
Jefferson, Thomas, 23
Jennings, Peter, 143
Jet, 66
"Jimmy's World," 117–118
Johnson, Hiram, 22–23
Johnson, Lyndon, 186–187
covert action programs, 7, 11
declining presidential nomination,
15
Ho Chi Minh and, 8, 10
King and, 73
moral authority, 12
Vietnam War falsehoods, 7–8
on voting rights, 72–73
on war ships, 4
Johnson City Press Chronicle, 182
Jones, Alex, 28–29
Jones, Doug, 60
Journalism
American Journalism Review,
173–174
Carnegie-Knight Initiative on the
Future of Journalism Education,
219
Columbia Journalism Review, 99,
203
Fund for Independence in
Journalism, 214

Journalism *(continued)*
  GIJN, 223
  public-service, 220–221
  See also Investigative reporting;
    News; Newspapers; Nonprofit
    journalism; Reporters and
    reporting
Judgment at Nuremberg (movie), 72

Kaden, Ellen, 146
Kalb, Marvin, 44
Kaplan, Joel, 213
Karamessines, Thomas, 94
Keith, Michael C., 158
Kellogg Pact, 17
Kelsey, Frances Oldham, 118–119
Kennedy, Edward M., 24, 46
Kennedy, John F., 3, 59, 69
Kennedy, Robert F., 15, 24, 76
Kerwin, Neil, 221–222
Kessler, David, 135–137
Khrushchev, Nikita, 183
King, Martin Luther, Jr., 77–78
  assassination, 24, 58, 60
  dramatic confrontations, 67
  emergence, 65
  Johnson, L., and, 73
  "Letter from Birmingham Jail," 68
  Nobel Peace Prize, 70
Kirkman, Larry, 221
Kirkpatrick, Jeane, 105
Kirtley, Jane, 52–53
Kissinger, Henry, 38, 85, 90
  on assassinations, 101
  on Chilean politics, 95–96
  domino theory, 91
  on FUBELT project, 93
Klibanoff, Hank, 63–64
Kluger, Richard, 128

Knight Ridder, 131, 172–173
Knightley, Phillip, 20–21
Koch, Charles, 151–152
Koch, David, 151–152
Koch Industries, 151–152
Koop, C. Everett, 125, 137
Kopechne, Mary Jo, 24
Korean War, 18, 159
Kornbluh, Peter, 101
Kotz, Nick, 67, 81
Koughan, Frank, 137
Koughan, Marty, 137–139, 147–148
Kovach, Bill, 28, 108, 181–182, 209
Kramer, Joel, 217
Krogh, Egil, 40–41
Ku Klux Klan, 74–75
Kuchma, Leonid, 210
Kuralt, Charles, 165

LaFeber, Walter, 103–104
Landau, Saul, 84
LaSalle, Lawrence Lee, 3, 24–25
LaSalle, Randy, 3, 24
Laurence, Jack, 12
League of Nations, 17
Lee, Ivy, 121
Legacy of Ashes (Weiner), 9
Lemann, Nicholas, 155
Letelier, Orlando, 84–87, 100–101
"Letter from Birmingham Jail," 68
Lewis, Al, 47
Lewis, John, 71, 73, 76–77, 82
Liddy, G. Gordon, 40, 48, 50
Liebman, Marvin, 102
Life magazine, 71, 79
Ligget, 200
Light, Gary, 135–136
Lincoln, Abraham, 2, 90
Liuzzo, Viola, 58, 73–76

Loeb, Vernon, 221
Loews Corporation, 200
Lorrilard, 200
Los Angeles Times, 74
Lumumba, Patrice, 97
Lung cancer, 122–123, 125, 128–129
Lying: Moral Choice in Public and Private Life (Bok), 11

MacArthur, Douglas, 56, 159
MacLeish, Archibald, 154
Madison, James, 23
The Making of the President, 1960 (Phillips), 205
Mandela, Nelson, 208, 226
Manning, Chelsea, 53
Maples, Marla, 208
Marder, Murrey, 16–17, 33
Martin, James, 237–238
Martin, John, 52, 136, 142
The Master Switch (Wu), 233
May, Gary, 59
Mayan massacres, 105
Mazdoor Kisan Shakti Sangathan (MKSS), 228
McCarthy, Eugene, 15
McCarthy, Joseph, 16, 157–158, 160–162, 190
McChesney, Robert, 170
McCone, John, 90
McCord, James W., 47
McFarland, Robert, 113
McGann, James, 231
McGill, Ralph, 63
McNamara, Robert, 5, 8, 10, 23–24
McNaughton, John, 10–11
The Meaning of the Twenty-first Century (Martin, James), 237
El Mecurio, 95

Meiselas, Susan, 107
Miami Herald, 112, 220
Michaels, David, 122, 124
Mickelson, Sig, 156
Milam, J. W., 65
Mintz, Morton
  on Dalkon Shield, 119
  fervor, 120
  Graham on, 119
  on Oralflex, 119
  on thalidomide, 118–119
Mississippi Burning (movie), 60–61
Mitchell, Jack, 135
Mitchell, Jerry, 60–61
Mitchell, John, 30–31, 38, 51, 90
Mitchelson, Marvin, 190
MKSS. *See* Mazdoor Kisan Shakti Sangathan
Mobil Oil, 117
Moffit, Michael, 86
Moffit, Ronni, 86
Mohr, Charles, 12
Monsanto, 149–150
Montgomery bus boycott, 65, 82
Morse, Wayne, 5
Mother Jones magazine, 218
Mudd, Roger, 165
Mueller, John, 18
Mulvad, Nils, 223
Murphy, Thomas, 139, 142–143
Murrow, Edward R., 44, 98, 183
  broadcast beginnings, 153–154
  at CBS, 155–156
  censored, 159
  death of, 163
  forced out of television, 176
  Halberstam on, 161–163
  "Harvest of Shame," 163, 165
  IIE and, 160–161

Murrow, Edward R., *(continued)*
  on lung cancer, 128–129
  McCarthy, J., and, 158, 160–162
  on television, 156–157, 167
  World War II reporting, 154–155
Muskie, Edmund, 46
My Lai massacre, 19–20
Myrdal, Gunnar, 62–63, 65, 82

Nader, Ralph, 200
Nation, 126
National Institute for Money in State
    Politics, 230
National Press Club, 201
National Public Radio (NPR), 45, 216
National Review, 102
National Security Agency (NSA), 7, 9
National Security Archive, 106,
    229–230
Nazi regime, 121
Negro newspapers, 63–64
Nelson, Jack, 74
Neoslavery, 62
New America Foundation, 232–233
New Republic, 126
New York Times, 20
  on confidence in president, 6
  on lung cancer, 128
  Pentagon Papers and, 28–32
  Pulitzer Prize, 37
  restraining order lifted, 36–37
  on Selma campaign of 1965, 71–72
News, 176
  commercials masquerading as, 171
  Cronkite News Service, 220
  Cronkite on, 185
  Dispatch News Service, 20
  gathering, 236
  INN, 223

television trends, 165–167
  See also ABC News
Newson, Moses, 64–65, 66
Newspapers
  churnalism, 170
  consolidations, 174–175
  corporatization, 175–176
  job cuts, 168–169
  need for profit, 172
  press releases and, 170–171
  serious reporting and, 168
  takeovers, 173
  See also specific newspapers
Newsweek, 20, 112, 128
NGOs. *See* Nongovernmental
    organizations
Nichols, John, 170
Nieman Watchdog Project, 17
Nixon, Richard
  Chilean politics and, 90–96, 99
  criminal misconduct, 49
  Ehrlichman and, 46
  on Ellsberg, 38–39
  on embassy break-ins, 85
  Enemies List, 44
  on illegal activities, 43
  moral authority, 12
  obsessions, 38
  plotting against Ellsberg, 39–42
  resignation, 25, 57
  White House Special Investigations
    Unit, 40
Nongovernmental organizations
    (NGOs), 231, 234
Nonprofit journalism, 216–218
  concerns and challenges, 224
  online publishing, 231
  university affiliations, 221–222
North, Oliver, 111

Index

Noyes, Dan, 218

NPR. *See* National Public Radio

NSA. *See* National Security Agency

OAO Alfa Bank v. Center for Public Integrity, 213–214

Obama, Barack, 126
  at Brown Chapel Church, 77
  election, 81
  transparency promise, 227
  WikiLeaks and, 53–54

Ober, Eric, 146

Obst, Davis, 20

On Bended Knee (Hertsgaard), 233

Open Democracy Advice Centre, 229

Operation Condor, 87, 100

Oralflex, 119

Ortega, Daniel, 104

Orwell, George, 83

Overholser, Geneva, 173

Pacino, Al, 146

Packwood, Bob, 181

Paley, William, 128, 154, 158–159, 161

Palm Beach Post, 220

Palos, Ricardo Sandoval, 232

Parker, Barrington, 98

Parry, Robert, 112

Patriot II draft legislation, 207

Patriotism, 2, 13

Pay-to-play, 171

Pearl, Raymond, 126–127

Pentagon Papers, 8, 21
  decision to publish, 28–29
  Ellsberg and, 30, 32–33, 38
  in federal court, 32
  New York Times and, 28–32
  overview, 27–28
  power and values struggle, 52

Sheehan and, 28–31
  Washington Post and, 33–37

Petersen, Henry, 42

Peterson, Pete, 193–194

Philadelphia Inquirer, 171–173, 222

Philip Morris, 52, 133, 137–142, 144–145, 148

Phillips, Kevin, 205

Picard, Robert, 166

Pinochet, Augusto, 86–87, 95, 100

Plame, Valerie, 52

Plugola, 171

The Politics of Lying (Wise), 24

Polston, Robert, 191–192

The Powers That Be (Halberstam), 161–162

Presidential Records Act, 114

The Price of Power: Kissinger in the White House (Hersh), 85

Primetime Live (television show), 139, 208

Project on Government Oversight, 230

Propaganda (Bernays), 120–121

ProPublica, 218, 233

Public accountability, 235–237

Public Broadcasting System, 216

Public Citizen, 200

Public Health Cigarette Smoking Act of 1970, 130

Public policy research organizations, 231–234

Public-service journalism, 220–221

Pulitzer Prize
  New York Times, 37
  number of entries, 169
  Philadelphia Inquirer, 171–172, 222
  ProPublica, 218
  Washington Post receiving, 50
  Washington Post returning, 117–118

Race relations
  Birmingham, Alabama, 67–68
  Civil Rights Act of 1964, 69
  civil rights movement, 60–61, 64–65
  Freedom Riders, 66–67
  history, 62–63
  Horton incident, 79
  Hurricane Katrina and, 80–81
  Liuzzo killing, 58, 73–76
  Montgomery bus boycott, 65, 82
  Negro newspapers, 63–64
  neoslavery, 62
  overview, 55–58
  revisiting Selma, Alabama, 76–78
  school desegregation, 65–66
  Selma campaign of 1965, 58, 70–73, 82
  Sixteenth Street Baptist Church bombing and, 58–60, 68
  Southern Strategy, 78–79
The Race Beat (Roberts, Klibanoff), 63, 64
Radulovich, Milo, 159–160, 190
Railsback, Tom, 57
Rampton, Sheldon, 150
Randolph, A. Philip, 63
Randolph, Eleanor, 112
Raphael, Chad, 164
Reader's Digest, 127–128
Reagan, Ronald
  on Castro, 104
  on Central America, 105
  on El Salvador, 107–108
  Reagan Doctrine, 110
  right agenda, 131
Realpolitik, 22
Red Channels newsletter, 157
Red Scare, 157
Redford, Robert, 116

Reeb, James J., 72
Reed, Roy, 71–72
Rehnquist, William, 36
Reporters and reporting, 216, 222
  hyper-local reporting, 220
  Iran-Contra scandal, 112
  IRE, 61
  numbers, 168–169
  Stone investigative report, 17–18
  on tobacco industry, 126–129, 136–141
  Vietnam War common commitment, 20–21
  Vietnam War skepticism, 12–17
  See also Investigative reporting; *specific reporters*
Reston, James ("Scotty"), 28–29
Richardson, Elliot, 57
Ridenhour, Ron, 20
Risen, James, 53
Rivera, Geraldo, 187–188
R.J. Reynolds, 133, 136, 150
Roberts, Chalmers, 35
Roberts, Gene, 63–64, 66, 71, 171–174
Robeson, Paul, 160
Rockwell, Norman, 1
Rodino, Peter, 49, 112
Roosevelt, Eleanor, 155
Roosevelt, Franklin D., 2, 155
Roosevelt, Teddy, 2
Root, Elihu, 161
Rosenthal, Abe, 28, 31–32, 108–109
Rosenthal, Robert, 217
Ross, Thomas B., 227
Roth, William, 55–56
Rowe, Gary Thomas, 74–75
Ruckelshaus, William, 57
Rules of Land Warfare manual, 17
Rusk, Dean, 88

Index

Russo, Anthony, 42
Ryan, Hewson, 100–101

Safer, Morley, 12
San Jose Mercury News, 172–173
Sandinista National Liberation Front, 104
Sarokin, H. Lee, 134–135
Sawyer, Diane, 142, 208
Scheffler, Phil, 134
Schlesinger, Arthur, Jr., 201
Schlesinger, James, 13
Schneider, René, 92–94, 97, 99
School desegregation, 65–66
    See also Brown v. Board of Education
Schorr, Daniel, 44–45, 97–98
    career, 182–183
    resignation, 98
    Wallace interviewed by, 145
Schudson, Michael, 168
Schulke, Flip, 71
Schulte, Brigid, 233
SEATO. *See* Southeast Asia Treaty Organization
See It Now (television show), 128–129, 156–157, 162–163
Segretti, Donald, 48
Seldes, George, 126–127
Selma campaign of 1965, 58, 70–73, 82
Senate Foreign Relations Committee, 4
Sevareid, Eric, 156
Shaw, John, 21
Sheehan, Neil, 12, 20–21
    Pentagon Papers and, 28–31
Shell Chemical, 150
Shepard, Alicia, 51
Sherman, Bruce S., 173
Shipler, David, 81

Silent Spring (Carson), 149–151
Simons, Howard, 36, 47
Sirica, John, 48, 50
Sixteenth Street Baptist Church bombing, 58–60, 68
60 Minutes (television show), 132–135, 143–145
    dictum, 189
    Emmy nominations, 193
    format, 165
    good-versus-evil genre, 190
    Hewitt and, 193–195
    quitting, 196–198
    ratings, 188
Slavery by Another Name (Blackmon), 61
Smith, Howard K., 156
Society of American Archivists, 114
Soloski, John, 175–176
Somoza dynasty, 104
South African Truth and Reconciliation Commission, 226
South Florida Sun-Sentinel, 220
Southeast Asia Treaty Organization (SEATO), 4–5
Southern Christian Leadership Conference, 68
Southern Strategy, 78–79
Stanton, Frank, 162
Starkman, Dean, 203–204
Starr, Paul, 224
Stauber, John, 150
Steiger, Paul, 217
Stewart, Potter, 37
Stockdale, James, 8
Stockman, David, 194
Stone, I. F., 17–18
Studds, Gerry, 107
Sullivan, John, 222

361

Sulzberger, Arthur ("Punch"), 28–29, 31, 108
Summa, Keith, 136
Sunlight Foundation, 229
Surine, Donald, 160
Surowicz, Simon, 194
Sussman, Barry, 39, 47, 48, 120

Tavoulareas, William P., 117
Taylor, Arthur, 13
Taylor, Maxwell, 10
Tea Party, 152
Teaching hospital model, 219
Television
    commercials masquerading as news, 171
    investigative reporting and, 185–186
    Murrow forced out of, 176
    Murrow on, 156–157, 167
    news trends, 165–167
    See also specific television shows
Tet Offensive, 12–14
Thalidomide, 118–119
The Therapeutic Nightmare (Mintz), 119
Think tanks, 231–232
Thomas, Eugene, 74
Tifft, Susan, 28–29
Till, Emmett, 64–65
Time magazine, 52, 128
Times-Picayune, 80
TIRC. *See* Tobacco Industry Research Committee
Tisch, Andrew, 144
Tisch, Laurence, 132–133, 196
Tobacco industry
    ABC News and, 141–143
    adverting ban, 129–130
    Bernays and, 120–123

CBS and, 143–149
cigarettes and women, 121–122
civil litigation, 132–135
corporate war on truth, 120–149
deaths and, 125–126
FDA and, 135–137
investigative reporting, 126–129, 136–141
libel lawsuit, 138–140
lung cancer and, 122–123, 125, 128–129
modus operandi, 124
testimony on addiction, 125
TIRC and, 123–124
Tobacco Industry Research Committee (TIRC), 123–124
Tomic, Radomiro, 89
Tomuschat, Christian, 105
Townley, Michael, 87
Transparency International, 229
Tri-State Defender, 64
Trump, Donald, 208
Truth, 1, 22–23
    commissions, 106, 226–227
    demand for, 225–226
    global right to know, 229–230
    government transparency, 227–228
    investigative reporting pursuit, 179–180
    light of, 238
    shared truths, 65
    See also Corporate war on truth; Values
Tunney, Gene, 127
Turning Point (television show), 137–141, 140–141
Tutu, Desmond, 226
20/20 (television show), 75, 187
Tyler, Patrick, 117

Index

Ungar, Sanford, 44
United Nations, 12
 truth commissions, 106
 United Nations Charter, 17
United Press International (UPI), 20
USS *Maddox*, 4–5, 7–8
USS *Ticonderoga*, 4, 7

Values, 1–2
 nonprofit journalism sharing, 223
 Pentagon Papers power struggle
  and, 52
 Watergate power struggle and, 52
Vanocur, Sander, 58, 74, 184
Velsicol, 149
Vietnam War
 air attacks, 10
 covert action, 7, 11
 Cronkite on, 14–15
 escalation, 15
 fake intelligence, 9
 Gulf of Tonkin Resolution, 4–6, 9,
  16–17, 23–24
 intelligence gathering, 6–7
 investigative reporting, 17–20
 Johnson falsehoods, 7–8
 lives claimed by, 3, 6
 living room war, 18
 My Lai massacre, 19–20
 reporters' common commitment,
  20–21
 reporters' skepticism, 12–17
 Tet Offensive, 12–14
 See also Pentagon Papers
Vineyard Gazette, 29
Voting Rights Act, 69–70

Wald, Richard, 140, 187
Wall Street Journal, 171

Wallace, George, 69, 71
Wallace, Mike, 132–134, 144, 188
 arguments with, 195
 interviewed by Schorr, 145
 interviewing at 90, 197
 respect for, 196
 subpoenaed, 191
Walsh, Lawrence E., 111, 113–114
Walton, Mary, 174
War, Presidents and Public Opinion
  (Mueller), 18
Washington, George, 2
Washington News-Journal, 56
Washington Post, 16, 30
 on confidence in president, 6
 courage of, 51
 Mobil Oil and, 117
 Pentagon Papers and, 33–37
 Pulitzer Prize, 50
 returning Pulitzer, 117–118
 university affiliations, 221–222
 Watergate head start, 47–48
Washington Star-News, 42
Wasilewski, Vincent T., 129
Watergate
 Bernstein, C., as reporter, 48, 115
 burglary, 46–47
 cover-up, 25
 overview, 38–40
 power and values struggle, 52
 Washington Post head start, 47–48
 Woodward as reporter, 48, 115
 Woodward on, 49–50
Waxman, Henry, 124, 144
Weekly newsletter, 17
Weicker, Lowell, 57
Weinberger, Caspar, 113
Weiner, Tim, 9
Weinstein, Henry, 218

Weir, David, 218
Welch, Joseph, 162
Wershba, Joe, 159–161, 190
Westfeldt, Wallace, 74
Westmoreland, William, 13, 189
Weymouth, Katharine, 222
What Is Happening to News (Fuller), 176
White, Theodore H., 49
White House Special Investigations
    Unit (plumbers), 46
  embassy break-in and, 85
  Nixon creation, 40
  psychiatrist office break-in, 40–42
Whiteside, Thomas, 129–130
Wigand, Jeffrey, 143–145
WikiLeaks, 53–54
Wikipedia, 235
Wilkins, Collie Leroy, 74
Williams, Edward Bennett, 35–36, 98
Williams, Hosea, 71
Wimert, Paul, 92–93

"Windfalls of War," 208–209
Wise, David, 24, 227
Woodward, Bob, 47
  fading of, 131
  ICIJ address, 115–117
  international celebrity, 50
  on "Jimmy's World," 117–118
  as watchdog, 55
  Watergate reporter, 48, 115
  on Watergate reporting, 49–50
World Bank, 12
World War II, 2
W.R. Grace, 150
Wu, Tim, 233
Wurtzel, Alan, 140
Wyatt, Clarence R., 19

The Years of Lyndon Johnson (Caro), 186
Young, David, 40

Zelkind, Matthew, 166

Charles Lewis is a professor of journalism and the founding executive editor of the Investigative Reporting Workshop at the American University School of Communication in Washington, DC. A former ABC News and CBS News *60 Minutes* producer, he founded the award-winning Center for Public Integrity and its International Consortium of Investigative Journalists, the first global network of premier investigative reporters to develop and publish online multimedia exposés across borders. He is the co-author of five Center books including *The Buying of the President* (1996), *The Buying of the Congress* (1998), *The Buying of the President 2000*, *The Cheating of America* (2001), and *The Buying of the President 2004*, a *New York Times* bestseller. He was awarded a prestigious MacArthur Fellowship in 1998, and in 2004, he was given the PEN USA First Amendment award, "for expanding the reach of investigative journalism, for his courage in going after a story regardless of whose toes he steps on, and for boldly exercising his freedom of speech and freedom of the press." In 2009, the *Encyclopedia of Journalism* called him "one of the 30 most notable investigative reporters in the US since World War I."

PublicAffairs is a publishing house founded in 1997. It is a tribute to the standards, values, and flair of three persons who have served as mentors to countless reporters, writers, editors, and book people of all kinds, including me.

I. F. STONE, proprietor of *I. F. Stone's Weekly*, combined a commitment to the First Amendment with entrepreneurial zeal and reporting skill and became one of the great independent journalists in American history. At the age of eighty, Izzy published *The Trial of Socrates*, which was a national bestseller. He wrote the book after he taught himself ancient Greek.

BENJAMIN C. BRADLEE was for nearly thirty years the charismatic editorial leader of *The Washington Post*. It was Ben who gave the *Post* the range and courage to pursue such historic issues as Watergate. He supported his reporters with a tenacity that made them fearless and it is no accident that so many became authors of influential, best-selling books.

ROBERT L. BERNSTEIN, the chief executive of Random House for more than a quarter century, guided one of the nation's premier publishing houses. Bob was personally responsible for many books of political dissent and argument that challenged tyranny around the globe. He is also the founder and longtime chair of Human Rights Watch, one of the most respected human rights organizations in the world.

⋅　⋅　⋅

For fifty years, the banner of Public Affairs Press was carried by its owner Morris B. Schnapper, who published Gandhi, Nasser, Toynbee, Truman, and about 1,500 other authors. In 1983, Schnapper was described by *The Washington Post* as "a redoubtable gadfly." His legacy will endure in the books to come.

Peter Osnos, *Founder and Editor-at-Large*